TOURISM DESTINATIONS

ROB DAVIDSON AND ROBERT MAITLAND

Hodder & Stoughton

A MEMBER OF THE HODDER HEADLINE GROUP

For Stuart and for Jane

British Library Cataloguing in Publication Data
A catalogue record for this title is available from The British
Library

ISBN 0 340 65475 9

First published 1997
Impression number   10 9 8 7 6 5 4 3 2 1
Year   2002 2001 2000 1999 1998 1997

Typeset by Fakenham Photosetting Limited, Fakenham,
Norfolk
Printed in Great Britain for Hodder & Stoughton Educational,
a division of Hodder Headline Plc, 338 Euston Road, London
NW1 3BH by Bath Press, Bath

Acknowledgements

A great many people have helped us in our research on tourism destinations and in preparing the text for this book. We are grateful to them all and thank them for their help and their ideas. Without wishing to exclude any by identifying only a few, we would like particularly to thank the following:

Jane Branton, North Pennines Tourism Partnership; Mike Cowlam Bradford MDC, and Maria Glot; Brian Human, Assistant Director of Planning, Cambridge City Council; James Overton, Tourism Marketing Manager, Dover District Council; Clive Wyatt, Head of Tourism, Winchester City Council for their help in the preparation of the case studies.

Wayne Dyer, now with Llewelyn Davies Planning, and David Smith, now with Drivers Jonas, for their diligence, resourcefulness and patience in providing excellent research assistance at the University of Westminster.

Steve Beioley, Director, The Tourism Company, who helped us develop a number of the ideas in the book, reviewed many initial drafts and provided thoughtful and positive suggestions for improvements.

Philip Goulding, Napier University; Michelle Grant, Michelle Grant Associates, Tim Heap, University of Derby School of Business, Laurent Queige, SETEL, France, who read drafts of their text and provided most helpful comments.

Colleagues at the University of Westminster, but especially Dimitrios Buhalis, Andy Coupland, Deborah Grieve, Tim Edmunsdson and Anne Graham for comments on early drafts, valuable ideas, insights and support.

Our students on whom we tried out some of the ideas and who provided helpful feedback.

Thanks finally to our partners for their patience and support and to our editors at Hodder. The responsibility for errors and omissions which remain despite all this help is, of course, ours.

R.D.
R.M.

The author and publisher would like to thank the following organisations and people for the use of illustrations and information in this publication:

WTO (World Tourism Organisation): Figures 2.1 and 2.5, 1996; Addison Wesley Longman Ltd: Figure 2.2, reprinted from *Business Travel*, Davidson R., 1992; The English Historic Towns Forum: Figure 2.3, taken from *Getting It Right*; Van Nostrand Reinhold: Figure 2.4, taken from *Tourism Planning: An Integrated and Sustainable Development Approach*, Inskeep E., New York, 1991; Reproduced by permission of the Controller of HMSO and the Office for National Statistics: Figures 2.6, 2.8, 2.10 and 2.11 (part of), taken from the International Passenger Survey (part of Figure 2.10 also taken from Day Visits Survey, Department of National

Heritage; United Kingdom Tourism Survey (English Tourist Board, Scottish Tourist Board, Northern Ireland Tourist Board, Wales Tourist Board): Figures 2.9, 2.10 and 2.11 (part of); Maison de la Géographie: Figure 3.1 taken from Miossec, 'Un modele de l'espace touristique' in *L'Espace Géographique*, vol. 6, part 1, pp. 41–8, Paris, 1976; Ritter, Wigand and Dewailly, Jean-Michel: Figure 3.2, adapted from: Schwarzenbach, Fritz Hans, 'Problem analysis of the control of regional tourist development in tourist regions of the Alps' in Brugger, E. A., ed, *The Transformation of the Swiss mountain regions*, Bern, 1984, pp. 619–37; Ritter, Wigand, *Allgemeine Wirtschaftsgeographie* second edition, München, 1993, p. 130; Dewailly, Jean-Michel, Flament, Emile, *Géographie du Tourisme et des Loisirs*, SEDES, 1993; Centre des Hautes Etudes Touristiques: Figure 3.3, reprinted from *La Consommation d'Espace par le Tourisme et sa Préservation*, Gormsen, 1981; University of Colorado: Figure 3.4, taken from Doxey G., 'A causation theory of visitor-resident irritants, methodology and research' in *Conference Proceedings of the Travel Research Association*, San Diego, 1975, pp. 195–8; Elsevier Science Ltd, The Boulevard, Langford Lane, Kidlington OX5 1GB: Figure 3.6, reprinted from *Annals of Tourism Research* 9, Butler, 1980; OECD (Organisation for Economic Co-operation and Development): Figure 4.1; Reproduced by permission of the Controller of HMSO and of the Office for National Statistics: Figure 4.2, reprinted from *Labour Market Trends*; The World Travel and Tourism Council: Figure 4.3; Elsevier Science Ltd, The Boulevard, Langford Lane, Kidlington OX5 1GB: Figure 4.4, reprinted from *Annals of Tourism Research* 9, Baretje, 'Tourism's external accounts and the balance of payments', 1982; Channel View Publications: Figure 6.1 taken from Human B., 'Visitor Management in the Public Planning Context: A case study of Cambridge' in *The Journal of Sustainable Tourism*, Vol. 2, No. 4, 1994; Commission of the European Communities: Figure 6.2; Décison Tourisme: Figure 6.3, taken from *Décision Tourisme*, no. 4, February 1996; Commission of the European Communities: Figure 6.4; Elsevier Science Ltd, The Boulevard, Langford Lane, Kidlington OX5 1GB: Figure 6.5, reprinted from *Tourism Management*, Baum T., 1994; Elsevier Science Ltd, The Boulevard, Langford Lane, Kidlington OX5 1GB: Figure 6.6, reprinted from the *International Journal of Hospitality Management* 12, Akehurst G., Bland N. and Nevin M., 'Tourism Policies in the European Community member states', 1993; The English Tourist Board: Figures 7.1 and A.2; Centre for Leisure and Tourism Studies, University of North London: Figure 7.2 adapted from Richards, G., 'The UK Local Authority Tourism Survey', 1992, PNL Press; The National Centre for Studies in Travel and Tourism (James Cook University, Australia): Figure 7.3 taken from Long, J., 'Local Authority Tourism Strategies – A British Appraisal' in the *Journal of Tourism Studies*, vol. 5, no. 2, 1994; Department of Employment: Figure 7.4 from 'Tourism and the Environment – Maintaining the Balance', DoE, 1991; Bradford Metropolitan City Council: case study A photo of Bradford, Figures A.2–A.6; Dover District Council: case study B photo of Dover, B.2, B.3, B.4, B.5, B.7 and B.8; South East England Tourist Board: Figure B.6; Cambridge City Council: case study C photo of King's College, Figures C.4, C.5, C.6, C.7, C.8, C.9 and C.10; Winchester Tourism, Winchester City Council: Figure D.1 (redrawn), case study D photo of Winchester cathedral; Clive Wyatt, Winchester City Council: Figures D.5 and D.7; Clive Wyatt: Figures D.6 and D.8; North Pennines Tourism Partnership: case study E photo of Holwick, North Teesdale; North Pennines Tourism Partnership: Figures E.2 and E.3 reprinted from *The Volume of Employment Attributable to Tourism and Leisure Day-Trip Activity in the North Pennines AONB: A Report of Research Findings*, Heap T. and Wylie R., 1992; North Pennines Tourism Partnership: Figure E.5 (data taken from Tourism Partnership News, Autumn 1994)

Every effort has been made to obtain permission with reference to copyright material. The publishers apologise if inadvertently any sources remain unacknowledged and will be glad to make the necessary arrangements at the earliest opportunity.

Contents

Introduction to destinations, management and planning

INTRODUCTION

On a sunny Sunday morning in late September 1972, the inhabitants of Holmfirth awoke to find an unusual level of activity in the narrow streets of their attractive West Yorkshire village. On what would normally have been a quiet uneventful day like any other, there were new faces peering in through the windows of the village's neat stone-built houses and an unfamiliar jostling for the few parking spaces available, as the local newsagent quickly sold out of the scant supply of postcards and rolls of film it had in stock. Holmfirth had become a tourist destination.

The previous evening, the first episode of the series *Last of the Summer Wine* had been shown on BBC television, and many people living in Yorkshire's Pennines and in the Peak district had recognised Holmfirth as the location where the series was filmed. From the next day on, they came in growing numbers for a glimpse of the houses and streets in which the series' redoubtable characters, Nora Batty *et al.* lived out the adventures of their twilight years. They were to be followed in the years ahead by rapidly growing numbers of visitors from further afield, as the series increased in popularity and Holmfirth's reputation spread.

By the early 1980s, the district of Kirklees, in which Holmfirth is situated, was marketing itself to potential visitors as 'Last of the Summer Wine Country', with guided tours of the series' locations. A Tourist Information Centre had opened and new attractions had been created in the town, including 'England's only postcard museum' based on the products of the local company Bamforths, publishers of 'saucy' seaside postcards. Holmfirth is now firmly established as a day-trip destination for independent day-trippers and coach parties, and tourism has replaced the village's textile industry, already in decline in the 1960s, as a major source of employment and prosperity for many local people. And if other residents are ruing that day in the early 1970s when the BBC cameras first appeared in the streets of Holmfirth, then they are mainly keeping their opinions to themselves.

Few places are transformed into tourist destinations as rapidly and unexpectedly as Holmfirth. But in the closing decades of the 20th century, with tourist activity expanding globally, more and more people around the world have been confronted with the reality that the places where they grew up, and in which they now live and work, have also become magnets for visitors, from neighbouring towns or from the other side of the planet, or both.

Places can become recognised tourist destinations in a variety of ways.

Some are 'discovered', when entrepreneurs or developers, feeding the tourism industry's voracious appetite for expansion, see in them an opportunity for development. There then may follow the construction of hotels, conference centres, recreational facilities and tourist attractions, whose appeal may only partly depend on the attractiveness of the place where they are located. For others, tourism development is driven by necessity, as traditional industries decline and new economic activities are needed to create employment and prosperity. Locally-elected representatives choose to market and develop the municipality, district or region for tourism, based on its natural, built and cultural resources.

Finally, in Western developed countries in particular, the general population's determination to exercise its freedom to travel and visit as it wishes, has resulted in many other localities becoming tourist destinations, in some cases, if not against the will of the localities' inhabitants then at least without their active encouragement. A population ever more mobile and ever more restless, well-informed, sophisticated and curious is increasingly given to seeking out new experiences in places previously untouched by tourism. Coastal areas, mountain and wilderness areas, inland rural areas, towns and cities … places offering the right type of resources are increasingly finding that they are attracting substantial numbers of visitors.

The expanding global appetite for travel and tourism is, of course, not only resulting in the creation of new destinations. Tourism has long been an established industry in many 'traditional' destinations such as seaside resorts, attractive country areas, historical towns and cities, where it is often a major economic activity. Tourism's continuing growth has, therefore, also fuelled increases in the number of visitors to many such long-established destinations, in particular those which have some unique quality or resource which retains, through time, the appeal they have for the travelling public.

Whether we are considering places where tourism is relatively new or places which tourists have been visiting for hundreds of years, it is clear that visitors have the potential to bring substantial benefits to the community and its residents. It is equally clear that, left uncontrolled, tourism can wreak damage to the very fabric of a destination, through the many negative impacts it can bring.

For tourism activity at any destination to be considered a *success* for all concerned, it must not only provide a satisfactory experience for visitors, but also maintain or improve the quality of life of residents and protect the local natural, built and cultural environment. Finally, and equally importantly, the tourism industry itself, in particular the private sector, must be rewarded, in the form of healthy profits, for the risks it takes in investing in commercial facilities at the destination. Only when tourism is developed in an integrated manner which respects the rights and wishes of all of these parties, can it be considered to be a success.

The effective planning and management of tourism at destinations is now widely regarded as the key to this overall success. How tourism is planned, guided, shaped and managed at destinations is therefore the subject of this book. It is a subject which is as relevant to the prosperity of all sectors of the tourism industry as it is to the wider, but related, issues of environmental protection and quality of life of resident populations. Moreover, the importance of understanding the need for, and the issues involved in, tourism planning and management becomes more urgent by the day, as tourism development marches steadily onwards, affecting increasing numbers of people and places.

WHAT IS A TOURIST DESTINATION?

What actually constitutes a tourist destination? In this section, we examine in more detail the questions of the attributes which can make places destinations for visitors.

We can use a modified version of Leiper's model of the tourism system to locate our discussion of destinations within tourism activity as a whole. The spatial elements of Leiper's model are a tourist generating region, and a tourist destination region which travellers reach via a transit region. Information flows back from the destination to the generating region, influencing the perception of the destination and stimulating visits.

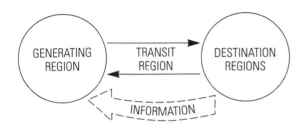

FIGURE 1.1 *The tourism system (after Leiper, in Cooper, C. et al., 1995)*

This approach emphasises that tourism results from the interaction of both demand and supply factors. There are a range of push factors stimulating demand for travel and tourism generally in the generating region – for example, disposable incomes, taste and demographic change (see Chapter 2). Changes in these factors will affect the potential demand for tourism trips, as will changes located in the transit region, such as easier or cheaper transportation. However, supply factors are crucial. At its most basic, tourism is about visiting places (destinations) and it is the desire to go to a particular place which lies at the heart of tourist activity. Destinations are a focus for attention since they stimulate and motivate visits, and are the location in which the major part of the tourist product is produced. As a result, much of the tourism industry is located in destinations, and most of its impacts are experienced in them.

Despite this, defining what actually constitutes a destination is problematic, and there is no agreed definition of the term. Nor is terminology clearly defined: the words 'resort' and 'destination' are often used interchangeably, for example. Since destinations motivate visits, they can be defined simply in terms of what they offer to tourists. Gunn (1994a) defines the destination zone as 'a geographic area containing a critical mass of development that satisfies traveller objectives', while Flament (1975) says:

> 'secondary home owners, walkers, hunters … the tourist is first and foremost a consumer of places and any place capable of satisfying the tourists' need [for relaxation] must be classed as a destination.'

However, definitions at this level of generality do not take us much further forward. We can get a clearer idea of what constitutes tourist destinations by considering their definition in spatial terms, and the attributes that distinguish destinations from one another and from other places.

The term 'destination' is applied at a bewildering variety of spatial scales, ranging from a country the size of India to an individual attraction occupying a few acres. At one extreme, national tourist organisations market and promote whole countries as destinations, and the benefits of tourism are often conceived on a national scale – for example, earning a country foreign currency. Within a country, whole regions may be seen as having an identity which means that they constitute destinations; tourists choose to visit the Dordogne or the Cotswolds more often than particular towns or villages within these areas. The boundaries of such tourist regions or *Pays* are often blurred, the more so when they are defined in cultural rather than strictly geographic terms. It would be difficult (and doubtless controversial) to attempt to establish with any precision the boundaries of Thomas Hardy's Wessex or 'James Herriot Country', yet these are both destinations in terms of Gunn's and Flament's definitions.

Cities, towns or villages seem to be safer ground. Their boundaries are clear, and the seaside town remains the popular archetype of a tourist destination. We need to bear in mind however, that tourism and tourist activity may be focused in just part of the place. While London and Paris are major tourist destinations, visitors are concentrated in comparatively limited areas. In a traditional or purpose-built seaside resort such as Scarborough or La Grande Motte, tourism is a much more pervasive activity. We must bear in mind though, that even in a traditional resort, tourism is never the only activity, and in other destinations, tourism will be just one of several ways in which the place makes its living. For example, Cambridge receives over three million visitors per year, and tourism is an important and highly visible activity – yet it accounts for only about 6% of the city's total employment (see case study). One important implication is that the interaction between tourism and other activities, and between tourism and the host community will be of particular importance.

Finally, a single attraction occupying a small geographic area may be seen as a self-contained destination. Disneyland Paris is an obvious example, but equally, a resort hotel, or a Center Parc can provide a visitor with accommodation, services and entertainment so that they need never leave the site. Unlike cities and towns, they do not encompass non-tourism activities and there is no host population to be taken into account.

In spatial terms, then, destinations overlap and interact, and can be defined at a wide variety of scales. As Gordon and Goodall (1992) say: 'each tourist destination may incorporate a mosaic of resorts or tourist areas, each of which in turn comprises a mosaic of tourism enterprises.' We can, however, move towards a sharper and more restricted definition. Our concern is with the management of destinations, and that allows us to eliminate both whole countries and attractions from consideration. Whilst it may be helpful to market whole countries as destinations, in reality tourism activity is concentrated in a rather limited number of tourist areas. It is within these areas that impacts are experienced and the tourism product produced, and so it is at this scale (rather than nationally) that management must be focused. Attractions may be destinations in the sense that they motivate a visit, but in reality they constitute hospitality management on a large scale. Single purpose, under single ownership and management, and purpose-built, they are more usefully seen as facilities rather than places.

Therefore, although all levels of planning are of relevance to the subject of this book, the text converges on the planning and management of local tourist destinations: a single district, town or city, or a clearly defined and contained rural, coastal or mountain area. These destinations all share a number of characteristics.

They have:

- a complex and multidimensional 'total tourism product' based on a variety of natural, social and cultural resources and services (which may include heritage attractions, leisure, entertainment and culture, shopping and business facilities) as well as hospitality and tourism services. These resources may be under a variety of ownerships (public, private and not-for-profit).
- other economic activities which may be complementary to or in conflict with tourism activities
- a host community which may be an integral element in the destination's attraction and which makes its own demands on the locality, its resources and facilities
- an elected local council (or other public authority or authorities) which can influence the destination's planning and management, particularly of its resources
- an active private sector which also has an important degree of involvement in the destination's planning and management

These characteristics are displayed by the vast majority of places located in Western industrialised countries currently attracting visitors.

It is worthy of note that, with the exception of traditional holiday resorts and tourist 'honeypots', many of the places attracting visitors may not even consider themselves to be, first and foremost, tourist destinations. For non-traditional destinations in particular, tourism is simply one of many forms of economic activity taking place in the locality. However, it is precisely in these non-traditional destinations that tourism is increasingly appearing as a powerful force, with the potential to alter radically the place itself, and the lives of those who live and work there.

The issues and problems explored in this book are therefore relevant, not only to 'traditional' resorts and tourist destinations, but also to the growing number of other places becoming desirable places to visit. Given the politico-economic profile of the places which display these characteristics, we are primarily concerned with tourism planning for destinations in Western industrialised countries (notably Western European) and focus more specifically on the UK. This sets the book apart from much of the academic literature on tourism planning and development, which places its emphasis on development planning in new destinations, often purpose-built resorts, and usually in developing countries. This type of development and *ex nihilo* planning has already been fully and admirably dealt with by a number of authors.

The context of tourism planning in the UK and other Western European countries is sufficiently distinct from that which exists in developing countries as to be treated as a quite separate case for analysis. The principal differences may be summarised as follows:

■ **Different forms of government intervention** – as Pearce notes,

'Public sector intervention in developing countries largely involves central government which acts to regulate or encourage tourist developers as well as directly participating in development . . . While central government is also involved in developed countries, regional government and especially local authorities tend to play a much greater role there than they do in the Third World . . .'
(Pearce, 1989)

■ **Different forms of private sector activity** – the importance of transnational developers (and therefore foreign control) in developing countries is not found to the same extent in developed countries which have mature, complex economies. In developed countries, 'external' developers are usually external to the region/community rather than to the country (*ibid*).

■ **Different forms of demand** – developed countries' tourism market is usually characterised by a strong domestic demand, a high level of day-visits, short breaks and independent (i.e. non-packaged) tourist activity, to a much greater degree than is generally found in developing countries. Business tourism is also more important.

■ **Different forms of supply** – developed countries' tourism products have evolved in a much more diversified manner than those of many developing countries, and include facilities and resources which stimulate visits based on many forms of recreation and sport, leisure and entertainment, culture and heritage, as well as business and commercial activities. Tourism activity also tends to be more dispersed throughout developed countries, with far less of the enclavic development typical of many developing countries' tourism product. Finally, in developed countries, the tourism product relies to a much greater extent on facilities which are shared with the local population. Foreign tourists in London, for example, may make use of the same transport, cinemas, theatres, and shopping facilities as Londoners themselves. Indeed, such facilities depend upon a market which is composed of both visitors and residents.

■ **Different impacts** – in developed countries, differences in culture and standards of living between hosts and guests are usually far less pronounced than in developing countries. This excludes many of the most extreme sociocultural impacts of tourism which affect many Third World destinations (see Chapter 4). Moreover, the influence of conservation groups and the political power of ordinary citizens in developed, democratic countries arguably gives these groups greater ability to defend the environment and their quality of life against tourism's excesses than is enjoyed by many of those living in developing countries.

The rationale for concentrating on the tourism planning and management of destinations in developed countries is, therefore, based on these differences. While this book focuses on tourism in the UK, many of the processes at work in shaping tourism in this country also operate in similar forms in other European states, in particular those which are members of the European Union.

TOURISM PLANNING AND TOURISM PLANS

Planning is central to the orderly development of tourism and to the benefit of all parties concerned. But what do we mean by 'planning'? What are the specific characteristics of tourism planning which distinguish it as an activity? Tourism planning has been succinctly defined as: 'a process, based on research and evaluation, which seeks to optimise the potential contribution of tourism to human welfare and environmental quality' (Getz, 1987).

The word 'process' is important here. Unlike Town and Country Planning, for example, tourism planning is not a specific profession; neither is it an activity undertaken by a single national or local government department, organisation or sector of the tourism industry. None of these can claim to offer the entire range of skills, powers, knowledge and experience vital to effective tourism planning.

Tourism planning is a process as complex and multifaceted as tourism itself. It takes place at a number of geographical levels, at each of which a large number of public agencies interact with private sector representatives to forge policies and plans to shape the development of tourism. The public/private aspect is essential. The planning and development of tourism at destinations is too important to be left entirely in the hands of private sector entrepreneurs, who are primarily concerned with the profit motive and often have no apparent allegiance to the destination as a whole. On the other hand, as Cooper *et al.* (1995) emphasise, if tourism development is dominated by the public sector, then it is unlikely to be developed at the optimum rate from the economic point of view (the public sector may lack a commercial or market focus for its activities). Public/private sector partnership as applied to the tourism planning and management process is therefore a key theme of this book.

Braddon (1982) elaborates on Getz's definition by providing an analysis of the constituent characteristics of effective tourism planning:

- 'The planning process needs to take account of very many factors ranging from topography to the economy and from tourists' needs to residents' needs. It is subject to a great many external influences which both modify the process and the outcome – the implementation of the plan.
- Tourism is a social, economic and environmental activity. Its planning has to operate at various levels: nationally, regionally, locally.
- Tourism planning must take account of conservation of the physical environment ... The spatial planning of tourism can be very effective in this regard.
- Ideally, tourism planning should be fully integrated with all socio–economic activities and at all levels of involvement. This would ensure the optimal use of tourist resources with least social, economic and environmental costs ...'

(Braddon, 1982)

The multifarious nature of tourism planning is also due, in part, to the many policy subjects which converge on the planning process. Braddon mentions conservation of the physical environment as an example. But Heeley (1981) develops this point in his description of tourism planning in the UK.

'The scope of existing arrangements for planning for tourism is an amalgam of economic, social and environmental considerations. Three distinct geographical planning levels (region, county and district) are discernible; a large number of public agencies is active at each level. Overall planning objectives in tourism vary from encouragement to restriction, while planning tools range from grants and other incentives to development control schemes and visitor management projects ... Moreover, tourism is not a self-contained policy area. It overlaps with policy fields such as transport, conservation, rural development, and so forth, so that only a small proportion of the sum total of plans affecting tourism are exclusively devoted to it.'

(Heeley, 1981)

Tourism plans abound the world over at all spatial scales, from plans affecting several countries to those for individual sites. As early as 1980, there were already over 1,600 such plans in existence, according to the World Tourism Organisation (WTO, 1980). Many of these were national tourism development plans, often linking land development plans with the country's objectives for tourism development and seeking to coordinate and optimise investment in tourism.

Tourism plans at the local level, however, are much more concerned with the needs of those living and running businesses in tourist destinations, and the impact which tourism has on them and the fabric of the destination itself. In the UK, for example, visitor management plans are increasingly used to maximise the economic and social benefits of tourism to the resident population, while at the same time mitigating or possibly eliminating the adverse effects on aspects such as the environment and the quality of life of the residents.

Nevertheless (as Heeley's quotation suggests), for every plan dealing solely with tourism there are many in which tourism features as only one element among several. For example, at the national level in the UK, tourism is an element in plans for the conservation and management of the country's forests, waterways, national parks, museums and many national monuments; and at the local level, tourism features, for example, in many individual counties', districts' and cities' economic development plans, taking its place alongside other activities such as attracting inward investment, developing the infrastructure and training.

The type of tourism-related plans which are of central interest to the subject of this book are all of those plans, polices and strategies which have as their objective, or as one of their objectives, the guiding and shaping of the development of tourism at destinations. Some of these plans are statutory and enforceable by law; but most are non-statutory, taking the form of agreements and guidelines for action.

TOURISM PLANNING AND SUSTAINABILITY

Until recently, the planning of tourism has been primarily oriented towards the intensive marketing and promotion of destinations and the satisfaction of the needs of the tourists themselves. Typically, politicians and tourism planners have, in the past, had as their priority the maximisation of the financial benefits of tourism for their country, region or locality, and the tourism industry has done its utmost to attract as many customers as possible, in order to receive the greatest returns on its investments.

Archer and Cooper (1994) observe, however, that:

'Fortunately, the climate of thought is changing, albeit slowly. Increasingly politicians and planners are becoming aware of the longer-term social, economic and environmental consequences of excessive and badly planned tourism expansion. It is crucial, if the adverse effects are to be prevented or remedied, that politicians and planners should become less preoccupied with increasing the numbers of visits (and indeed with volume as a yardstick of success) and devote more time to the long-term welfare of the resident population.'

(Archer and Cooper, 1994)

Gunn (1994b) also notes the move away from the strong preoccupation with *promotion* as the sole key to development, and the growing tendency for tourism planners to recognise several goals, in addition to that of an improved economy: increased visitor satisfaction, integration with existing local social and economic life, and protection and better utilisation of basic natural and cultural resources.

There are several factors which, in the past few decades, have changed this general approach to tourism planning. But most significant among them is the rise of environmentalism and sustainability as major global issues.

Sustainable development refers to development which takes place without the degradation or depletion of the resources that make the development possible. It involves the conservation of resources for future as well as present generations to use and enjoy. It also involves taking a long-term view of economic activity and questions the imperative of continued economic growth. Concepts of sustainability are now widely accepted as an essential approach to any type of development, including tourism.

It is now generally accepted that it is no longer admissible for the tourism industry to exploit and 'use up' destinations without due consideration of the long-term consequences of such an approach for the environment and the community. Sustainable tourism sees tourism within destination areas as a triangular relationship between host areas and their habitats and peoples, holidaymakers, and the tourism industry. In the past, the tourism industry dominated the triangle. Sustainable tourism aims to reconcile the tensions between the three partners in the triangle, and keep the equilibrium in the long term. It aims to minimise environmental and cultural damage, optimise visitor satisfaction, and maximise long-term economic growth for the region. It is a way of obtaining a balance between the growth potential of tourism and the conservation needs of the environment (Lane, 1994).

An unregulated market will not deliver sustainable development (see Chapter 5). Environmental concerns have stimulated greater interest in tourism planning and management as an effective way of ensuring that principles of sustainability are observed in the manner in which tourism evolves at destinations. The same concerns have also changed the nature of tourism planning itself. The broadening of tourism planning's scope to embrace more social and environmental issues has already been mentioned. In addition to this change, many commentators have noticed the trend away from the rigid 'grand design' master plan in favour of a more flexible, integrated approach, with planning for tourism taking its place alongside other forms of planning in the locality. Gunn notes the growth in interest in planning for tourism at the local destination level – which he neatly defines as 'a community and surrounding area', and the proliferation of destination plans:

> 'Now there is greater sensitivity to visitor capacity management, integration of tourism with the local society and economy, and protection of natural and cultural resources as foundations for more and better travel experiences. New organisational mechanisms that foster collaboration on planning are appearing. More areas are seeing the value of planning that utilises input from local citizens as well as planning specialists and consultants.'
>
> *(Gunn, 1994b).*

The last point is very significant and points to another noticeable trend of recent years. Professionals involved in tourism planning having been increasingly moving from an elitist approach to greater involvement of all parties involved in and impacted by their decisions. Public participation in tourism planning decisions has come to be widely regarded as an essential ingredient in tourism planning and policy making. Simmons (1994) suggests that this has come about for two reasons: first, the recognition that the impacts of tourism are felt most keenly by those living in the local destination area; and second, the realisation that community residents are an essential ingredient in the 'hospitality atmosphere' of a destination. Public participation refers to 'decision making by the target group, the general public, relevant interest groups, or other types of decision makers whose involvement appeals to our desire to use democratic procedures for achieving given goals' (Hall and Jenkins, 1995, citing Nagel).

Any involvement of a wide cross section of participants in the planning system will necessarily bring not only goals which are conflicting, but also incompatible perceptions about the development of the tourism industry. Genuine public participation can therefore require a consensus-building approach to tourism planning and policy making. This gives professionals involved in planning an additional role to play, that of catalytic agents for new solutions to planning problems: resolving conflicts by bringing opposing factions together to agree a plan which is acceptable to all sides.

In conclusion, the drive towards sustainability has meant that all of those involved in planning and policy making for tourism have been presented with not only new challenges, but with new roles and responsibilities. For the many applications of tourism planning and management which will be described in this book, sustainability as a desirable goal is the common thread running through them all.

Although the vast majority of our examples are taken from UK tourism development, the trend towards sustainability in tourism is international and growing. The OECD summed up the situation in 1996 as follows:

> 'One of the priorities of Member countries is sustainable development. First of all, tourism should be part of a planning process which pays particular attention to the environment. The tourism industry and those responsible for policy are attaching growing importance to the quality of tourism developments and are implementing major schemes to protect and enhance the natural and cultural heritage. Through the concept of quality in development, adopted in most countries, social issues are now fully taken into account in economic assessments. Tourism development must live up to the expectations of local citizens as well as foreign visitors. It must protect and enhance a nation's heritage.'
>
> *(OECD, 1996)*

BOOK STRUCTURE

This book examines the challenges facing those responsible for the planning and management of tourism in destination areas, and the way in which they have responded to those challenges. Chapter 2 describes the diversity of tourism demand, the variety of elements which constitute the tourism product, tourism's historical development and the dimensions of tourism in the contemporary world. Chapter 3 focuses on the dynamics of tourist destinations and how they evolve. It outlines and reviews various models of destination development, emphasising the dynamic nature of that development and its interaction with external factors. The economic, sociocultural and environmental impacts of tourism development are examined in Chapter 4, together with a consideration of how the tourism industry interacts with other economic activities taking place at the destination. Chapter 5 makes the case for intervention in the form of tourism planning and management, as the most effective means of reducing tourism's negative impacts and maximising the benefits which tourism can offer. It emphasises the role that tourism has come to play as part of a wider process of regeneration in non-traditional destinations. Chapter 6 outlines the various policies and strategies for the management of tourism which exist on the international and national scale and which provide the context within which the planning and management of tourism at the destination level takes place. The various actors responsible for the planning and management of tourism at the local level in the UK are described in Chapter 7, which ends with a survey of some of the main collaborative measures they employ in order to carry out this task. The five case-studies illustrate examples of the challenges and opportunities tourism presents in the destinations where it takes place, and the way in which effective planning and management have been used to deal with these.

REFERENCES

Archer, B. and Cooper, C. (1994) 'The positive and negative aspects of tourism' in *Global tourism: the Next Decade*, William Theobold (ed), Butterworth-Heinemann, Oxford.

Braddon, C.J.H. (1982) *British Issues Paper: Approaches to tourism planning abroad*, British Tourist Authority, London.

Cooper, C. *et al.* (1995) *Tourism: Principles and Practice*, Pitman, London.

Flament, quoted in Cazes, G. (1992) *Fondements pour une geographie du tourisme et des loisirs*, Breal.

Getz, D. (1987) 'Tourism planning and research' in *Proceedings of the Australian travel workshop*, Bunbury, Western Australia.

Gordon, I. and Goodall, B. (1992) 'Resort Cycles and the Development Process' in *Built Environment* 18, 1.

Gunn, C.A. (1994a) *Tourism planning: basics, concepts, cases*, Taylor and Francis, Washington and London.

Gunn, C.A. (1994b) 'The emergence of effective tourism planning and development' in *Tourism: The State of the Art*, Seaton, A.V. *et al.* (eds), Wiley & Sons, Chichester.

Hall, C.M. and Jenkins, J.M. (1995) *Tourism and public policy*, Routledge, London.

Heeley, J. (1981) 'Planning for tourism in Britain' in *Town Planning Review*, 52: pp. 61–79.

Lane, B. (1994) 'Sustainable rural tourism strategies: a tool for development and conservation' in *Journal of Sustainable Tourism (2)* 1 & 2.

OECD (1996) *Tourism Policy and International Tourism in OECD Countries 1993–1994*, Organisation for Economic Co-operation and Development, Paris.

Pearce, D. (1989) *Tourist development*, Longman, Harlow.

Simmons, D.G. (1994) 'Community participation in tourism planning' in *Tourism Management*, 15 (2): pp. 98–108.

WTO (1980) *Physical planning and area development for tourism in the six WTO regions*, World Tourism Organisation, Madrid.

CHAPTER

2 *Tourists and tourism*

INTRODUCTION

From its early origins as an indulgence restricted to the rich and leisured classes, tourism has grown to become an inseparable part of modern life and an integral part of social, cultural and economic activity in Western Europe, as in other parts of the developed and developing world. The European Union 1995 Green Paper on tourism remarked that:

> 'More than a matter of habit or a heterogeneous set of economic activities, tourism has become, within less than a century, a determining factor in the life of millions of people. Tourism changes with the improvement in living and working conditions and is simultaneously an essential element of this improvement and a result of it.'

> *(Commission of the EC, 1995)*

As the 20th century draws to its end, very few countries have remained untouched by tourism in one or several of its many forms. Increasingly, the inhabitants of rural and coastal regions, towns and cities are becoming aware that these places are not only their homes, but also the destinations for sometimes substantial numbers of visitors – whether from a neighbouring town or the other side of the world.

It has by now become commonplace to claim that tourism is the world's largest economic activity and employer, and that it will maintain that status well into the 21st century. When these claims come from the industry itself, there may be some justification for treating them with a degree of healthy scepticism (*The Economist*, 1995a). But increasingly, more objective commentators are coming to similar conclusions. For example, according to futurologist John Naisbitt, author of *Megatrends* and *Global Paradox*, three 'paradigm industries' will drive the service-led economies of the 21st century: telecommunications, information technology and *travel and tourism*.

The economic aspects of tourism are of central interest to the following chapters of this book, but it is important to remember that tourism is more than an economic activity. The 1980 Manila Declaration on World Tourism (WTO, 1980) described tourism as being, in essence, a massive interaction of people, demanding a wide range of services, facilities and inputs which generate opportunities and challenges to destinations (these too are key themes which will be explored in later chapters).

This chapter examines the tourism phenomenon: the nature of tourism demand and supply, and dimensions of tourism activity as well as tourism's historical development.

TOURISM AND TOURISTS: DEFINITIONS

Despite the near omnipresence of tourism on the global scale, universally accepted definitions of 'tourism' and 'tourist' have yet to be agreed by governments, researchers and commentators on this activity.

From the earliest awareness of tourism as a distinct phenomenon, many definitions have been suggested, some conceptual and others more technical, some comprehensive and others more partial in scope. One of the first attempts to define a tourist was that put forward by the League of Nations in 1937: 'one who travels for a period of 24 hours or more in a country other than that in which he normally resides' (Holloway, 1989). The limitation of this definition is that it excludes two important categories of visitors: domestic tourists (those travelling to destinations in their own country), and day-trippers or 'excursionists' (those visitors who arrive at the destination and leave the same day). These could be people who leave their home to visit a nearby town and return home in the evening; or those who visit a particular destination while on holiday, or while *en route* to, or from, their final holiday destination. Since both domestic tourists and day-trippers are clearly of considerable importance for the type of destinations with which this book is concerned, a wider definition is called for.

One of the most useful working definitions of tourism is that given by Mathieson and Wall:

'Tourism is the temporary movement of people to destinations outside their normal places of work and residence, the activities undertaken during their stay in those destinations, and the facilities created to cater to their needs.'

(Mathieson and Wall, 1981).

This statement contains the four key elements which appear in most conceptual definitions of tourism and which are now generally agreed to be defining features of tourist activity: travel or movement, stay (even if only for a few hours), destination activities, and the short-term, temporary nature of tourism and travel. In addition, the definition is particularly appropriate to the subject of this book, as it explicitly mentions tourist facilities, which, as will be seen, are of central concern to the planning and management of destinations.

The World Tourism Organisation's (WTO's) definition of tourism which was adopted by the Statistical Commission of the United Nations in 1993 contains the same elements, but places the emphasis on tourism demand, adding the tourist's activities carried out while travelling to and from the destination, as well as the different purposes of tourist trips. According to the WTO, tourism includes:

'... those activities deployed by people during the course of their journey and their stay in the place situated outside of their usual environment, for a continuous period of less than one year, for leisure or business purposes or other reasons.'

However, for the purpose of data collection more technical definitions are required to estimate, for example, the volume of foreign tourists visiting a particular country during a particular period. Accordingly, these focus on *'tourists'* rather than tourism. The WTO has produced a schematic classification of international visitors which divides these into tourists and same-day visitors. Its technical definition of a **tourist** includes the length of time someone must stay at the destination in order to qualify as such (more than 24 hours but less than one year) and altogether excludes certain categories of travellers from the definition of a 'tourist'. Nomads, refugees, diplomats, members of the armed forces on duty, transit passengers and border workers do not figure in WTO tourism statistics. Figure 2.1 shows the WTO's classification of international tourists.

The WTO definition's separation of visitors into 'tourists' and 'same-day visitors' is, of course, an important one, not least for those concerned with the marketing, planning and

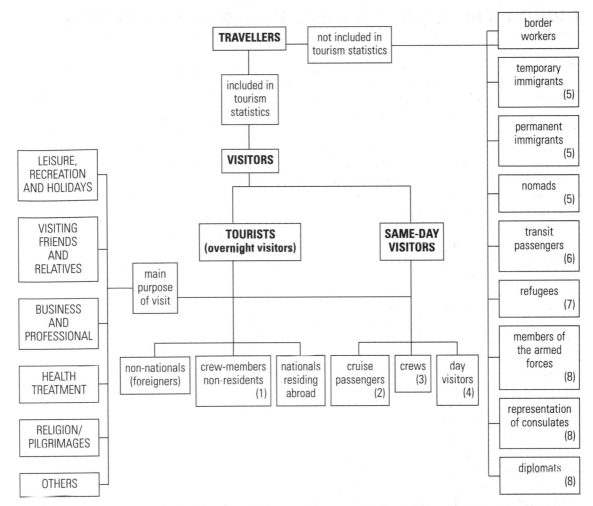

FIGURE 2.1 *Classification of international visitors*

1. Foreign air or ship crews docked or in lay over and who use the accommodation establishments of the country visited.
2. Persons who arrive in a country aboard cruise ships (as defined by the International Maritime Organization (IMO 1965) and who spend the night aboard ship even when disembarking for one or more day visits.
3. Crews who are not residents of the country visited and who stay in the country for the day.
4. Visitors who arrive and leave the same day for: leisure, recreation and holidays; visiting friends and relatives; business and professional; health treatment; religion/pilgrimages and other tourism purposes, including transit day visitors en route to or from their destination countries.
5. As defined by the United Nations in the Recommendations on Statistics of International Migration, 1980.
6. Who do not leave the transit area of the airport or the port, including transfer between airports and ports.
7. As defined by the United Nations High Commissioner for Refugees, 1967.
8. When they travel from their country of origin to the duty station and vice versa (including household servants and dependants accompanying or joining them).

Source: WTO, 1996

management of destinations. However, for the purposes of this book, the terms 'tourist' and 'visitor' will be used interchangeably, and, where it is important to make the distinction, the words 'staying visitor', 'day-tripper' or 'excursionist' will be used. This usage reflects the reality of the situation pertaining to many of the destinations with which this book is concerned, where day-trippers qualify as 'tourists' just as much as staying visitors do – both categories may use Tourist Information Centres, visit tourist attractions and use other facilities which come under the management of the tourist industry. And, perhaps, most significantly of all, both categories are likely to be classified as 'tourists' by those who live at the destination.

We are also concerned with the activities of a group of people who would be more likely to describe their pursuits as 'leisure' rather than 'tourism'. Tourism and leisure are, of course, closely related. Tourism is one form of activity undertaken in leisure time; tourists often use the same leisure facilities as local residents, for example restaurants, theatres, parks and swimming pools. Not all forms of leisure activity overlap with tourism – clearly, two people travelling to the end of the road where they live in order to go to the cinema can hardly be said to be indulging in tourist activity. But two others who drive or travel by public transport from their suburban home into the city centre, indulge in some non-essential shopping, and then have a meal in a restaurant followed by a visit to the cinema or theatre, are engaged in a *different* pattern of behaviour, which is of significant interest and relevance to those planning and managing tourist facilities in that city. It is here that our wide definition of tourists and visitors may be seen to overlap with what is more commonly thought of as 'leisure' or 'recreation'.

These suburbanites would most probably not consider themselves to be either tourists or visitors or even day-trippers. Nevertheless, the fact that they are outside their usual environment means that their impacts and needs are very similar to that of tourists visiting the city from the other side of the planet: their physical presence is added to that of local residents, commuters and shoppers; they need information on where things are and what to do; they are enjoying free time in the midst of others who are working; and they have an expectation of fun and enjoyment – and are prepared to pay for it.

All of these characteristics imply that a significant proportion of those indulging in leisure and recreation activities outside their immediate place of work and residence must also be taken into account in the planning and managing of places which have become destinations.

We are therefore interested in the activities of a wide range of visitors to destinations, including day-trippers and staying visitors, domestic and international tourists, all of whom may be visiting the destination for a wide range of purposes.

TOURISM DEMAND

It clearly emerges from the WTO chart in Figure 2.1 that the demand for tourism takes many forms, each with its own particular spatial and temporal pattern. The determinants of that demand may be examined from two different but complementary perspectives. Firstly, it is possible to consider the demand for tourism according to the *purpose* of the trip. Secondly, the demand may be described through an examination of the various factors which contribute to the tourist's propensity to travel – the tourist's different *motivations*.

DIFFERENT PURPOSES

The WTO definition of a tourist, as shown in the table in Figure 2.1, suggests a number of purposes which determine why people travel:

LEISURE BREAKS AND HOLIDAYS

These create the demand for the greater part of the tourism which takes place in many destinations.

The individual needs which determine where and how visitors spend their holidays include the following categories:

- **Sports and recreation:** destinations, with a combination of natural resources (such as beaches, mountains, forests, and rivers) and man-made facilities (ski-lifts, swimming pools, hiking paths), attract visitors whose principal holiday purpose is physical activity in any form, from simple walking or fishing to hang gliding and bungy-jumping, or even physical inactivity, such as sunbathing and relaxation. The increasing emphasis which has been put on health and fitness in Western society at the end of the 20th century has meant a general move in favour of stimulating activities.

  However, sports-related tourism may also include spectator sport, when a trip is made outside the spectator's usual place of residence in order to attend a sporting event. Such events can be major tourist attractions in themselves. For example, during the 1996 European Football Championship, increased business from visiting supporters led to a rise of 57% in hotel room revenue in Manchester alone (Greene Belfield-Smith, 1996).

- **Culture**: in the widest sense, the culture of a destination may be taken to mean any aspect of it which visitors are keen to see or experience during their stay. General sightseeing – appreciating the natural and built environment, particularly when the latter is of historic interest – may be the most basic and most widespread tourist activity. It is certainly the 'been there – done that' factor behind the 'milk-run' tour of Britain, which is popular with many overseas visitors who undertake the London–Oxford–Stratford–Chester–Lake District–Edinburgh–York–London circuit at a pace which astounds many of the British themselves. (This does not prevent the latter from doing the Florence, Sienna, Pisa and Assisi run in Tuscany!)

Sightseeing may or may not be supplemented by more conventionally 'cultural' activities, such as visiting museums and art galleries or attending musical, dance or theatre performances. Many cities have gained their reputations by holding arts and cultural festivals, which attract visitors as well as the local population.

- **Visiting friends and relatives (VFR)**: VFR is an important purpose behind much of the inbound tourism to the UK. In 1994, about one in five overseas visitors to the UK were visiting friends and relatives (IPS). A substantial proportion of inbound tourists come to visit friends and relatives who have settled permanently in the UK, as a result of governments' immigration policies of the 1950s and 60s. Conversely, the UK's past history as a country of emigration also means that there are people in most countries of the world who have family links with Britain and who are often motivated by the idea of tracing their family 'roots' in the UK, or simply visiting friends and family.

  Clearly, family links and friendships also stimulate outbound tourism by British nationals as well as a very high proportion of domestic trips to visit friends and family within the UK: in 1994, VFR was given as the purpose of visit by 27% of those domestic staying visitors interviewed in the UK Tourist Survey.

The rationale behind deploying the VFR category in statistical analysis is to identify a group of visitors who, spending nothing on board and lodging and little on tourism activity overall, need to be differentiated from 'pure holiday' visitors, whose average spending per trip in the UK is almost three times greater than that of their VFR counterparts. Clearly, this places a significant limit on their potential for revenue-generation for the destination. Nevertheless, as Seaton (1994) points out, the VFR market can be influenced by tourism marketing, for example, by the promotion of local restaurants for meals out, attractions to visit and excursions to take once visitors reach their destination.

BUSINESS TRAVEL AND TOURISM

After leisure, the next most common purpose for travelling is *business*. Business travel and tourism involve people travelling for work-related purposes, such as attending meetings and conferences or being present at trade fairs and exhibitions.

More similar to leisure travel, yet no less work-related than the other forms of business travel, are the incentive trips used by employers to reward or motivate their staff for special achievements. These tend to take the form of short, luxury trips to exotic locations for companies' high achievers, often sent in groups (accompanied, or not, by their partners) and given a memorable travel experience designed to forge company loyalty and spur them on to even greater efforts on the company's behalf.

Those travelling on business share many of the characteristics of leisure travellers: they travel, they stay temporarily, and they engage in specific activities at the destination. Nevertheless, there are considerable differences between leisure and business tourists, as shown in Figure 2.2.

As a result of some of these differences, business tourism and leisure tourism can have contrasting impacts on the destinations they visit. In financial terms, it is business travellers who appear to bring the more favourable benefits. Since in most cases their employers are paying their travel and accommodation expenses, they have a much higher average spend per day than leisure tourists.

By comparison with leisure tourism, business tourism also tends to be more evenly spread throughout the year, with only a slight 'low season' during the summer months, when conferences and trade fairs are less numerous. Many destinations (such as Brighton, Harrogate, and Bournemouth) are both business and leisure destinations and they benefit from the 'dovetailing' effect of these two complementary markets. Business tourism's same temporal complementarity with leisure tourism is also seen on a days of the week basis – the destination's Monday to Friday business visitors are replaced at weekends by day-trippers and those on short breaks.

However, attracting large volumes of business visitors is not an option for every type of destination. Unlike leisure tourism, which can thrive in many different types of environment – urban,

	Leisure tourism	Business tourism	but ...
Who pays?	The tourist	The traveller's employer or association	Self-employed business travellers are paying for their own trips
Who decides on the destination?	The tourist	The organiser of the meeting/ incentive trip/conference/ exhibition	Organisers will often take into account delegates' wishes
When do trips take place?	During classic holiday periods and at weekends	All year round, or Monday to Friday	July and August are avoided for major events
Lead time (period of time between booking and going on the trip)?	Holidays – usually a few months; short breaks – a few days	Some business trips must be made at very short notice	Major conferences are booked many years in advance
Who travels?	Anyone with the necessary spare time and money	Those whose work requires them to travel, or members of associations	Not all business trips involve managers on white-collar duties
What kinds of destination are used?	All kinds: coastal, city, mountain, and countryside locations	Largely centred on cities in industrialised countries	Incentive destinations are much the same as for up-market holidays

FIGURE 2.2 *Leisure tourism and business tourism*

Source: Davidson, 1992

rural and coastal – business tourism tends to be concentrated in those towns and cities with a substantial industrial and commercial base, and/or with conference and exhibition facilities as well as suitable accommodation. Destinations aiming at the international conference and trade exhibitions markets need to have, or be within easy access of, an international airport. Although most large cities have the facilities to attract conferences and trade exhibitions, many destinations have specialised in these markets: Paris, London, Dallas and Singapore are among the world's most successful conference cities, while half a dozen German cities between them have all but cornered the European and world markets for trade fairs (*The Economist*, 1996).

OTHER CATEGORIES

Although leisure breaks, holidays, VFR and business constitute the main purposes for travel and tourism globally, there are other purposes, which, for certain destinations, can be just as, if not more, important than those already described. These other categories, although relatively minor by comparison with those already mentioned, nevertheless have a long history and in some cases pre-date leisure and holidays as reasons for travelling.

- **Health-related** travel was one of the earliest types of tourism, with visits to spas and holidays in the pure air of the Alps being examples of this purpose behind travelling. Modern examples of health tourism are visits to centres offering specialised medical or therapeutic treatments, such as health farms or even hospitals. For example, certain Eastern European hospitals which have earned a worldwide reputation for treating particular disorders (especially childrens'), receive substantial numbers of patients from other countries whose prime purpose for visiting is to receive medical treatment.
- The **religious** purpose behind some forms of tourism is another of the earliest reasons for travel, and still manifested today in pilgrimages to holy places such as Mecca and Jerusalem or, in the UK, Canterbury or the Shrine of Our Lady at Walsingham in Norfolk.
- Travel for **educational** purposes includes attending language courses, lectures and short training courses held outside the student's normal place of work and residence. Many towns on England's south coast attract vast numbers of young foreigners whose purpose in visiting the UK is to improve their command of English at an English language summer school.

Naturally, the above categories are not mutually exclusive. More commonly, visits to destinations combine several different purposes. A delegate at a conference in Rome may visit the Vatican in his or her spare time, as well as doing some shopping and sightseeing. One of the reasons why many cities have been successful in tourism terms is that they offer the critical mass of different facilities and attractions, which bring visitors with a variety of motivations and encourage them to stay and return there.

DIFFERENT MOTIVATIONS

While his or her *purposes* for travelling are usually clear to the individual tourist, their *motivations* can sometimes be much less apparent. Motivations are the factors which (whether people are aware of them or not) incite them to travel, for whatever purpose. While the stated purpose of a trip may be given as 'holiday in the sun', the underlying motivation for making the trip could be any one, or several, of a whole series of social, psychological and economic factors, such as, the need to spend more time with one's partner, the desire to impress the neighbours, or the wish to use up some surplus income in a pleasurable way. As in the case of tourism purposes, several motivations can contribute to the tourist's decision to travel.

PSYCHOLOGICAL AND SOCIAL FACTORS

The topic of tourists' social and psychological motivations has been widely researched in the area of consumer behaviour in marketing studies.

Hudman (1980) is one of several authors who argue that Maslow's (1943) hierarchy of needs provides a useful framework for understanding psychological motivational factors in tourism. In particular, the upper levels of Maslow's pyramid of needs may be used as a framework for classifying tourists' psychological motivations in terms of their desires (conscious or not) for: *self actualisation* (the wish to fully develop one's capabilities and potential), *self-esteem*, *recognition and status*, and *belonging*.

Thus, for example, although the apparent purpose of a trip may be to visit friends and relatives, the underlying psychological motivation may be a need for belonging and the desire to reinforce family links.

Social factors which can motivate the traveller may include the desire to spend time with like-minded people who share the same interests and values – an important motivating factor behind many decisions to take part in conferences. Similarly, one reason why *group* incentive trips are used to motivate employees is that the employer hopes to harness this social factor in order to create or reinforce the *esprit d'équipe* of those who undertake the trip together. However, more often, the social factor which motivates the tourist is the need for escape, for a break from routine, to 'get away from it all' – 'it all' often being the stress and crowds of modern city life. The theme of 'escape' is an important one in describing tourists' motivations, and is often used in tourism promotional literature.

SOCIOPOLITICAL FACTORS

Cooper (1989) points out that tourism demand is influenced by the society and the political system in which the individual lives. Countries differ widely, for example, in the degree of tacit encouragement which is given to citizens to go on holiday. To take two extremes, a country such as France may be contrasted with Japan. The French have more public holidays than any other Western European country; the social security system partly refunds treatment in France's vast supply of spas and thalassotherapy centres; and the generous funding of social tourism from the public purse means that those otherwise unable

to afford holidays are able to do so, through State aid. The Japanese, by comparison, typically have only 12 days annual leave plus six or so days paid company holidays. However, they rarely take all of their leave entitlement, usually preferring to save some days in case of illness, since there is little paid sick leave in Japan (Craig-Smith and French, 1994).

Other relevant factors in countries' socio-political systems are the length of school and university holidays and the way in which the school week is organised. For example, again in the case of France, to what extent does the obligation for pupils there to attend schools on Saturday mornings act as a disincentive for families to take weekend breaks?

ECONOMIC FACTORS

Without doubt, economic factors play a key role in determining the propensity to travel of most people. Money is necessary for access to most forms of tourism and its abundance or scarcity is therefore an important motivating factor for those considering a holiday or any other form of tourist activity. But, as emphasised by Peat and Mullan (1995), the relationship between availability of money and spending on tourism is not necessarily simple:

'Clearly an increase in Real Personal Disposable Income (RPDI) brings with it the opportunity to spend more, and hence is favourable ... for the tourism outlook. But money alone is not the whole story. Consumer confidence is an important matter, as that encourages – or discourages – spend from income and changes in the savings rate. When confidence is low, expenditure can be restrained, despite RPDI growth, as savings are built up and debts repaid – to pay for expected hard times ahead. But the contrary is also feasible. Factors influencing confidence – and 'feel good' – include interest rates (actual and expectations) and unemployment, or wider labour market considerations such as job security. The housing market will also come into play.'

(Peat and Mullan, 1995)

For international tourism, exchange rates are clearly a major factor in influencing relative costs and therefore an important demand determinant, whether for inbound or outbound visitors to or from a country. During the mid-1990s, devaluations of several Western European countries' currencies gave certain destinations an advantage (albeit temporary) over their competitors, by simultaneously encouraging incoming tourism and discouraging residents to travel outside the country, where their devalued currency bought less.

Business travel too is influenced by economic factors, and is:

'... likely to be highly correlated with GDP or economic activity/output trends. This combines with business confidence ... (which) will again be influenced by interest rates and crucially by market expectations ... Generally, the health of the business sector, and hence its propensity to travel, will be influenced by competitiveness at home and overseas. Competitiveness, in turn, will be influenced by the sterling exchange rates.
(Peat and Mullan 1995)

However, once again the relationship is not a simple one. When business is bad for companies, there may be more urgency than ever to go out seeking new customers and conquering new markets; similarly, in tough times, there may be a perceived need to motivate staff more and drive them to new records of achievement by sending them on incentive trips, for example. In both cases, the result will be an increase in business travel and tourism.

An understanding of the various types of tourism purpose and motivation is vital for those planning and marketing tourist destinations. Not only do planners need to understand tourism demand in order to make investment decisions, for example, but they need to be aware of the different kinds of impact which different types of tourist have on the destinations they visit. This is the theme of Chapter 4, and will only be illustrated here in general terms. However, it is necessary first to highlight some other important distinctions between different types of tourists.

OTHER FACTORS

Although the purpose and motivation behind tourist trips are key indicators of differences between individual visitors, they are not the only factors which a destination must take into account when planning for tourism. Other important distinctions which may be made between visitors are as follows.

DIFFERENT LENGTHS OF VISIT

Tourists can differ from each other in terms of the length of time they spend at their destination. To the WTO distinction of 'tourist' and 'same-day visitors', may be added the 'short-break' visitor, who spends from one to three nights at the destination.

For destinations, the impact of receiving visitors will to a certain extent depend on whether those visitors stay for less than a day, for two or three days, or for longer. At the most basic level, day-trippers' spend nothing on accommodation and perhaps little in shops and restaurants; yet their impact on aggravating problems of congestion and overcrowding can be considerable. For example, since the day-trip market is overwhelmingly one using private transport, destinations targeted by this market (such as Windsor or Mont St Michel), must make a particular effort to deal with traffic and parking problems.

Short breaks, on the other hand, may provide a useful source of tourism revenue for destinations such as Bradford (see case study A). They would have little hope of attracting holidaymakers on their annual two-week break from work, but, with some distinctive attractions and imaginative marketing, might successfully establish themselves as short-break venues.

DOMESTIC AND OVERSEAS VISITORS

Knowing the geographic origin of tourists is another important key to successfully managing their visits to particular destinations. For example, unless they are day-trippers or VFR visitors, tourists from overseas are likely to use hotel accommodation. Depending on their country of origin, they may be high spending,

Type of visitor	Market targets	Age range	Level of interest in historic towns	Spend pattern	Impact	Visiting season considerations	Other
domestic long holiday visitors	general independent or special interest visitor	all	low	high	low	high season	declining UK market
domestic short holiday visitors	general independent or special interest visitor	35+ (professional/ retired)	high	high	low	off-peak, shoulder months, weekends	developing UK market – trend to take more holidays
conference, business & exhibition	corporate, association and incentive visitors – via conference organisers/ buyers/ placement agencies	35+ (professional)	high (subject to suitable facilities)	high (when not confined to hotels)	low	out of main season	developing market – can act as ambassadors
group travel	short breaks, excursion, overseas, domestic day visitors via coach and tour operators	50+	high	medium – low	low (subject to good coach parking facilities, etc)	high season (developing off-peak)	require information prior to visit to manage impact
overseas holiday visitors	general independent – via incoming tour operators and transport sector	all	very high	high	low	high season	volatile market dependent on rates of currency exchange – difficult to target – require information in a variety of languages
domestic leisure day visitors	general independent	all	high	low	high (tend to come by car)	throughout the year	need for local information
visiting friends & relatives (VFR)	general independent	all	N/A	low	low	throughout the year	need for local information and education of local community

Source: Getting it Right, *English Historic Towns Forum*

FIGURE 2.3 *Impacts of different tourists*

and therefore of interest to the owners of local shops. On the other hand, they may have special needs related to language. At the most basic level, non-English speaking visitors may need to be shown around by guides fluent in their own language and may require explanatory signs at tourist attractions, for example, to be written in their language, in order to get the maximum benefit from their visit.

ORGANISED GROUPS AND INDIVIDUAL VISITORS

The high visibility of groups of visitors can have a major impact on destinations such as villages and small towns, and this can be a source of conflict with the local population. Groups arriving by coach also create their own demands for parking spaces or coach parks, which local residents can find unsightly. However, in certain cases, it may be easier to control the flow of visitors arriving in organised groups, than vast numbers of individual, independent tourists using their own cars to get to the destination.

It is already clear that visitors to a destination will have different impacts according to the range of factors described above. A general example of how these impacts can differ according to the type of tourist in question is given in Figure 2.3. The information contained in the table is based on an examination of different groups visiting a particular type of destination – historic towns in the UK.

TOURISM SUPPLY

THE TOTAL TOURISM PRODUCT

From a destination point of view, one way of thinking about what Middleton (1988) calls the **total tourism product** is as a combination of resources and services. Resources constitute the initial attraction that the destination has for visitors, whilst services are provided to make possible or enhance the visit, and are provided mainly or entirely for tourists. We can consider the elements of resources and services in turn.

RESOURCES

Natural resources include the area's climate and its setting, landscape and natural environment (including wildlife). Natural resources are frequently the most important or key elements in a destination's attraction – seaside resorts, ski resorts and spas are obvious examples. It is worth noting, however, that in many cases 'natural' environments have been deliberately created and depend on continuing management. In the UK, almost all landscape is the outcome of thousands of years of human adaptation (Hoskyns, 1955), and changes in farming practices have had a profound effect on landscape and wildlife.

Built environment resources include the area's built stock and physical infrastructure, excluding that provided specifically for tourists. In historic cities and towns, the built stock is the fundamental attraction, but an attractive built environment is important to most destinations.

Sociocultural resources include intangible elements of the visitor experience which contribute to the attractiveness of a destination – pleasures derived from high and popular culture, from the atmosphere of the destination and from contact with the host population. Cultural resources include the arts, festivals, shops and special services and cuisine. Cultural resources cover a wide range of elements, catering for many different visitors. Amsterdam's resources, for example, range from high culture such as the art of the Rijksmuseum and music in the Concertgebouw to a tolerant, liberal and youthful counter-culture. Finally, the hospitality and perceived warmth and friendliness of the host community affect both image and attractiveness of the destination and the satisfaction tourists gain from their visit. A place's image is of fundamental importance, since tourists do not visit places of which they have never heard, or which they find unattractive. Image can affect both numbers and types of visitor.

SERVICES

Transport services are needed to allow visitors to get to the destination, and to move around once they are there. Transport services include the provision of infrastructure, such as new roads or facilities such as charter flights.

Hospitality services are provided to support visitors' stays in the destination. They include accommodation provided specifically for visitors and provision of food, drink and entertainments.

Support services aim to attract visitors and enhance their experience. They include information services such as Tourist Information Centres or *Syndicats d'Initiatives*, conference or convention bureaux and guide services.

We can identify three types of organisation involved in providing, developing and managing tourism services and resources.

VOLUNTARY AND NOT-FOR-PROFIT SECTOR

The voluntary and not-for-profit (NFP) sector in many countries has become a major stakeholder in the provision of tourism resources, offering many opportunities for events and activities, such as visits to historic properties (e.g. the National Trust), cultural exhibitions run by arts foundations, and pilgrimages organised by religious groups. However, the vast majority of tourism industry actors operate in either the public sector or private sector.

PUBLIC SECTOR

Public sector involvement in tourism has a long history in the UK, particularly at the local government level. For example, the provision of tourism-related infrastructure, such as piers, parks and gardens, in the 19th century was an essential public sector contribution to the success of many UK resorts. Since that time, national and local governments' tourism-related roles have extended greatly to include a wide range of services and functions, many of which cannot or would not be provided by the private sector. Swarbrooke (1993) lists these as follows:

- 'Marketing the country or area as a tourist destination . . .
- Developing and managing major tourist attractions, such as museums, galleries and historic buildings
- Providing and operating the infrastructure that is required by tourism, including the transport network
- Organising international events and festivals
- Linking tourism to rural development, regional policy and urban regeneration
- Stimulating tourism demand by operating subsidised "social tourism" schemes
- Educating and training the workforce for the tourism industry
- Encouraging private-sector investment through a range of financial and non-financial incentives
- Using planning controls to protect the natural and built environment, which are key tourism resources
- Collecting and disseminating market research data to help those responsible for both tourism marketing and development
- Levying local taxes on tourists, which can be used to fund tourism-related projects
- Using nationalised industries such as railways to stimulate tourism.'

We shall return to a consideration of many of these roles during the course of this book, since they are all relevant to the planning and development of tourism. At this point, however, it is important to emphasise that in Western industrialised countries, many of the functions listed above are increasingly carried out in partnership with the private sector actors in the tourism industry.

PRIVATE SECTOR

Private enterprise sector involvement in tourism includes the provision of an enormous variety of facilities and services, such as accommodation, transport, tour operations, entertainment and business-related services for tourists.

Some of the businesses providing these are locally owned and operated; others are part of national and international networks. Some are small family-run enterprises, while others are large corporations. In Western Europe, businesses stretch from giant companies, including airlines such as British Airways and hotels chains such as Forte, Accor and Club Méditerranée, to tens of thousands of family firms, including the proverbial British whelk stalls (*The Economist* 1995b).

Although many of the tourism multinationals have become household names, tourism is above all a major activator of small- and medium-sized enterprises. For example, a recent EU survey showed that in the hotel and restaurant sector, 80% of the hotel beds available throughout the EU were provided by independent hotels, and 'micro-enterprises' (0–9 employees) made up 96% of the businesses. These businesses accounted for 57% of turnover in the hotel and catering sector and 63% of the estimated total labour force of 4.6 million people (EC DG XXIII-Eurostat, Enterprises in Europe, 3rd report, 1994). In the UK, 70% of hotels and guest houses, for example, have 10 or fewer bedrooms (McIntyre, 1995).

Looking at destinations in this way draws attention to three important points.

1 The attraction of a destination arises from a mix of resources and services. Without such a mix, a place will not work as a destination. The mix varies from one place to another, and this variation gives each destination its individual character – its different total tourism product. In some cases however, the distinction between resources and services may be blurred. In many cities, for example, services like restaurants, bars and cafés are not provided specifically for visitors, but constitute one of the destination resources which attract tourists (see Chapter 5). Similarly, while the attraction of a place as a destination derives from the exploitation of its resources, what constitutes a 'resource' is ambiguous, and depends upon the perception of the visitor. A particular feature – whether it is natural, built or sociocultural – exists as a tourist resource only if it is valued and demanded by visitors. The value or very existence of 'tourist resources' in a destination thus changes as visitor perceptions change. In the nineteenth century, one of the major reasons for the development of seaside resorts as places devoted to leisure and recreation was the change in perceptions brought about by the Romantic Movement. Romantics liked the seaside because of its picturesque and enchanting natural landscape, and as such perceptions became more widespread, seaside holidays became attractive to more and more people (Soane 1992).

The growth in interest in industrial and social heritage is a more recent example. As popular interest in heritage has grown, new tourist resources have been created in non-traditional destinations. In Wigan, once derelict canal freight warehouses are now a popular visitor attraction. In Wakefield and at the Scottish Mining Museum near Edinburgh, redundant coalmines have been re-opened as attractions. Industrial cities such as Halifax, Bradford or Lille use their built heritage to attract visitors. Equally, changing perceptions can mean that resources are attenuated or disappear. Changing tastes mean that many spas can no longer attract visitors to take their waters, and the climate and setting of many cold water seaside resorts have been declining assets as warmer alternatives have become accessible. The dynamic nature of the process is emphasised by the publicity surrounding the possible ill effects of exposure to the sun. Perhaps warm water resorts will begin to lose popularity, offering a new competitive advantage to places – like many traditional UK resorts – where excessive exposure to the sun is an uncommon problem.

All this means that the resources available to attract visitors or to make a place a destination in the first place can vary over time, as visitor tastes and perceptions change. What constitutes a destination is in part a matter of 'cultural appraisal' (Cooper *et al.*, 1993). Equally, in many urban destinations, there is little distinction between tourist resources and those used by local people – shops, restaurants, cultural facilities and entertainments, historic buildings and the atmosphere of the place are used by the host population and visitors alike.

2 Tourism must compete with other industries for the use of a destination's resources. In many cases, resources which have tourism potential may also be attractive to other kinds of enterprise. An obvious case is the conflict between 'dirty' industries such as mineral extraction in beautiful and remote rural areas, and the unspoilt and peaceful landscape sought by visitors. Lime quarrying in the Peak District is a well known instance. A less familiar case is the potential conflict between tourism and high technology growth industries in attractive locations. Such industries are geographically mobile and heavily dependent on highly skilled labour for whose services there may be fierce competition. They frequently seek locations with an attractive climate, physical or cultural environment, often favouring historic towns, especially those with established Universities. Cambridge and the area known as 'Silicon Fen' in England, and Montpellier in southern France exemplify this trend. While there may be potential complementarity between different users of resources, there is also the potential for considerable conflict. In the case of attractive historic towns and cities, for example, preserving their character may require considerable restriction on new development. This can mean fierce competition between tourism and other industries over the use of sites that become available for development (see Cambridge case study). Seeking complementarities or synergies, and resolving conflicts are key tasks for destination management.

3 Although resources are the key to a place's attractiveness as a tourist destination, they are frequently not under the control of or produced by the commercial tourist industry. The commercial tourist industry is mainly involved in, and profits from, the provision of transport, hospitality and support services but it is dependent on destination resources, which constitute its basic capital.

Tourism is an unusual industry because it depends on the use of resources which it does not own. In terms of resource ownership, we can see the industry as depending on four distinct sets of resources:

- **Resources owned by the tourism industry**, and designed to attract visitors. These include bars, restaurants and other hospitality services, and attractions such as Theme Parks, commercial entertainment and resort developments.
- **'Free' resources**, to which there are generally no defined rights of ownership. These include the most familiar tourism resources – things like climate, fresh air, scenic views, culture, heritage or a friendly host population. Although these things are clearly valuable resources and fundamental to the tourism industry, they are not traded directly through the market, and can be used by anyone without payment.
- **Publicly owned resources**. Destination infrastructure is largely provided by public authorities. This includes transport and access, many of the elements which contribute to a destination's ambience (such as street furniture, planting, street cleaning), and frequently facilities like parks and open spaces, galleries, theatres and concert halls.
- **Resources owned by organisations outside the tourism industry**. The owners of resources which are fundamental to a destination's attraction may not be mainly (or at all) in the business of tourism. In Cambridge, for example, the colleges are the most important visitor attraction – but their key purpose is scholarship, not visitation. In the North Pennines, much of the land is owned by the National Trust, a body which must balance the demands of visitors against its main role of safeguarding heritage. Such resources are free from the point of view of the commercial tourism industry. Thomas makes the point in discussing Oxford's main attractions, the colleges, the Ashmolean Museum, the Sheldonian Theatre and the Bodleian Library:

'These "tourist attractions" were not conceived as tourist attractions. They serve a dual function – in the case of Oxford, education/tourism – and as such are a free resource to the tourism industry. That there is an admission charge to some of these buildings does not detract from the fact that they are essentially a free resource to the industry, as the admission charge is primarily directed at controlling admission, with the charge being directly related to the cost of extra staff for its collection. Nowhere is the admission charge related to the cost of upkeep of the buildings, and that is why it is still valid to designate all historic buildings as free resources.'

(Thomas, 1992)

In other words, 'tourism is frequently built upon a basis of free resources with ... a mixture of publicly and privately owned scarce resources superimposed' (Bull, 1991).

This gives rise to problems of protecting and managing tourism resources. One view of tourism is as an extractive industry, mining the destination's resources to create a tourism product. The eventual result of mining is resource depletion, and this can happen with tourism resources. Natural environments are vulnerable to volumes of visitors who can disturb wildlife and physically wear out footpaths; historic buildings can be worn away by the sheer pressure of visitor numbers; and visitor numbers and congestion may fundamentally change the nature of the place tourists wish to see – Venice is the most quoted example. Resources are particularly likely to be over-used since many of them are free to users, such as beautiful landscape, peace and quiet, and attractive city streets. These are essentially externality issues, and are discussed in Chapter 5. An alternative model for tourism is as a farming industry, cropping from a resource base which is constantly renewed and replenished. The problem is how to bring about this renewal, since the resources are not owned by the tourism industry which conse-quently has neither direct incentive nor direct means to renew them. We discuss later the way in which a destination's resources can be protected, managed and renewed, and how conflicts between different users, and between visitors and the host community can be resolved.

The availability and use of resources and services are influenced by the *institutional elements* of the overall tourism product, which are a focus of this book and which give a degree of unity to all of the other components. These essentially include the public and private organisational structures for promoting and supplying information on the destination; the suppliers of tourism education and training; and the various plans and programmes which determine the development of tourism at the destination – marketing and development plans, tourism-related legislation and regulations, incentive and grants schemes, and public awareness programmes on tourism.

Tourism planning involves consideration of all of the above elements, considered in relation to domestic and international tourist markets, as well as local residents' use of the various elements. All the components relate to and impact upon the natural, built and socioeconomic environments. This basic framework for the planning of tourism, expressed in terms of the tourism product's component parts is shown in Figure 2.4.

Taken together, all of the above elements may be understood to compose the global tourism product which is 'consumed' by the visitor at a particular destination. Certain characteristics of the global tourism product set it apart from other types of product, however. The tourism product is:

- **Non-transportable** – in order to consume a tourism product, the customer must travel to the point of production. Tourists wishing to visit a specific historic town such as Chester, or a monument such as Stonehenge, have no choice but to travel to these places. Only tourism products comprising events such as the Olympic Games are mobile. All other types of tourism product are firmly fixed in space.

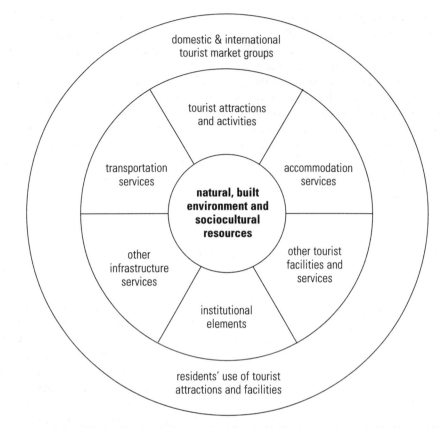

domestic & international
tourist market groups

tourist attractions
and activities

transportation
services

accommodation
services

**natural, built
environment and
sociocultural
resources**

other
infrastructure
services

other tourist
facilities and
services

institutional
elements

residents' use of tourist
attractions and facilities

Source: based on Inskeep, E. (1991) Tourism Planning: An Integrated and Sustainable Development Approach, *Van Nostrand Reinhold, New York*

FIGURE 2.4 *Components of a tourism plan*

- **Non-storable** – unlike manufactured products, the tourism product cannot be stocked: a seat on a charter flight or a room in a hotel are highly perishable, and are lost for ever if they remain unsold at the critical moment.
- **Inelastic** – another key characteristic of tourism is the inelasticity of its supply, both in quantitative and qualitative terms. In the short term, the tourism product cannot be quickly and easily adapted in response to substantial changes in the volume of demand for the product. While a sudden surge in demand for a certain type of car, for example, may be met by the manufacturers investing in new plant, taking on new staff or encouraging existing staff to work overtime, the tourism product is not so easily adaptable.

In the longer term, the inelastic nature of the tourism product (which is fundamentally based on the type of natural, infrastructural and built elements listed above) means that it cannot respond readily to changes in taste or fashion. Repositioning a destination in order to meet the changing demands of the market presents immense problems when the destination has a very strong image or has created its infrastructure to suit a very specific market. For example, many of the UK's small- and medium-sized seaside resorts, built to support the Victorian and Edwardian growth in holidays by the sea, entered a period of decline during the 1970s, when several factors, including competition from foreign markets, created the situation where the image and facilities offered by these resorts no longer matched the demands of the market (Lane, 1992).

But resorts, for example, are not so easily

transformed as, for example, the design of a car, and consumers are more likely to switch to other destinations than to believe that a destination with a previously strong established image has changed in line with their new tastes and needs.

All of the above factors explain the considerable inflexibility of supply which characterises tourism products. And the situation is exacerbated by the inflexibility and unpredictability of much of the *demand* for tourism. The highly *seasonal* nature of certain types of tourism demand (highly peaked at particular times of the week or year) means that destinations can be faced with serious problems of adapting themselves to large fluctuations in the level of that demand.

The problems of equating supply and demand are therefore considerable. One of the functions of tourism planning is to attempt to attune these two factors, since doing so is one of the ways in which negative impacts from tourism can be minimised and benefits maximised. This theme is developed in Chapter 4.

THE DIMENSIONS OF TOURISM

Since the end of the Second World War, international tourism has grown spectacularly in scale, now ranking alongside the petroleum industry and aeronautics as one of the world's major export industries.

The World Tourism Organisation is the source of the most comprehensive statistics for international tourism, although, on its own admission, these are 'fraught with gaps, divergent definitions and lack of uniformity in methods of data collection' (WTO, 1996). Given that note of caution, the global figures published by the WTO are nevertheless impressive.

According to the WTO, there were about 25 million international tourism trips made in 1950 and 561 million in 1995. Some 60% of international travel is for holiday purposes, 30% for business and the rest for other purposes (McIntyre, 1993).

Spending on international tourism has risen even faster than the number of trips. While it has taken over 40 years for the number of international tourism trips to increase 20-fold, the same growth in terms of spending has happened in the past 23 years alone. Spending on international tourism rose from US$ 18 billion in 1970 to US$ 381 billion in 1995. These figures do not include expenditure on international transport, which amounted to almost US$ 57 billion in 1994 (WTO, 1996).

In the 10 years leading up to 1995, worldwide tourist arrivals grew at an average rate of 5.5% a year and international tourist receipts, excluding transport, at 12.5%. International tourism has shown itself to be strongly resistant to fluctuations in economic conditions. Declines in the growth rate for international tourism were recorded only in 1991 as a result of the Gulf War and in 1993 under the influence of the economic recession in the industrialised countries (*ibid*).

However, this growth rate is not evenly spread throughout all world regions. The East Asia and Pacific region is the world's fastest-growing tourism region, having increased the number of its international tourist arrivals five-fold between 1970 and 1994 (WTO, 1995). This is partly due to a local boom in tourism created by the new holiday-making middle-classes of the region. But the expansion is also due to Europeans and North Americans attracted to countries such as Thailand and Malaysia, which have been brought within the spending power of much of the internationally travelling public by falling long-haul air fares and cheaper local labour costs.

EUROPEAN TOURISM

By comparison with the East Asia and Pacific region, the growth rate for tourist arrivals in Western Europe is weak, attributable, according to the WTO, not only to competition from new destinations but also because of saturation effects and high prices.

However, Europe is still the world region which receives the greatest share of the world's international visits – almost 60% of the total in 1995, according to the WTO (although as many authors have pointed out, the continent's concentration of relatively small countries with good transport links between them, means that Europeans cross national frontiers relatively easily and frequently, thus boosting international tourism statistics in this world region). But this compares unfavourably with 1960 when 72.5% of the world's international tourism trips were made within or to Europe. In terms of revenue, Europe's share of the world's total expenditure on international tourism has fallen from almost 60% to just over 50% between 1960 and 1995, and, if the WTO's predictions are accurate, it could fall even further.

Since 1985, tourism in the countries of Central and Eastern Europe has been growing faster than in all the other parts of the continent, with arrivals rising by an average of 10% a year and receipts by 19%. The WTO (1995) points out that these are the highest increases in receipts registered in any European sub-region and represent over double the continental average.

Figure 2.5 shows the top twenty destinations in Europe, in terms of numbers of international tourist arrivals.

Despite the emphasis put on international tourism statistics, the domestic tourist market is by far the largest source of demand for business tourist and leisure tourist facilities in most Western European countries. Pearce (1989) notes that 'Domestic tourists are generally several times more numerous than international tourists in most developed Western states'; and Vellas and Bécherel (1995) estimate that, globally, 'Domestic tourism ... represents, on average, over 80% of all tourism movements.'

Although in many countries, including the UK, the number of main annual holidays taken by nationals in their country of residence is declining, second holidays, short-breaks and business tourism are boosting the level of domestic tourism. OECD (1994) figures show that in non-Mediterranean countries in particular, the domestic tourism market is more important than the incoming, international tourism market. *Foreign* tourists were responsible for less than 50% of all nights spent in the various forms of tourist accommodation in Finland (21.8%), France (37.1%), Germany (12.6%), the Netherlands (30.8%), Norway (37.2%), Sweden (19.7%) and Switzerland (48.6%). In the UK, spending on tourism by the British themselves regularly outstrips the amount spent by foreign visitors. The figures for 1994 were £13.2 billion and £9.9 billion respectively. Even on accommodation, spending by the British (£4.9 billion) was higher than that of overseas visitors' (£3.6 billion) (International Passenger Survey and UK Tourism Survey).

However, in all Western European countries, a major domestic tourism market is that comprising day trips, which are overwhelmingly taken by those countries' own residents. For the UK, for example, the 1991/92 Leisure Day Visits Survey estimated the value of domestic day visitor spending in 1992 to be £9 billion, just under the UK's entire earnings from incoming tourism that year.

UK TOURISM

The numbers of incoming visitors to the UK has grown steadily since the Second World War. There were just under 10 million foreign visitors to the UK in 1975, rising to over 15 million in 1987 and to 21 million in 1994. The average annual growth for overseas visits to the UK was 4.4% between 1984 and 1994. However, between 1989 and 1994, it was 3.9%, showing a slight slowing down of growth in the 1990s, compared with the 1980s.

The number of overseas visits to the UK rose by 20% between 1989 and 1994, and associated spending rose by over 40% in nominal terms, although this represented an increase of only 8% once the effects of inflation were stripped out (Peat and Mullen, 1995). Visitors from the EU make up the majority of visitors, but their expenditure per head is markedly lower than visitors from North America and the rest of the world.

Figure 2.6 shows the principal countries of

Rank 1985	Rank 1995	Country	Arrivals 1000s 1995	% change 1995/94	% of total 1995
1	1	France	60,000	−2.1	18.0
2	2	Spain	44,886	3.8	13.5
3	3	Italy	29,953	9.0	9.0
5	4	United Kingdom	23,746	12.9	7.1
8	5	Hungary	20,700	−3.4	6.2
17	6	Poland	19,200	2.1	5.8
4	7	Austria	17,173	−4.0	5.2
12[1]	8	Czech Republic	15,500	−8.8	4.7
6	9	Germany	14,847	2.4	4.5
7	10	Switzerland	11,500	−5.7	3.5
10	11	Greece	10,130	−5.4	3.0
11	12	Portugal	9,706	6.3	2.9
20	13	Turkey	7,083	17.4	2.1
16	14	Netherlands	6,574	6.4	2.0
13	15	Belgium	5,224	−1.6	1.6
14[2]	16	Russian Federation	4,796	3.3	1.4
18	17	Ireland	4,231	−1.8	1.3
15	18	Bulgaria	4,125	1.7	1.2
21	19	Norway	2,880	1.8	0.9
19	20	Romania	2,608	−6.7	0.8
		Total 1–20	**314,862**	**1.3**	**94.5**
		Total Europe	**333,299**	**1.1**	**100.0**

(1) Former Czechoslovakia. (2) Former USSR.

Source: World Tourism Organisation (WTO)

FIGURE 2.5 *Top twenty tourism destinations in Europe. International tourist arrivals (excluding same-day visitors)*

residence of overseas visitors to the UK, with comparisons between the first three quarters of 1994 and 1995.

According to the WTO, the UK is fifth in the world in terms of earnings from international tourism. The most popular attractions of the UK for foreign visitors depend on which segment of which nationality is under consideration, as its image changes from country to country. Some examples in Figure 2.7, taken from BTA Market Guides, demonstrate this diversity and give some indication of the complexity in marketing overseas a tourist 'product' such as the UK.

In general terms, the trend is for a growing proportion of the UK residents' main holidays to be taken overseas, as foreign destinations become

	1994 quarters				1995 quarters				Cumulative (1 + 2 + 3 quarters)		
Visits to UK by residents of ...	1st '000	2nd '000	3rd '000	4th '000	1st '000	2nd '000	3rd '000	4th* '000	1994 '000	1995 '000	Change %
USA	506	788	1,050	634	609	824	1,147		2,344	2,580	+10
Canada	91	163	210	107	97	198	197		464	492	+ 6
Belgium/Luxembourg	142	367	280	245	203	298	432		789	933	+18
France	708	754	752	565	604	974	829		2,214	2,407	+ 9
Germany	415	691	789	622	411	795	888		1,895	2,094	+11
Italy	133	153	358	182	169	173	406		644	748	+16
Netherlands	228	305	364	306	270	339	364		897	973	+ 8
Denmark	86	78	83	86	70	83	93		247	249	*
Greece	40	36	55	35	43	31	52		131	126	− 4
Spain	143	123	205	210	147	134	285		471	566	+20
Portugal	30	35	39	39	34	33	53		104	120	+15
Irish Republic	322	410	573	371	342	426	621		1,305	1,389	+ 6
Austria	42	68	85	48	44	79	91		195	214	+10
Switzerland	87	141	135	110	85	156	151		353	392	+ 8
Norway	58	74	101	103	65	97	136		233	298	+28
Sweden	82	115	161	158	132	141	137		358	410	+15
Finland	15	27	32	32	19	34	34		74	87	+18
Rest of W. Europe	69	51	84	75	79	54	117		204	250	+23
Middle East	105	92	281	124	139	116	277		478	532	+11
North Africa	15	12	32	15	18	18	39		59	75	+27
South Africa	53	56	98	54	45	64	93		207	202	− 2
Eastern Europe	60	147	206	131	84	150	280		413	514	+24
Japan	140	107	203	139	155	128	211		450	494	+10
Australia & N. Zealand	87	171	270	141	114	199	277		528	590	+12
Latin America	57	61	108	56	73	67	96		225	236	+ 4
Rest of World	172	303	415	259	219	401	508		890	1,128	+27
Total	3,888	5,327	6,972	4,848	4,270	6,013	7,814		15,187	18,097	+12

* Not available.

Source: International Passenger Survey

FIGURE 2.6 *Principal countries of residence of overseas visitors to the UK*

more accessible and relatively cheaper. The numbers of their visits abroad have risen constantly since the 1950s, at the beginning of which only 5% of UK residents travelled overseas. Between 1980 and 1992, the tourism expenditure of UK residents at home rose by 12%, as against an increase in their overseas expenditure of 66%. 45% of total UK tourism expenditure is now domestic, compared to 55% in 1983 (McIntosh, 1995).

In 1993, just under 36 million overseas visits were made by the British, a rise of 6% on the previous year. Their areas of destination are given in Figure 2.8. The substantial growth in 'Rest of World' destinations in a single year testifies to the UK residents' increasing enthusiasm

WHAT ATTRACTS VISITORS TO BRITAIN?

Australia and New Zealand – Australians are more likely than the average visitor to stay in Scotland, Wales and all regions of England outside London. They plan their trips in detail. Cultural links are strong and castles, gardens and historic houses have particular appeal. New Zealanders also like waterways and walking; younger visitors may be interested in tracing their ancestors and all of them are environmentally conscious, expecting the clean and unpolluted countryside they find at home.

Thailand – Britain's royalty, nightlife and quality brand shopping offer the most recognisable and positive aspects of Britain to the Thai traveller. Britain is seen as a top quality destination and most Thais travel to London for the variety that it offers.

Malaysia – strong Commonwealth links make most Malaysians familiar with Britain through the education system and the fact that English is their second language. Students in particular are interested in travelling around Britain during term time. There is a growing interest in touring holidays.

Greece – about half come to Britain for medical care or to learn English. London's shopping is as much a draw as minor surgery, but usually little interest is shown in historic buildings, museums and theatre. However, day trips to places such as Windsor, Stratford and Bath do raise some interest.

Canada – family ties and theatre attractions contribute to their capacity to travel off-season. Canadians have greater knowledge of Britain than their American neighbours and seek new experiences rather than traditional sights. They are also likely to be older than the average visitor, since 30% are aged 55+, double the average.

Source: Bresh, 1995

FIGURE 2.7 *What attracts visitors to Britain?*

for long-haul destinations in the East Asia and Pacific region, for holidays as well as business tourism.

The table in Figure 2.8 indicates global figures for all tourism purposes. Focusing specifically on leisure tourism, Figure 2.9 compares UK residents' holiday trips in the UK with their holiday trips abroad from 1990 to 1994.

Although Figure 2.9 may appear to indicate that, contrary to what was previously stated, the British are taking more holidays in their own country year after year, in fact the majority of residents' 'holiday trips' in the UK are of one to three nights in length, in other words, short breaks. The number of such domestic short

breaks has risen gradually, to finally outnumber domestic holidays of four plus nights in 1994. The increased emphasis on short break holidays (encouraged by advertising campaigns) taken especially by 'career couples' and 'empty nesters' (couples whose children have grown up, left home and become financially independent of their parents), added an estimated £8.5 million to domestic tourism expenditure in 1994. Real spending on short breaks had already increased by nearly 15% between 1990 and 1993.

Regarding business tourism in the UK, most commentators stress the contrast between the lavish spending levels of the 1980s and the belt-tightening which has characterised the 1990s.

Year	Total	Destination area		
	('000)	North America	Western Europe	Rest of World
1992	33,836	2,813	27,675	3,347
1993	35,842	3,050	28,869	3,922
Change (%) 1993/92	+6	+8	+4	+17

Source: International Passenger Survey

FIGURE 2.8 *Tourists in North America, Western Europe and the rest of the world*

	1990		1991		1992		1993		1994	
	m	Index	m	Index	m	Index	m	Index	m	Index
UK holidays	58.4	100	58.3	100	59.9	103	54.9	94	62.8	108
Overseas holidays	16.1	100	17.0	106	19.9	124	19.7	122	23.3	145
All holidays	74.0	100	74.9	101	79.4	107	74.2	100	85.6	116

Note: Some trips involved both staying in the UK and overseas visits, therefore the sum of UK holidays and overseas holidays is greater than the figure for all holidays.

Source: UKTS

FIGURE 2.9 *Comparison of UK residents' holiday trips from 1990 to 1994*

Peat and Mullan (1995) add a more optimistic note:

'On the business side, associated spending fell by 11% in real terms between 1989 and 1994, but that masks an increase of 29% between 1993 and 1994. There is a strong suggestion here of a link to the business cycle and economic activity generally'.

(Peat and Mullan, 1995)

As the UK's domestic and overseas markets for business tourism emerge from the recession, it would appear that those responsible for the marketing and planning of tourism can be reasonably optimistic of modest growth in this segment.

The different segments of the tourist market for the UK, in terms of revenue, are shown in Figure 2.10.

The importance of the day visitor market is clearly indicated. It is the largest domestic category, and, in terms of revenue, amounts to almost the same as the spending of all overseas visitors to the UK.

Naturally, this tourism activity, either inter-

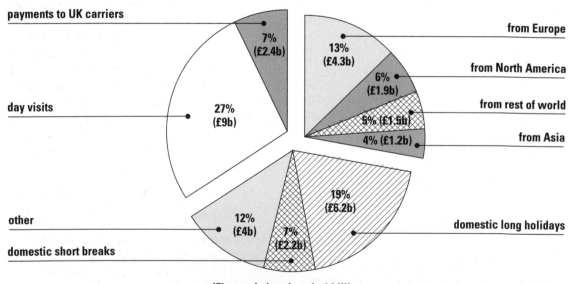

(Figures in brackets in £ billions, totals are approximate because of rounding)

Source: IPS, UKTS and DVS

Total £33bn (1993)
Other includes domestic business travel and visiting friends and relatives

FIGURE 2.10 *Segments of UK tourism industry*

national or domestic, is not spread evenly across the country as a whole. The tables in Figure 2.11 indicate the disparities which exist between the tourism visits, nights and expenditure of overseas visitors in the different regions.

The pattern of the regional distribution of overseas visitors to the UK is marked by the domination of London as a major draw, especially for first time visitors. In 1993, the capital accounted for 53% of all staying visitors to Britain and 52.6% of all expenditure. Among the English regions, those nearest the busy Channel ports, South East England and Southern region attract the largest proportion of overseas visitors – 10.7% and 9.2% respectively in 1993.

Concerning domestic tourism, the West Country of England is by far the principal destination, particularly for holidays. Almost one in three holidays of four plus nights was spent in that region in 1994. For business-related tourism, London, the Heart of England, the North West and Southern England are all important regions.

Many of the tourism patterns which emerge from this brief survey have their roots in the historical development of tourism in the UK and other countries. This chapter concludes, therefore, with a historical review of tourism, with particular reference to the UK.

TOURISM: A HISTORICAL PERSPECTIVE

Although the word 'tourism' did not appear until the 19th century, tourism as an activity has its roots in the ancient worlds. However, then, and up until the 20th century, the temporary movement of people to destinations for rest and recreation was confined to the privileged few who had the leisure and money to indulge in tourist activity. Classical scholars have shown that wealthy Greeks and Romans travelled to Egypt on holiday, spent the summers in second homes in locations such as the Bay of Naples, and visited spas – more often for leisure than for health reasons (Py, 1992). Ancient Greece was the destination for those attending the Olympic Games and other major festivals (Craig-Smith and French, 1994). Even for the elite, journeys were, for many centuries, slow, uncomfortable and often dangerous. An indication of the arduous conditions of most travel up until the 19th century is contained in the origin of the word 'travel', which is linked to the Old French verb *se travailler* meaning to put oneself through torture.

Apart from travel for trading purposes and the pilgrimages of the early Middle Ages (with Jerusalem, Rome, Canterbury and Santiago de Compostella as main destinations) little is known of the subsequent development of tourism until the advent of the educational and cultural trips, known as the 'Grand Tour' of Europe, undertaken by young members of the aristocracy of the 17th and 18th centuries. For British travellers, the tour began in France and continued on to Italy, where they would spend about a year visiting cities such as Rome, Venice and Turin, finally to return via Switzerland, Germany and the Netherlands.

A common theme in tourism histories is the gradual extension of tourism to other social classes, beginning with the rise of the bourgeoisie. Steinecke (1993), for example, notes that, due to socio-economic structural changes in Middle and Western Europe at the end of the 18th century, the exclusivity of travelling for leisure altered to a certain extent:

'Merchants and others with urban or trading occupations gained economic influence and status due to the increased ownership of factories and the expansion of national and international trade. By imitating the behaviour of the former noble elite, the bourgeoisie tried to increase their status. This ... influenced travelling behaviour. The 'Grand Tour' destinations also became popular destinations for the travelling bourgeoisie.'

(Steinecke, 1993)

Region	Visits %	Nights %	Expenditure %
England	**87.2**	**86.4**	**89.6**
London	53.0	36.6	52.6
Rest of England	**44.3**	**49.8**	**37.0**
Northumbria TB	2.0	2.0	1.4
Cumbria TB	1.3	0.8	0.6
North West TB	5.4	4.8	3.3
Yorkshire & Humberside TB	4.5	4.0	2.6
East Midlands TB	3.3	3.0	2.2
Heart of England TB	6.9	5.5	4.2
East Anglia TB	6.9	6.4	4.3
West Country TB	7.0	5.8	4.2
Southern TB	9.2	8.3	7.0
South East England TB	10.7	9.1	7.0
Isle of Man	0.1	0.1	0.1
Channel Isles	0.2	0.2	0.2
Scotland	**8.6**	**9.6**	**7.2**
Wales	**3.5**	**2.8**	**1.9**
Northern Ireland	**0.5**	**0.7**	**0.4**
	100.0	100.0	100.0
Total	**19,488**	**185,217**	**£9,278m**

Note: County/region/country figures are rounded to the nearest 10,000 (staying visits), 100,000 (nights), £m (expenditure). The survey excluded Irish Republic residents, but the bases in this table include them.
The expenditure base excludes spending by visitors departing directly from the Channel Islands and nil-nights transit visitors.

Source: International Passenger Survey 1993 Regional Analyses

	All tourism			Holidays			Short holidays (1–3 nights)			Long holidays (4+ nights)			Business and work			VFR		
	trips %	nights %	spending £ %	trips %	nights %	spending £ %	trips %	nights %	spending £ %	trips %	nights %	spending £ %	trips %	nights %	spending £ %	trips %	nights %	spending £ %
Cumbria	3	4	4	5	5	5	4	4	5	5	5	5	1	1	1	1	1	1
Northumbria	3	3	3	3	3	2	4	3	2	3	3	2	3	4	4	4	4	5
North West England	10	8	9	9	8	9	10	10	12	9	7	7	12	11	11	10	9	10
Yorkshire & Humberside	10	10	10	11	10	10	12	12	11	10	10	9	8	8	10	9	8	10
Heart of England	11	8	9	8	6	6	9	9	9	6	5	4	17	16	16	15	13	13
East Midlands	8	7	7	9	8	7	9	9	9	8	7	6	7	5	6	9	7	9
East Anglia	11	11	10	12	11	11	12	12	11	11	11	10	8	7	6	11	12	11
London	10	7	9	5	4	5	7	6	10	3	3	3	17	17	21	13	11	14
West Country	17	23	21	22	28	29	14	16	15	31	32	35	9	9	7	11	12	9
Southern	12	11	10	12	11	10	11	10	9	13	11	11	12	13	10	11	11	8
South East England	9	8	8	9	8	7	9	9	8	8	7	7	9	9	6	9	10	10

FIGURE 2.11 *Regional pattern of domestic tourism, 1993*

In an early manifestation of the tendency noted by Thurot (see Chapter 3) for social classes to succeed one other at destinations, the British travelling nobility increasingly abandoned the Grand Tour cities in favour of a wider choice of destinations, often in the UK, many of which have survived to the present day as venues for tourist activity:

- **Inland spas** – originally visited because of the healing effects of their mineral springs, inland spas in 18th century Europe became destinations for members of the nobility, not only for medical reasons but more importantly as centres of entertainment and social intercourse. Facilities in spas such as Bath and Tunbridge Wells in the UK and Baden-Baden, Marienbad, Aix-les-Bains, and Vichy on the Continent reflected the demands of their aristocratic guests: bathing houses and swimming baths, but also large parks, concert halls and casinos (Steinecke, 1993). Spa towns were therefore the first settlements to reflect a specific tourism function in their layout.

  The growth and spread of wealth in society allowed more people to follow the fashion for taking mineral waters, and by the mid 18th century, there were more than a hundred spa towns in the UK, ranging from those such as Bath, which enjoyed international renown, to those of a more local reputation, such as Buxton, Leamington and Malvern.

- **Seaside resorts** – by the middle of the 18th century, there began the growth of small seaside 'watering places', linked to the advocacy of the curative virtues of sea water, which was found to contain many of the minerals found in spa waters. Indeed, Scarborough, as the only English spa bordering the sea, was the first to exploit this facility for its medical benefits (Cooper, 1989). By 1750, Brighton, Margate, and Weymouth were also being used by wealthy visitors, following the invention of the bathing machine.

  As in the case of inland spas, royal visits played a role in establishing such resorts as fashionable destinations. For example, Lavery (1987) describes how the arrival of the Prince of Wales in Brighton in 1784 accelerated the growth of the town as a fashionable resort:

'In 1760, Brighton consisted of a large village with a population of 2,000. By 1820, it had over 3,000 houses, a population of over 24,000 and more than 10,000 visitors a year. During the late 18th century, many other coastal towns realised the potential of their seaside, and Lewis' *Topographical Dictionary* of 1835 lists dozens of former hamlets and small fishing villages, from Bognor Regis to Rhyl, that were transformed as seaside watering places.'

(Lavery, 1987)

Steinecke quotes Cosgrove and Jackson, who showed that between 1801 and 1851, UK seaside resorts experienced the highest rate of growth compared with other cities. Continental Europe also developed its own seaside resorts, many with a distinctive image, such as Scheveningen, Ostend, Biarritz and Deauville. Berry (1992) describes the role of British travellers in exporting the concept of the seaside resort to the French and Italian Riviera and to the north coast of France.

As with the spas, a specific seaside resort infrastructure was developed, the fundamental elements being bathing facilities, promenades, reading and conversation rooms, libraries, concert halls and theatres. Berry (*ibid*) notes that in many instances, the same people ran the facilities at a spa and at a seaside resort, since the seasons were sequential. For example, the first library opened in Brighton was owned by a librarian from Tunbridge Wells, and facilities in Weymouth were developed by entrepreneurs from Bath.

Much of the development of spa towns and seaside resorts took the form of public sector/private sector collaboration, with public money paying for infrastructure and private entrepreneurs funding the construction of facilities.

Other forms of holiday-making developed during this period. Parallel to the development of the coastal resorts, came the 'discovery' of the Lake District and the Alps as regions rich in the wild, romantic aspects of nature, the appreciation of which had become fashionable by the 19th century. Later in that century, the growth of mountaineering and winter sports led to the spread of resorts catering for enthusiasts, in the Alpine regions of France, Switzerland, Italy and Austria.

Most of the UK spa and seaside resorts were situated one or two days' journey by coach or horseback (the only available forms of transport) from the major towns or cities. The absence of a cheaper form of transport was a major factor in limiting the number of people who could afford to travel to such destinations. But from the 1840s, the faster, cheaper transport provided by the invention of the railway considerably boosted the number of middle-class tourists visiting UK seaside resorts, which as a result prospered and grew rapidly in size. Lavery (1987) gives the example of Southend, which, with the opening of the London, Tilbury and Southend Railway, saw its population grow in the space of a few years from 4,000 to 20,000 in 1901. The same pattern occurred at many other, now familiar coastal resorts such as Brighton, Southport and Blackpool.

Regular cheap-day excursions to the seaside and other destinations were soon being organised by the railway companies and entrepreneurs, most famously by Thomas Cook with his one shilling return Temperance Association excursion from Leicester to Loughborough. The result of such ventures was a substantial movement of pleasure-seekers travelling to the seaside for day trips, weekend trips and longer journeys.

However, as Cooper (1989) remarks, accommodation in centres served by the railways was initially found to be woefully inadequate to meet the needs of the new rail travellers. Consequently, a period of hotel construction began, led by the railway companies themselves, building the great terminus hotels which were to play a significant role in the UK hotel industry over the following 100 years. He adds that, 'The high capital investment called for by this construction programme led to the early formation of the hotel chains and corporations in place of the former individual hotel proprietors.' The industrial age of tourism thus began.

By the end of the 19th century, the fundamentals of modern tourist activity were established: sightseeing, bathing, culture and education, health and winter sports.

In the first half of the 20th century, certain socioeconomic factors operating in Western Europe led to a rapid growth in the numbers of people able to participate in tourism activities:

- increases in leisure time due to the reduction in working hours and paid holiday regulations – the first Holidays with Pay Act of 1938 encouraged voluntary agreements on paid holidays for employees, and set the target of an annual two-week paid holiday for all workers (an ambition not realised, however, until after the end of World War II)
- increases in real average income levels, particularly following World War II
- greater mobility as a result of the growth in motorised public transport and in the rate of private car ownership.

This was the period of growing access to holidays for ordinary working people. Between the wars, the seaside holiday became firmly established as the traditional annual break for the mass public in Britain, and numerous towns developed as 'new' resorts to meet the burgeoning demand, including Bournemouth, Broadstairs, Clacton, Skegness and Colwyn Bay. Generally, people travelled by rail or car or coach and stayed in guesthouses, or with friends and relatives. An alternative form of accommodation was provided by the holiday camps which sprang up during the 1930s, popularised by Billy Butlin, who built his first camp in Skegness in 1936. The main distinguishing characteristic of such camps at the time was the provision of indoor and outdoor entertainment and amusement facilities, which quickly gained the widespread approval of the British public used to the risk of bad weather while on holiday. By 1939, there were 200 such camps scattered around the coasts of Britain, catering for 30,000 holiday-makers a week during the season (Brunner, 1945).

Ironically, it was a by-product of World War II which was to create competition for Britain's seaside resorts and finally bring about the demise of many of them. The technological breakthroughs in aircraft design during the war meant that air travel finally emerged as a viable, afford-able alternative to sea travel. The large number of aircraft and pilots made available by the return of peace, helped the growth of the major national airlines in Europe and North America, many of which invested in the new jet aircraft, selling their propeller aircraft to entrepreneurs such as Freddie Laker. Private airline companies such as Freddie Laker's pioneered the develop-ment of charter services (an essential element in the Mediterranean package holiday business) which, by the early 1960s, had transformed the annual holiday pattern of the British holiday-maker. By the 1970s, winter package tours, prin-cipally for skiing holidays, were also accelerating the exodus of UK holiday-makers from their tra-ditional destinations.

The growth in, and affordability of, overseas holiday packages contributed to the decline of many of the UK's traditional seaside resorts. However, the substantial rise in the number of visits to the countryside and historic towns was a simultaneous phenomenon linked to another post-war trend – the rapid growth in car owner-ship.

As post-war standards of living rose in the UK, private car ownership expanded rapidly, rising from about 2 million in 1950 to over 11 million vehicles by 1970 and over 20 million in 1990. Individual transport by car on this scale opened up almost unlimited spatial opportunities and brought about a corresponding decline in demand for both coach and rail services. The ease and flexibility of private car transport en-couraged the growth of day trips, as destinations such as historic cities and rural villages became quickly and easily accessible to millions. It soon became clear that car parking (for visitors and residents) was to become a serious problem for towns designed in the pre-motor age, a problem with which most are still struggling at the end of the 20th century.

Car ownership on a massive scale had other far-reaching consequences. Ferry companies flourished with the growth in the trend of using the family car for holidays abroad. The develop-ment of motorway links to the Channel ports in the UK and similar improvements on the motor-ways of France, Belgium and the Netherlands brought more continental resorts within driving distance from Britain, making independent foreign travel easier and more attractive.

Camping and caravanning holidays also grew rapidly in popularity. By 1995, approximately 15% of all UK holiday trips used these forms of accommodation. Nevertheless, this form of tour-ing holiday has come in for much criticism from those responsible for tourism planning, not only for its impact on congestion on the roads, but also concerning the aesthetic question of caravan sites' impact on the landscape.

Growing recognition by the government of the importance of the tourist industry, both as an employer and as a major contributor to the national economy, led to the 1969 Development of Tourism Act which developed a framework for public-sector planning for tourism on the national level. In the decades which followed the UK's entry into the European Union, the legislation and policy of that body was also to have an impact on the development of tourism in the UK and other member states (see Chapter 6).

In the past few decades, changing socio-economic conditions, as well as changing values, have continued to create new forms of tourism demand: from special-interest and activity holi-days, to long-haul trips, short breaks and second holidays.

The tourism market is in a state of constant flux. McIntyre, commenting on global trends in tourism, notes that:

'The inclusive tour, typical of mass tourism of the past 30 years, is becoming somewhat outmoded. These tour packages were designed to suit everyone – usually a sun, sea and sand package and resort-based with relaxation as the main activity. But there is growing evidence that more tourists desire individual expression, more possibilities to learn something new, and greater activity ... Increasingly, tourists are separating into different markets ... More tourists are now activity and learning oriented, wanting to participate in recreation and sports and understand the areas which they visit. Smaller families, two-income households and women as travel decision-makers are other major trends which affect travel patterns.'

(McIntyre, 1993)

He predicts that even established forms of tourist activity are set to undergo a qualitative change:

'At the same time, the conventional forms of resort, sightseeing and urban tourism will remain popular, but tourists will expect a higher level of environmental quality than they have done in the past. Already, tourist destinations that exhibit environmental and social problems because they were unplanned and poorly managed are being bypassed by many tourists for the better planned and managed destinations.'

(ibid)

The tourism industry in the widest sense has responded to these changes in demand by inventiveness and innovation, as a number of new types of tourism products and tourist destinations have been developed in the UK and overseas. Many of these are based on areas not traditionally associated with tourism as defined by the coastal resort model. The private sector has added to the supply through the development of such products as theme parks, farm tourism, inland holiday centres (such as the Center Parcs chain), and time-share developments.

There has also been significant contribution to tourism supply through private sector/public sector initiatives in the UK. For example, tourism has often been included as a major element in urban renewal projects and conservation schemes, such as St Catherine's Dock in London and the Piece Hall in Halifax.

Similar private-sector and public-sector partnerships have been behind the UK's burgeoning supply of industrial heritage areas and open-air museums, such as the North of England Open Air Museum at Beamish, County Durham; garden festivals including the National Garden Festivals held in Stoke-on-Trent, Glasgow, Gateshead, and Wales; and inner-city tourism – dockland developments such as the revitalising of the harbour area of Merseyside.

Forecasters generally support the view that the evolution of tourism demand and supply will continue and that tourism activity will expand. Crawshaw summarises the reasons for this optimism as follows:

'Although there are discernible limits to the growth of tourism demand, new markets will emerge, due to changing economic conditions, new technologies and consumer behaviour. It is predicted that even moderate levels of growth would support an expansion of tourism. There will be a lot more people in age groups with a greater propensity and financial ability to travel, particularly retired people and single adults. New technologies such as computerised reservation systems ... will make tourism more accessible. Legislative changes, deregulation and privatisation are expected to increase competition within the industry. It is anticipated that greater individuality in consumer behaviour will encourage greater segmentation in tourism markets. It is also predicted that there will be more tourist destinations, new products and greater competition at the international level and within the United Kingdom.'

(Crawshaw, 1993)

Tourism destinations play a vital part in the constantly shifting equation of tourism supply and demand. The dynamics of their evolution is the subject of the next chapter.

REFERENCES

Berry, S. (1992) 'The impact of the British upon seaside resort development in Europe', in *Proceedings of the 1992 Tourism in Europe Conference*, Centre for Travel and Tourism, Tyne and Wear.

Bresh, L. (1995) 'What attracts visitors to Britain?' in *Insights*, May 1995, English Tourist Board, London.

Brunner, E. (1945) *Holiday Making and the Holiday Trades*, Oxford University Press, Oxford.

Bull, A. (1991) *The economics of travel and tourism*, Pitman-Wiley, London.

Commission of the EC (1995) *The role of the Union in the field of tourism: Commission Green Paper*, Brussels.

Crawshaw, C. (1993) 'Tourism and the Environment' in *Town and Country Planning 1993 Summer School Proceedings*.

Davidson, R. (1992) *Tourism in Europe*, Pitman, London.

Economist, The (1995a) 'Faulty holiday towers' in *The Economist*, 29 July 1995, p. 15.

Economist, The (1995b) 'A place in the sun' in *The Economist*, 29 July 1995, p. 56.

Economist, The (1996) *Messe business*, pp. 71–2, The Economist.

Greene Belfield-Smith (1996) *The Impact of Euro '96 on the Hotel Industry*, Greene Belfield-Smith, London.

Hoskyns, W.G. (1995) *The Making of the English Landscape*, Hodder & Stoughton, London.

Hudman, L.E. (1980) *Tourism: a shrinking world*, Grid Inc, Columbus, Ohio.

Lane, P. (1992) 'The regeneration of small to medium sized seaside resorts', in *Proceedings of the 1992 Tourism in Europe Conference*, Centre for Travel and Tourism, Tyne and Wear.

Lavery, P. (1987) *Travel and Tourism*, Elm Publications, Kings Ripton.

McIntosh, S. (1995) *London and the tourism policy of the European Union*, London and Europe Research Programme, London.

McIntyre, G. (1993) *Sustainable Tourism Development: Guide for local planners*, World Tourism Organisation, Madrid.

Maslow, A.H. (1943) 'A theory of human motivation', in *Psychological Review* 50(4).

Mathieson, A. and Wall, G. (1982) *Tourism: Economic, Physical and Social Impacts*, Longman, London.

Peat, J. and Mullan, G. (1995) 'Tourism and the economy' in *Insights*, September 1995, English Tourist Board, London.

Poon, A. (1994) 'The "new tourism" revolution' in *Tourism Management* 15(2) pp. 91–92.

Py, P. (1992) *Le tourisme – une phénomène économique*, La Documentation Française, Paris.

Richards, G. (1992) 'European Social Tourism: Welfare or Investment?' in *Proceedings of the 1992 Tourism in Europe Conference*, Centre for Travel and Tourism, Tyne and Wear.

Seaton, A.V. (1994) 'Are relatives friends? Reassessing the VFR category in segmenting tourism markets' in *Tourism: the State of the Art*, John Wiley and Sons, Chichester.

Smith, V.L. (1977) *Hosts and guests: the anthropology of tourism*, Blackwell, Oxford.

Soane, J. (1992) 'The Origin, Growth and Transformation of Maritime Resorts since 1840' in *Built Environment*, 18, 1.

Steinecke, A. (1993) 'The historical development of tourism in Europe', in *Tourism in Europe: Structures and developments*, Pompl, W. and Lavery, P. (eds), CAB International, Wallingford.

Swarbrooke, J. (1993) 'Public sector policy in tourism – a comparative study of France and Britain', in *Insights*, March 1993, English Tourist Board, London.

Tocquer, G. and Zins, M. (1987) *Marketing du Tourisme*, Gaëtam Morin, Quebec.

Vellas, F. and Bécherel, L. (1995) *International Tourism*, Macmillan, Basingstoke.

WTO (1995) *Tourism Market Trends: World 1994*, World Tourism Organisation, Madrid.

WTO (1996) *Tourism Market Trends: World 1995*, World Tourism Organisation, Madrid.

The dynamics and evolution of tourism destinations

INTRODUCTION

In Chapter 2, we looked at the nature of tourism and at how the demand for tourism has changed and grown. We pointed out that we can see destinations satisfying tourism demand by supplying the experiences, or products, which tourists seek. These tourist products comprise a mix of tourism services and resources – but many of the resources are not owned by the tourism industry. In this chapter we look more closely at destinations and their tourism products. We begin by reviewing a number of ideas about how destinations develop over time. We argue that most models of tourism development are oriented toward resorts – which are simply one type of destination – and do not properly acknowledge that tourism now involves a wide

variety of destinations where it is simply one industry amongst many – just one of the ways in which the place makes its living. Finally, we suggest that it makes sense to see destinations as places which offer a portfolio of tourism products – a portfolio that has to be renewed and updated as tourists' demands change. Since the products in the portfolio rely heavily on destination resources, and since those resources are not owned or controlled by the tourism industry, the industry alone cannot ensure that resources are protected and enhanced; nor can it resolve conflicts over their use and/or bring about sufficient investment in new resources. Management and planning at the destination level is needed.

THE GROWTH AND DEVELOPMENT OF DESTINATIONS

With these points in mind, we can go on to examine how destinations develop and change over time. Several descriptive models of the dynamics of tourism development have been devised over the past few decades, in the attempt to account for, and explain, destinations' historical

development. One of the most useful of these is that of Miossec (1976). As well as providing a descriptive framework for the development of a destination's tourism facilities through time, Miossec's **tourism development model** (see Figure 3.1) has the additional value of describing

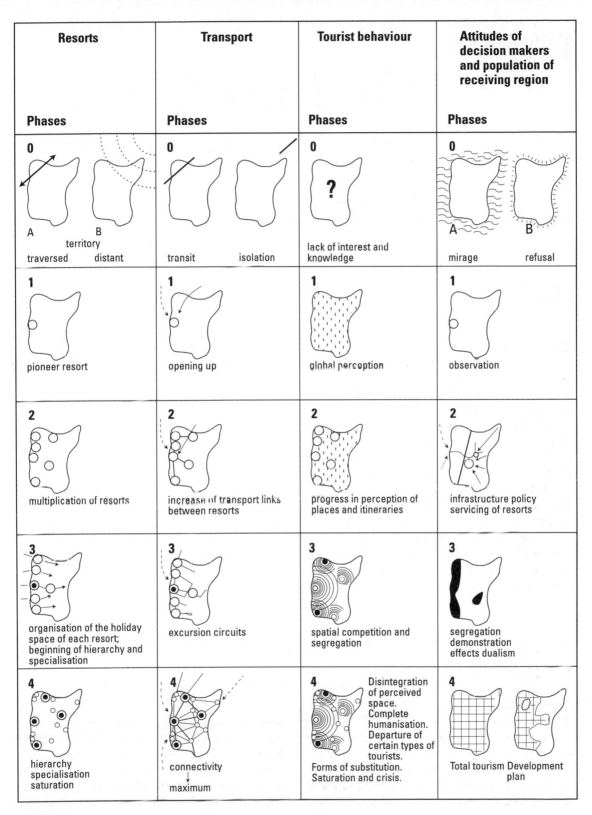

FIGURE 3.1 *Tourism development model (after Miossec, 1976)*

the behaviour of tourists and the attitudes of host populations over the same phases.

Initially, in the early phases 0 and 1, there is little or no tourism development in the region in question. It is practically unrecognised as a tourist area and its residents tend to have polarised opinions of tourism's potential effects, either viewing these through rose-coloured spectacles or with a blinkered refusal to accept that there might be any positive impacts at all. Following the advent of tourism in the area (either as a result of chance discovery or as a deliberate development policy by the destination itself) a pioneer resort is first developed, then others are established, as visitor numbers increase and awareness of the areas as a tourist designation spreads (Phase 2). As local attitudes towards tourism change with experience however, the result can be either positive acceptance of this phenomenon, outright rejection, or the demand for planning controls to guide or limit tourism development (Phases 3 and 4). By this time, tourists have become more aware of the area's attractions and facilities, and this results in a degree of specialisation and hierarchy between different centres, finally leading to development saturation being reached. At this last phase in Miossec's model, the region is characterised by a clearly-defined hierarchy of interconnected centres operating as a unified destination area with a strong tourism image. Miossec suggests that by Phase 3 it is this very image – rather than the original attractions – which is attracting visitors, and that as a result, certain categories of visitors abandon the destination in search of less-developed regions.

Many authors, including Pearce (1989) and Craig-Smith and French (1993), commend Miossec's model for its simplicity and its ability to be applied to empirical studies of tourism development in specific regions. However, as a simplified framework of tourist development, some issues of relevance to the planning process are necessarily omitted from this model. One of the most important of these is the identity of the actors in the development process – those who build and own the resorts and facilities. Are they local or non-local, public sector or private sector? What are their motivations for investing in tourism development?

There are other models which do incorporate this particular issue. Regarding the local/non-local issue, several models, including that of van Doorn (1979), based on studies of tourism in developing countries, suggest a progressive reduction in local participation over time, as external developers take control of the development process. **Schwarzenbach's spiral** (see Figure 3.2), as illustrated in Ritter (1991) represents this tendency in terms of investment in tourism facilities, with the development being driven by investment and promotion carried out by agents from levels of administration which are increasingly remote from the destination itself.

However, in Gormsen's (1981) model of the **spatio-temporal development of international seaside tourism**, which is taken from a mainly European perspective, regional (i.e. local) initiative is shown to actually *increase* over time (see Figure 3.3). Unlike Miossec's model, Gormsen's is specific to particular times and places. Approximate dates are given, and the four diagrams refer to particular destination areas:

- Periphery 1 represents tourism development on both sides of the English Channel
- Periphery 2 represents the coasts of southern Europe
- Periphery 3 represents the North African coastline and the Balearic and Canary Islands
- Periphery 4 represents destinations in West Africa, the Caribbean, the Pacific and Indian Oceans, South East Asia and South America.

The model reflects Gormsen's findings that, in the destination areas observed, the initiative for tourism development first comes from actors who are external to the destination itself, but that local initiative gradually takes over (Column A). However, acknowledging the continuing importance of external capital and international investment in these destination areas, Gormsen points out that: 'the population (of these areas) is gradually becoming involved in independent (tourism business) activities, which are however limited chiefly to secondary, less profit-making tourist services.'

Linked to the question of control of the development process is the issue (included but greatly simplified in the Miossec model) of how

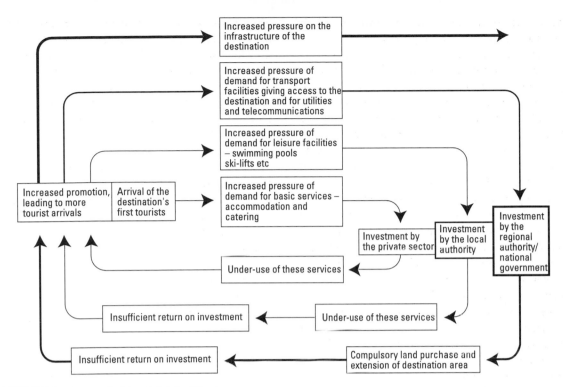

FIGURE 3.2 *Schwarzenbach's spiral (after Ritter)*

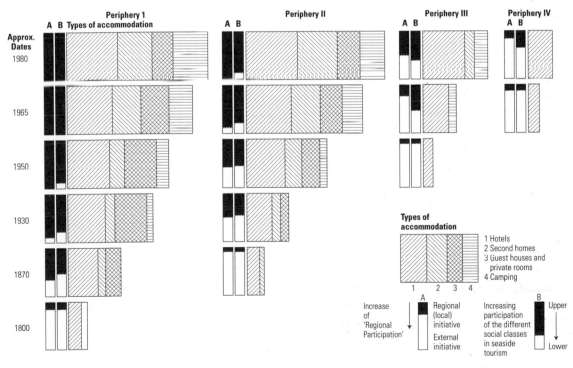

Source: redrawn from Gormsen, 1981

FIGURE 3.3 *Schematic representation of the spatio-temporal development of international seaside tourism*

residents' and policy-makers' attitudes towards tourists affect the planning process. Doxey's (1975) **Irridex model** (see Figure 3.4) identifies four attitudes commonly held by local residents towards tourists. The first of these, Euphoria, occurs when visitors are few in number and the extra income and stimulation they bring are welcomed by residents. At this stage, there are few negative impacts of tourism, and regulation and control are regarded as unnecessary. The positive attitudes of the Euphoria phase makes the destination more popular with visitors, who increase in number, leading to the phase of Apathy. By this stage, the residents' initial enthusiasm has cooled and more commercial transactions characterise the destination's approach to visitors. However, as the destination is still eager to maximise the economic benefits from tourism, policy for this sector is primarily concerned with marketing. But as tourist numbers continue to grow towards saturation point and the disbenefits of tourism, such as congestion and competition for local resources, become more apparent, Annoyance becomes the dominant attitude.

Nevertheless, the planners' reaction, portrayed in this model, tends to be one of simply increasing the infrastructure at the destination, rather than tackling the thornier question of limiting growth (we examine their ability to do so later). If continuing growth causes further problems, putting an intolerable pressure on resources and services, the outcome may be open antagonism, particularly among those residents who derive no direct benefits from tourists. The case of the residents of Royal Crescent in Bath who threw buckets of water over the passengers on open-top tour buses, claiming that the noise of the guides' commentaries coming every ten or fifteen minutes was driving them to distraction, is one of the more well-publicised examples of

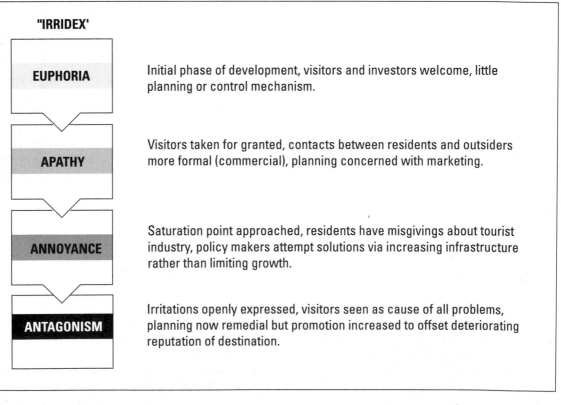

Source: After Doxey (1975)

FIGURE 3.4 *Irridex model*

openly-expressed antagonism towards tourists. Doxey considers that such manifestations of anti-tourist sentiments bring about a deterioration in the destination's reputation and that, side-by-side with planning measures to remedy such negative impacts, tourism promotion is also increased to offset this. But while this may be true of destinations which are very dependent on their tourism industry, in places where tourism accounts for a far less important proportion of the local economy, remedial measures need not necessarily be accompanied by increased tourism promotion (see the Cambridge case study for an example).

The destiny of tourist destinations is also determined to some extent by the profile of the visitors they tend to attract. Not only do different types of visitors have different types of impact on destinations, but the needs and motivations of those visitors also determine the range of facilities which the destination must provide for them. Several models include different aspects of visitors' characteristics in their description of tourism development, the most commonly-cited of these being tourists' socioeconomic and psychological profiles.

Gormsen's model shows the development of wider participation in tourism by other social classes apart from the élite who comprised the initial visitors to the destinations he describes. As new affluent middle class and working class travelling publics emerge in society as a whole, the proportion of visitors from these classes increases. An example of how changes in the socio-economic profile of visitors can alter the very nature of the destination area itself is shown in Gormsen's model, in the different types of accommodation provided to meet the demands of different social groups of visitors.

Reflecting the generally recognised tendency for the arrival of one social class to drive away the destination's existing class of visitor, several models present tourism in terms of class succession. One such scheme is that of Thurot (1973), who suggests that destinations pass through three successive phases:

- Phase 1: Discovery by rich tourists and the construction of an international class hotel
- Phase 2: Development of 'upper middle class' hotels (and expansion of tourist traffic)
- Phase 3: Loss of original value to new destinations and arrival of 'middle class' and mass tourists.

As in the case with many of the models under consideration here, Thurot's model most accurately describes tourism development in simple, resort-type destinations, where tourism is a dominant element in the local economy and where the image of the destination itself derives mainly from its reputation as a place worth visiting. However, the applicability of these ideas to all types of designation is questionable and even for resorts, the progression through a succession of phases ending in decline is far from being predestined and inevitable. These points are taken up in the following examination of one of the most widely-used models of destination development; the tourist area life cycle.

THE LIFE CYCLE OF DESTINATIONS

The **tourist area life cycle (TALC)** is probably the most widely-used model of destination development. It incorporates several of the ideas discussed previously, including the notion of a place progressing from a pioneering to an established destination, the crucial role of investment, and changes in the type of visitor attracted. It is intended to provide an organising framework for understanding the historical development of destinations, and for analysing their current position and for considering strategy. It is derived from the **product life cycle (PLC)** which has been influential in marketing and corporate strategy. We will argue that whilst the TALC can be extremely helpful in thinking about the development and management of destinations, some of its most important implications have received insufficient emphasis. We will describe the PLC and how the TALC is derived from it, discuss criticisms of the concepts, and go on to consider what they can contribute to our understanding of destination management.

PRODUCT LIFE CYCLE (PLC)

The PLC suggests that all products have a 'life cycle' which begins with their introduction or 'birth', and ends with their withdrawal or 'death'. The biological analogy is deliberate, and the PLC is seen as in some way mimicking biological life cycles. The PLC describes sales of a product over time, and in the classic case this follows an 'S' shaped curve – again, common in the natural world. The PLC is composed of several phases, typically: Introduction, Growth, Maturity, Saturation and Decline (Palmer, 1994). Whilst there is general agreement among commentators on this shape, the phases are difficult to identify with precision. Some versions of the PLC may have only four phases (e.g. Baker, 1992), others as many as nine (Wells *et al.*, quoted Baker, 1992).

The essential elements are common to all versions, however, and an example of the PLC is shown in Figure 3.5.

The PLC assumes that all products will tend to follow a similar path: the 'S' shaped curve. Initially sales are zero or low and climb slowly

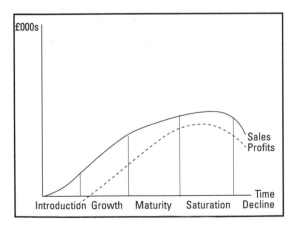

£000s

Sales
Profits

Time

Introduction Growth Maturity Saturation Decline

FIGURE 3.5 *Product life cycle*

through the Introduction phase. They expand rapidly through the Growth phase, continue to increase through Maturity, and peak when Saturation is reached. Sales then decrease in the Decline phase until the product is withdrawn. The PLC is highly generalised and shows a pattern with units of time left undefined, but it clearly implies that eventually all products will reach the end of the Decline phase if no action is taken.

It is important however to be clear at the outset about the PLC's limitations. According to Baker:

> '[it] is one of the most widely known yet most misunderstood theoretical constructs in marketing . . . misinterpretation arises from the mistaken belief that the PLC is a precise forecasting tool . . . it may be regarded as an important tool for planning at the strategic level always recognising that it is not of itself deterministic and may be influenced significantly by environmental changes and/or marketing action'
>
> *(Baker, 1992)*

Cooper (1989) also emphasises its attractions and limitations: '. . . despite its logical and intuitive appeal, it is difficult to operationalise and use the PLC for, say, forecasting or decision taking'.

From a firm's point of view, the value of the PLC is that it is helpful in thinking about the marketing conditions and problems associated with each phase of the cycle, and about the cash flows involved. In terms of marketing, the firm will seek to understand its potential consumers at each phase of the cycle. One means of differentiating consumers is through 'adopter' categories, which divide consumers on the basis of their willingness to try new products. It is argued that as the product moves through its life cycle it will be taken up successively by: Innovators, Early Adopters, Early Majority, Late Majority and Laggards (Baker 1992). The point is not that the same people fall into the same 'adopter' category for each product – on the contrary, the composition of each category will vary from product to product. Rather, once this categorisation is accepted, it provides a framework which allows the firm to identify more clearly its target consumers at each stage of the cycle.

The firm will have to manage the conflicting demands of its cashflows through the cycle. In the Introduction and Growth phases, demands for cash will be heavy to meet costs of promotion and investment. Revenues will be very limited in the Introduction phase, so cash flows will be negative; as Growth picks up revenues will increase, but they are unlikely to do more than service investment requirements. It is only in the Maturity phase that substantial positive cash flows can be achieved.

For our purposes, there are three main implications to be drawn from the PLC concept:

1 Change is inevitable, as products pass through the stages of their life cycle.
2 Firms reliant on a single product will thus eventually, but inevitably, go out of business as their product reaches the end of its life cycle – unless the product can be continually rejuvenated.
3 Funding the development of new products or the rejuvenation of existing products requires significant cash flows.

We take up these issues after our discussion of the tourist area life cycle.

TOURIST AREA LIFE CYCLE (TALC)

The TALC is explicitly derived from the PLC, and has been widely discussed following Butler's introduction of the concept (1980). Applying the notion of the PLC to tourism immediately raises the question of how the 'tourism product' should be defined and how its sales should be measured (a question to which we return later on). The TALC asserts that the product is the destination (or tourist area) and that destinations experience life cycles which are analogous to product life cycles. Accordingly to Cooper:

> 'Although it could be argued that the tourism product is the sum of travel experiences from anticipation to recall, the destination is a key element in the product. Destinations go through a cycle of evolution similar to the product life cycle ... simply, numbers of visitors replaces sales of a product'
>
> *(Cooper, 1989)*

In considering the development of a destination over time, the TALC attempts to model the interaction between demand for and supply of the tourism product. It considers changing patterns of demand generated by changing visitation (different types of visitor with different needs and expectations) and changing patterns of supply which arise as destination characteristics and facilities are modified. In other words, like the PLC, it is concerned with changing marketing conditions at different phases of the cycle, and thus by implication with the cash flows involved.

A depiction of the TALC is shown in Figure 3.6 (based on Butler, 1980).

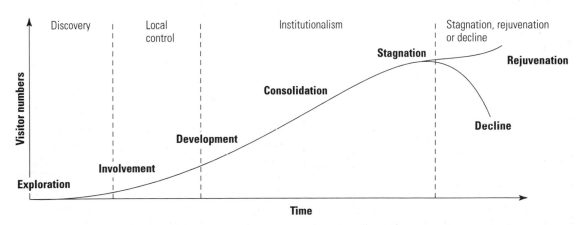

Source: Butler (1980). (Reprinted with permission from Pergamon Press Ltd.)

FIGURE 3.6 *Tourist area life cycle*

The similarity with the PLC is clear. Success is now measured not by sales volume, but by numbers of visitors, and the curve depicts visitation to a destination over a period of time. The phases of development are depicted as Exploration, Involvement, Development, Consolidation, Stagnation (the latter two sometimes combined as a Maturity phase), and Decline. Visitation begins slowly in the Exploration phase, grows more rapidly to peak in the Stagnation or Maturity phase, and then falls as the destination enters a period of Decline. We can consider each of these phases in turn.

- In the **Exploration phase**, the place starts to become a tourist destination – in other words, a new tourist product is introduced. This phase is normally depicted in terms of small numbers of intrepid visitors 'discovering' some new destination, attracted in part by the lack of other visitors.

  '... small numbers of adventurous visitors are attracted by the unspoilt natural beauty or culture of the destination. At this stage numbers are restricted by lack of access and facilities, and the attraction is that it is as yet unchanged by tourism and contact with local people will be high ... Parts of Antarctica, Latin America, and the Canadian Arctic are examples here.'

  (Cooper, 1994)

At this point in the cycle, a key role is played by the small number of adventurous visitors. They are the equivalent of the innovators in the PLC's Introductory phase, and have a crucial role in starting to establish the new product in the market. The obvious difference is that in the case of the PLC, a considerable promotional effort is made to identify and catch the attention of innovative consumers (producers are seeking to develop the market) whereas the TALC sees consumers themselves developing the market through seeking out new destinations (we consider this further below). Cash requirements present another contrast. At this phase of the TALC, there is little need for investment in facilities for visitors, since the lack of such facilities provides much of the area's attraction.

- The **Involvement phase** sees visitor numbers beginning to build up, and facilities are provided (largely by local operators). There is an identifiable tourist season and the place is marketed as a destination although visitors are still attracted to its novelty and the fact that it is not an established resort. Impacts from tourism begin to become significant, and public authorities may become involved, either through infrastructure provision, or control and management of development.

- The **Development phase** sees the most crucial change. Visitor numbers are substantial as the destination becomes better known. The visitor profile begins to change, and there is greater appeal to the less adventurous traveller. This is in part because services and facilities are expanding, and are increasingly being provided by major operators who are able to offer familiar and reliable levels of service. Increased involvement of larger firms means that investment, and thus ownership and control of the industry, comes from outside the destination. The higher levels of visitation means that destination resources begin to come under pressure, and may start to become degraded, depending on visitor numbers and the resources' fragility. The natural and built environment may suffer wear and tear, and conflicts between tourism and the host population (or non-tourism industries) may begin to emerge. Public policy and investment to protect resources and manage conflict will be required if the destination is to sustain continuing development. Long haul destinations like the Seychelles or Bali are frequently quoted examples.

- At the **Consolidation phase**, visitor numbers continue to increase, although growth is much less rapid. The area is now firmly established as a destination and is attracting more conservative visitors seeking the familiar. Many tourism services are provided by large national or international companies, although smaller and local operators still play a significant role. The continuing increase in visitation will place further demands on the destinations' resources, and the way these have been or are managed will determine its future.

- The **Stagnation phase** occurs when visitor numbers peak. The destination now relies principally on unadventurous travellers who are attracted by its reassuring familiarity and extensive facilities. There is likely to be a need to promote the place and to identify potential new products and markets, in order to sustain visitation. The extent to which resource management has been effective is likely to be crucial. If the resources which initially made the place attractive have been substantially conserved, then the destination may be able to sustain a stable or gently growing level of visitation indefinitely. However, this will require continuing protection and renewal of resources, and adaptation of products and markets.

- The **Decline phase** occurs as visitor numbers fall. There will be a move down market, and there is likely to be continuing promotion in an attempt to attract sufficient visitors to meet the capacity of available facilities. The extent to which such promotion succeeds depends partly on how far the destination's original resources have been degraded. Destinations in decline may seek Rejuvenation through a shift in products or markets and they may accept continued decline of their tourism industry or they may ultimately move out of the tourism

business altogether. In any case, significant involvement of municipalities will be required to manage change. This may involve rejuvenation strategy through major new investment in partnership with the private sector.

Central to the TALC analysis is the interaction between different types of visitors and the nature of the destination. The development of the destination proceeds as a few adventurous visitors sampling a new product are replaced with larger volumes of visitors consuming a product which becomes increasingly standardised. The growth of visitation stimulates the provision of more facilities for tourists, which itself feeds the growth in visitor numbers. The combination of more visitors and more facilities means that the nature of the destination changes.

This view clearly sees the market as segmented in terms of visitors' adventurousness, or their willingness to try a new destination product. In one sense, this simply borrows the PLC's classification of new product adopters (ranging from Innovators to Laggards). The idea has been taken further by linking destination life cycles to Plog's well-known **classification of tourists' characteristics**.

Plog (1973) broadly categorised tourists along a spectrum of personality types ranging from Psychocentrics to Allocentrics. The former are self-inhibited, nervous and lacking in the desire

Experience	Demands	Destination impacts
Explorer	Quest for discovery and desire to interact with hosts.	Easy to accommodate in terms of numbers, acceptance of local norms.
Elite	Tour of unusual places, using pre-arranged native facilities.	Small in number and easily adapted into surrounding environments.
Off-beat	Get away from the crowds.	Minor because willing to put up with simple accommodation and service.
Unusual	Occasional side trips to explore more isolated areas or undertake more risky activity.	Temporary destinations can be simple but support base needs to have full range of services.
Incipient mass	Travel as individuals or small groups; seeking a combination of amenities and authenticity.	Numbers increasing as destination becomes popular; growing demand for services and facilities.
Mass	Middle-class income and values leads to development of a 'tourist bubble'.	Tourism now a major industry, little interaction with local people beyond commercial links.
Charter	Search for relaxation and good times in a new but familiar environment.	Massive arrivals; to avoid complaints hotels and facilities standardised to Western tastes.

FIGURE 3.7 *Interaction of tourist type and destination*

for adventure, preferring well-packaged routine holidays in popular tourist destinations. The latter are more outgoing and independent, have varied interests and are keen to explore new places and find new things to do. Since the needs of these two groups differ so much, they will need to visit different destinations at any given time. But Plog suggests that the same destination can appeal to different categories of tourist at different times: being 'discovered' by Allocentrics, popularised by Midcentrics and then finally adopted by the Psychocentrics (by which time the Allocentrics will have long since moved on to other destinations). Since, according to Plog, the population is distributed normally along this spectrum (that is the bulk of the population is in the mid-ranges), the implication is that by the time the destination is attracting predominantly Psychocentrics, its market is already in decline. Thus, he maintains

> 'we can visualize a destination moving along the spectrum, however gradually or slowly, but far too often inexorably towards the potential of its own demise. Destination areas carry with them the potential seeds of their own destruction, as they allow themselves to become more commercialised and lose their qualities which originally attracted tourists.'
>
> *(Plog, 1973)*

An alternative model of the relationship between different types of tourists and destinations is that suggested by Smith (1977). He identifies seven types of tourists seeking different types of experiences, making different demands and creating different impacts on the destination. (Figure 3.7).

Just as destinations can move along Plog's allocentric-psychocentric spectrum, so may they begin their involvement in tourism by being visited by a few Explorers and finish up as havens for vast numbers of Charter tourists. The relationship between visitor types and stages in the TALC is shown in Figure 3.8.

Considered in this light, the TALC seems a convincing means of explaining the development of destinations:

- it draws on an apparently generalisable set of observations about the range of visitors' personalities and preferences
- it links tourism products to a wider analysis of consumer behaviour
- it links consumer preferences with the provision of services at destinations and changing types of operator
- it is intuitively appealing and can be simply and clearly expressed.

It does, however, have a number of deficiencies; we discuss these next, and then go on to consider how they can be addressed.

WEAKNESSES OF TALC IN ACCOUNTING FOR DESTINATION DEVELOPMENT

It is a 'resort' model

'Tourist area' is a vague term, but its advantage is that it can encompass a wide variety of destinations. However, a disadvantage is that implicit definitions of 'tourist area' can come to be accepted without sufficient justification. In practice, 'tourist area' frequently seems to include the

Adopter category	Destination stage	Visitor type	
Innovator	Exploration	Allocentrics	Explorer/Elite/Off-beat
Early adopter	Involvement	Allocentrics	Unusual
Early majority	Development	Midcentrics	Incipient mass
Late majority	Consolidation	Midcentrics	Mass
Laggards	Stagnation	Psychocentrics	Charter

After Baker (1992), Plog (1976), Smith (1977)

FIGURE 3.8 *Classification of tourists' characteristics*

assumption that destinations follow a 'resort' model – probably a new or rapidly growing resort in the developing world or an under developed area in Europe. Thus the destination's (tourist area's) overall development is depicted as driven primarily by the tourism industry. However, as we pointed out earlier, in the UK and the rest of Western Europe (and elsewhere in the developed world), many destinations are established places and tourism is just one of a number of activities driving their development. This is true of capital cities like London and Paris, historic towns and cities like Cambridge or Montpellier, and increasingly of places which began as holiday resorts, such as Brighton or Nice. In non-traditional destinations like Halifax or Lille, tourism is a new or growing industry in a long established city. Understanding the development of tourism in destinations like these means seeing the industry as part of the local economy as a whole, and not as the dominant force driving change.

Progress through the life cycle is not inevitable

The TALC depicts inevitable movement along the curve from the Exploration to the Decline phase, a movement which results from forces outside the destination's control. Unless growth can continually be stimulated, decline may be postponed but will eventually occur. This view stems in part from the biological analogy on which the PLC and TALC are based: 'decline is ultimately inevitable, and tends to mirror the growth phase in that it accelerates over time' (Baker, 1992). This means that, like ageing movie stars, destinations can for a time stave off decay with a series of face lifts, but must in the end accept their demise. The idea that there are inevitable phases of destination development is reinforced by the TALC's resort bias, for that gives it an implicit supply and demand agenda. Since resorts are mainly reliant on tourism, they often lack alternative investment opportunities, and that means there is a tendency to retain existing tourism facilities, and develop new ones, which in turn means visitor numbers must continually increase, so that the resort is driven toward the Stagnation phase.

These perspectives are at best partial. Places are not natural organisms and there is no reason to suppose that they must inevitably die. The apparently inevitable class or personality-type successions described by Thorot, Smith or Plog seem rooted in 'resort' models of destinations. They are less applicable to more complex destinations where tourism represents only one aspect of the economy and image of the area. Most cities, for example, receive visitors from a wide variety of socioeconomic backgrounds and with different motivations – ranging from shopping, to conferences, to high cultural pursuits. At such destinations, the different social classes coexist without, in many cases, even being aware of each others' existence. Equally, in these more complex economies, tourism is simply one of a variety of investment opportunities and it is much easier for existing tourism enterprises to diversify into other markets – this removes the tendency to oversupply tourism facilities.

Even traditional resort-type destinations, on close examination, may be able comfortably to accommodate visitors from different social classes; indeed they may depend on doing so for their continuing success in tourism. Alan Bennett could perceive a whole range of subtle distinctions regarding the different areas of a destination as apparently homogeneous as Blackpool:

> 'which my mother always thought a bit common. If we ever went to Blackpool, she made sure we stayed at Cleveleys or Bispham – "the refined end". The era of package holidays came too late for my parents and they never went abroad, but had they done so the same standards would have applied. Mam would soon have sussed out the refined part of Torremolinos or a select end to Sitges.'
>
> *(Bennett, 1994)*

Places can exert some control over their own destiny through managing the supply of the tourism product (resources and services) and by influencing demand. This can make it possible to stabilise their position at a chosen point in the life cycle, or to influence the rate of progress along it. The role of management throughout the life cycle (and not simply as a reaction to decline) must be recognised.

Visitor numbers are an ambiguous measure of success

The PLC measures a product's progress in terms of sales volumes and revenues generated. The TALC uses visitor numbers as a proxy for sales, but this is an unreliable guide to success. In the case of a product, sales usually provide the firm with a good measure of success, since increased sales result in increased revenues and increased profits (as unit costs are likely to be falling or at least static). Rising sales will almost always signal net benefits to the firm.

From a destination's viewpoint, things are different: increased visitation in itself does not necessarily generate revenue, but may well generate costs. Visitor revenue may be a better success measure but, ideally, a destination will want to maximise the net benefits it gains from *each* visitor (that is, the benefits each visitor generates, less the costs they impose). On this basis, success should be measured not simply in terms of the quantity of visitors, but in terms of visitor quality (defined by the net benefits they generate for the destination). This is illustrated by the efforts many destinations make to attract business and conference visitors; a group which generates substantial benefits through high spending per capita, and imposes comparatively few costs. Once quality and net benefits are considered, it is clear that from a destination perspective, it may be preferable not to maximise visitation, but to stabilise visitor numbers to below their maximum potential, to focus on maximising benefits from tourism and to seek complementarity between tourism and other activities. However, the issue is complicated by the fact that the benefits and costs of visitation are unevenly distributed, especially in destinations other than resorts. The commercial tourism industry may gain continued benefits from increasing visitor numbers, and suffer few costs – but for the host population, the reverse can be true. We discuss how destination management can tackle this conflict in subsequent chapters.

The tourist area is not an integrated product

The destination or tourist area is depicted as a single integrated product in which all the elements develop consistently and at similar speed. This is a simplifying assumption which makes the model clearer, but which obscures three important points.

1 It assumes that all services required by visitors are equally demand-responsive, so that an increase in visitation will call forth supply as required. In practice, this is unlikely to be so. Provision of infrastructure and other public goods will tend to lag behind the provision of direct tourist services such as accommodation because of the difficulties in recovering investment costs. In an unregulated market, accommodation and other services may advance quickly from Exploration to Development whilst infrastructure remains little changed. The result is likely to be congestion, pollution and long-term damage to the destination's resources.

2 Different elements of the destination may have different carrying capacities and thresholds preventing balanced growth. This is clearest in the case of natural resources. Johnson and Spengler (1993) show in their study of Yellowstone National Park that whilst visitor services have only reached the stage of Development, from the point of view of the area's ecology visitor numbers are at Saturation, and causing damage. Some means of recognising and acting upon these conflicts is required. Other destinations have different inconsistencies: a non-traditional destination seeking to develop its market (such as Bradford in the early 1980s) may have many services at the Consolidation stage (hotels, restaurants, entertainment) whilst visitation is at the Exploration stage.

3 It is misleading to think in terms of the destination as a single product serving a single market, differentiated mainly by the adventurousness of visitors. Whilst this may be true for purpose-built resorts where tourism is the dominant industry, it is not always the case. A single destination may, in fact, offer a series of different products to different markets, each at a different point in its life cycle. For example, a British seaside destination may provide a series of products: long family holiday (in de-

cline); weekend breaks (mature); business and conference tourism (consolidation); educational tourism (growth). The destination's position on the life cycle depends on the net outcome of this series of products, which serve widely differing markets. In this sense, it is helpful to think of a destination as a series of products, or a system of tourism components, existing at several points on the TALC curve at any one time, and with a series of potentially conflicting demands on the destination's resources. We take up this point in the next section.

The role of resources is neglected

The TALC sees the development of tourism products as driving destination development. It focuses on the provision of additional tourist services and facilities over the life cycle, and pays comparatively little attention to resources, although the need to deal with problems of overuse or depletion are acknowledged. However, as Gordon and Goodall (1992) point out, it is possible to view destination development as driven at least in part by cycles in the development of the destination's resources.

In general, the natural environment, the built environment and sociocultural resources are all subject to degradation as the destination develops. An unspoilt natural environment which attracts visitors in the first place is vulnerable as the destination develops. As visitor numbers increase, peace and quiet and the sense of being in an unspoilt area will be diminished, and there may be pressure on wildlife and on natural habitats. The provision of infrastructure to cope with more visitors may itself be intrusive. The value of the built stock can also decline as the destination develops. Historic or vernacular buildings are subject to the same sort of pressures as the natural environment as visitation increases – they suffer wear and tear, and may be damaged by conversion to inappropriate uses to serve visitors. New facilities built to serve the growing market face

different problems – their attractiveness to tourists will decline as time passes if their facilities become outdated, forcing operators to shift down-market in their search for customers. Sociocultural resources can also be affected. For example, the image of a place will change as visitation increases and it becomes, necessarily, less unusual and exotic. This shift down-market will be reinforced if the built and natural environments are also being degraded. Equally, high levels of visitation may mean cultural facilities become crowded and over-used, and the host population may become less hospitable.

All this will occur if investment, maintenance and management are inadequate, but it is not inevitable. The key problem is that as resources are not generally under the control of the tourism industry, they have tended to be treated as constraints to be dealt with as tourism services expand. However, there is a strong case for seeing management of resources as being at the centre of destination development.

Overall, the TALC has a number of serious weaknesses. Its attraction is that it offers an easily comprehensible and intuitively appealing model of destination development. Its drawback is that this requires simplification which can be misleading. In particular, the TALC does not come to grips with the fact that tourism occurs not only (or primarily) in purpose-built monofunctional resorts, but in places where it is just one of a number of activities. Nor does the model acknowledge that the destination offers a composite series of tourism products, serving different markets and making different demands on its resources. To get a clearer view of how destinations can develop, we need to look in more detail at these problems. Next we will consider the different components which make up the destination's tourism product: the 'tourism product portfolio'. Later on we will consider the relationship between tourism and other economic activities in destinations.

TOURISM PRODUCT PORTFOLIO (TPP)

The **tourism product portfolio** (TPP) comprises all the tourism products which a destination supplies. Analysis of the TPP can be used to help clarify a destination's current position and the strategic choices it faces. Portfolio analysis was initially developed as an aid to corporate strategy, and is based on seeing the corporation as a series of products or businesses. In this section we discuss product portfolio analysis, and apply the ideas to the analysis of destinations.

As we pointed out previously, the logic of PLC is that a one-product firm is eventually doomed to extinction. If all products eventually follow the life cycle from birth to death, the firm which relies on a single product must itself follow that same life cycle. Of course, the notion that progress through the life cycle is inevitable is questionable, as we pointed out above, and it is easy to think of firms which have survived very successfully with a single product: Morgan, the car builders and Purdey, the shot gun makers are examples. In any event, few firms are entirely reliant on a single product. The more general point is that a firm is vulnerable if its product range consists of a series of related products each of which follow the life cycle in a similar way. Unless the firm can find means constantly to rejuvenate these products, it again faces eventual extinction. Product portfolio analysis was developed as a means of addressing this problem. If all products inevitably follow the product life cycle, then it is in the firm's interests to develop a complementary range of products, each at different stages in the cycle. Thus, as one product

reaches stagnation and decline, and sales revenue falls, another will be approaching maturity and revenue will be increasing. As products reach the end of their life cycle and are discontinued, new products are brought to the market.

The principle of portfolio analysis is simple and clear: by creating a balanced product range, a firm can ensure that the inevitable death of particular products does not bring about its own demise. Achieving such a balanced portfolio is obviously much more difficult. The key point from the firm's point of view will be how to fund the development of the new products which will be brought to market to replace those which are being retired. An influential aid to dealing with this problem was devised by the Boston Consulting Group and is known as the Growth Share Matrix, or 'Boston Box'. The Boston Box plots products' place on the PLC (their market growth rate) against their dominance, or competitive position in the market place. This allows products to be differentiated in terms of their need for cash resources or their ability to supply resources for development. A version of the Boston Box is shown in Figure 3.9.

In this depiction, 'dominance' indicates the product's share of the market. The analysis depends on high market share (a high level of 'dominance') generating high profits and cash flows. High market share generates high profits because costs are driven down by scale economies and also by experience effects. Increasing scale of production tends to lower the

		Dominance	
		high	**low**
Annual market growth	high	**Stars** (cash flow modest ±)	**Queries?** (cash flow −)
	low	**Cash Cows** (cash flow large +)	**Dogs** (cash flow modest ±)

FIGURE 3.9 *Boston Box*

unit cost, through economies of scale. As plant size increases, cost per unit decreases (doubling the size of a facility usually costs much less than double the unit cost). Scale economies may also occur in other areas, such as R&D. Experience effects stem from the cumulative volume of production (at whatever scale): as a result of experience, the firm gets better and better at producing the product, and costs per unit are driven down. The result is that products with a high market share enjoy a double advantage, and should generate high profits and cash flows.

The other axis in Figure 3.9 depicts growth in the market for a particular product, and is derived directly from PLC analysis. Individual products will experience different rates of growth depending upon their position in their life cycle: growth will be most rapid in the Introduction and Growth phases, and will slow down in Maturity and Saturation.

Given these pairs of characteristics, we can identify different types of product in terms of their current contribution to cash flow and profit, and their possible future role.

- **Cash cows** are successful products which have reached maturity and saturation. They are dominant in their market, with a high market share, and therefore costs have been driven down through scale and experience effects. The product is produced at, or near, its maximum volume, and growth is slow. There is little need for additional investment or promotion, so that there is large positive cash flow, since the product generates substantially more cash than it needs. Firms will seek to maintain the dominant position of 'cash cows' in their markets, and to extend their life. This will lead to strategies which include promotion to reinforce brand loyalty, and encouraging new uses or more frequent purchases to maintain or extend product life.
- **Dogs** are products which also form part of slow growing markets but, unlike cash cows, they have not developed a dominant position. Since their share of the market is low, they have not benefited much from scale or experience effects, and at best are likely to be generating very modest profits and positive

cash flows. Since the market overall is growing only slowly, and rival products have established dominance, there is little opportunity for 'dogs' to improve their position. In these circumstances, the firm's basic strategy will be to terminate the product. This can be done in a variety of ways: the product could be sold to a rival; a harvesting strategy could be employed, designed to maximise the returns from a restricted market; or production could simply be ended.

- **Queries** (aka problem children) are products which currently have a small share of a market which is growing rapidly. The growth in the market means that potentially, production could be expanded considerably, leading to cost reductions through scale and experience effects. However, these products are not generating profits, and will require large injections of cash from another source if they are to improve their market share. The strategic problem from the firm's point of view is whether to make this investment. If it is successful, then the product can be transformed into a 'star' and later a 'cash cow'. However, there is no guarantee of success – other firms will be promoting rival products in the market, also aiming to create 'stars'. If the strategy does not succeed, considerable investment will be wasted.
- **Stars** have a large share in a rapidly growing market. That means they are generating positive cash flows, which will increase if they can maintain their dominance and begin to benefit from scale and experience effects. Firms will seek to promote their growth and will use all the cash flow generated by the product (and perhaps more) to do so.

Portfolio analysis requires firms to assign their products to one of these categories. This allows the interactions and potential complementarity within the product range to be considered, especially in terms of how it may be developed in the future: which products should be promoted, and how currently available cash flows can best be used. Thus, from the firm's point of view, the value of this analysis is that it identifies its current strategic position in terms of its product range, and does so in a way which focuses attention on the crucial issue of the resources which will be required for future development, and from where they can be obtained. This leads to decisions about the current and future composition of the product portfolio.

It should be noted that portfolio analysis has, however, been subject to a number of criticisms. Briefly these are as follows:

■ The approach oversimplifies a complex reality. It is seen as reducing corporate strategy to choices about products, depicted in four crude, stereotypical positions derived from a simplified view of markets and competitive positions.

■ Product positions and characteristics are described mechanistically, and often inaccurately. For example, dominance in the market is not necessarily the most effective route to profitability and positive cash flows – niche marketed products can also be highly successful.

■ Factors which are essential to long-term strategy are not included. For example, changing technologies and changes in the social, political and economic environment will be at the heart of a firm's consideration of its future, but are not encompassed in the analysis.

■ The basic assumption that a balanced and diversified product portfolio is the most appropriate strategy may be incorrect. During the 1980s, analysts drew attention to the potential problems of firms operating in series of markets with a range of different types of product, not all of which they understood well. It was argued that a better strategy was to focus on a limited number of products. The influential Peters and Waterman (1982) argued that diversification by acquisition (sometimes motivated by a desire to achieve a more balanced portfolio) had generally had disastrous outcomes for firms, and that a more effective strategy was to 'stick to the knitting' i.e. remain within areas that the company understands and in which it has particular skills. These criticism were reinforced by the observation that many single or limited products were able to survive the severe recessions of the 1980s more effectively than their diversified counterparts.

These criticisms clearly have validity, but apply more to the abuse of the portfolio concept than to its use. The value of portfolio analysis is not that it provides answers automatically – it does not. Rather, it sets a valuable structure for strategic questions, and a useful and readily comprehensible analysis of the current position. As such it is a valuable tool for *thinking* about strategic problems and strategic possibilities, and not a device to determine strategy automatically.

Portfolio analysis is a logical development of ideas which flow from the PLC. Since the TALC itself derives from the PLC, can we use portfolio analysis to help understand the problems of destinations? In Chapter 2 we argued that tourism is becoming increasingly diverse, and that there is an increasing range of tourism products. Whilst pleasure travel has continued to grow and to become more varied, there has in addition been rapid expansion in other categories of tourism: business tourism and educational tourism have expanded rapidly; the distinction between leisure and tourism has become increasingly blurred; and day visitors typically undertake a variety of activities from visiting a museum to going shopping.

This diversity is reflected in, and stimulated by, an increasing diversity of tourism products. Just as firms have a portfolio of products, we can see each tourism destination as offering a unique range of tourism products: its tourism product portfolio (TPP). The current strength or weakness of tourism in the destination will be the result of its current portfolio, and tourism's potential in the destination will depend on the possibilities of adapting the portfolio in the future. Destination management is thus in a real sense concerned with the management of a portfolio of products in a destination.

This idea is straightforward enough. However, as with other models of destination development, there are difficulties in making it operational. Examining the market position of a destination's products raises two problems. First, how do we define and measure the products? There is no unambiguous answer, since we can define products at a more or less detailed level. We might see 'business tourism' as a single product, but it could then be broken down into a series of components – for example overseas and domestic business tourism. The appropriate definition of the product will depend on the destination we are considering. We can measure changes in the significance of products to a destination either by numbers of visitors or by their spending. Spending will generally capture the significance of visitation more effectively. However, this brings us on to the second difficulty: finding reliable, consistent data on tourism in destinations. Collecting information about visitors, their spending and their behaviour is difficult and expensive; the result is that the data available for most destinations are limited in scope and accuracy. Information on type of visitors and their spending, or even the numbers of visitors, is often based on dated surveys which have been fairly crudely updated. This situation may change in the future. Models are now being designed and tested which estimate the volume and value of tourism activity in destinations, as well as the employment it creates. An example is the Cambridge Local Area Tourism Model (Cambridge Economic Consultants, 1996). This seeks to overcome the lack of regularly collected local information by using information from national tourism surveys and data held by Regional Tourist Boards. 'It distributes regional activity as measured in those surveys to local areas using "drivers" such as accommodation available which influence the distribution of tourism activity at the local level' (Cambridge Economic Consultants, 1996).

If models like this are brought into widespread and successful use, it will be possible to examine change in destinations' tourism product portfolios in much more detail. Until then, we must accept that for most destinations, any model of development must rely on broad estimates. Provided we are using the model as an aid to understanding and to clarify strategic choices, this is not too severe a disadvantage. In any event there seems little choice, since we can hardly use lack of data as an excuse for not trying to understand destination development.

We begin by defining products in a way which is appropriate to the destination we are examining. We can then look at the portfolio using Boston Box principles. We make two slight modifications. First, the Boston Box depicts market growth as a range from high to low. However, some tourism products can be in absolute decline – for example long family holidays at cold water resorts – so we depict market growth as stretching from high growth to actual decline. Second, we look at a product's market share in terms of the importance of its contribution to the destination's total tourism activities. A high share thus means a product is especially important. This allows us to examine the current product portfolios of different destinations.

Figure 3.10 below represents, in simplified form, the tourism product portfolio for London. In this case it is possible to base the model on

FIGURE 3.10 *Schematic tourism product portfolio: London*

quantified information, since the statistics for London tourism are unusually good. Here we have defined five products – overseas leisure visits, business tourism, visiting friends and relations (VFR), day visits and long domestic holidays, and measured their share of London's total tourism activities in terms of expenditure.

Overseas leisure visits (which are a strong growth market) account for a high share of London's tourist market. Business tourism is also very significant, but is a slow growing or static market. Day visits are a growth area, but account for a smaller share of the London tourism economy. VFR is more or less static in growth terms, and of limited significance since expenditure per visit is relatively low. Long domestic holidays, a declining activity, are of little importance. Thus the general position is a healthy one. In BCG terms, overseas leisure tourism is a 'star', business tourism hovers between being a 'cash cow' and a 'star', day visits are 'queries' and domestic long holidays and perhaps VFR are 'dogs'. Strategic issues revolve around whether to accept business tourism is destined to be a 'cash cow'; whether day visits can or should be developed as 'stars'; and potential problems of success created by the overseas tourism market.

Figure 3.11 below illustrates a contrasting situation – that of a cold water seaside destination.

Although the domestic long holiday is declining, it still represents a large share of the resort's business. The resort is poorly represented in the rapidly growing overseas leisure market, and in the slower growing business tourism, and short break products. Its only area of high growth is in the DSS market – the conversion of holiday hotels to long-stay establishments for claimants. In this case short breaks are a dog and may have little growth potential. Overseas and business tourism are 'queries', but the key question is the level of investment needed to expand the markets. The DSS claimants market probably has prospects of continuing growth, but is unlikely to be an acceptable product for marketing, and is probably incompatible with other product development. Domestic long stay holidays, though in decline, do still represent sources of profits and cash flows, and can be seen as a 'cash cow'. Strategic issues revolve around the need to recast the product portfolio. As things stand, the destination seems likely to decline; if that is to be avoided, ways of developing new products with growth potential must be found.

Looked at from this point of view, the success of a destination thus depends not so much on having a single successful product as on having a successful portfolio of products. Whilst we tend to think of destinations in overall terms (they are growing, or declining, or holding their own), it is helpful to disaggregate this performance: different products are at different points in their life cycles, and are more important (or less) to the destination's tourism economy. It is clearly possible to make a much more detailed analysis than that presented here e.g. overseas visitors could be segmented by their country of origin (see

FIGURE 3.11 *Schematic tourism product portfolio: cold water resort*

Grabler, Mazanec and Wober 1996, for an example). The overall position of a destination is in fact the result of the performance of the whole of its tourism product portfolio (TPP). The range of possibilities is summarised in Figure 3.12.

- **The upper left quadrant** shows the position if the destination's portfolio is dominated by products in rapidly growing markets. There is scope for continued expansion and growth products can act as a dynamo for the whole industry. Possible problems will focus on the potentially disruptive effects that growth in particular products may cause – on the remainder of the industry, on the destination and its resources or on other destination activities. Policies to manage visitors and the pace and nature of development are likely to be needed.

- **The upper right quadrant** shows the position if the destination's portfolio has only a few products in rapidly growing markets: as things stand, the industry will be able to enjoy modest growth, which will be comparatively easy to manage. The dilemma is whether to attempt to become a bigger player in the growth markets by developing the products. This would offer more potential benefits, but may require very significant investment with the risk of costly failure. For example,

attempting to exploit growth in the business and conference market might require investment in a conference centre – a substantial and potentially high risk project. Policies will be required to establish partnerships to share or reduce risks, share costs and maximise potential benefits.

- **The lower right quadrant** shows the position when some tourism products are focused in declining markets. The nature of the problem depends on the speed of decline, and the potential for adaptation or the introduction of new products. In some cases the best strategy will be to exit from the market, but the problem is comparatively manageable since declining products do not dominate the portfolio.

- **The lower left quadrant** shows the position when the industry's main products are in declining markets. This is potentially a serious position, although the speed of decline is again crucial. An exit strategy is unlikely since so much of the industry is dependent on the product or products. Much of the tourism industry comprises small- and medium-sized enterprises (SMEs) which are often strongly rooted in the local area, and lack the willingness or ability to shift investment as markets change. They will continue trading even when returns are very low. The key issue for the destination is likely to be how to develop appropriate substitute products to compensate

Market	growth	Rapid expansion in products with good prospects for further growth, affecting whole industry. Possible adverse impacts and dislocation.	Modest growth, but scope for significant increase – if investment forthcoming.
		Serious long-term decline in key tourism product(s). Significant long-term threat to industry in destination.	Gradual decline in tourism product. Manageable shift to other activities.
	decline		
		high	low
		Share of destination's tourism portfolio	

FIGURE 3.12 *Possible tourism product portfolios*

for decline. Inaction will lead to a depressed and shrinking industry. Policy responses will focus on attempts to adapt or re-launch the products, and to seek funding and subsidy to make this possible.

This analysis is of course a simplification, and focuses on a series of polarised positions. Its purpose is to identify the different problems that arise as the composition of the portfolio varies. The tourism product portfolio helps analyse a destination's current position, and the strategic choices which it faces. In that sense, it does for a destination what business portfolio analysis does for a firm. There are however four crucial respects in which devising and implementing strategies for destinations is more complex and difficult.

1 Implementing a strategy to change the product portfolio is much more difficult. For an individual firm, business portfolio analysis can be used to review the current product portfolio to decide on new products and how their development can be financed. Once the firm has adopted a corporate strategy and selected the products to be developed, the Chief Executive Officer (CEO) and the board can ensure compliance with the strategy, even if it is unpopular in some parts of the company – for example, because some products are to be phased out and jobs will therefore be lost, or because the type or location of new products is disputed. (In practice, of course, gaining organisational consensus and carrying through the strategy can prove problematic).

Things are much harder in a destination, since the product portfolio derives from the activities of not one, but many, different organisations some of which do not even see themselves as being in the tourism business (Cambridge colleges or upland farmers, for example). Even if a strategy for changing the destination's portfolio is agreed, there is no straightforward means of assuring that all the organisations involve comply with it, since there is no true equivalent of the CEO and board. As Gordon and Goodall say:

'at critical stages in the cycle ... long term

success rests on organisational factors. Neither fragmented local competition nor dependence on the strategies of externally controlled oligopolies can ensure either innovation to replace obsolete products or coordinated redevelopment and upgrading of decaying resort areas, or avoiding of overdevelopment, crowding and environmental degradation.'

(*Gordon and Goodall, 1992*)

The centrality of the organisational factors means that the role of local authorities or other public bodies is critical in initiating and coordinating destination management and development – taking on the role of the CEO and Board.

2 Financing new product development is much more difficult – this is a reflection of fragmentation. In the case of a firm, once new products to be developed have been identified, cash can be channelled in their direction. Using Boston Box terminology, the 'cash cows' can be milked in order to promote 'queries' or reinforce the performance of 'stars', through new investment, advertising or other means. Again, the firm's senior management will ensure compliance. In the case of a destination, matters are much more complex: a mix of tourism products means that some are enjoying positive cash flows which could be used to develop new products for the future. The problem is that key elements of the product are derived from the destination's resources, whilst profits and cash flows accrue largely to the service-providing tourism industry. Generally, the industry does not own the resources, and that means there is no straightforward way of ensuring that investment funds are channelled in the right direction. There is, in other words, a classic externality problem: the market will tend to under-invest in the resources which provide the basis for the destination's tourism product, so that resources are degraded. For example, the natural environment will be damaged by over-use, the built stock will be under-maintained, or cultural resources will be devalued and commercialised. Equally, assem-

bling the funds for significant new investment to enhance or reconfigure the destination's product portfolio will be difficult. Instead, there will be a tendency to over-invest in individual facilities owned by the industry, to channel investment elsewhere (in the case of externally owned companies), or simply to reduce overall investment levels.

In the case of our declining seaside resort, it may be that the long-stay domestic holiday market, though in decline, is still providing positive cash flows to the accommodation sector. But if the destination's strategy is (for example) to promote business tourism by providing additional facilities, there is no straightforward way of making use of the cash flow to achieve that. In principle, the 'cash cow' could fund the development of a 'query'; in practice there is no market solution which will ensure that it does. This points to the need for destination management to coordinate individual actions and build partnerships.

3   There is also the broader issue of the distribution of costs and benefits. For any firm, a change in corporate strategy will produce winners and losers, but, in principle, the firm can make a judgement about whether overall benefits outweigh costs, and if they do, push the change forward. The firm can, if it wishes, then ensure that the losers are compensated, for example through attractive redundancy packages. In the case of destinations, matters are again more complex. Change will generate winners and losers, but they will be different individuals and organisations (both within and outside the tourism industry). For example, externally-controlled hotels may squeeze out local operators as a destination develops, or visitors flocking to a popular attraction may cause congestion which has adverse effects on residents and firms outside the tourism industry. There may be a net benefit overall, but there is no means of winners compensating losers so that the benefit is equally shared. One consequence is that change which results in significant costs or losses for a particular group or groups will be strongly resisted. Destination management, again with public bodies playing a leading role, is thus required to address the question of the costs and benefits of change, and to find ways of generating sufficient consent and consensus for change to allow effective progress to be made.

4   We must remember that destinations have products other than tourism. The tourism product portfolio helps us to understand change in the tourism sector, but by itself says relatively little about the overall impact of tourism in the destination. For this wider perspective, we need to look at the relationship of tourism with other activities and to consider its importance in the destination as a whole – it is to this which we now turn.

THE IMPORTANCE OF TOURISM IN DESTINATIONS

The TALC is an effective means of thinking about the development of tourist destinations, and the TPP helps us understand the interaction between different components of tourism. The final element to be considered is the relative significance of tourism in a particular place (its dominance) and its growth or decline (the rate of change). Both dominance and rate of change have important implications for tourism management.

DOMINANCE

Dominance is an assessment of how important a role tourism plays in the destination. Its basis is the economic function of tourism, which includes direct economic effects, and indirect effects including intangibles such as image. Lack of adequate economic and other data means that dominance cannot be measured precisely, but must be estimated, for example on the basis of the proportion of local jobs attributable to tourism. Such broad estimates are sufficient for our purposes. Usually, dominance measured in economic terms will act as an effective proxy for other elements, but this may not always be so; there are broader issues, such as the environmental effects of tourism and the perceptions of the host community of its role and significance. For example, if a small village is a popular part of sightseeing routes for coach and car visitors, tourism may be dominant in terms of environmental impacts and residents' perceptions whilst playing little or no role in the local economy.

Why is dominance important for problems of destination management? There are two general reasons.

1 Impacts, whether positive or negative, are partly a function of the relationship between the scale of tourism and the scale of a place. For example, an additional 10,000 visitors a day will have greater impacts in Chipping Camden than in the London Borough of Camden.

2 The extent to which tourism dominates the destination crucially affects options for future development. Destinations in which tourism plays a very dominant role will have difficulty re-orientating themselves in a completely new direction, whereas those in which tourism plays a lesser role may have a wider range of development strategies open to them.

In this context, it is important to note that changes in tourism dominance can occur in either of two ways. Most obviously, there can be change in the industry itself. Tourism may grow or decline in a destination as a result of changing demand for its products (the TPP helps us to understand this). However, the role of tourism may alter as a result of changes in its external environment – factors outside the industry. For example, during the 1980s tourism became more dominant in industrial towns and cities such as Bradford, Halifax and Wigan, as tourism initiatives were used to counter the decline in traditional economic activities (Buckley and De Witt, 1985; Beioley, Maitland and Vaughan,

1990). In a real sense, these places became tourism destinations as much because of the decline in other parts of their economies as because of tourism industry driven changes. Equally, the role and dominance of tourism may be diminished as a destination becomes more attractive to other activities. For example, the Isle of Man has proved attractive to financial services, and tourism is now a less important (though still vital) part of its economy. Some seaside destinations, such as Brighton and Eastbourne, now attract many people looking for a pleasant place to retire, as well as holidays-makers and other tourists.

RATE OF CHANGE

Rate of change encompasses the direction and speed of change. Again, we are considering change in all aspects of the tourism industry, but with an emphasis on its economic elements. We can consider growth or decline in terms of visitor numbers, the economic impacts of visitation, and the broader impacts of tourism. Rate of change is important for policy. The direction of change determines the nature of the problems to be dealt with and affects policy options. A declining industry may require measures for rejuvenation, or movement away from tourism, and sources of funds for investment will be a particular concern. Growth will see problems of accommodating increased tourism activity, perhaps including issues of capacity limits.

Whatever the direction of change, its speed will be significant. Very rapid change will be likely to require urgent and skilful management action if problems are to be avoided, whether tourism is growing or declining. Market processes left to themselves rarely result in appropriate adaptation to rapid changes. If change is taking place at a gradual rate, there is more likelihood of a market-based adaptation, and more time for management actions to be considered and implemented.

Looking at dominance and rate of change allows us to identify some of the policy problems that destinations are likely to face. They are illustrated in Figure 3.13.

	high	Rapid expansion, attractive to investors in tourism services; spin-off to other economic activities. Danger of environmental and infrastructure problems, community backlash. Reliance on external investment.	Interest and excitement in tourism as the new growth sector. Entrepreneurial investment. Complementarity and synergy with other activities. Potential problem of over-supply.
Tourism growth		Potentially serious problem of economic decline. Deteriorating environment through lack of investment. Closure/ downsizing tourism enterprises.	Little interest. Tourism not a central issue for place. Possible development of specialist markets.
	decline		
		high low	
		Tourism dominance in destination	

FIGURE 3.13 *Tourism dominance and growth*

Tourism dominance is shown on the horizontal axis. High dominance means that a destination is heavily dependent on tourism, which makes up a significant part of its economy. Low dominance means that tourism is simply one among a number of the destination's activities. A position at the extreme right on the axis will mean that there are few tourism activities, and tourism does not have significant impacts on the destination. As we move left on the axis, there will be cases where tourism is still significant in absolute terms though not dominant in the destination either economically or in terms of its other impacts. The vertical axis shows the rate of growth of tourism, ranging from rapid decline to rapid growth.

- **The top left quadrant** includes destinations which are likely to experience the problems of success. Tourism is a dominant feature of the destination and is growing rapidly. This will create benefits in terms of incomes, profits, employment and a positive image, but may also lead to problems. Rapid growth can lead to a series of environmental problems – ranging from pressures on natural habitat to infrastructure problems, to pressures for excess or inappropriate new developments. Since benefits and costs fall on different groups, there may be resentment from local residents and non-tourism businesses which are forced

to bear the problems of expansion of tourism. Growth has many positive features, but there are difficult problems concerned with controlling and managing development, creating public infrastructure, and managing competing and often conflicting interests. In extreme cases, there will be issues of carrying capacity and loss of authenticity (e.g. York and Bath).

- **The bottom left quadrant** represents destinations which are heavily dependent on tourism, but suffering problems of decline or low growth (several English seaside resorts face this problem). They will tend to experience a series of often interlinked difficulties. Since tourism is dominant, its decline will have multiplier effects on the whole economy, as spending is reduced by individuals and firms in the industry. Low or zero profits will result in deferred maintenance and lack of modernisation of buildings and facilities, and the public infrastructure will follow the same pattern. All this will tend to give the destination a negative image and, in the worst case, it can fall into a cycle of decline, making it difficult to introduce and market new tourism products – some UK seaside resorts fall into this category. Strategies for development will be concerned with arresting the cycle of decline, and finding ways to encourage regeneration: these may include consideration of alternatives to tourism, and trying to attract external finance (usually from public agencies) to promote the regeneration of tourism or to facilitate conversion.

- **The top right quadrant** includes destinations in which tourism is growing from a comparatively low base. In some cases, rapid growth will be associated with the reinvention of a place not previously seen as a tourist destination. The growth of tourism in industrial towns and cities in Britain and elsewhere in the 1970s and 1980s is an obvious case in point. In these cases, the growth of tourism is likely to generate excitement and enthusiasm and be seen as an opportunity for wider regeneration and developmental efforts. Issues will include means to foster development, to ensure new facilities are provided, and to achieve the maximum spin-off benefits from tourism's growth (e.g. Halifax and Bradford).
- **The bottom right quadrant** represents places where tourism is currently of little importance, and where there is little sign of growth. This clearly implies that it will be of little concern to policy makers, local business and local residents. However, there are now relatively few places where this is wholly true. Rapid and continuing economic change fosters a constant search for new types of economic activity, and towns and cities have become increasingly imaginative in their views of what can be achieved. Tourism (especially defined in our broad terms) has, over the last 20 years, begun to make a significant contribution to places which previously would not have been regarded as destinations. Most places currently within our lower right quadrant will at least keep under review the possibility of achieving tourist development, and thus moving toward the top right quadrant. Dartford, on the Thames and well known for its M25 bridge and tunnel is an instance. We discuss the increasing role of tourism in local economics in Chapter 5.

CONCLUSIONS

There has been a tendency to see destinations as synonymous with resorts. However, in Britain and much of mainland Europe, tourism is an increasingly pervasive activity, and a much wider range of places are now tourism destinations. Traditional seaside and ski-resorts have been joined by historic cities, capital cities, rural areas, and industrial towns and cities. Places in which tourism does *not* play a role are increasingly becoming the exception. This is not a new phenomenon, but much of the literature on destination development still focuses on a resort model.

We can use the idea of a portfolio of tourism products to help us understand change in a broad range of destinations. Each destination faces a particular set of challenges, depending on the nature of its tourism product portfolio, the growth or decline of tourism products, and the dominance of tourism in the destination. The value of the portfolio idea is that it provides a means of focusing on the key issues for a strategy of destination development; it is essentially schematic, an aid to thinking, rather than a model offering quantified measures of development and change. Such quantification would require detailed statistical data, regularly collected – and for most destinations, those data are simply unavailable.

We have argued that moving away from the resort model has some important implications:

- It focuses attention on the fact that the commercial tourism industry is primarily dependent on destination resources which are not in its ownership. Sustainable destination development thus requires some means of protecting and enhancing those resources.
- Whilst it makes sense to think of destinations in corporate terms (offering a portfolio of products) the reality is that the different products may be produced by different organis-

ations. This means that it is difficult to develop and adapt the destination's portfolio, since there is no straightforward means of using funds from currently successful products to develop new ones for the future.

- Destinations are complex places which earn their livings in many ways, of which tourism is only one. We need to see tourism as part of a broader local economy and set of activities.

We have argued that an increasingly varied range of destinations face a variety of problems – ranging from coping with decline, to dealing with rapid growth, to introducing new products or establishing tourism as a significant part of the local economy. The problems are varied but they have a common factor: the tourism industry alone cannot respond effectively to them. Management at the destination level is required. There may be a need for regulation to influence the nature and amount of new development. Visitor management may be required so that large numbers of people can be accommodated in popular destinations without causing unacceptable ill effects. Public-private partnerships may have to be initiated to resolve conflicts between tourism, residents and non-tourism industries and to find means to fund investment in destination resources. Strategies and action programmes may be needed to adapt a destination's product portfolio or develop tourism from a low base, often with public funding. We will examine the need for, and practice of, destination management in Chapters 5, 6 and 7. We will then illustrate what can be done through detailed case studies of a series of destinations, each facing a series of different problems. In the next chapter we will consider the nature of the impacts that tourism can have on a destination.

REFERENCES

Baker, M.J. (1992) *Marketing Strategy and Management*, 2nd edn. Macmillan, London.

Beioley, S.J, Maitland, R.A. and Vaughan, R. (1990) *Tourism and the Inner City*, HMSO, London.

Bennett, A. (1993) *Writing home*, Faber & Faber, London.

Buckley, P.J. and De Witt, S.F. (1985) 'Tourism in Difficult Areas' in *Tourism Management* 6, 3.

Butler, R.W. (1980) 'The concept of a tourism area cycle of evolution: implications for resources', *Canadian Geographer* 24, 1, pp. 5–12.

Cambridge Economic Consultants (1996) *Cambridge Local Area Tourism Model*, Cambridge City Council.

Cooper, C., Fletcher, J., Gilbert, D. and Wanhill, S. (1993) *Tourism Principles and Practice*, Pitman, London.

Cooper, C. (1989) 'Tourism product life cycle', in *Tourism Marketing and Management Handbook*, Prentice Hall, Hemel Hempstead.

Cooper, C. (1994) 'The destination life-cycle: an update' in Seaton A.V. *et al.* (Eds) *Tourism: The State of the Art*, John Wiley and Sons, Chichester.

Craig-Smith, S. and French, C. (1993) *Learning to live with tourism*, Pitman, Melbourne.

van Doorn, J.W.M. (1979) *The Developing Countries: Are they really affected by tourism? Some critical notes on socio-cultural impact studies,* paper presented at seminar on Leisure Studies and Tourism, 7–8 Dec. 1974, Warsaw.

Doxey, G. (1975) *A causation theory of visitor-resident irritants, methodology and research,* Conference proceedings of the Travel Research Association, San Diego.

Gormsen, E. (1981) 'The spatio-temporal development of international tourism: attempt at a centre-periphery model', pp. 150–70 in *La Consommation d'Espace par le Tourisme et sa Préservation*, CHET, Aix-en-Provence.

Grabler, K, Mazanec, J. and Wober, K. (1996), 'Strategic marketing for urban tourism: analysing competition among European tourist cities' in Law, C.M. *Tourism in Major Cities*, International Thompson, London.

Johnson, J.D. and Spengler, D.J. (1993) 'Application of the Tourism Life Cycle Concept in the Greater Yellowstone Region', in *Society & Natural Resources,* Vol 6, pp. 127–148.

Miossec, J.M. (1977) 'Un modèle de l'espace

touristique', *L'Espace Géographique*, 6(1), pp. 41–8.

Palmer, A. (1994) *Principles of Services Marketing*, McGraw-Hill, London.

Pearce, D. (1980) *Tourism Development*, Longman, Harlow.

Plog, S.C. (1973) 'Why destination areas rise and fall in popularity, in *Cornel HRA Quarterly*, Nov., pp. 13–16.

Ritter, W. (1991) 'Recreation and leisure in the interior deserts of the Arab Gulf countries' in *Union Géographique Internationale*, Marrakech.

Smith, V.L. (1977) *Hosts and guests: the anthropology of tourism*, Blackwell, Oxford.

Thurot, J.M. (1973) *Le Tourisme Tropical Balnéaire: Le Modèle Caraïbe et ses Extensions*, Thesis, Centre d'Etudes du Tourisme, Aix-en-Provence.

4 *The impacts of tourism*

INTRODUCTION

All types of human activity, and particularly economic activities, can have impacts on the people who undertake them and on the places where they are carried out. They can have both positive, negative, direct, and indirect impacts. These impacts not only affect the consumers and producers of the goods or services in question, but also other people who actually live in the places where these are produced, transported and consumed. The economic, physical and natural environment can also be changed by the production, transportation and consumption of goods and services.

Indeed, where tourism takes place the tourism industry is not usually the only economic activity having an impact on the destination. For example, the fragile turf in the High Fell area of the Lake District is not only damaged by too many walkers, but also by the presence of too many sheep. Water and air pollution in Venice is mainly due to the Mestre-Marghera industrial complexes – the *vaporetti* which drive tourists around the city's canals only add to the problem. Tourism is an important source of income for many businesses in Aberdeen, but the most significant boost to the local economy came from the oil industry in the 1970s.

Tourism is a complex phenomenon with varying positive and negative impacts; it is not a simple matter to determine what the net balance is. It is necessary to ask the questions: 'Where?', 'When?' and 'For whom?'.

An awareness of the forms tourism's impacts can take is essential to the understanding of the rationale for tourism planning and management. In this chapter, we explore the issues, with particular emphasis on tourism's impacts on Western European destinations.

Academic opinion is divided over the question as to whether tourism's impacts are, on the whole, more or less damaging or beneficial than those of other economic activities.

- Turner and Ash (1975) maintain that 'Tourism ... is no less an industry than steel manufacture, and its introduction ... has been no less destructive of total population patterns and traditional culture than if each hotel had been a blast furnace.'
- Other writers, presenting tourism's positive as well as negative impacts often conclude that the negative effects of tourism on destinations are generally exaggerated. For example, Mathieson and Wall (1982) assert that even if tourism's negative impacts are admitted, they are probably nowhere near as damaging as those produced by industrialisation and urbanisation.

A more pertinent question is: which features make tourism's impacts different in nature to those of the manufacturing sector or other service sector economic activities (e.g. retailing or banking). The characteristics of tourism's impacts setting them apart from those of other sectors are as follows:

- concentration in space
- concentration in time
- the rapid growth in scale and intensity of the industry
- visibility
- the extraneous nature of tourism.

CONCENTRATION IN SPACE

In tourism, both production and consumption take place in the same location – the visitors 'consume' the product in the tourism destination. The impacts of tourism are therefore spatially concentrated in the places visited by the tourists. This contrasts with agriculture and the manufacturing industry, where most of the products are consumed outside the region where they are produced.

Naturally, impacts from tourism are not *exclusively* confined to the destination itself, or parts of the destination. For example, transport from the tourist's home to the destination has an effect on the transit zone, and money spent on buying a package trip benefits the tour operator and travel agency (which are usually based outside the tourist's destination). Tourism can also have an effect on the visitors themselves, who may be changed to some extent by what they see, do, or learn and by the people they meet (whether these are other tourists and/or residents).

These 'additional' impacts lie beyond the scope of this book. Our principal concern is with the impact that tourism has on the destinations – on the locality where tourism takes place and on the people who live there.

CONCENTRATION IN TIME

Much tourism is characterised by seasonality or periodicity (the high concentration of visitor activity at particular times of the year or week). This is the result of two factors:

- the climatic features of the destination (e.g. the presence of sunshine or snow at certain times of the year)
- the potential tourist's motivation and ability to visit (e.g. the annual leave-taking period, school holidays or days of the week which are free from the constraints of work and school).

Thus, in Europe, the vast majority of the demand for annual holidays is concentrated in the peak summer months, while short breaks and day trips are most likely to be taken at weekends. To these classic periods of concentration may be added the other 'mini-seasons' associated with Easter and winter breaks, skiing holidays, and specific annual events such as festivals and major trade fairs.

The degree of seasonality varies with the type of destination. For example, large cities have a less seasonal pattern of tourism than tourist resorts – they depend on a more diversified demand and include business travel as well as short breaks, and day trips based on cultural, shopping and entertainment facilities which are open all-year round. However, tourism at most destinations is characterised by some degree of seasonality and/or periodicity, creating surges of visitors which may be either foreseen (as in the case of an organised festival or a Bank Holiday) or unexpected (as in the case of a surprisingly sunny Saturday in the month of November).

Whatever the causes of these peaks and troughs of visitation, they lead to an unevenness of demand which creates perturbations throughout the destination as well as difficulties for those running tourism-related businesses (cashflow, problems of capacity). This concentration in time of tourism's impacts (often for reasons completely outside the control of those living and working at the destination) sets it apart from most other economic activities, and adds to the intensity of those impacts on the destination.

THE RAPID GROWTH IN SCALE AND INTENSITY OF THE INDUSTRY

Increasing discretionary income and free time means that tourism is already a huge industry, is growing rapidly and is voraciously reaching into new locations to satisfy the escalating global demand for places to visit. Safier's description of urban tourism's spread and growth shows the extent of this phenomenon on one type of destination:

> 'The most dramatic – indeed exponential – increase in scale and reach of tourism in cities, has occurred over the past century and a half, dwarfing the entire preceding build-up. From a fortunate few hundred people pottering about places like Athens, Florence, Paris and Vienna, and then a still fortunate few thousand following in their footsteps courtesy of Messrs Cook and others, to the globetrotters of the inter-war years with their widened horizons, we have now accelerated up to the point of achieving universal mobility on a global scale. 'Le weekend' visitor can now choose from destinations around the world and the urban 'pleasure periphery' has been expanded from Acapulco and Beijing to Vancouver and Vladivostok.'
>
> *(Safier, 1994)*

Few other industries can match the worldwide growth in tourism's scale and intensity. Air travel means that practically overnight, the inhabitants of an island destination hitherto untouched by tourism can suddenly find themselves playing hosts to large numbers of foreign visitors. Individual regions and towns can also become major destinations just as suddenly. For example, in the space of only a few years, the French *département* of Vienne found itself transformed from being a sleepy part of rural France, completely passed over by most tourists, to being the location of the country's most successful home-grown theme park, the Futuroscope, with over three million visitors a year.

The enormous scale and rapid pace of much tourism development are inevitably reflected in the sheer extent of tourism's impacts, as well as in the difficulty in bringing its negative effects under control.

VISIBILITY

The extremely visible and pervasive nature of tourism as an activity means that it enters into the daily lives of *all* of those living and working in destinations, in a way in which other economic activities do not. With the exception of destinations which restrict visitors to certain controlled enclaves, tourists and tourism are highly visible. A further consequence of tourism's high visibility is the impact not only on the self-image of the residents, but also on the image of the destination itself, as a place to live and work in. The presence of tourism as an activity in a town or region can have an impact on how the destination is perceived by those seeking a place to move to, for residential purposes or for industrial relocation.

THE EXTRANEOUS NATURE OF TOURISM

Not only are tourists highly visible at the destination, they are also by definition from 'elsewhere', if only from a neighbouring town or region. Tourism has therefore this extraneous nature which makes it different from other industries.

Many civilisations have evolved through contact with 'outsiders': these have ranged from the more or less well-intentioned (e.g. pilgrims, travelling traders, explorers, missionaries) to the more or less aggressive (e.g. foreign armies, colonialists). As residents have interacted with these outsiders, a number of sociocultural impacts have resulted in sometimes profound changes, for good or bad. Trade has been the cause of the displacement of many people and the modern-day equivalent may be the globalisation of the world economy, which explains, for example, why car manufacturing workers on Tyneside have become used to taking orders from Japanese bosses. But tourism as an industry is unique in bringing its customers from their own places of residence to the destination, and this characteristic gives it much more potential to modify the sociocultural aspect of the destination than 'home-grown' economic activities.

All of the characteristics of the tourism industry discussed previously distinguish its impacts from those of other economic activities. This makes an understanding of those impacts all the more essential for the planning and managing of tourism at destinations. Moreover, as impact assessment is now a key element in many planning processes for tourism, as for other forms of development, this makes an understanding of tourism impacts all the more indispensable.

The literature on tourism and its impacts has grown very considerably in the last two decades, in part indicating the growing appreciation of the significance of the industry in terms of its size and the effects it can have on destination areas. Pearce (1989) identified the impacts of tourism as the most extensive theme in academic tourism literature.

The first impacts of tourism to be studied were the economic ones. Two explanations are usually given to explain why this was so:

- economic impacts were easiest to measure
- the sponsors of such impact studies were often governments or developers who were fairly certain that the results would be positive.

However, in the late 1970s, a growing awareness developed regarding the social, cultural and environmental impacts of tourism. With the realisation that the continued support of residents is essential to tourism's success, studies increasingly focused on residents' perception of the impact of tourism on their community. At the same time, increasing concern over the state of the environment itself heightened interest in the impact that all activities (including tourism) have on the physical and man-made environment of the destination.

Evaluating tourism's impacts means setting the benefits against the costs, both within and between the different types of impact. Since the traditional approach has been to compare the economic benefits of tourism with the sociocultural and environmental costs, this is the order we follow in this book – although in each case the other side of the argument is also presented, resulting in a more dialectic approach to the complex question of tourism impacts.

ECONOMIC BENEFITS

Tourism clearly represents a source of potential economic benefits to the destination where it takes place, and those advocating tourism as a development option (e.g. developers, entrepreneurs and national and local politicians) commonly use tourism's economic benefits as one of their most powerful arguments.

From the point of view of destinations, tourists' spending is a valuable source of additional income brought into the destination area from another town, region or country. This redistributive effect of tourism brings with it a range of potential economic benefits which manifest themselves in several different ways:

- the balance of payments

- employment
- income
- multipliers
- regional development.

THE BALANCE OF PAYMENTS

At the national level, these benefits are most often considered in terms of the foreign exchange earnings which *foreign* tourists' spending brings into the destination country. The prospect of making substantial amounts of foreign currency is often a major factor in the decision of national governments to promote their countries as international destinations. The impact of such earnings is measured in the contribution they make to the current account of the destination's balance of payments: where these contributions are higher than citizens' spending on tourism abroad, a country may be said to have a net positive balance for tourism. Reasoning in this way, each country's net balance of payments for tourism can be calculated simply by subtracting its citizens' expenditure on tourism abroad from its own receipts from foreign visitors. Moreover, since these two figures are often presented together, the temptation to make this calculation is considerable.

On this basis the OECD's figures shown in Figure 4.1 would appear to divide European member countries into those having a positive balance of payments for tourism (e.g. Austria, Ireland and the Mediterranean countries) and those with a negative tourism balance (all other countries, including the UK).

Since 1980, Britain's net balance of payments on the tourism account has been mainly in deficit, as the spending of British tourists on holidays overseas has increased faster than the spending of incoming visitors to Britain.

Country	1995 receipts from international tourism (US$ millions)	1995 expenditure on international tourism (US$ millions)
Austria	14 630.7	11 704.5
Belgium–Luxembourg	5 593.7	9 038.1
Denmark	3 672.0	4 279.3
Finland	1 716.2	2 382.8
France	27 510.4	16 089.5
Germany	12 267.8	48 066.4
Greece	4 300.0	1 295.5
Iceland	166.4	275.6
Ireland	2 192.7	2 000.9
Italy	28 504.8	12 911.6
The Netherlands	5 523.5	11 383.5
Norway	N/A	N/A
Portugal	4 404.0	2 156.4
Spain	24 713.3	4 300.4
Sweden	3 474.2	5 453.1
Switzerland	N/A	N/A
Turkey	4 956.0	912.0
United Kingdom	17 835.8	24 465.0

Source: OECD press release SG/COM/NEWS(96)21, 7 March 1996

FIGURE 4.1 *Tourism in Europe*

EMPLOYMENT

An inflow of tourists to a destination creates employment opportunities. Tourism, as a service industry, is labour intensive and, in times of concern over high unemployment rates in certain countries and regions, the job creation characteristic of tourism is a powerful argument in favour of its development. For example, the World Travel and Tourism Council, a powerful industry lobby group, claims that tourism was directly and indirectly responsible for some 19.4 million jobs in the EU in 1995, amounting to 13.2% of the workforce or one in every eight EU jobs (WTTC, 1995).

In the UK, in September 1995, there were an estimated 1,545,300 employees in tourism-related industries, excluding the self-employed (Tourism Intelligence Quarterly). This represented an increase of 54,500 jobs over the previous year. The various categories of employees included in these statistics are shown in Figure 4.2. Employment in these categories, plus the self-employment in tourism-related industries (estimated at 186,000 in 1995), amounted to 6% of the entire employed labour force in the UK.

Job creation or job retention is a benefit experienced mainly in the destination itself, although those living at the tourists' place of residence and in the transport zone may also benefit through the creation of employment in travel agencies, tour operations and transport. The various forms of employment created by tourism may be classified according to type, as proposed by the WTO (1994):

- **direct employment** – the persons who work in tourism enterprises (such as hotels, restaurants, tourist shops and tour and travel agencies)
- **indirect employment** – jobs generated in the supplying sectors (such as agriculture, fisheries and manufacturing)
- **induced employment** – additional people supported by the spending of income made by the direct and indirect employees
- **construction employment** – jobs generated in the construction of tourist facilities and infrastructure.

Claims based on the current or potential *quantity* of tourism jobs are often supplemented by other assertions regarding the *quality* and *variety* of tourism employment. Tourism is thus portrayed as an industry using computerised global-distribution systems and sophisticated transportation equipment, and as a high-tech employer of the most technically- and technologically-qualified staff.

By the same token, tourism may also be said to produce large numbers of the type of low-tech, entry-level service jobs which are important in addressing problems of structural employment (particularly in city centres and rural areas where these problems are often most severe). Holloway (1989) adds yet another advantage of tourism employment in emphasising that, while advances in technology may have had some impact on reducing labour requirements in tourism, the high degree of personal service which characterises certain sectors of the industry makes it relatively protected (in terms of job losses through technological change).

An additional advantage often vaunted for tourism as an employer is that it may create jobs more cheaply than other sectors of the economy. However, calling this characteristic of tourism into question, Pearce (1989) is among the many commentators who have highlighted the 'conflicting evidence regarding the capital-employment ratio advantages of tourism relative to other sectors'.

The most pertinent point on this issue may be that made by Hughes (1982) who points out that comparisons between employment generation in tourism and in other sectors are limited by the choice of opportunities for job creation in particular regions – cost per job does not imply that there is a choice of job type that can be created. It may be cheaper, in theory, to create tourism jobs rather than jobs in hi-tech industries, but if the region in question is one in which tourists show little or no interest, then the question of relative cost of job creation remains an academic one.

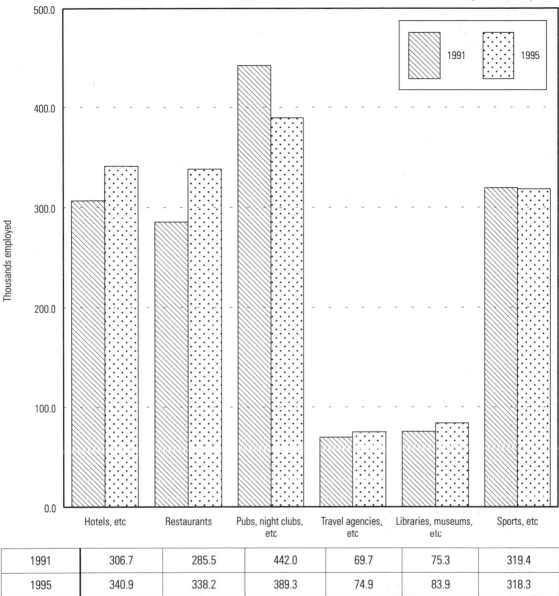

Sept 1991 and Sept 1995

	Hotels, etc	Restaurants	Pubs, night clubs, etc	Travel agencies, etc	Libraries, museums, etc	Sports, etc
1991	306.7	285.5	442.0	69.7	75.3	319.4
1995	340.9	338.2	389.3	74.9	83.9	318.3

Source: CSO Labour Market Trends

FIGURE 4.2 *Employment in tourism-related industries*

INCOME

Tourism is a source of personal income for those employed in the industry, and in some destinations, may represent the main source of wages and salaries for a substantial proportion of the workforce. But tourism also generates income for businesses (in the form of profits) and for governments.

The creation of tourism-related tax income for national governments arises in three main ways:

■ indirect taxes, such as VAT, levied on, for

example, restaurant meals and entry fees to tourist attractions
- direct corporate taxes based on travel and tourism companies' profits
- personal income taxes based on tourism employees' wages and salaries.

To these may be added income from the kind of charges and user fees which are levied directly on travellers in some countries (e.g. the departure tax which is imposed on airport passengers in the UK). Local authorities have less scope for making revenue through this kind of tourism-related taxation, although local tourism taxes added to hotel bills are applied at some destinations. (e.g. the *taxe de séjour* in certain French cities or the Austrian *Kurtaxe*). Local authorities with significant numbers of second homes in their territory may also earn revenue through property taxes charged to their owners, as well as property taxes on tourism establishments, such as hotels and tourist attractions operating commercially.

Taxes earned from tourism in EU member countries are shown in Figure 4.3, along with other economic indicators. (The figures shown for 'Employment' include direct, indirect and induced employment created through tourism.)

MULTIPLIERS

Just as tourism creates direct, indirect and induced employment at the destination, so it leads to different kinds of expenditure in the destination's economy. Of the money received by tourism businesses, individuals and governments, a certain portion is re-spent within the destination economy, thereby creating further rounds of economic activity. For example, hoteliers may buy food locally (indirect expenditure) and part of a tour guide's salary may be spent in local shops (induced expenditure). This is known as the **multiplier effect** of tourism: a measurement of the extent to which tourist expenditure (as measured, in economists' terminology, in 'units of final demand') filters through the national, regional or local economy and generates other economic activities there. A variety of multiplier values may be calculated for tourism:

- **income multipliers** – as described in the above example, are the most often quoted type
- **employment multipliers** – show the direct, indirect and induced effect of one additional unit of final tourism demand upon the level of employment
- **output multipliers** – the ratio of change in total productive output throughout the whole economy brought about by the initial change in tourism expenditure
- **government revenue multipliers** – show the total effect of a unit change in final tourism demand upon government revenue from all sources.

Such multiplier values therefore give a more comprehensive picture of the stimulus which the external source of tourism income has on the economy of the destination (whether this is an entire country, a region or a single town or city). Whatever the geographical scale used, the principle remains the same: an increase in inbound tourism expenditure will cause an increase in national/regional/city income by an amount larger than the original increase in tourism expenditure.

Methods for calculating tourism multiplier values are based on traditional approaches used in economics. These methods lie beyond the immediate scope of this book, but Archer and Fletcher (1991) provide a detailed technical investigation of multiplier analysis in tourism in general. Several authors have calculated multiplier values for specific tourism destination areas. Sadler *et al.* (1973) examine regional income multipliers, with a detailed case-study of Anglesey. More recently, Parlett *et al.* (1995) have generated income, output and employment multiplier values for Edinburgh's Old Town, as part of their assessment of the economic impact of tourism on this destination.

As in the case of cost per job created, the issue of cross-industry comparisons arises when measuring multipliers for tourism against those for other sectors. Does tourism have a higher general multiplier value than, say, agriculture or the construction industry? If anything, such comparison are even more difficult to make in the case of

	Gross output* (ECU billions)	GDP (ECU billions)	Employment (millions)	Investment (ECU billions)	Total taxes (ECU billions)
Austria	29.79	25.34	0.46	6.71	6.78
% of total	3.1%	15.45%	13.07%	16.46%	17.85%
Belgium	31.02	29.11	0.60	7.27	8.46
	3.2%	15.55%	16.17%	21.02%	16.08%
Denmark	17.48	14.84	0.28	3.26	4.71
	1.8%	11.50%	10.98%	16.55%	11.47%
Finland	11.97	10.47	0.22	2.81	2.65
	1.2%	12.16%	10.89%	21.27%	14.03%
France	189.82	164.26	2.96	39.18	40.95
	19.6%	14.17%	13.31%	18.18%	15.47%
Germany	242.20	220.80	4.31	50.06	45.16
	25.1%	12.91%	12.38%	12.50%	15.94%
Greece	10.98	9.36	0.48	2.43	2.34
	1.1%	14.60%	13.28%	19.00%	17.22%
Ireland	6.45	5.64	0.13	2.45	1.75
	0.7%	12.80%	10.91%	32.84%	13.05%
Italy	142.56	120.92	2.68	27.25	32.22
	14.8%	12.98%	13.13%	16.56%	14.64%
Luxembourg	1.43	1.34	0.03	0.33	0.36
	0.1%	15.55%	16.17%	21.02%	15.96%
Netherlands	35.94	33.18	0.74	7.29	9.81
	3.7%	11.98%	11.33%	13.32%	12.55%
Portugal	10.79	9.55	0.64	3.51	2.40
	1.1%	14.27%	13.70%	16.78%	14.82%
Spain	85.66	76.78	2.36	21.44	19.25
	8.9%	18.86%	19.92%	24.91%	23.02%
Sweden	22.80	18.98	0.40	3.01	4.37
	2.4%	10.51%	10.05%	12.13%	12.43%
United Kingdom	126.56	109.33	3.13	14.31	32.11
	13.1%	12.02%	12.19%	10.41%	12.69%

* Gross output percentages are expressed as proportion of total EU market. All other percentages are expressed as proportion of national market.

Source: WTTC

FIGURE 4.3 *Tourism-related economic indicators in EU member countries (1995)*

multipliers, due to the many different ways used to calculate these. Komilis (1994) cites the Tourism and Recreation Research Unit of the University of Edinburgh with regard to this problem: 'The absence of a standard procedure for preparing multipliers poses considerable difficulties in any attempt to compare the multiplier effects of different industries.'

REGIONAL DEVELOPMENT

In most countries, socioeconomic indicators demonstrate that there are inequalities between different regions, some enjoying much higher average standards of living, employment rates and salary levels than others.

International and domestic tourism has demonstrated its potential for counterbalancing regional imbalances in terms of income and employment levels. Williams and Shaw (1991) quote Peters who states that 'tourism, by its nature, tends to distribute development away from the industrial centres towards those regions in a country which have not been developed'.

Archer and Cooper (1994, p. 73) also stress this particular advantage of tourism: '. . . tourism seems to be more effective than other industries in generating employment and income in the less developed and often outlying regions of a country where opportunities for development are more limited. Indeed, it is in these areas that tourism can make its most significant impact.'

The many contributors to Williams and Shaw's (1991) volume demonstrate in their case studies tourism's potential to bring development to the more economically-neglected regions of European countries. Tourism's role as a key to regional development within the European Union is examined in Chapter 6, while, on a more localised scale, its role in urban regeneration is investigated in Chapter 5.

ECONOMIC COSTS

The impacts of tourism on the economy of a destination are by no means exclusively positive. For example, national and local governments incur many different *costs* in developing, marketing and maintaining themselves as tourist destinations. A major cost at the national level is that of maintaining a National Tourism Organisation (NTO) to promote the country as a tourist destination. To this may be added the costs of providing the transport infrastructure required by tourists to enable them to get to the country and travel around it. At the level of the individual town or city, as well as incurring marketing costs, the local authority that is faced with the presence of tourists must provide them with a number of extra services, such as more parks maintenance, car parks, police patrols and public toilets. Local residents, who pay for most municipal services may find themselves confronted with vast numbers of short-staying visitors who contribute very little to the local economy, but do add to the overcrowding, pollution and demand on services. Tourism can have negative economic effects on:

- the balance of payments
- inflation of prices
- employment.

THE BALANCE OF PAYMENTS

Such tourism-associated costs as those described previously have caused many commentators to call into question the simplistic method (see page 71) of calculating the net contribution which tourism makes to a country or a destination area's balance of payments. That method ignores all of the associated costs incurred in first of all attracting and then providing services to visitors. Such costs must be deducted in order to calculate a more accurate level of net earnings from tourism. **Leakage** must also be taken into account. This is the sum of tourism earnings which does not remain at the destination, but drains away through the importing of goods and services that are required to satisfy incoming tourists' needs (e.g. food items, hotel equipment and supplies) and through the repatriation of foreign workers' salaries and of profits of foreign-owned facilities.

Although problems of leakage are clearly of less concern to countries such as the UK (which has a well-developed and diverse national economy), the general concept is important in calculating tourism's economic impact more accurately. In addition, even in developed countries, individual regions (which are usually less economically self-contained than entire countries) must allow for regional leakage, in order to calculate the net as well as the gross earnings generated by tourists arriving from other regions.

Ownership of tourism facilities is also a key factor in the balance of payments – fewer economic benefits accrue to destinations (whether they are countries or regions) where substantial parts of the tourism product are owned and managed by outsiders. Hotels owned by transnational corporations which repatriate profits out of the tourist destination, are most often identified as a cause of leakage, but other less evident examples abound. For example, Swarbrooke (1992) identified the issue of leakage in connection with the increasing number of British-owned second homes in France, which are being let out as holiday homes to visitors, either directly through newspaper advertisements or through tour operators. Most of the rental money paid for these properties never reaches the local economy, but instead accrues to their British owners in Britain.

Baretje (1982) incorporates these associated costs of tourism into his 'tourism external account' (see Figure 4.4) which proposes a broader system of accounting, including not only leakages but also indirect transactions resulting from tourism.

The value of this system of accounting lies in its comprehensive nature. However, while attractive in theory, the calculation of 'tourism's external account' in practice presents enormous difficulties, particularly when it is applied to large, complex economies such as those of Western European countries.

INFLATION

As tourism grows within a destination area, it makes increasing demands upon the scarce resources of that area. Land in particular is required, and land prices can rise as a consequence. This places an additional financial burden on residents. For example, increase in property values caused by the buying up of second homes can mean that prices rise to the level where they are no longer affordable by local people and resident communities are driven out as a result. Swarbrooke identified this problem as another of the impacts which British second-home ownership has had on parts of rural France.

'The main deterioration in the (British visitor/French host) relationship begins with the rise of second-home ownership by British tourists, because of their tendency to congregate and take over areas. Although

Expenditures	Receipts
Expenditures by tourists abroad	Expenditures 'at home' by foreign tourists
Transportation	Transportation
Investments (outward)	Investments (inward)
Dividends, interest and profits paid out	Dividends, interests and profits received
Commodity imports (tourism induced): – capital goods – consumption goods	Commodity exports (tourism induced): – capital goods – consumption goods
Salaries repatriated	Salaries sent abroad
Training	Training
Publicity and promotion	Publicity and promotion
Miscellaneous services	Miscellaneous services

Source: Baretje, 1982

FIGURE 4.4 *Components in tourism's external account*

second-home ownership saves old buildings, the fact that such homes are occupied for only a few weeks each year means that they contribute little to the local economy. As many buyers are relatively affluent, property prices are forced up beyond the level that young people can afford ... Many villages are beginning to look like holiday villages for foreigners.'

(Swarbrooke, 1992)

(However, it is interesting to note that Swarbrooke's emphasis on the role of the British visitor in France obscures the fact that this phenomenon is also due to the spread of *French*-owned holiday homes, purchased by affluent city-dwellers wanting second homes in rural areas or beside the sea.)

EMPLOYMENT

The type of employment created by tourism has come under criticism from various commentators who have drawn attention to the quality of some jobs. Representative of these are Craig-Smith and French, who list their main objections to the tourism industry as an employer:

'Employment is often advocated as one of the primary benefits of the tourism industry to a community but many jobs are unskilled, lowly-paid and part-time. Managerial positions tend to go to outside personnel and in Third World economies they often go to overseas managers, usually from the country which provided the investment capital. Much tourism employment is also highly seasonal and this presents special problems'.

(Craig-Smith and French, 1994)

To these objections can be added several other characteristics, identified by the European Institute of Education and Social Policy (EIESP, 1991) in their survey of careers in the European travel and tourism industry: 'Many (tourism) jobs are seen to offer little training and career prospects are limited; jobs in this sector have a poor image as a result of long and unsocial working hours and below-average pay; staff turnover is often high, leading to recurring recruitment difficulties.'

Calculating the overall impact on the local or regional economy of tourism-related employment is a complex task, involving a whole range of variables and assumptions. What value should be placed on part-time as opposed to full-time work? How much seasonal employment is taken by those, such as students, who are only available for work during the summer months? What percentage of tourism wages are supplementary to the main source of income and are used to support another enterprise, such as a farm or craft workshop? And, perhaps most pertinently of all, how many tourism jobs are created in areas offering few or no alternative employment opportunities?

DETERMINANTS OF ECONOMIC IMPACT

An understanding of the factors which determine the nature and the extent of tourism's economic impact is essential when considering the tourism planning and management process, as they are part of the key to optimising tourism's financial contribution to the destination. These factors relate to:

- the type of tourism demand
- the type of economy operating at the desti-

nation and the destination's capacity (local, regional, or national) to respond to tourism demand.

THE TYPE OF TOURISM DEMAND

The type of tourist visiting the destination is a major determinant of the economic contribution which tourism makes there. Many different categories of tourist and tourism exist (see Chapter 2). The form of tourism in which they participate largely determines their economic impact.

■ **Duration** – the duration of the visit is a factor of the utmost importance, since short-staying day-trippers usually contribute very little to the local economy (but can create environmental pressures and social problems of the type discussed later in this chapter). Accordingly, more and more destinations are reacting to this problem by attempting to attract the longer-staying visitor while discouraging day-trippers.

■ **Purpose of trip** – different types of tourist (in terms of purpose of visit) make strikingly different contributions to the national, regional and local economy. For example, business visitors are among the most profitable categories of tourist. In the UK, business visitors spend on average more than twice the average daily expenditure of all types of visitors (BTA, 1993). Although business travel accounted for only 11% of UK trips in 1994, it represented 15% of tourism-related spending (The UK Tourist). These tourists may be contrasted with people visiting and staying with friends and relations, who can make a minimal impact on the economy.

■ **Origin of visitors** – domestic tourists and foreign visitors are two distinctly different types of visitors when considering the national level of economic impact. On the national scale, the level of visitation from foreign visitors is a vital factor in calculating the balance of payments for tourism. Similarly, a high degree of domestic tourism, such as that found in France, also helps the balance of payments when it is a substitute for trips abroad, since this keeps money in the country. However, from the point of view of the more immediate destination area, the domestic/foreign visitor distinction is less important, for example, a Londoner's spending on tourism in Stratford-upon-Avon brings money into the town in the same way that a Japanese tourist's spending does. However, the spending characteristics of different nationalities (see below) can make some tourists more economically beneficial than others.

■ **Tourist spending** – the level of economic benefits are, of course, related to the volume of tourist spending which takes place at the destination. The spending power of individual tourists is therefore of relevance here – more relevant than their absolute numbers, since the contribution made by some tourists is well out of proportion to their numbers. Spending varies according to the combination of a wide range of sociodemographic variables, including age, social class, and nationality. For example, American visitors to the UK tend to be higher spending than the French. Not only is the American market on the whole composed of older, wealthier visitors than the French, but Americans are also more likely to spend freely in shops.

Given the above determinants, those responsible for the planning and managing of destinations can undertake deliberate measures to increase the contribution which visitors make to the local economy. The WTO (1994) lists three ways in which tourists' expenditures can be increased by adapting the product available to them at destinations:

■ shopping opportunities, especially of local arts and crafts
■ expansion of tourist activities – more attractions and tours, enticing tourists to stay longer
■ tourism product enrichment and diversification – expanding and upgrading tourism.

The attempts by destinations to boost tourists' spending are clearly seen, for example in their efforts to persuade conference delegates to bring their spouses with them on their trip and/or to extend their visit by spending some time exploring the destination before or after the conference. Parallel 'spouses' programmes' of cultural and shopping activities, as well as offers of add-on week or weekend packages, are often sent along with details of the conference itself.

THE TYPE OF ECONOMY OPERATING AT THE DESTINATION

LEAKAGE

The economic gains from tourism often depend not only on how much visitors spend, but what they spend it on. The key issue here is that of leakage. For example, money spent on campsite fees will contribute more effectively to the local economy than money spent on petrol (which may have to be imported into the destination area either from other regions or from abroad).

A loss of economic benefits can occur for the destination if a large proportion of tourist facilities are owned and managed by outsiders, and if there is a high import content of goods and services used in tourism at the destination.

The degree to which foreign ownership of tourist facilities is a feature of the destination is in part the result of the policy of the destination itself. National, regional and local ownership of tourist facilities can be encouraged in a number of ways, notably through adapting economic policy. The WTO suggests various techniques:

> '... providing investment incentives; organising stock companies with sale of shares to the general public; and requiring joint ventures of local and foreign companies ... If local capital is very limited, then a policy can be taken of initially allowing foreign ownership but requiring purchase by local owners when capital is available.'
>
> *(WTO, 1994)*

The education and training of indigenous tourism staff to supervisory and management level is also an important technique in seeking to maximise local employment in the tourism industry, and avoid the necessity of employing foreign nationals.

Pearce (1989) quotes various sources in compiling a list of those factors at the national level which determine the extent to which goods and services consumed by foreign tourists can be provided domestically:

- the size of the nation
- the structure and diversity of the national economy
- the nation's import policy
- whether or not supply can keep pace with demand
- the type of tourism and process of development
- the class of visitor
- the location of development – remote areas may draw more on imported goods due to the uncertainty of domestic supplies.

Clearly, for a modern, diversified national economy such as the UK, import leakages due to tourism pose far less of a problem than they do for the much less developed economies. For example, in certain small Caribbean and Pacific island destinations leakages can represent between 25% and 50% of gross foreign exchange receipts from tourism.

While leakages for developed countries are generally assumed to be much lower (although actual studies are rare), at the regional or destination area levels, the same seven characteristics listed above will determine the extent to which earnings from tourism remain in the local economy, to the benefit of residents.

LEVEL OF INVESTMENT

Continuing investment in tourism is required for two reasons:

- to keep pace with or increase the numbers of visitors to a particular destination
- to allow the destination to respond to tourists' demands for higher quality facilities and services.

Williams and Shaw (1991) stress that 'the ability of the national economy to benefit from tourism depends on the availability of investment to develop the necessary infrastructure (hotels, golf courses, etc.) and on its ability to supply the needs of tourists, whether for food, souvenirs or hotel beds'.

The main question is who will finance such investment and on what terms. In general, there are two types of tourism investment possible:

- **public capital investment** is undertaken by national, regional and local governments and tends to be associated with infrastructure (e.g. airports, ports, roads and highway construction)
- **private capital investment** is undertaken by companies and individuals, and tends to include such elements as aircraft, hotels and caravans, certain types of tourist attractions, and second homes.

Where the capital available for investment is limited, or where there is strong competition from other sectors for its use, the destination may be required to seek foreign investors. However (as indicated above), foreign investment means a degree of foreign control and this represents another form of leakage of economic benefits from the destination.

While tourism development is usually justified on the basis of the type of economic benefits we have just discussed, it is most often challenged on the grounds of its social, cultural or environmental costs. Although such costs are difficult if not impossible to quantify in money terms, consideration of them is vital to the tourism planning and management process.

In recent years, the negative effects of tourism on the environment and host populations have been increasingly set against the more tangible economic gains. Cause for concern has arisen wherever there has been any perception that short-term economic advantages are outweighed by more permanent problems, or that the sociocultural and environmental costs of tourism outweigh the economic benefits. For example, in some established historic tourism cities, such as York, Bath and Oxford, the significant economic benefits are clouded at times by the environmental problems and social tensions that tourism can cause. These costs of tourism will now be examined, and set against the benefits accruing to the destination.

SOCIOCULTURAL COSTS

Tourism involves a range of human interactions. Bringing together hosts and visitors, it can create the conditions for exchanges of views, ideologies, customs, traditions and lifestyles. Taken together, these elements may be said to represent the cultures of the two populations on opposite sides of the tourism equation.

Cultural differences between the visitors and the visited often constitute the major motivation behind a tourist trip being made. The different lifestyles, traditions and customs of the host community can be a source of fascination for visitors. But where these differences are great, tourism's legacy can be a range of negative impacts leading to serious problems in the host society.

Negative (and, arguably, positive) sociocultural impacts tend to be most significant where cultural and social differences between the visitors and the visited are most substantial, and as a result the vast majority of tourism-impact litera-ture focuses on the impact of international tourism, most often north-south, between markedly-different cultures. To what extent can the impacts identified in this literature be assumed to be transferable to tourism in the type of developed countries with which this book is mainly concerned? After a brief review of the sociocultural costs and benefits of tourism, we shall return to this question.

THE DEMONSTRATION EFFECT

Among the potential negative consequences of tourism for the host community is the loss of authenticity and identity of traditional cultures, resulting from the destination's inhabitants' tendency to imitate tourists by aspiring to their values. The reason given for this so-called 'demonstration effect' by the many commentators who have identified this phenomenon is that, where tourists clearly enjoy a standard of living which is significantly higher than that of the host population, visitors can come to represent for their hosts a 'higher', more modern or more desirable civilisation than their own. Increasing materialism and dissatisfaction among the hosts are said to be among the consequences of this phenomenon. Craig-Smith and French comment that:

'... demonstration effects can lead to unrealistic expectations by local people. Expensive cameras, Walkmans, ghetto blasters, watches and jewellery worn or carried by tourists can lead to local people demanding similar luxuries. In many cases, the local economy cannot support such aspirations ...'

(Craig-Smith and French, 1994)

Nevertheless, as many commentators have pointed out, the demonstration effect of tourism is notoriously difficult to disentangle from other forces for change acting upon destinations, notably advertising and the media. For example, do young Indonesians chew gum and wear personal stereos and baseball caps because they see tourists doing so or because they watch *Baywatch*?

STAGED AUTHENTICITY

MacCannell's (1976) 'staged authenticity' or instant culture phenomenon involves the local culture becoming degraded and stylised to suit a pattern of tourism-related entertainment, with the host population providing experiences for tourists which are not authentic but commercialised and trivialised. The result may be seen in the many 'culture shows' and 'authentic' folk dances as well as the ubiquitous 'typical' restaurants of many popular holiday resorts.

CHANGES IN COMMUNITY ORGANISATION

Tourism has also been blamed for disrupting the traditional norms of host communities and thereby weakening mutual help and cooperation based on these norms, increasing intergenerational conflicts and damaging the quality of personal relations. One way in which this is said to occur is when the job opportunities provided by tourism result in young people from rural backgrounds being tempted into tourism-related employment in cities and resorts. Not only can this lead them to abandon traditional skills, but

'... freed from the restrictions of their family and the familiarity of their home environment, (they) may abandon their traditional values. One result of this is an increase in the breakdown of marriage and in divorce.

(Cooper, 1989)

SOCIAL PROBLEMS

Substantial increases in the scale of crime, prostitution (finding its most heinous expression in child sex tourism), gambling and drug trafficking can be imported into destination areas with the advent or rapid growth of tourism, which brings with it a supply of new victims or markets for these activities. Standards of moral conduct may decline temporarily as tourists find themselves less restrained in the anonymity which prevails at a destination far from home.

The general deterioration in moral behaviour can cut both ways, bringing with it not only negative impacts for the host population, but also for the visitors themselves. The same anonymity, coupled with the presence of a transient population of vulnerable strangers apparently enjoying a more leisured and luxurious lifestyle, is a recipe for crime against tourists. Such crimes range from the level of petty pickpocketing and overcharging, to the far more serious use of tourists as targets caught up in the political crossfire of volatile countries, or used as hostages. Safier stresses this point:

'When the forces making for inequality, division and disrespect reach a certain point, then the reactions can be correspondingly cumulative and ultimately dangerous to all. From Miami to Moscow, and Rio to Cairo, the impact of social and cultural dislocations has led to tourists being targeted as actual and potential victims – innocent individuals caught up in collective confrontations.'

(Safier, 1994)

For destinations suffering from these negative impacts of tourism on their cultural and social structures, the problems are undeniably severe. Third World countries in particular are vulnerable to assault through tourism, and examples abound of destinations where 'culture' has become devalued and divorced from everyday life, where communities' traditions and lifestyles have become fossilised, and where racial and communal tensions have flared up with the arrival of tourism development.

Most research and concern over these negative impacts of tourism are (justifiably) focused on destinations which, for Europeans, are remote and exotic, often with fragile indigenous cultures. To what extent do such problems arise as a result of tourism in developed countries such as the UK, where, although social and cultural differences between tourists and the host community can exist, they are usually far less marked than in the case of international tourism to developing world destinations?

When the social values, habits and mores of the visited and the visitors are close, the demonstration effect is far less of a problem issue for destinations. For example, day-trippers visiting Chester are hardly likely to leave the inhabitants of that town feeling dissatisfied with their lot following exposure to the values of a higher civilisation. Similarly, UK examples of staged authenticity feature comparatively rarely in the tourism impact literature. Instances of this phenomenon in Britain might include the infamous Cockney Shows and the kilts-and-haggis parodies of 'Scottish evenings'. But these tend to be restricted to major cities, where they constitute only one very small aspect of a vast and complex tourism product (although, it is interesting to speculate whether the recent suggestion that London's 'Changing of the Guard' ceremony be performed by actors, since the Ministry of Defence can no longer afford the manpower to provide the ceremony every day (Goldring,

1995), represents another, more literal, example of staged authenticity).

Nevertheless, while the sociocultural problems caused or exacerbated by tourism in countries such as the UK may be less striking than those affecting developing countries, there is no room for complacency. For instance, when a remote village suddenly becomes the destination for several coachloads of tourists every day, because of its associations with, say, a popular TV series, what is the impact on the quality of village life? When sports enthusiasts find themselves excluded from well-known events such as the Henley regatta or Wimbledon, because places are increasingly reserved by companies for their corporate entertainment, what are the consequences? When the residents of historic towns, such as the Old Town of Edinburgh, increasingly have to travel further afield for the weekly shopping because of the steady growth of souvenir shops at the expense of all other types of retail outlet, what effect does this have on their attitude towards tourists? And what is the long-term impact on British culture of being prettified and packaged for tourism through the renaming of regions, such as 'Jane Austen', 'Constable', and 'James Herriot' country? The comparisons with the different 'lands' of so many theme parks is inevitable and has brought the expression 'Theme Park Britain' into popular usage. When a country's 'heritage' becomes an *industry*, how does that affect the way it is perceived by visitors and visited alike?

Social problems caused by tourism are no less a problem for destinations in the developed world. It may simply be that, sadly, such problems have become an unremarkable part of the tourism landscape. Examples of tourism-related crime may range from the street vendor fraudulently charging foreigners £10 for an ice-cream outside Madame Tussaud's, to the notorious organised gangs of pickpockets which operate during events such as Wimbledon or the Chelsea Flower Show. And while organised child prostitution may not exist on the scale found in certain destinations in the developing world, who can tell to what extent prostitution in UK cities depends on conference delegates and other business travellers as a constantly self-renewing pool of clients?

Tourism undoubtedly does bring with it negative impacts on the sociocultural fabric of the destination. Left unchecked, these impacts can result in serious damage to the destination and its image, from antagonism being expressed towards visitors by local people, to the debasing of the destination's culture and traditions.

However, the principle is the same, whether the destination is Bali or Blackpool: tourists will desert a destination which they find unfriendly or degraded, and move on to other places. Planning and management of the destination are vital, in order to minimise the types of impacts mentioned in this section.

SOCIOCULTURAL BENEFITS

Tourism's sociocultural impact is far from being entirely negative. Claims for international tourism's potential sociocultural benefits range from its role as a major force for world peace (WTO, 1980), to its power as a catalyst for cultural exchange, understanding, appreciation and respect, nurturing understanding between countries.

As in the case of tourism's negative effects on host cultures and societies, certain positive impacts are also most commonly found where visitors from the industrialised developed world travel to developing countries. There, the need to adapt in order to attract tourists, as well as inhabitants' exposure to new ideas and values has been credited with a whole range of benefits including an accelerated pace of modernisation, a more democratic and tolerant political climate, the development of the education and training system, and the emancipation of women.

However, many of tourism's socioeconomic benefits apply, more generally, to a wider range of types of destination. These benefits include:

- demographic regeneration
- service retention
- revitalisation.

DEMOGRAPHIC REGENERATION

Depopulation is a serious problem for many rural areas of Europe, as young people leave home to find elsewhere the work which is not available in their home region. Cazes (1992) makes the claim that wherever tourism has been significantly de-

veloped, it has put an end to depopulation and has brought about a sometimes spectacular demographic revival, as in the case of the northern Alpine regions, the French and Spanish Mediterranean coasts and the Balearics.

For example, in the effort to use tourism as a policy tool, the French government seeks, by giving grant-aid towards holiday villages being built in remote areas, to help keep rural economies viable and reduce de-population. Nevertheless, tourism's potential for stopping depopulation must be treated with some caution. Destination areas can receive a demographic boost partly as a result of an influx of elderly and retired people to the destination area, attracted by its climate and facilities such as golf courses, restaurants, shops, health care, etc. As an illustration of this tendency, Cazes (*ibid*) quotes from a source claiming that one and a half million foreigners (three-quarters of them retired) live on the Spanish coast and on the Canary Islands.

Prentice pursues a similar theme, identifying tourism and day trips to the countryside as a background factor in counter-urbanisation ('population transfusion' from cities to rural areas) for villages in the North Pennine and Cheviot Uplands.

'... Tourism, as holidaying and leisure, particularly as day-trip making, would seem to be of importance in spreading an awareness of the availability of attractive environments locally for residential relocation. As such, the impacts of tourism and leisure extend into counter-urbanisation and into the latter's impacts in both population and social terms.'

(Prentice, 1992)

SERVICE RETENTION

The influx of tourists to a destination can create new markets for services shared with local inhabitants and provide a strong case for retaining or strengthening such services. In rural areas, services such as transport and the retail sector may benefit from the presence of new markets generated through tourism, while visitors can help develop and maintain museums, sports facilities and cultural venues (such as the theatres in London's West End).

REVITALISATION

Tourism can be a factor in the preservation of the host population's traditional culture. It can reinforce or renew residents' sense of pride in their culture, when they see it being appreciated by visitors. Traditions, customs and institutions in the process of vanishing can be revived and can gain new meaning when they become tourist attractions in themselves. Historical celebrations, festivals, religious ceremonies: tourism provides the opportunity to exhibit these resources to others, and this in turn can boost the cultural self-confidence of the destination's inhabitants. For example, Scotland's New Year celebration, Hogmanay, has shaken off its maudlin, self-parodying image and received a new lease of life since the city of Edinburgh launched its annual Hogmanay Festival, Britain's biggest street party of free musical concerts and fireworks. Another impact is that every hotel and guesthouse in the capital is now fully-booked at a time of year when the tourism trade used to be relatively quiet.

When traditional culture itself becomes a tourist attraction, the result can be that local people begin to value elements of their culture and increase identification with them, since they see their traditions being appreciated by visitors. Examples abound in the tourism-impact literature, of the revitalising effect which tourism has had on the various aspects of a destination's cultural fabric – from crafts and traditional dances to folklore and ceremonies. The reinforced sense of pride which tourism can stimulate in such aspects of the host population's heritage can also be accompanied by an increasing local acceptance of tourism, particularly when the economic benefits arising from tourism are evident.

Moreover, although the policy decision to encourage domestic tourism (as well as or as opposed to international tourism) may have at its base economic motives, this type of tourism can play an important part in strengthening national identity and values. For example, Lickorish (1994) notes that in India, the strengthening of national identity through domestic tourism has long been an important feature of policy, while the Australian Bi-Centenary Year and European Tourism Year are further instances of tourism being used, in part, to strengthen national or regional identities.

DETERMINANTS OF SOCIOCULTURAL IMPACT

Some of the factors which determine the nature and the extent of tourism's sociocultural impact have already been discussed. One of the most important of these is the degree to which cultural similarities exist between hosts and visitors. This factor is perhaps the most important one distinguishing the difference between tourism's sociocultural impacts in developed nations and in Third World countries. For example, most domestic tourism in European countries (or even intra-European tourism) is likely to be characterised by hosts and visitors sharing similar values, beliefs and often language. The sociocultural effects of this form of tourism will, consequently, be less striking than those of international tourism in the developing countries of Southeast Asia or Africa, for example, where there is a much lesser degree of sociocultural homogeneity between visitors and visited.

TYPE OF TOURISM

The type of tourism developed at the destination is clearly of the greatest importance – the degree of exposure which residents have to visitors will in part determine the impact of tourism on the host culture. **Enclave tourism**, (which implies a conscious decision to segregate tourists from the general population) aims to reap the economic benefits of tourism for the destination without the culture being overwhelmed by foreign visitors. Most examples of enclave tourism are to be found in developing countries, although, interestingly, Lickorish (*ibid*) gives as examples from the developed world the many Club Mediterrannée developments, as well as Butlins Holiday Camps in the UK. To these might be added the Center Parc type of holiday village found in Northern Europe, as well as certain types of exclusive timeshare development.

SCALE OF TOURISM DEVELOPMENT

The scale of tourism development, in the sense of the ratio of visitor numbers to the local population, is equally important in determining tourism's sociocultural impact. In its simplest expression, the hypothesis is that mass tourism will have a far greater sociocultural impact on a destination than a lower level of visitation, which allows for a more harmonious and equitable exchange between hosts and visitors. The apparently commonsense appeal of this notion must be qualified by taking into account the degree of contact which exists between hosts and visitors. Certain tourists may have an impact which is out of proportion to their numbers. For example, a

few dozen backpackers interacting with local inhabitants, staying as their guests, eating and conversing with them, can have a greater sociocultural impact than many thousands of enclave tourists who rarely leave their compound and the beaches. Similarly, despite its relatively small scale, farmhouse tourism, with the opportunities it provides for interaction between hosts and guests, may impact more, socially and culturally, on a country than city-centre conference tourism, where contact with the local population is minimal.

NATURE OF THE DESTINATION

The nature of the destination itself is equally important in determining tourism's ability to generate sociocultural changes. For example, cities may be more immune to negative impacts of this kind, not only because of their scale, but also due to their sheer cultural complexity. Safier (1994) remarks that: 'Because cities are such powerful and complex constructs, they can accommodate immense shifts in circumstances. And city dwellers are generally a diverse and dynamic lot, able and willing to live with great multitudes of visitors.' Smaller-scale and more culturally homogenous destinations, such as villages, on the other hand, are less able to absorb tourists and are therefore correspondingly more sensitive to their impacts.

SOCIAL CARRYING CAPACITY

A key issue in this respect is the 'social carrying capacity' of destinations. Cooke and d'Amore, as cited by Pearce (1989) define **social carrying capacity** as: 'that point in the growth of tourism where local residents perceive, on balance, an unacceptable level of social disbenefits from tourist development'. As the level of tourism's sociocultural costs is perceived to rise, residents' tolerance of tourism will correspondingly decrease, leading to the general deterioration in their attitude towards tourists, as described by Doxey (see Chapter 3). Planning for tourism must, therefore, include the attempt to determine the social carrying capacity of the destination, although, as many researchers have emphasised, this presents enormous operational difficulties. However, one interesting attempt to incorporate social carrying capacity into a tourism planning and managing tool is made by Saleem (1994), who includes in his model indices such as the visitor/resident ratio of the destination, and sets these against the destination's 'economic carrying capacity'.

Finally, the way in which tourism is perceived at the destination depends on a number of characteristics inherent in the local population itself, as follows.

- **The level of exposure to tourists** – Belisle and Hoy's study quoted by Snaith and Haley (1994) showed that the distance of residence from the central tourist zone was a significant predictor of residents' perceptions of tourism development.
- **Degree of economic dependence on tourism** – Brown and Giles (1994) cite a number of commentators who have segmented the local resident population on this basis and have generally found that the favourable attitudes towards tourism increase with the individual's economic dependence on tourism.
- **Age differences** – this is identified by Dogan (1989) as a factor in determining attitudinal differences towards tourists. He concludes that the curiosity and adventurousness of the young make them more liable to come into contact with tourists and to be open to having their world-view changed.
- **The ability of residents to organise themselves to resist undesirable development** – communities in control of the level of tourism they live with are more likely to feel positive towards those visitors who come within the limits which they (the residents) impose. For example, in Austria, following a period of rapid growth in the buying of second homes in the 1970s, two out of three communes ruled against any more purchases by foreigners; and, several times, residents of certain Swiss towns have voted against competing to be the venue for the Winter Olympics, because of the cost of holding these, the potential damage to the environment, and the possible disruption for the local population (Dewailly and Flament, 1993).

ENVIRONMENTAL COSTS

Tourism, more than any other industry, relies upon the attractiveness and overall image of the place where it is produced. Landscape and natural beauty are key elements, and the protection of these elements is essential for the continuing success of tourism. Gratton and van der Straaten emphasise the role of the environment in economic terms:

> '. . . nature and the environment are used as an input in the production process of the tourism sector. This implies that a good functioning nature and a clean environment are important economic production factors in the tourism sector, as are labour and capital'.
>
> *(Gratton and van der Straaten, 1992)*

But Plog's (1972) observation that tourism has the potential to 'create the seeds of its own destruction' has become a basic axiom of all tourism research, and most relevant studies have focused on the tourism's environmental *costs* for destinations, and its negative impact on the natural and built environment.

TOURISM AS A CONSUMER OF SPACE

The tourism industry's voracious need for land, for the construction of hotels, leisure complexes, golf courses and the development of infrastructure has, in extreme cases, led to the expropriation and expulsion of local communities, and the loss of access to public space for large numbers of residents. The problem of the destruction of habitat and displacement of host communities is most acute in Third World countries, where, according to Keel (1995) hundreds of thousands of people are facing malnutrition and starvation because they have lost access to the land and resources that could sustain them. She cites as examples Kenyan fishermen being dispossessed and losing their livelihood through the creation of national marine parks, and the forced eviction of Ugandan tribes when the valley they inhabited was declared a national park for hunting safaris for European and North American tourists.

Compared to these examples, instances of population displacement through tourism in the developed world may appear mild and trivial. Nevertheless, the principle is the same, whether we are considering residents in rural England, priced out of the local housing market by the buying of second homes by affluent city-dwellers looking for a weekend retreat in the countryside, or Goan farmers evicted from their land to make way for golf course development.

The problem is not confined to the countryside. In Europe, as in other continents, the regeneration and preservation of historic areas of cities has been an important factor in attracting visitors. But once the houses and apartments in these areas have been renovated, the new rents are often no longer affordable by the tenants. Previous working-class neighbourhoods can, as a result, become gentrified into middle class areas and the working classes are pushed to the periphery.

In examining the impact which tourism has on the environment where it takes place, Cazes' (1992) schema is a useful one to follow. He classified tourism's environmental impacts according to the actual *degree* of those impacts, as follows.

- **Pressure** on the destination's physical resources may range from the increased requirements for parking spaces to the added demand for natural resources. Water is a key issue. For example, hotels are major consumers of water:

for guests' showers, swimming pools, frequent washing of bedlinen and cleaning of floors, and constant watering of gardens and golf courses. Cazes (1983) demonstrated that tourists in Tunisia, although representing only 0.5% of the population consumed 7% of the water supply. As many resorts are situated in regions which already suffer from water shortages (sometimes seasonal but, increasingly, chronic), water must often be diverted from other users, often local farmers and inhabitants.

- **Damage**: the OECD's (1980) classification lists tourism's detrimental effects on the physical and built environment:
  - **Pollution**: for example, water, air and noise pollution caused by the various forms of transport which bring tourists to destinations and take them around destinations during their stay, and by the waste they produce there.
  - **Deterioration** in the appearance of the destination through overbuilding of/inappropriate design or scale of facilities (such as hotels, car parks, snackbars). Without rigorously-applied planning controls, the destination's visual aspect can be compromised. For example, the *ad hoc* development of second homes and holiday cottages can lead to the unsightly condition described in French as *mitage*, the nibbling away at the landscape.
  - **Overcrowding and traffic congestion**: many forms of tourism bring substantial numbers of cars and coaches into towns which can barely cope with their residents' own requirements for roads and parking spaces, with well-known results. Individual attractions, too, suffer from the sheer numbers of visitors they receive. For example, Westminster Abbey, a World Heritage Site, perfectly illustrates the problem with three million visitors a year, far outnumbering those who come for the purposes of worship. Wear and tear caused by vast numbers of visitors is also a constant problem for the UK's National Trust, who have a legal obligation to protect the properties under their stewardship from the type of damage

wrought, for example, by the 90,000 people who visit Beatrix Potter's tiny house in the Lake District every year.

- **Destruction**: rapid or badly-conceived tourism development can lead to irreparable destruction of land, particularly in fragile areas such as dunes and wetlands, and the depletion of wildlife, both fauna and flora. Damage to the ecology is often irreversible and a permanent loss to the whole life-supporting natural system and community. Those responsible for this type of destruction are not always the developers. The tourists themselves also bear some of the responsibility, through, for example, thoughtless souvenir hunting leading to the destruction of coral reefs in some areas.

ENVIRONMENTAL BENEFITS

The well-documented catalogue of tourism's detrimental effects on the environment is notoriously long, and western industrialised countries have not been spared. However, there is another aspect to this issue: the environmental *benefits* brought about by tourism.

CONSERVATION

Tourism can also be a positive force in helping to conserve the environment of destination areas. Tourists are attracted to areas of scenic beauty, regions of historical and architectural interest, and places offering abundant and interesting wildlife. Satisfying tourists' desires to visit such areas is one of the motivations behind destinations' moves towards the conservation of their environment. For example, there are the many steps taken in the UK to protect rural areas through designation as Areas of Outstanding Natural Beauty and the moves to conserve certain historic parts of industrial cities. Tourists' spending in such places can provide the necessary means to conserve and improve the natural and built environment.

ENVIRONMENTAL ENHANCEMENT

Any destination wishing to attract visitors, whether for leisure or business-related purposes, must present itself as an attractive place to be, and for this reason, tourism has played a large part in improving the appearance of the environment of many destinations. For example, the resident population as well as visitors benefit from the general landscaping and the cleaning of buildings and rivers, which often follow the decision to turn a city into a venue for visitors.

Perhaps the most striking example of this type of environmental enhancement has been the facelifts given to many of the derelict and redundant 19th century riversides which have been transformed in cities ranging from Sydney, Vancouver and Baltimore, to Bristol, Liverpool and Leeds. Although tourism is only one of the reasons for developing these waterside areas (retail and office development being others), its importance can be seen in the many maritime museums, restaurants and historical trails which have accompanied such renewal schemes.

DETERMINANTS OF ENVIRONMENTAL IMPACT

The extent of the environmental and ecological impact of tourism on any destination is related to some of the same factors already identified in the case of tourism's sociocultural impacts:

- type of tourism
- scale of tourism development
- volume and concentration of visitors
- the concentration in space and time.

The type of environment in which tourism development occurs is also an important consideration. Many tourist regions are located in areas with vulnerable ecosystems (e.g. mountains, natural reserves, islands, coastal areas). As with all resources, there is a finite level of use of such systems, beyond which permanent damage will occur. This once more raises the issue of **carrying capacity**. Cooper *et al.* (1993) provide the following definitions of the carrying capacities relevant here.

- **Physical carrying capacity** relates to the amount of suitable land available for facilities, and also includes the finite capacity of the facilities (such as car parking spaces, covers in restaurants, or bed spaces in accommodation).
- **Biological carrying capacity**: the biological capacity of a site is exceeded when environmental damage or disturbance is unacceptable. This can relate to both flora and fauna, although more work has examined the capacity thresholds of vegetation (e.g. at picnic sites, along paths, or in dune ecosystems) than has looked at the tolerance of animals or birds to tourism in their habitats.

All destination areas must be checked for their capacity to absorb tourist and tourist facilities, and both of these types of carrying capacity are relevant to the kind of environmental analysis of a destination area which provides part of the basis for tourism planning. Physical carrying capacity is perhaps the most straightforward of all capacity measures, and can be used for basic planning and management control, for example, by limiting the number of car parking spaces at sensitive sites or visitor numbers in fragile historic properties. (Nevertheless, when attempts are made to determine, for example, the carrying capacity of an entire destination such as York or Torquay, the process becomes much more complex and open to controversy.)

The assessment of biological carrying capacity is even less simple, due to the composite character of tourism and the complex nature of most ecosystems. Pearce (1989) quotes various attempts to measure the carrying capacities of dune systems, coral reefs and coastal waters, and Inskeep (1987) cites a number of authors who have attempted to determine the carrying capacity standards for various types of tourism development. Naturally, the assessment of carrying capacity is only part of the process. Regulations and controls which prevent these capacities being exceeded are of equal importance if the situation described by Safier (1994) is to be avoided: 'The attempted exploitation of market opportunities has thus a tendency to extend beyond the overall carrying capacity of the local area and its attractions, to the point where overcrowding and decline in atmosphere become all too familiar.'

The importance of the role of planning in protecting destinations from environmental damage is generally acknowledged by all authors examining this subject, and their conclusions may best be summed up by Inskeep:

'Many governments realise that tourism and the environment are inseparably related and that tourism must be carefully planned to avoid problems of air, water, noise and visual pollution, congestion and ecological damage, and disruption which have been experienced by certain tourism areas. It is also recognised that planning of tourism is necessary not only for scientific purposes and to conserve the environment for the benefit of residents, but also for the protection of long-term investments in tourism infrastructure, attractions, facilities, services and marketing programmes. Increasingly, tourists are demanding that their environment be high quality and pollution-free as well as inherently interesting, and some tourists will change travel patterns if environmental quality expectations are not met. Therefore, it is in both the developer's and governments' long-term financial interest to plan projects]...'

(Inskeep, 1987)

TOURISM'S IMPACT ON OTHER SECTORS

In comparison with the very extensive literature which exists on tourism's economic, sociocultural and environmental impacts, very little has been written on the relationship between tourism and other forms of economic activity. Two main themes may, however, be identified:

1 The links between tourism and agriculture, usually in the context of tourism providing access to new markets for local agricultural products
2 Tourism's ability to attract labour and other resources away from other forms of economic activity.

CONFLICT

The 'opportunity costs' of tourism may be considered as the value of the output which could have been obtained from the use in other sectors of the resources and factors of production employed in establishing and operating the tourism sector: including capital, grants, skilled labour and land.

Where these resources are scarce, it is claimed that the sudden advent of tourism at a destination can create problems for other more evolutionary industries, by the competition it creates for manpower or investment capital. This 'cuckoo-in-the-nest' image of tourism has been created by several authors, cited in Pearce (1989) in connection with tourism's arrival in Spain in the 1970s, when agricultural labour shortages and enormous rises in farmland prices were said to be the result of tourist development. But Pearce *(ibid)* also quotes Hermans who suggests that such judgements were based on very little evidence, and (in a well-documented case study of Cambrils on the Spanish Costa Dorada) shows that tourism actually promoted agriculture directly and indirectly (for example by allowing diversification of markets through improved access).

Evidence of tourism's ability to damage other industries' prospects is, therefore, inconclusive, although the general view is that it is seductive, perhaps too seductive, as a development option:

'In those situations in which tourism is seen to be in competition for resources with other activities, it is often tourism which emerges as the victor, in part because, as a new activity, it has momentum and change on its side, and partly because by the time its demands may be appreciated, it may have preempted the resources beyond the possibility of a return to the status quo.'

(Butler and Fennel, 1992)

SYNERGY

More frequently, tourism's synergetic qualities with other industries are lauded. On a simple level, tourism, by helping justify and pay for transportation facilities and other services, can serve as a catalyst for expansion of other economic sectors. Archer and Cooper sum up this point thus:

'... these utilities are economically indivisible in the sense that, in providing them for the local tourism industry, they at the same time become available for the use of local people. Thus ... highways and airfields, constructed primarily to cater for tourism, ... provide an access to wider markets for locally-produced goods.'

(Archer and Cooper, 1994)

Clearly, the factor which most determines the level of synergy between tourism and other industries is the strength of the linkages which exist between these. Strong linkages between tourism and other sectors operating in the area (such as agriculture and handicrafts) can provide new markets for local products. One example of what may be achieved is France's hi-tech theme park, the Futuroscope; a range of locally-produced farm produce is for sale in its souvenir shops, and local farmers do a thriving business in bed and breakfast accommodation for visitors to the park – despite being originally opposed to the theme park's development. More generally, tourism and the retail sector co-exist, in many destinations, in a clearly synergetic relationship – the distinction between the two becoming blurred in the modern concept of 'leisure shopping'. The Dover case study demonstrates the importance of shopping as an attraction for visitors.

However, the most vivid example of synergy between tourism and other sectors may be the countless examples of industrial or workplace tourism, which involve companies (mainly, but not exclusively, in the manufacturing sector) attracting visitors to the contemporary workplace to see products being made. These range from Stoke's ceramics factories, to the vineyards of Champagne and Scotland's distilleries. Not only does industrial tourism provide destinations with new and diverse visitor attractions, but it also provides the participating industries with a range of tangible and intangible benefits, including increased sales of their products, increased customer loyalty, improved public relations and better staff morale.

Finally, tourism can have an impact on other sectors by creating a positive image for the destination, thus serving as a magnet for other economic activities. For example, there is no doubt that the concentration of hi-tech industries in Sophia Antipolis, near Nice, is in no small part due to the image of that area, as transmitted by tourism, just as in the case of Florida and California. In the UK, the trend towards corporate city marketing, as identified by Bramwell and Rawding (1994) shows that cities such as Bradford (see case study) and Sheffield are increasingly using tourism marketing as a means of attracting new economic investment.

It is worthy of note here that the impact between tourism and other sectors is not all one-way: other economic activities can have an impact on tourism. Very little has been written on this aspect, but one shining example is Butler and Fennel's (1992) study of the effects of North Sea oil development on tourism in the Shetland Isles. The oil industry all but obliterated the entire holiday market during the 1970s, as accommodation, transport and ancillary services overwhelmingly geared their efforts towards the lucrative and burgeoning business travel market created by the oil boom in Shetland. But the authors conclude that:

'In many respects, (tourism) is in a much stronger position than it would have been without the intervention of oil. In the first case, the pressure (to provide accommodation and transport facilities) and subsequent financial rewards both forced and allowed the operators to improve and expand their facilities ... Some of the self-catering establishments which were established initially for the oil-related workers have since been given over to tourist accommodation.'

(Butler and Fennel, 1992)

CONCLUSION

Tourism, in common with other economic activities, has the potential to impact both positively and negatively on the place where it is carried out, on the people who live there, and on other economic activities at the destination.

In general, the tourism industry has been successful at attracting visitors to destinations, but has been less successful at protecting those destinations from the negative impacts of tourism. Examples abound of tourism's harmful effects on the environment and the quality of life of those living in places which have become tourist destinations.

Chapter 5 describes how the planning and management of tourism has a role to play in intervening to limit these negative impacts of tourism and help the destination reap as many benefits as possible from this activity. In this way, it will be argued, tourism can be successfully developed in a carefully planned and controlled manner.

REFERENCES

Archer, B.H. and Fletcher, J.E. (1991) *Multiplier Analysis in Tourism*, Cahiers du Tourisme, Centre des Hautes Etudes Touristiques, Université de Droit, d'Economie et des Sciences, Aix-en-Provence.

Archer, B.H. and Cooper, C. (1994) 'The positive and negative impacts of tourism' in *Global Tourism: The Next Decade*, William Theobold (ed), Butterworth-Heinemann Ltd, Oxford.

Baretje, R. (1982) 'Tourism's external account and the balance of payments', in *Annals of Tourism Research*, 9(1), pp. 57–67.

Bramwell, B. and Rawding, L. (1994) 'Tourism marketing organisations in industrial cities' in *Tourism Management*, 15(6), pp. 425–434.

Brown, G. and Giles, R. (1994) 'Resident responses to the social impact of tourism' in *Tourism: The State of the Art*, John Wiley & Sons, Chichester.

BTA (1993) *Promoting your business travel facilities in overseas markets*, British Tourist Authority, London.

Butler, R.W. and Fennel, D.A. (1992) 'The Effects of North Sea Oil Development on the Development of Tourism – The Case of the Shetland Isles', in *Proceedings of the 1992 Tourism in Europe Conference*, Centre for Travel and Tourism, Tyne and Wear.

Cazes, G. (1992) *Fondements pour une géographie du tourisme et des loisirs*, Bréal, Paris.

Cazes, G. (1983) 'Le tourisme international en Thaïland et en Tunisie. Les impacts et les risques d'un développement mal maîtrisé' in *Travaux de l'Institut de Géographie de Reims* (pp. 53–54).

Craig-Smith, S. and French, C. (1994) *Learning to live with tourism*, Pitman, Melbourne.

Dewailly, J-M. and Flament, E. (1993) *Géographie du Tourisme et des Loisirs*, Sedes, Paris.

Dogan, H.Z. (1989) 'Forms of adjustment: Sociocultural impacts of tourism', in *Annals of Tourism Research*, 16(2).

EIESP (1991) *Education for careers in European travel and tourism*, European Institute of Education and Social Policy and American Express Foundation, London.

Goldring, M. (1995) *The Goldring Audit: Tourism*, BBC Television, London.

Goodall, B. and Stabler, M. (1992) 'Environmental auditing in the quest for sustainable tourism: the destination perspective', in *Proceedings of the 1992 Tourism in Europe Conference*, Centre for travel and Tourism, Tyne and Wear.

Gratton, C. and van der Straaten, J. (1992) 'Changing tourist patterns in Europe and environmental impact' in *Proceedings of the 1992 Tourism in Europe Conference*, Centre for travel and Tourism, Tyne and Wear.

Inskeep, E. (1987) 'Environmental planning for tourism' in *Annals of Tourism Research* (14).

Komilis, P. (1994) 'Tourism and sustainable regional development' in *Tourism: The State of the Art*, John Wiley & Sons, Chichester.

Lane, P. (1992) 'The regeneration of small to

medium sized seaside resorts' in *Proceedings of the 1992 Tourism in Europe Conference*. Centre for Travel and Tourism, Tyne and Wear.

MacCannell, D. (1976) *The Tourist: A new theory of the leisure class*, Schoken, New York.

Mathieson, A. and Wall, G. (1982) *Tourism: Economic, Physical and Social Impacts*, Longman, New York.

OECD (1980) *The impact of tourism on the environment*, Organisation for Economic Co-operation and Development, Paris.

Parlett, G, Fletcher, J. and Cooper, C. (1995) 'The impact of tourism on the Old Town of Edinburgh' in *Tourism Management*, vol 16, no. 5, pp. 355–360.

Plog, S.C. (1972) *Why destination areas rise and fall in popularity*, presented before the Travel Research Association, Southern California Chapter.

Prentice, R. (1992) 'Tourism and counter-urbanisation: the case of the North Pennines and Cheviots' in *Proceedings of the 1992 Tourism in Europe Conference*, Centre for Travel and Tourism, Tyne and Wear.

Sadler, P.G, Archer, B.H. and Owen, C.B. (1973) *Regional Income Multipliers: The Anglesey Study*, Bangor Occasional Papers No 1, University of Wales Press, Cardiff.

Safier, M. (1994) 'Tourism in cities: an unequal exchange' in *Tourism in Focus* (12), Tourism Concern, London.

Saleem, N. (1994) 'The destination capacity index' in *Tourism: The State of the Art*, John Wiley & Sons, Chichester.

Snaith, T. and Haley, A.J. (1994) 'Tourism's impact on host lifestyle realities' in *Tourism: The State of the Art*, John Wiley & Sons, Chichester.

Swarbrooke, J. (1992) 'The impact of British visitors on rural France' in *Proceedings of the 1992 Tourism in Europe Conference*, Centre for Travel and Tourism, Tyne and Wear.

Thomas, J. (1992) 'Tourism and the environment: an exploration of the willingness to pay of the average visitor' in *Proceedings of the 1992 Tourism in Europe Conference*, Centre for Travel and Tourism, Tyne and Wear.

Turner, L. and Ash, J. (1975) *The golden hordes: international tourism and the pleasure periphery*, Constable, London.

WTO (1980) *Manila Declarations on World Tourism*, World Tourism Organisation, Madrid.

WTO (1994) *National and Regional Tourism Planning, Methodologies and Case Studies*, Routledge, London.

5 The need for destination management

INTRODUCTION

We argued in Chapter 3 that successful destination development depended on a portfolio of tourism products that had to be constantly modified and updated. Tourism products rely heavily on the destination's resources, but the tourism industry frequently does not own or control them, and it alone cannot ensure that the best use is made of them. In Chapter 4, we discussed the impacts that tourism can have on destinations and showed that, compared to many other industries, tourism impacts can be especially intense and visible. We also pointed out that they are becoming more significant and pervasive with the growth of tourism and leisure and as more and more places take on a role as tourist destinations. In this chapter we argue that making the best use of destination resources and dealing with the impacts that visitors create cannot simply be left to the market: destination management and planning are required.

What do we mean by management and planning? In the most general sense, we mean some form of intervention in the market by public agencies (like a local authority) to bring about outcomes different from those which would occur in an unregulated market. The need for planning and management in capitalist economies is widely acknowledged, although the extent and form of intervention varies considerably from country to country (Keegan, 1992; Hutton, 1995). An obvious example of the effect of management and planning on tourism in the UK can be seen in National Parks and designated Areas of Outstanding Natural Beauty (AONBs). These areas are popular with visitors, but there is the danger that catering for visitors' demands will create developments damaging the very attractiveness of the areas – their landscapes and the peace and quiet they offer. Town planning legislation has been used over the last 50 years to restrict development in National Parks (and elsewhere) and to balance the broader public interest (in maintaining peaceful and attractive areas) with the demands of the market (to create profitable developments). The Peak District, the Lake District, the North Pennines and other beautiful rural areas would look very different today if there had been no regulation of their development.

One reason tourism needs to be managed then, is that the market response to increasing demands for tourism activities often leads to unacceptable adverse impacts: to the environment, to the local economy or to the host population. This can occur in urban as well as rural areas. Increasing visitor numbers to historic cities like Bath, Cambridge or York (or Venice or Florence) can cause physical damage, a series of problems for the host population, and create a visitor experience that is tawdry and inauthentic.

Similar problems can arise in and around popular attractions in large cities like London or Paris; the chaos of crowds of visitors, coaches and local traffic that for so long surrounded the Changing of the Guard at Buckingham Palace is one example. In all these cases, problems arise from continuing and rapid growth in visitor numbers putting greater pressures on finite tourism resources. The management problem is concerned with how to accommodate visitors whilst minimising the adverse impacts they cause. Attempts may be made: to reduce or at least stem the growth in visitation, to influence the type of visitor attracted, to change visitor behaviour at the destination, to restrict development of new attractions or facilities for tourists, or to divert visitors to areas which have spare capacity. We will examine in detail how this can be achieved when we look at destination management in Chapter 7 and we will provide practical illustrations in the case studies of Cambridge, Winchester and the North Pennines.

But dealing with visitor pressures is not the only reason that tourism management is important – at the other end of the scale, management can be used to create tourism demand and establish a new destination. Over the last 20 years, more and more non-traditional destinations (such as industrial cities) have sought to build up their attraction for visitors and to establish themselves as destinations. The American cities of Baltimore and Lowell are often seen as the pioneers, but they were quickly followed by British cities. They sought tourism because of the positive impacts it can have, especially on local economies; as a growth industry, tourism offers a potential source of new economic activity and can be a direct source of new jobs. However, it can also play a broader role – by helping to change a place's image, and because of the complementarity it can have with other growing economic activities, tourism can play a key part in the process of regenerating the economies of towns and cities, or of rundown

areas within them. As the pace of global economic change continues to quicken, and as traditional manufacturing industries move, down-size or disappear, this is an increasingly important role – during the late 1970s and the 1980s industrial cities like Wigan, Bradford and Sheffield turned to tourism and leisure as part of broad regeneration strategies, whilst in Bristol Docks and London's Covent Garden, for example, tourism was at the centre of projects to create new uses in former industrial or commercial areas.

In these cases too, management is required – but its role is to create demand rather than to regulate it. Tourism management in these cases is about identifying the resources a place has that could be attractive to tourists, and finding ways to make use of them so that the place can become (or develop as) a destination. Whilst the involvement of the tourism industry and other private sector players is essential, the market alone will not create demand in non-traditional destinations. Management and intervention is needed to create a vision of what might be, to identify how it could be achieved through specific projects and developments and to create the means to bring it about – by building partnerships, securing grants and gaining investment. This is a role for a local authority or other public sector agency. We will examine this approach (sometimes known as entrepreneurial planning) in Chapter 7, and will illustrate it in the case studies of Bradford and Dover.

Destination management, then, takes a variety of forms: it may involve regulating and channelling heavy tourism pressure, or it may involve creating tourism demand where none currently exists. The common factor is that there are problems and challenges which the market alone cannot meet. In the rest of this chapter we will explain why this is so, and why destinations must be deliberately managed: to make the most of their resources, minimise the adverse impacts and maximise the favourable impacts of tourism.

TOURISM AND MARKET FAILURE

Markets provide a means of dealing with the problem of scarcity: scarcity exists because (in materialist societies) wants are infinite whereas the resources that can supply those wants are finite. The goods and services which people want are produced using a combination of the economic resources of land, labour and capital. Since the combination of unlimited wants with limited resources means that, even for the well-off in rich societies, not all wants can be met, economists refer to resources as 'scarce'. Since resources are scarce, decisions need to be taken about how they should be used, and it makes sense to use them in a way which satisfies the most wants. A perfectly functioning market provides a means to do this.

In a perfectly functioning competitive market the goods and services produced are determined by the individual preferences of consumers. Markets allow consumers to express their preferences through the price mechanism, which acts as a signal between consumers and firms (the organisations which use resources to produce goods and services). Consumer preferences are signalled to firms through price, and firms adjust their production (and thus their use of resources) accordingly. This ensures that in individual markets, and across the whole economy, the demand for, and supply of, goods and services is in balance i.e. there are neither surpluses nor shortages. Changes in consumer preferences resulting, for example, from changes in taste, are also met through the price mechanism. An increase in demand for a particular good means that it will initially be in short supply, so that prices are bid up and firms can make greater profits. This attracts more firms to producing the particular good, supply is increased and prices begin to fall. Competition between profit-maximising firms will ensure that goods and services are produced at the lowest possible cost. The change in consumer taste thus brings about a change in resource use by firms so that they meet consumer demand more effectively (see Le Grand, Propper and Robinson (1992) for a more detailed but non-technical discussion of the market model).

The **market model** provides an elegant solution to the complex problem of the allocation of scarce resources, since it achieves maximum efficiency through a mechanism which is decentralised, largely automatic, and based on the interaction of buyers and sellers acting in their own self-interest. It is intuitively convincing as an explanation of changes in the real world. For example, over the last 30 years or so, consumer preferences for family holidays have changed, with package holidays to warm destinations replacing holidays at UK resorts. For many resorts, like Morecombe, this is reflected in disinvestment as resources are withdrawn (firms investing elsewhere) or are unused (unemployment and derelict sites). Meanwhile, investment in warm water resorts has increased.

However, in reality, the market model does not always mirror reality accurately. The model is based on a series of assumptions and its accuracy depends upon the realism of those assumptions. If the real world is broadly similar to the model's specifications, then the market will be the most effective way of solving real world problems. However, if reality and the model diverge significantly, then there is no reason to suppose that the market, left to itself, will necessarily bring about the most efficient use of resources or will be the best way of reflecting consumer preferences. These circumstances are known to economists as **market failures**, and where they exist, there is a case for introducing intervention into the market – through planning and management – to achieve a better use of resources. There are a number of types of market failure which apply to tourism and these are discussed below:

- externalities
- sustainability
- public goods and free resources
- nature of demand for tourism resources.

EXTERNALITIES

Externalities exist when the production or consumption of a good or service gives rise to costs or benefits which are not reflected in the market price, and which impinge on those not involved in its production or consumption. Externality effects are common in tourism, and can be beneficial or adverse. For example, a market transaction between visitors and a local hotelier may give rise to externalities which affect third parties, e.g. local residents. **Negative externalities** caused by tourism typically include noise, overcrowding, litter and congestion, while **positive externalities** may be such aspects as a lively and cosmopolitan atmosphere. In both cases, the third party has no control over the externalities.

Externalities can be created by producers (firms in the tourist industry) and by consumers (the tourists themselves). The externalities can affect either producers or consumers or both. Figure 5.1 shows these interactions, with examples of the external costs and benefits which producers and consumers can impose upon one another.

The key to the externality problem is that external costs or benefits are not reflected in market prices. This means that the private cost of production or consumption (to the firm or individual) differs from the social cost of production to society as a whole. If hotels can discharge raw sewage into a lake or the sea, the cost to them of sewage disposal is low, and this can be reflected in lower prices for accommodation. However, costs are imposed on visitors using the sea, who will find bathing unpleasant or may even be made ill. Other firms in the tourism industry may also be affected, for example if visitors are deterred from taking part in water sports. Externalities mean that production is set at an inefficient level. Firms will over-produce goods or service with external costs (because they do not have to pay for the externality) and under-produce those with external benefits (because they receive no share of the external benefit). There is too little incentive to remedy pollution and too little to carry out environmental upgrading.

Excessive negative externalities can lead to the destruction of the resources which formed the basis of the destination's original attractiveness. We take up the point in our discussion of public goods which follows. The market mechanism must be adjusted or regulated if negative externalities are to be avoided and positive externalities encouraged.

PUBLIC GOODS AND FREE RESOURCES

The term **public goods** refers to goods or services with particular characteristics which mean

	Producers	Consumers
Producers	Positive: Development in new resort or rundown area increases confidence of other developers	Positive: Restoration of historic buildings improves environment for all visitors to the area
	Negative: Water skiing on a lake reduces visitation to anglers' hotels	Negative: Caravan parks in prominent locations spoil views; pollution from sewage discharge
Consumers	Positive: Tourism increases the number of potential customers to all retailers in an area	Positive: Crowds are part of the excitement in carnivals, festivals and city centres
	Negative: Congestion from tourist traffic causes delays to all firms in other industries	Negative: 4 × 4 vehicles and motor bikes on country trails cause nuisance to walkers and horse riders

FIGURE 5.1 *Examples of positive and negative externalities*

that they cannot be charged for through the market. A public good has two main aspects:

- consumption is normally non-rival – that is use by one person does not prevent use by another (the opposite of positional goods, below)
- the goods are non-excludable – their benefits cannot be confined only to those who pay.

As Goodall and Stabler (1992) put it: 'access cannot be excluded and ... in abundant supply, users can normally consume without reducing the amount available to other users'. Street lighting is a classic example. If lighting is provided, the streets are necessarily lit for everyone (non-excludable) and 'consumption' of the light by one person does not reduce the light available for others (non-rival). These qualities mean that public goods are free to all who want to use them – and since firms cannot charge individual users, they will not be provided through the market.

We noted the importance of free resources in Chapter 2, and Bull (1991) is among the many commentators who point out that 'tourism is notable, compared with many other sectors of the economy, in that it calls upon many free resources or public goods in order to satisfy the wants and requirements of tourists'. For the tourism industry, much of the physical, built and 'cultural' environment used to promote destinations are examples of public goods: beautiful scenery, quaint village streets, the ambience of an attractive city like Cambridge or Montpellier, the sight of an historic building like the Observatory at Greenwich or the sound of the one o'clock cannon nearby. Some of the services used by tourists, such as signposting, are also public goods. Many of these resources have no individual owners (e.g. peace and quiet, ambience, history) whilst others are 'free' to the commercial tourist industry only in the sense that they are owned and maintained by others. For example, in historic towns, the architecture and history of the destination are important free resources.

Such 'attractions' are often vital components of the tourism product and the main reason for the tourist trip being made, but they give rise to two sets of problems.

- Since they are 'free' resources they may be over-used and exploited. At a price of zero, users have no incentive to economise on their consumption of the resource, and will keep on using it even if they derive little benefit from doing so. If public goods are in truly abundant supply, like light from street lamps, this does not matter. No matter how many people 'use' the light, it will not run out. However, many public goods are in fact in limited supply, since they have a finite carrying capacity, and use beyond a certain point will deplete the resource, e.g. views are spoilt, picturesque village streets become crowded with people and tour buses, peace and quiet becomes noise and bustle. There is, in other words, the familiar problem of tourists destroying what they have come to visit, and at root this is a problem of free resources and the overlapping question of externalities.
- Since public goods are 'free', there is what economists call the 'free rider' problem. If there is no means of preventing people from using the resources, no charge can be made and thus there is no means of recovering the cost of maintenance, new investment, or indeed, providing the resource in the first place. This is true even of public goods in abundant supply (e.g. street lights have to be provided and maintained) but is a particular problem for resources which require renewal and maintenance to protect or enhance their carrying capacity.

There are, in principle, two ways of dealing with the problem of public goods.

- Privatise public goods and confer rights of ownership and thus establish a more effective market. This is most commonly seen in private resorts or purpose-built destinations. For example in Centre Parcs entry is confined to paying visitors, unlike public parks, and their payment allows the company to recover the cost of providing a pleasant ambience and attractive views (as well as other services). Ski-resorts are frequently able to limit the numbers of people using the slopes through lift capacity and pricing policy. However, in most cases such an approach is impractical or unacceptable. Whole cities and villages cannot be privatised with entry charges and access restrictions, and the same applies to much of the countryside and the coast.

■ In most cases, public goods are provided and managed by government and public bodies. They seek to use regulation and management to prevent over-use of 'free' resources, and they can fund provision and maintenance of public goods through various forms of taxation which everyone has to pay (thus eliminating the free rider problem).

It should be clear from this discussion that not all the tourism resources and facilities provided by public bodies are 'public goods'. Signposting provided by a local authority on footpaths in the countryside is a public good, because consumption is non-rival and non-excludable. However a book of countryside walks published by a local authority is not — like most goods, use by one person precludes its use by others, and it is available only to those who pay; non-payers are excluded.

SUSTAINABILITY

The problem of sustainability arises from related weaknesses of the market mechanism. Not only does it fail to take account of externalities and 'free' resources, it also tends to undervalue the future in favour of the present — this can lead to the over-use or destruction of resources. The problem of potential resource depletion has been debated for at least 30 years. Mishan (1969) drew attention to the problem in his influential discussion of the limits to economic growth, and the Meadows' (1974) prediction that world population would reach the limits of the Earth's resources in less than a century promoted widespread debate and research. More recently, concern about potential damage to key elements of the biosphere (issues such as global warming and ozone depletion) led to the publication of the Brundtland Report (WCED 1987) which stressed the need for development to be sustainable. The report defined **sustainable development** as 'development which meets the needs of the present without compromising the ability of future generations to meet their own needs'.

This idea of sustainable development stresses both the importance of valuing the future so as to take account of the needs of future generations ('inter-generational equity') and the importance of conserving resources. This is of particular relevance for tourism, since it is often characterised as an extractive industry like mining or quarrying — using up scarce resources in particular places and moving on when they are exhausted. Sustainability means moving towards an agricultural model of 'good husbandry' — using the resources of a destination to produce an annual crop of tourism benefits whilst ensuring that the resources are replenished and undiminished when handed on to future generations. This is most obvious in terms of natural resources — maintaining the quality of seas and rivers, and protecting wildlife and the countryside. However, it can apply equally to built and cultural resources. Historic cities can be physically damaged by visitors and their vehicles, and the insensitive introduction of tourism may change a place's culture and way of life forever.

Sustainable development cannot be achieved through the market alone, because prices fail to reflect accurately the value society places on resources continuing to be available in the future. If current prices do not reflect the future value of resources, there will be a tendency for them to be over-used or depleted altogether. There are two elements to the problem: in the first place, the value ascribed to a resource in the future may simply be too low; second, in order to compare future and present values, a discount rate must be used, and this may be too high. The present valuation of future costs or benefits depends upon how far in the future they occur and the discount rate used. This is intuitively obvious. If we are to be paid a fee for a task we have performed, we would prefer to be paid now rather than in 10 years time. If we are to be paid in 10 years time, we would expect the fee to be increased by the prevailing annual rate of interest (the discount rate) to reflect the time we have had to wait for payment and the increased uncertainty involved. The same argument applies to costs: a cost which arises 10 years in the future is of less importance than one that arises immediately.

This is a rational approach to dealing with investment decisions and assessing competing calls for scarce investment funds. The difficulty is that, even at comparatively low discount rates, little value is placed on the future. For example, at a discount rate of only 5%, a cost or benefit of £100,000,000 that occurs in 100 years' time will have a current value of just £3,802. On this basis, there is little reason to be concerned about resource depletion towards the end of the next century (e.g. the destruction of a habitat which would cost £100 million to put right). Equally, there is little incentive to invest in improvements which will not bring benefits for many years (e.g. planting a new forest). Such outcomes are not an accurate reflection of society's demands (see the discussion in the next section) and this has led to calls for low or zero discount rates when environmental and other scarce resources are being considered. How far the market can be adapted to reflect sustainability concerns is a complex debate, involving consideration of how future values are estimated, discount rates set and whether a 'sustainability constraint' should be introduced in appraising investment projects (see Pearce *et al.* 1989 for a discussion).

In thinking about sustainability, it is helpful to distinguish between renewable and non-renewable resources. **Renewable resources** are those which can be used and replenished, whilst **non-renewable resources** are those which, once used, can never be replaced. The distinction between renewable and non-renewable resources is not clear cut, and the rate at which a resource is used can be crucial. For example, a path through a meadow can take a number of walkers each year and still recover from the damage they cause. Beyond that point (the 'physical carrying capacity'), more walkers will cause damage that is not made good until the path becomes a quagmire and is effectively destroyed. Similarly, if the number of boats using the Norfolk Broads becomes excessive, wildlife habitats are destroyed. The key issue is matching the use of the resource to its regenerative capacity. Some resources are non-renewable – obvious examples are wilderness areas, plant and

animal species, and historic buildings. Once lost, they cannot be replaced in the same form – although similar substitutes may be provided. Some resources can be seen as both non-renewable and inherently scarce. According to Hirsch (1978), some goods are **positional**, in that their supply cannot be increased and their use by one person diminishes their availability to others. Remoteness and exoticism are obvious examples: places are only remote if few people visit them; it is not very exotic to do what most other people do. When places become easily accessible, the resource of remoteness is lost forever. Hirsch argued that the market was ineffective in limiting the use of such resources.

Moving towards sustainability therefore requires policies that limit the use of non-renewable resources, and encourage activities that depend on renewable resources (which can absorb more visitors). After all, as Urry (1990a) points out, many tourist and leisure activities do not have positional goods aspects, and indeed are enjoyable partly because large numbers of people are involved, e.g. carnivals, funfairs or the excitement of a big city. At the same time, renewable resources must be protected so that use does not exceed their regenerative capacity. Whilst in some cases market mechanisms can be used to promote sustainability, regulation and management are essential. We discuss the range of policies that can be used in Chapter 6.

NATURE OF DEMAND FOR TOURISM RESOURCES

The demand for some tourism resources is more complex than for many other goods and services, and this gives rise to conflicts which are difficult to resolve through the market. Consumers generally want a good because they want to use it (although speculative motives can complicate the issue in some cases). People buy hamburgers because they want to use them to satisfy their hunger; they rent cars because they want to use them to get around. However, there are some tourism resources which face a more complex set of demands. They are generally resources which are seen as particularly important, or of symbolic value, and may often be resources which are non-renewable, for example historic buildings and monuments, familiar landmarks, famous views, or areas of coast and countryside. In these cases, four types of demand exist.

1 **Use demand** – people want to be able to take a walk along their favourite stretch of coastline or visit an historic building. In this case, visitors may pay for the use they make of the place or site (within the limits we discuss above).

2 **Option demand** – people who do not visit the place and who have no definite plans for doing so nonetheless value having the option to do so; that option confers a real benefit on them. (I have never been to the Taj Mahal, and have no plans to go, but knowing that I can is of some importance).

3 **Existence demand** – people can gain benefits from knowing that a particular building, or species, or place continues to exist and is in good condition, even though they do not visit it themselves. (I come from Yorkshire and York Minster has important symbolic significance for me even though I have not visited it for years and have no plans to do so.) Few people have ever seen a whale (as opposed to images of whales), yet hundreds of millions are concerned for their existence.

4 **Bequest demand** – if the existence of something is valued, there is a desire that it should be maintained and passed on to future generations (existence and bequest demands are clearly closely related to sustainability).

There can be conflicts between these different types of demand. 'Use demands' can conflict with 'option demands' and 'bequest demands' if the resource is fragile or in limited supply. If too many people use an attractive area of countryside or an historic building now, it will be damaged, and not be able to satisfy the other forms of demand (see case study C, Cambridge and case study E, North Pennines). These conflicts cannot be mediated through the market, since option, existence and bequest demands cannot be priced and thus in market terms cannot be articulated. Some form of planning and management is needed to resolve the conflicts.

The normal role of governments, therefore, is that of *regulator* of the market mechanism, in other words, to intervene in the market to correct for market failure when this is thought necessary and to minimise the effects of the negative externalities of tourism. This intervention is the basic principle of all tourism planning and management described in this book.

It is clear from this discussion that the market, left to itself, will not manage resources efficiently, so there is strong justification for intervention to manage market processes. In general, the tourism industry has been successful at attracting visitors to destinations, but it has been less successful at protecting those destinations from the negative impacts of tourism. One of the reasons for this is that tourism operates within a market which suffers from the severe failures we discussed above, and that means that unregulated tourism development is often seen as a threat – either through tawdry development or simply the impact of very large numbers of people on fragile environments. The transformation of Spanish Costas from rural areas interspersed with fishing villages to continuous strips of intense and poorly-designed urban development provides a vivid image of the dangers of uncontrolled market-led development.

Governments (national, regional or local) must intervene to modify market processes, and to plan and manage the resources on which tourism depends. If this is done successfully, it is likely that the local population will be more positive in their attitude to tourism. Local inhabitants' reactions to tourism's impacts on their lives are vitally important, not least because the inhabitants themselves are part of the tourism 'product'. It is they who, consciously or not, weigh up the benefits and costs of tourism development in their home areas, before concluding whether or not it is desirable. All this adds to the case for destination management we set out in Chapter 3. However, we must remember that effective management is easier to call for than to achieve, and intervention can itself give rise to problems. As Hartley and Hooper remind us:

'Inevitably, tourism creates debates and controversy about 'rights', particularly the rights of locals or nationals versus 'outsiders', and such controversies are often resolved through the political process ... In this context, there are dangers that market failure will be used to justify and rationalise any form of state intervention at the national and local levels and that tourism policy will reflect the lobbying and influence of vested interests.'

Hartley and Hooper, 1993)

We will examine approaches to destination management in detail in Chapters 6 and 7. In the remainder of this chapter, we will look at a further reason for its increasing importance – the growing role of tourism and leisure in regeneration and economic development.

TOURISM AND REGENERATION

For many places the problem is not excessive development and over-used resources, but little or no development and idle resources. Rapid changes in the world economy, accompanied by the continued poor performance of the UK has 'raised the importance of the promotion of development in contrast to its control' (Cullingworth and Nadin, 1994). Economic change has affected cities, towns and rural areas alike, encompassing traditional tourist destinations and places with which tourism would once never have been associated. A consistent element in the change has been the growing importance of tourism and leisure industries, which have come to play an increasingly significant role in the economies of a wider range of destinations. As a consequence, tourism and leisure have played an important part in strategies for economic development and regeneration. We will now look at the economic changes that have taken place and how and why tourism has become more important. There is a particular stress on the importance of tourism in cities and non-traditional destinations, since it is here that the main effects of change have been focused.

CHANGING ECONOMIES

The effects of restructuring have been especially noticeable in cities in Britain and other industrialised countries. Whilst cities have seen the rise of new industries and occupations, they have also

been the focus of decline, as previously dominant economic activities (especially manufacturing and dock industries) shrank in importance or shifted from urban areas to more rural locations or to other parts of the world. The rapidity and severity of this economic restructuring has caused strains for the populations and workforces of cities, and required major adaptations of their physical fabric. For example, in Britain, government policies for cities from the late 1970s onwards sought to deal with these problems through policies for urban regeneration which tackled social, physical and economic decline. The need for economic regeneration was, however, consistently seen as the key to a more general regeneration, and was the main focus of policy.

The economic changes experienced in cities and other urban areas form part of a global economic restructuring sometimes described as a shift from Fordist to post-Fordist patterns of production and consumption. The changes are poorly understood, but the main features are relatively easily summarised as follows:

- Changing industrial and employment structures, with continuing decline in manufacturing employment, and increases in service sector employment (Marshall and Wood, 1995). However, service job replacement has been insufficient to compensate for jobs lost, and new service jobs have often required new skills. The result has been persistent and high levels of unemployment, especially amongst male and unskilled workers.

- Counter-urbanisation – the shift of economic activities away from cities to small towns and semi-rural locations. Whilst the trend began with manufacturing industry (Fothergill and Gudgin, 1982, Fothergill, Kitson and Monk, 1985), subsequently some service industries followed, including office-based services and retailing.

- The demise of the classical specialised local economy – certain industries heavily concentrated in particular cities or sub-regions (for example cotton textiles in Lancashire in Britain, or in Lowell, Mass. in the USA) were replaced with a 'geography of corporate function'. **A geography of corporate function** means that large corporations distribute their different functions spatially on a global basis, with, for example, routine manufacturing activities in a low labour cost location, headquarters in a world city (such as London or Paris), and research and development in an area with a concentration of highly qualified labour and close links to leading academic research (such as the Cambridge sub-region in the UK) (Allen and Massey, 1988).

- Significant restructuring of public and private sector organisations, emphasising the externalisation of activities which used to be carried out in-house, and continuing labour force reductions ('downsizing' or 're-engineering'); and a trend toward a workforce employed on short term contracts ('flexibility'). The effect has been to reduce the proportion of the UK workforce in full-time and secure employment, and increase the proportion in contract, casual or self-employment (Hutton, 1995). One consequence has been that traditional distinctions between industrial sectors associated with secure and well-paid jobs (e.g. much of the manufacturing industry and public services) and those associated with insecure and poorly paid jobs (e.g. the tourism and leisure industries) has started to break down.

These trends have resulted in fundamental changes to the character of urban areas. The ex-

tensive literature on economic restructuring in the UK has emphasised that a great variety of restructuring strategies can be adopted within these general trends, and that each locality will have a unique experience, resulting from its inherited industrial structure and the roles it plays in the new corporate geography (Massey, 1984, Allen and Massey, 1988). The experience of change is variable, with market driven changes producing localities which gain economic activities and jobs, and those which lose them. However:

> 'Most of the larger cities in the industrialised world were confronted in the 1970s and early 1980s with the symptoms of what has frequently been called 'the urban crisis'... In the second half of the 1980s on the wave of world-wide recovery, some of the principal cities in western Europe and the United States regained something of their former leading position [but] the process of urban revival seems much more selective than that of urban decline'
>
> *(van den Berg, et al. 1994)*

Policy has focused on regeneration in localities which have been losers in the process of creating post-industrial cities.

Both the analysis of economic restructuring and the design of policy have generally relied implicitly or explicitly upon distinguishing 'basic' and 'dependent' economic activities within an economy (which may be a city, sub-region or region):

- **basic industries** are those which earn external income by exporting goods or services to the rest of the world
- **dependent industries** are those which serve the local market only (Kaldor, 1966).

The importance of the distinction is that basic industries are the key to growth in the economy. For any particular locality, they are the propulsive industries which generate growth since they can expand by selling more into the external market and thus earning more external income. Non-basic industries on the other hand simply sell the goods or services they produce to local consumers or to other local firms. Whilst this meets market needs and demands, it does not in itself generate growth in the local economy. These industries are therefore dependent in the sense that their size and structure is ultimately determined by basic propulsive industries.

It follows that the fortunes of a local economy are determined by basic industries. A decline in basic industries (e.g. through closure of mines or manufacturing plants, or out-movement of mobile firms) will result in direct job losses and also consequential job losses in dependent industries, as income earned from the rest of the world falls. Equally, growing basic industries will propel the whole economy, creating jobs themselves and further employment in dependent industries. As a result, the analysis of economic change and the focus of economic policy has been on those industries identified as basic, with dependent industries seen as relatively unimportant.

For many years, this translated into a preoccupation with manufacturing industry as the key to local regeneration. In principle, basic industries can be part of the agricultural, extractive, manufacturing or service sectors, but manufacturing has conventionally been seen as much the most important. Fothergill and Gudgin (1982) estimated that most manufacturing industry was basic, but most services were dependent. This meant that despite the continuing growth in service industries and service employment (Marshall and Wood, 1995), most service industries were seen as at best unimportant in economic regeneration, and at worst parasitic activities which did not provide 'real jobs' (Williams, 1994). Those service industries which clearly were basic (like many of the financial services in the City of London) tended to be regarded as exceptions. As Urry (1990) argues: 'implicit in the restructuring . . . literature is a presumed hierarchy of industrial sectors, with extractive-manufacturing seen as basic . . . and service industry as relatively unimportant.'

Williams (1994) points out that over the last decade this view of services has begun to break down.

- A wider view is now taken of what constitute basic services. Producer services (frequently closely associated with manufacturing) are now widely acknowledged as trading inter-regionally (and internationally), and thus as income-earning basic industries (e.g. business and financial services). In addition, some consumer services have been recognised as basic, since they attract consumers into the locality where they spend money, earning external income for the locality. Tourism is the most widely recognised 'basic consumer service' industry, but some leisure and retailing (part of our wide definition of tourism) fall within the same category. Tourism is capable of generating income from across regional and national boundaries, and is thus an export industry in the fullest sense.

- Services are propulsive and contribute to economic growth if they prevent the leakage of income outside the locality. They can do that by providing consumer services that otherwise could only be purchased elsewhere. Thus a city's shopping and leisure facilities are basic to the extent that they result in residents spending money in the city that they would otherwise have spent elsewhere. A similar argument can be made about changes in rural areas which have seen decline in employment in agriculture or mining industries, for example the uplands areas of North Pennines. Agriculture and extractive industries are basic industries, exporting their production outside the local area, so their decline has a depressing effect on other dependent industries in the locality. Tourism (such as farm holidays, cottage lets or bed-and-breakfast) and leisure (such as riding or fishing facilities) are new basic industries which can generate growth in the local economy.

The presumed hierarchy of industrial sectors is thus based on inaccurate assumptions. Services are of increasing significance in regeneration, and consumer services as well as producer services can have an important propulsive role.

CONSEQUENCES OF ECONOMIC CHANGE

Radical and rapid change in city economies from the 1970s onwards meant that there was an increasing concern to generate new investment and to attract mobile economic activity. That in itself was not new. National and local government, and local business interests have traditionally been concerned to attract new investment to areas where industries are in decline, but the novelty arose from the fact that economic change was sufficiently rapid, widespread and severe to prompt innovative responses from policy makers. There were three main factors involved in the UK.

1 There was an increasing awareness that total manufacturing employment would continue to decline whilst competition between cities to attract mobile investment would intensify (both nationally and internationally). As a result, individual cities could not expect that job losses in traditional manufacturing (and associated extractive and distribution industries) could be made good by new manufacturing investment. Conventional policy responses based on luring in new manufacturing firms through subsidy and the provision of premises were thus at best a partial solution. This forced policy makers in the late 1970s and early 1980s to look creatively at other sources of potential employment and regeneration, and this focused attention on activities lower down the conventional hierarchy of industrial sectors – consumer service industries such as tourism and leisure. In 1980, the English Tourist Board was able to review a series of examples of tourism-based regeneration initiatives and argue that whilst tourism was not a panacea for inner city problems, it could play an important role in creating employment and income and in revitalising an area (ETB, 1980). In many cases, however, tourism and associated arts, culture and entertainment (ACE) industries were promoted with reluctance and for the want of alternatives. There was a view that service jobs, and leisure jobs in particular, were 'candyfloss', not real jobs. This perspective was partly based on a culture of manufacturing and heavy industry (which defined 'proper jobs'), and partly on the reality that many leisure and tourism jobs have been of low quality (in

terms of pay, security or working conditions). In the mid-1980s, the Civic Trust's initial programme for regeneration in Halifax was modified to exclude an emphasis on the promotion of tourism because public consultation showed there was a feeling that 'job creation in tourism and retailing was a poor substitute for the employment in manufacturing that had been lost' (Lockwood, 1992). These ideas have persisted and even in 1994, Williams was calling for an end to 'erroneous prejudices' against service jobs in local economic development, and arguing that 'the service sector must be reconceptualised as a vibrant dynamic sector which can strengthen the health of a local economy'.

2 The intense competition for inward investment led to a concern with city marketing and promoting a positive image of a locality. Promoting the (alleged) advantages of locating in a particular town or city was not new. The 1950s and 1960s had seen local authorities advertising the availability of new industrial units and serviced sites, and in the 1960s and 1970s most places found some means to claim that they were located at the heart of Britain's motorway network. The novelty of city marketing was that it sought to promote a place to investors not through specific industrial or 'business' attributes (like sites and roads) but with the overall image and the general virtues of the place as somewhere to live or to visit. 'Place marketing [came to be] recognised as a key component of the post-industrial city' (Smales, 1994). This concern naturally meant an increasing interest in those aspects of places which were attractive to visitors or potential investors, which created positive images or which could be used effectively in marketing.

3 The loss of traditional industries left a legacy of vacant buildings and sites, for example, empty warehouses, mills, market buildings, railway stations, and factories. These vacant buildings and derelict sites were very visible signs of economic decline, and an obviously wasted resource, leading to pressure to create new and productive uses. In many cases buildings and sites were ramshackle and polluted, attractive only to the most dedicated

industrial archaeologist, so solutions required clearance and redevelopment. However there were also many instances of buildings with clear potential: frequently they were of historic interest (whether or not they were statutorily listed); well-known locally and symbolically important; structurally sound and adaptable; clustered in recognisable districts; within or close to city centres; and cheap (Beioley, Maitland and Vaughan, 1990; Urry, 1990). In such cases, the need for economic regeneration was not translated into proposals for comprehensive redevelopment, as would have been the case in the 1960s. Attitudes to the built heritage had changed, public money was scarce and such proposals mostly far too risky for the private sector to undertake without public guarantee or subsidy. Instead, the requirement was to find new activities and uses which could capitalise on the potential of the inherited stock of buildings. Ideas of 'adaptive re-use' of buildings (Cantacuzino, 1975) became widespread, often drawn from early US initiatives such as Baltimore's Harbour area or Boston's Quincy Market (Urbed, 1994; Colquhon, 1995).

The combination of these factors led to attempts to identify types of economic activity which could use the built heritage of past industry, and so turn it into an asset and a new source of competitive advantage which contributed to a positive image for the city. Above all, there was a concern to create new jobs, and an interest in industrial sectors which were growing rapidly in post-industrial circumstances. This inevitably led to an interest in tourism and ACE industries, which are large and rapidly growing in Britain and on a world scale.

TOURISM, ACE AND REGENERATION

The potential of tourism and ACE industries within economic development and regeneration strategies arises from two interlinked elements:

- **Realising potential tourism resources in a wider range of destinations** – the decline in traditional industries together with the growing importance of tourism and leisure means that more and more places are coming consciously to see themselves as destinations, and to accept that visitors generate a significant element of their economic activity. Rural and urban areas not traditionally associated with, or welcoming to, tourism and leisure have seen the industries as potential sources of growth to replace employment lost in agriculture, manufacturing industries or other service industries. This has led them to review and promote their tourism resources.

- **Tourism as a regeneration catalyst** – in industrial towns and cities particularly, the changes we have just discussed were fundamental. The response required not only new basic industries, but physical changes to cope with derelict land and buildings, image changes to promote new types of investment, and improvement in the morale of local people. Tourism initiatives have the potential not only to 'create jobs, [but] have a positive impact on the local environment, help change the image and perception of the area ... in some cases have been instrumental in attracting other investment ... and have the potential to provide facilities for local people' (Beioley, Maitland and Vaughan, 1990). It is this potential multiplicity of benefits which has helped account for the rapid increase in interest in tourism as part of regeneration initiatives.

We will now examine these two elements in turn. However, it is important to remember at the outset that estimates of the potential of tourism to promote regeneration need to be treated with some caution. Optimistic projections of continuing growth in tourism and leisure, often derived from industry sources, together with the genuine difficulty in defining the industries and their impacts (Goodall, 1987) naturally leads sceptics to argue that their significance may be overestimated. Even from a sceptical point of view, however, it is clear that tourism and ACE industries are already a substantial part of the UK economy, have grown rapidly, and seem likely to be a comparatively rapid growth sector in the future. They potentially constitute a basic consumer services sector which can propel the growth of city economies both directly and by their ability to encourage growth in other sectors.

REALISING TOURISM RESOURCES

Tourism and leisure growth depend on attracting visitors from elsewhere, whilst retaining the leisure spending of the domestic population. What are the attractions that are required to achieve this? As we said in Chapter 2, destinations are composed of a mix of resources and services: in principle, resources constitute their attractions and services make a visit possible. However, in practice, it is difficult to separate resources from services; it is also difficult to define the resources which are provided for or which attract mainly tourists and leisure visitors. The range of destination resources is extensive and include the following:

- **Physical characteristics and setting** – coastal or river locations, or proximity to attractive countryside have particular potential.
- **Built environment and the urban fabric** – architectural heritage has long been important in historic towns and cities like Chester, Norwich or York (EHTF, 1995), but a growing public interest in Victorian heritage has meant that the 19th century industrial architecture of cities such as Bradford, Glasgow, Halifax and Manchester has become an attraction for visitors. Industrial engineering and artefacts can also be turned into tourism attractions, for example, the Transporter Bridge in Middlesborough (English, 1995).
- **History, archaeology, and literary associations** – attractions may be of varying degrees of authenticity. They can be based on 'real' historic buildings and sites (e.g. castles, cathedrals, ruins) or interpretations based on real sites and artefacts (such as the Jorvik Viking Centre in York), or museums and interpretation centres. However, they may be themed entertainments based on elements of a

past (such as the London Dungeon a 'truly horrible experience' housed not in a dungeon, but in railway arches under London Bridge station), or a mix of historical and literary inspiration (such as the Canterbury Tales Experience, loosely based on Chaucer and the idea of pilgrimage).

- **Shops** – there has been a continuing growth in shopping generally, and in 'leisure shopping' in particular (Cairns, 1995). Leisure shopping is undertaken not just to purchase goods, but because the experience is enjoyable in itself – it thus excludes routine food, grocery and convenience goods shopping. For most holiday-makers, shopping is rarely the prime purpose of travel, but it 'tends to be a predominant time-use for many tourists, irrespective of their primary travel motive' (Jansen Verbeke, 1994). Leisure shopping is generally a more important element in the motivations of day visitors, and in the case of some cities it can be the main motivation for the visit (whether a day visit or overnight stay) or at least a secondary attraction (EHTF, 1995).

Some of the growth of leisure shopping has been accounted for by new monocultural retail developments. Many out-of-town shopping malls, or the growing factory outlet developments have no significant mix of uses, and are often closed entirely outside shopping hours. However, for many people, leisure shopping requires a mix of shops with some unique qualities (real or illusory), a positive image, supporting amenities (like pubs and restaurants) nearby, pedestrian areas and 'multi-functionality of the environment which guarantees the place feels alive' (Jansen Verbeke, 1994).

- **Cultural, entertainment and sporting facilities** – which can include museums, cinemas and theatres, arts centres, sports stadia, concert halls and night clubs. A number of these elements may be combined in leisure complexes (including, for example, cinema, bowling, nightclubs, bars and restaurants), and new types of entertainment centres are being developed (such as the Segaworld at London's Trocadero). Attractions may be created by packaging or marketing elements of a place's social characteristics to form a leisure experience, for example Bradford's 'Flavours of Asia', which provides an introduction and guide to the city's Asian shops and restaurants, and includes a 'Curry Tour' (Smales, 1992).

- **Characters and events** – whether real or literary. For example, Middlesborough has used its association with Captain Cook (who was born there) in marketing and as the basis of several visitor initiatives, whilst also promoting its association with popular novels as the 'Catherine Cookson Country' (English, 1995). Authors, works and characters as diverse as the Brontes, Emmerdale, and Sherlock Holmes have been used to help create images of places. In some instances, the 'place' to which tourists are attracted may be an artefact (like Granada's 'Coronation Street' studio set).

  Regular events such as festivals can be a major and long lasting-attraction, as the Edinburgh Festival illustrates. There has however been a growth of interest in high-profile single events which generate visitation, spending and a high profile, and which contribute to changes in image, e.g. Garden Festivals, Glasgow's year as 'European City of Culture', Manchester's bids for the Olympic Games (and securing of the Commonwealth Games), and Greenwich and Birmingham's rival bids for a Millennium Festival.

- **Facilities for business tourism and conferences** – such as hotels, conference and exhibition centres, and support services. Business and conference tourism has grown rapidly over the last decades, and is particularly important to cities. Business tourists generally spend more per day than leisure travellers, and are sought after. Whilst the supply of business and conference facilities is the most important attraction, an attractive physical environment, a range of other attractions, good evening facilities and a good image are also important (Law, 1993).

The tourism and leisure resources of some destinations (and cities in particular) are complex and interlinked. The attraction for visitors frequently arises from the combination of several, or all of these elements, in the right place and at the right times. Visitors are attracted to a well defined area (or areas) offering a range of activities for much of the day and evening. There are several implications which follow on from this.

- It is difficult to separate elements of the 'total tourism product'. What appear to be services or complementary elements (such as shopping) may in fact constitute a major part of the attraction of visiting the city or remaining there for leisure activities. It may be most sensible in cities to see primary and complementary elements together forming total 'urban leisure supply' (Margot Jokovi, 1992).
- It is difficult to separate those elements which cater for overnight visitors, day visitors and others, as many of the facilities will be used by all of them. Many of the aspects of the city which are attractive to visitors are also valued by others, whether residents or potential investors.
- Tourism and leisure resources are to be found in a wide variety of places. The expansion in what constitutes 'tourism or leisure resources' means that many more places can lay claim to being a tourism destination. This possibility is reinforced since 'tourism and leisure resources' derive partly from users' perceptions, and thus can be created or modified as perceptions change.
- There is a clear and strong association between tourism and leisure uses, and the overall development of areas – the attraction of the city for visitors, and for residents seeking entertainment, depends strongly on a combination of attractions that is convenient and coherent from a user's point of view.

TOURISM AS A REGENERATION CATALYST

Law (1993) has summarised the way in which tourism has been seen as fundamental to regeneration in cities. Faced with the decline of traditional industries, cities needed to develop new sources of employment and attract inward investment, whilst dealing with the physical problems of dereliction and decay, and social problems including the low morale of residents who had experienced the effects of economic decline. Tourism development can provide employment directly, but also contribute to resolving other problems. The process is outlined in Figure 5.2, adapted from Law (1993).

1 Developing a place's tourism resources can improve its image. As cities become increasingly competitive on a global as well as national scale, the image presented to potential inward investors becomes more and more important. Tourism development can initially gain attention and make a city stand out from the crowd, whilst continuing tourism marketing and promotion continues to emphasise the attractions of the city. It thus has a central role in place marketing. For example, the marketing of industrial cities has involved changing

negative images to positive ones – in the case Bradford, from one of derelict mills set in a decaying industrial wasteland, to one of interesting Victorian heritage surrounded by magnificent open countryside with strong literary associations. Both images, of course, include a mix of reality and interpretation. Bradford gained a particular advantage from being one of the first in the field. At the start of the 1980s, the idea of the city seeking to attract tourists under the slogan 'Bradford – a Surprising Place' was itself pretty surprising. (see case study A for a full discussion). Business tourism can be especially important here, since it involves people who will have a role in deciding on the location of new investment and facilities – images that they form of the places they visit can be an important influence in decision making. In short:

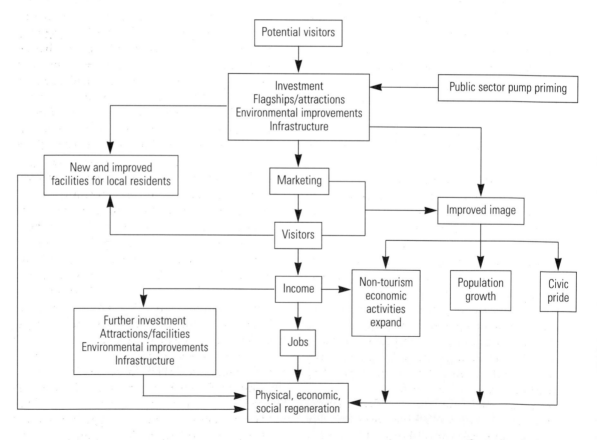

FIGURE 5.2 *Tourism as a regeneration catalyst*

Source: based on Law, 1993

'Tourism, including arts and leisure has become central in forming people's experience of place, of the natural and built environment, the range of services available locally, the transportation infrastructure, the degree of congestion and the attractiveness that such a place has for inward manufacturing investment'.

(Urry, 1990)

2　Individual tourism attractions can act as 'flagships' – prominent developments which symbolise change for a whole city and act as a catalyst for regeneration in a particular area. Bianchini, Dawson and Evans (1992) describe **flagships** as high-profile, prestigious developments which can play a catalytic role in urban regeneration, and which justify their flagship role only if they succeed in attracting a 'flotilla' of other development in their wake. This means, as Smyth (1994) argues, that flagships have the twin purposes of leverage (attracting further development) and providing a marketing tool for an area or whole city. Tourism and leisure developments are often seen as particularly appropriate flagships, since they are generally high-profile and attract attention.

Flagships confer status and can help build confidence, but more broadly, tourism and leisure uses can assist area regeneration because they are frequently good neighbours, especially for office, retailing and professional service activities. The need to attract visitors means they pay particular attention to their physical environment and often place a particular premium on good design. Some uses (like museums and galleries), may add to their neighbours' status, and visitor facilities (like cafés and restaurants) may be used by people living and working in the area. High volumes of visitors, on foot or coach-borne can cause difficulties in heritage cities, but rarely seem to be a problem in industrial cities (Beioley, Maitland and Vaughan, 1990).

3　Much tourism development involves the provision or renewal of infrastructure and the physical improvement of derelict land or redundant buildings – an 'adaptive re-use'. As growing economic activities, tourism and leisure require space. Any growth industry interests those seeking new uses for vacant floorspace, and tourism and leisure uses have often been the outcome of attempts to find some viable function for an historic building that has been 'saved' (Beioley, Maitland and Vaughan, 1990). More directly, they may capitalise directly on the building's history, its form or its status as part of the city's history and heritage. There has been a very rapid growth in the number of museums, heritage and interpretation centres. Urry (1990b) points out that a 1987 survey found 1,750 museums in Britain, of which half had been started since 1971. The redundant building itself may be an integral part of the museum or interpretation – as when a textile museum is housed within a former textile mill, and attempts to recreate industrial processes using authentic or original plant and equipment (Lowell, Styall in Cheshire, and New Lanark all offer examples). Equally, the building may be less directly associated with exhibits, but be appropriate in a more general way. For example, Manchester's Science and Industry Museum is housed partly in a railway station and railway warehouses, but also in a former wholesale market – not so directly related to science or industry, but certainly part of the city's past. Finally, many leisure uses gain interest and potential selling points from being housed in older or historic buildings. Hotels, bars, restaurants and shops can all gain from such locations and associations, although these advantages may be offset by high costs of conversion and operation compared to purpose-built premises. Some showpiece developments (such as Terence Conran's conversion of the former Michelin building in London) to shops, restaurants and offices illustrate the potential in this area.

A further advantage is that some tourism and leisure uses may attract public or non-commercial funding, especially if they are involved in arts and entertainment. The National Lottery is now an appealing source of cash for projects which would not meet commercial funding criteria – such as the Tate

Gallery's proposed conversion of the former Bankside power station. Public funding may be used for setting up or operating the activities (some museums or galleries, for example) or to assist in the costs of conversion of historic buildings. In either case, this may permit the conversion of a building which would not be viable on purely commercial criteria because the publicly funded use can act as an anchor tenant; capital costs of conversion are reduced; or developer confidence is increased. The tourism elements of Liverpool's Albert Dock development which included offices, shops, a studio, maritime museum and art gallery, can be seen in this light (Beioley, Maitland and Vaughan, 1990).

4 Tourism and leisure development can bring benefits to local people by adding to cultural, sporting or entertainment facilities, or by increasing audiences and attendances and so making the facilities more viable. They can also increase civic pride and attract local support: by re-using and revitalising buildings associated with industries which have declined or vanished, they offer a positive response to de-industrialisation which can be an antidote to feelings of social and cultural loss (Urry, 1990c). Bringing such buildings back into use for tourism also fosters the view that the city has something to be proud of, and which is attractive to the outside world. When residents of Manchester and Liverpool were asked about the redevelopment of former industrial areas for tourism, over 80% said that the developments were something to be proud of (Beioley, Maitland and Vaughan, 1990).

Heeley, in discussing Sheffield's experience, summarises the contribution that tourism and ACE can make to urban regeneration.

'The rationalisation of the steel and metal manufacturing industries in the two decades which followed the nineteen sixties led to unemployment and industrial unrest, localised dereliction, and to generally lower morale and pride. The city's response was an approach to urban regeneration based on partnership with a powerful alliance of local businessmen and civic leaders evolving a bold strategy based on an expensive and high risk use of leisure and tourism as a means of diversifying the economy and "imaging the city".'

(Heeley, 1995)

Tourism, then, is seen as more important in more places and as essential to economic regeneration in cities. This means that it has come to play a more important role in strategies for development, and that partnerships between public and private sectors to develop and manage tourism resources have become increasingly significant.

As we said at the start of the chapter, destination management is needed both to regulate high levels of tourism demand and to create demand as part of a wider process of regeneration. The scope for management in any destination is set by its potential resources and potential tourism demand, but also by the broader policy context: tourism policies at the national and international level. In the next chapter, we will examine that policy context before moving on to look at destination management in Chapter 7 and the case studies.

REFERENCES

Allen, J. and Massey, D. (1988) *The Economy in Question*, Sage, London.

Beioley, S.J. Maitland, R.A. and Vaughan, R. (1990) *Tourism and the Inner City*, HMSO, London.

Bianchini, F., Dawson, J. and Evans, R. (1992) 'Flagship developments in urban regeneration' in Healey, P. *et al. Rebuilding the City: Property-led urban regeneration*, E. & F. Spon, London.

Bull, A. (1991) *The Economics of Travel and Tourism*, Longman, London.

Cairns, S. (1995) 'Travel for food shopping: the Fourth Solution' in *Traffic Engineering and Control*, July/August, pp. 411–418.

Cantacuzino, S. (1975) *New Uses for Old Buildings*, Architectural Press, London.

Colquhon, I. (1995) *Urban Regeneration*, Batsford, London.

Cullingworth, J.B. and Nadin, V. (1994) *Town and Country Planning in Britain*, 11th ed. Routledge, London.

EHTF (1995) *Historic Towns – Mixed Uses and Vitality and Viability*, English Historic Towns Forum.

English, R. (1995) 'Tourism for Economic Regeneration: the Middlesborough Experience' in *RTPI Summer School Proceedings*, pp. 36–41.

ETB (1980) *Tourism and the Inner City*, English Tourist Board, London.

Fothergill, S. and Gudgin, G. (1982) *Unequal Growth: Urban and Regional Employment Change in the UK*, Heinemann, London.

Fothergill, S., Kitson, M. and Monk, S. (1985) *Urban Industrial Change: the causes of the urban rural contrast in manufacturing employment trends*, HMSO, London.

Goodall, B. (1987) 'Tourism Policy and Jobs in the United Kingdom' in *Built Environment* 13, 2, pp. 109–123.

Goodall, B. and Stabler, M. (1992) 'Environmental auditing in the quest for sustainable tourism: the destination perspective' in *Proceedings of the 1992 Tourism in Europe Conference*, Centre for Travel and Tourism, Tyne and Wear.

Hartley, K. and Hooper, N. (1993) 'Tourism Policy: Market Failure and Public Choice in *Perspectives on Tourism Policy*, Johnson, P. and Thomas, B. (eds) Mansell, London.

Hirsch, F. (1978) *Social Limits to Growth*, Routledge and Kegan Paul, London.

Hutton, W. (1995) *The State We're In*, Jonathan Cape.

Jansen-Verbeke, M. (1994) 'The synergy between shopping and tourism: the Japanese experience' in Theobold, W.F. ed. *Global tourism – the next decade*, Butterworth-Heinemann, Oxford.

Kaldor, N. (1966) *Causes of the slow rate of growth in the United Kingdom*, Cambridge University Press, Cambridge.

Keegan, W. (1992) *The Spectre of Capitalism*, Radius.

Law, C.M. (1992) 'Tourism as a Focus for Urban Regeneration' in *The role of tourism in the urban and regional economy*, Regional Studies Association, London.

Law, C.M. (1993) *Urban Tourism*, Mansell, London.

Le Grand J., Propper, C. and Robinson, R. (1992) *The Economics of Social Problems*, 3rd edn., Macmillan.

Lockwood, J. (1992) 'Holistic Regeneration: the experience of Calderdale, United Kingdom' in Berry, J., McGreal, S. and Deddis, B. (eds) *Urban Regeneration: Property investment and development*, Spon., London.

Maitland, R.A. (1991) 'Tourism and Urban Regeneration: the contribution of tourism to economic development in inner city areas in the UK', paper given at *Planning Transatlantic Conference*, Oxford.

Margit Jokovi, E. (1992) 'The Production of Leisure and Economic Developments in Cities' in *Built Environment* 18, 2, pp. 138–144.

Marshall, N. and Wood, P. (1995) *Services and Space*, Longman, London.

Massey, D.B. (1984) *Spatial Divisions of Labour: Social structures and the Geography of Production*, Macmillan, London.

Meadows, D.H., Meadows, D.L., Randers, J. and Behrens, W. (1972) *The Limits to Growth*, Earth Island; London.

Middleton, V. (1988) *Marketing in Travel and Tourism*, Heinemann, Oxford.

Mishan, E. (1969) *The Costs of Economic Growth*, Penguin.

Morrell, J. (1985) *Employment in Tourism*, British Tourist Authority, London.

Pearce, D., Markandya, A. and Barbier, E.B. (1989) *Blueprint for a Green Economy*, Earthscan, London.

Smales, I. (1994) 'Desperate pragmatism or shrewd optimism? The image and selling of West Yorkshire' in Haughton, G. and Whitney, D. (eds) *Reinventing a Region: Restructuring in West Yorkshire*, Avebury Press, Aldershot.

Smyth, H. (1994) *Marketing the City: the role of flagship developments in urban regeneration*, E. & F. Spon, London.

Thomas, J. (1992) 'Tourism and the environment: an exploration of the willingness to pay of the average visitor' in *Proceedings of the 1992 Tourism in Europe Conference*, Centre for Travel and Tourism, Tyne and Wear.

Urbed (1994) *Re-using Derelict Urban Buildings*, Department of the Environment, London.

Urry, J. (1990a) 'The "Consumption of Tourism"' in *Sociology*, 24, 1, pp. 23–35.

Urry, J. (1990b) *The Tourist Gaze*, Sage, London.

Urry, J. (1990c) 'Work, Production and Social

Relations' in *Work, Employment and Society*, vol 4, no. 2, pp. 271–280.

van den Berg, L., van der Borg, J. and van der Meer, J. (1994) *Urban Tourism*, Erasmus University, Rotterdam.

Ward, S.V. (1990) 'Local industrial promotion and development policies 1940-1988' in *Local Economy*, 5, 2, pp. 100–118.

Williams, C.C. (1994) 'Rethinking the role of the service sector in local economic revitalisation' in *Local Economy*, 9, 1, pp. 73–82.

World Commission on Environment and Development: Brundtland Report (1987) *Our Common Future*, Oxford University Press, Oxford.

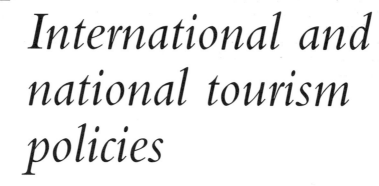

CHAPTER
6

International and national tourism policies

INTRODUCTION

Chapter 5 demonstrated the need for tourism industry planning as a means of promoting orderly development which optimises the benefits tourism can bring and reduces its negative impacts on destinations. We are primarily interested in how tourism can best be controlled and managed at the level of the individual destination, but in order to understand this fully we need to:

1 take account of the policy frameworks at international and national levels. This is a vitally important step, because policies and programmes enacted at these levels can affect tourism at the level of the destination – each geographical layer influences and defines the parameters for the layer below. In particular, attention will be given to the European Union's priorities and measures for tourism; an understanding of these is crucial to the understanding of the policy framework within which tourism is developed in all member states.

2 look horizontally within each geographical level at a number of programmes and policies devised for tourism. We also need to look at those programmes and policies which have an impact on the wider context within which the tourism industry operates: including policies for the economy, the environment and transport.

This interaction of spatial and sectoral elements is illustrated in Figure 6.1.

This chapter examines planning and policy contexts, starting at the worldwide scale and working down to the national scale: at each level tourism-specific policies are analysed, as well as other areas of activity which impinge on tourism. These international and national policies constitute the context of the management and development of tourism at the local level (see Chapter 7). They are important external influences acting upon individual destinations. They may either reinforce or frustrate the efforts of local authorities (and other policy makers involved) in seeking to manage tourism – indeed, if tourism management at the local level is too inconsistent with the external policy framework, it may be largely ineffective.

For this reason, those responsible for managing and developing tourism at the local level tend to take one (or sometimes both) of two approaches:

■ if their own policies are broadly compatible with international, national and regional policies, they can harness these in order to reinforce their own approach
■ if their own policies differ too much from those in the external policy framework, they can work to change the external policy framework itself.

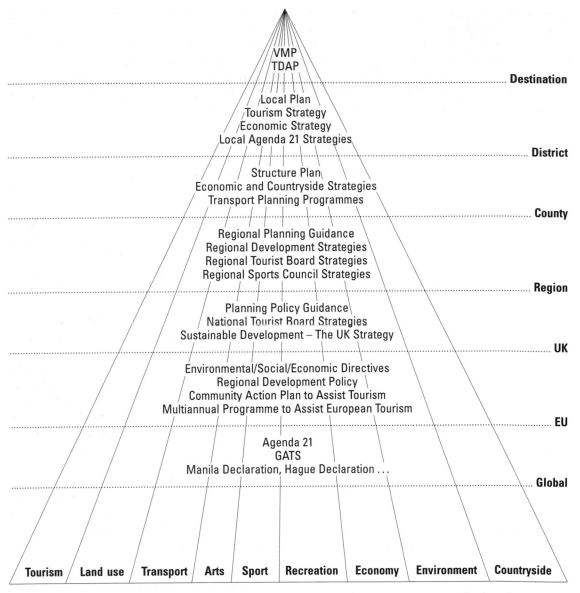

Source: Human, B 'Visitor Management in the Public Planning Policy Context: A Case-study of Cambridge', in The Journal of Sustainable Tourism, Vol. 2, No. 4, 1994 (adapted)

FIGURE 6.1 *Destination management and planning in the public policy context*

Clearly, there are advantages for destinations with tourism objectives which are supported by (rather than in conflict with) policies at the international, national and regional levels. These benefits for the destination have been summed up as follows:

'This results in an integrated policy framework that ensures consistency, encourages cooperation and long-term planning, makes the best use of resources, opens up additional sources of finance and provides a firm justification for refusing undesirable development.'

(Human, 1994)

When there are inconsistencies between the destination's own objectives and those of other agencies at other spatial levels, the local authority or other policy makers can seek to change or influence those other polices, for example, through commenting on draft national and EU policy statements and/or ensuring that all relevant policy documents include tourism issues. However, it must be admitted that the power of individual local authorities to change the polices of other agencies beyond the regional scale, is fairly limited. Nevertheless, an indispensable first step is to be aware of these policies – that is the theme of this chapter.

THE GLOBAL POLICY FRAMEWORK

GLOBAL TOURISM POLICY

Despite the essentially transnational nature of much tourism activity, very few binding regulations and agreements concerning tourism services exist at the global level, with the notable exception of the civil aviation conventions covering technical cooperation, and the safety and well-being of airline passengers. These conventions apart, other tourism-related policies at this level tend to be fairly weak in structure and lacking in enforcement, due to the almost complete absence of truly global mandatory authorities.

Nevertheless, due to the efforts of a number of inter-governmental agencies, certain international tourism policies in guideline form are slowly emerging on a worldwide scale. Most of these concern issues which transcend purely local or national considerations, such as freedom of movement and broad environmental matters.

National governments' moves toward worldwide economic and political cooperation and coordination, during the immediate aftermath of the Second World War, at first included no significant consideration of the tourism industry. Since then, as the importance of tourism has increased, international organisations have developed a growing interest in it and new structures have been established to attempt to guide tourism development on the international scale.

For most of these international organisations, tourism represents only one area of cooperation among others. For example, international aid agencies and inter-governmental organisations (such as the World Bank, the European Investment Bank and the United Nations), through their investment programmes, fund tourism infrastructure and technical expertise in (mainly) developing countries in the same way as they support the development of a number of other industries (such as agriculture and manufacturing).

However, other international and inter-regional organisations entirely concerned with tourism (in particular its promotion) have been established during the past 50 years. The European Travel Commission, the Caribbean Tourism Organisation and the Pacific Area Travel Association are all examples of inter-regional tourism organisations jointly promoting their world regions to third markets.

While these organisations play a part in the promotion of tourism in particular world regions, the global policy framework within which the world's tourism industry operates is essentially shaped by two institutions:

- the World Tourism Organisation
- the Organisation for Economic Cooperation and Development.

As international organisations, both place an overwhelming emphasis on *international* tourism issues.

WORLD TOURISM ORGANISATION

The world's leading inter-governmental organisation specifically oriented towards the promotion and development of travel and tourism is the Madrid-based **World Tourism Organisation (WTO)**.

Founded in 1975, when it replaced the International Union of Official Travel Organisations, the WTO is recognised by the United Nations Organisation as the official voice of tourism in discussions with governments. Its membership now includes over 120 countries. There are, in addition, 250 non-governmental affiliate members, including representatives from all sectors of the tourism industry as well as academia.

The WTO's overall aim is 'to promote and develop tourism as a significant means of fostering economic development and international trade, as well as international peace and understanding'. To achieve these objectives, the WTO is committed to taking 'all necessary measures', with particular considerations for the interests of *developing countries* (Article 3.2 of the WTO constitution).

Its work programme covers six main areas of tourism-related activities and services:

- statistics and market research
- education and training
- technical co-operation
- environment and planning
- quality of tourism services
- communication and documentation.

The results of these activities are presented at WTO seminars, which provide an important forum for discussion of global matters pertaining to tourism. The WTO also produces an extensive range of publications containing information on all aspects of tourism.

In addition to funds generated through membership fees, the WTO receives an annual budget from the United Nations Development Programme, although, as Cockerell (1994) points out, this funding source is in danger of drying up.

Developing countries represent the majority of members of the WTO, although their own share of international tourism arrivals and receipts is small. Frangialli (1991) suggests that for this reason, the WTO has been principally regarded by the industrialised nations as a source of aid for developing countries. Partly in order to correct this image, the WTO decided, at its General Assembly in 1989, to concentrate on providing those services most in demand by its members in industrialised countries:

- the compiling of statistics
- marketing activities
- environmental matters
- the creation of a computerised database.

However, the WTO does have an input into the development of policies on issues affecting global tourism, by issuing policy statements and publications on a range of matters which concern tourism on the worldwide scale. One of the most important of these publications is generally recognised to be the Manila Declaration on World Tourism of 1980, which is often cited as a turning point, explicitly linking the prevalent mood on environmental protection with global tourism development. It stated that:

'... the satisfaction of tourism requirements must not be prejudicial to the social and economic interests of the population in tourist areas, to the environment and, above all, to natural resources, which are fundamental attractions of tourism, and historical and cultural sites.'

(WTO, 1989)

This declaration formalised a new wider concept of tourism impacts, broadening it out from a preoccupation with the physical environment alone to one which included sociocultural dimensions. As such, it represented an important contribution to the development of worldwide tourism policy. Nine years later, the WTO was instrumental in bringing about the signing of the Hague Declaration on tourism, which reflected the call of the Brundtland Commission for Sustainable Development to integrate environmental dimensions into all areas of economic decision making.

Nevertheless, despite its unique position, the WTO has been criticised on two main fronts.

1 Many commentators have expressed the view that the WTO has an entirely expansionist tendency which leads it indiscriminately to advocate tourism development, without due consideration of whether this is the best development option for the countries con-

cerned. A possible explanation for this orientation is succinctly proposed by Burns, reviewing a WTO publication:

'It is clear . . . that WTO is actively promoting the expansion of tourism at a global level. WTO survives not so much through its membership fees (governments and affiliates) but through spin-off activities such as consulting and project management. It therefore actually needs more tourism!'

(Burns, 1994)

2 Some have expressed reservations over what they perceive as the WTO's governmental bias. Lickorish, for example, believes that:

'. . . the work of official international agencies tends to suffer from the one-sided nature of government-controlled bodies which concentrate on political rather than practical aspects. Errors are compounded because they rarely provide adequate machinery for consultation and cooperation over the range of official series concerned with tourism and with the operating and private sectors.'

(Lickorish, 1994)

A more balanced approach might be achieved through increasing the role of the WTO's non-governmental affiliate members, but meetings are infrequent and the active involvement of operators in the tourism industry itself is, in fact, very limited. Lickorish has advocated an expansion of the role played by the affiliate members, turning the WTO into a worldwide 'Parliament of Tourism', to improve cooperation through a 'partnership approach'.

The WTO's future effectiveness will always depend on the willingness of governments to accept its advice, and this in turn will depend on the organisation being able to convince national governments that it is uniquely placed to comment upon, and provide guidelines for, a range of global tourism issues. The battle is far from won. Funding from national government members is precarious, with several developed countries unconvinced that they are getting value for money for their contributions. Britain, for

example, remains to be persuaded that the WTO has a useful role to play.

ORGANISATION FOR ECONOMIC COOPERATION AND DEVELOPMENT

The **Organisation for Economic Cooperation and Development (OECD)** was created in 1961, when the USA, Canada, Japan, Australia and New Zealand were admitted as members to the former Organisation for European Economic Cooperation (OEEC), whose membership comprised 19 European countries. Its principal objective is to contribute to the development of the world economy.

Out of all the world's international tourism trade, 70% takes place in the OECD area, (in which the main sending and receiving countries are found). Reflecting the importance of the tourism industry for many of its members, the OECD has its own Tourism Committee, which was part of the former OEEC and is composed of senior tourism policy-makers drawn from all member countries. The mission of the Tourism Committee is to promote action to maximise the benefits of tourism to the economies of OECD Member countries by:

- increasing the understanding of the economic importance of tourism
- promoting the liberalisation of policies towards international tourism flows
- fostering international cooperation in these fields
- providing a forum for dissemination, analysis and benchmarking of the tourism policies and administration of member countries against comparable economies.

Since the 1960s, the OECD (through the Tourism Committee) has been the source of useful annual reports including two main types of information:

- a review of members governments' policies in the field of tourism
- details of statistical trends in international tourism in member countries.

Between them, the WTO and the OECD represent the two main sources of international tourism statistics – these have proven to be of use as supplementary data in, for example, the construction of broad marketing and development programmes.

Since the 1970s, the OECD Tourism Committee has also turned its attention towards tourism's environmental impact, publishing reports on tourism's impacts on the environment and making recommendations on this issue. For example, as part of a major research and policy programme on tourism and the environment, the Tourism Committee sponsored a 1990 series of seminars with the title 'Tourism Policy Issues to the Millennium: Keys to Successful Strategies', aimed at giving 'policy makers in the countries responsible for the most of the world's tourism trade a chance to exchange views and possibly coordinate their action in areas of common concern' (OECD, 1990).

However, beyond these activities, the OECD's further involvement in tourism matters has often been restricted both by a lack of resources allocated to this issue, and by the standing of the OECD itself. Cockerell (1994) notes that the OECD's Tourism Committee does not carry the weight it deserves. During the 1990s, the organisation's investment in tourism-related activities has been in decline, and its very involvement in tourism has been continuously called into question. Enjoying neither the benefits of worldwide membership nor the advantages of geographical concentration in a single world region (although half of its member countries are also members of the EU), the OECD's power and influence are limited. Frangialli sums up the OECD's tourism identity problem as follows: '[The OECD] has difficulty in finding a role for itself between, on the one hand, the more binding, statutory measures which apply to EU member countries ... and the work assigned to the WTO on a worldwide basis' (Frangialli, 1991). Nevertheless, he concedes that the OECD has succeeded in identifying a specific domain in which it has an important contribution to make to the development of the international policy framework within which tourism operates, namely the liberalisation of international tourism within the OECD area.

Liberalisation

Although international tourism is, by comparison with other service sectors, relatively free from protectionist and discriminatory practices, it is affected by measures which work against a completely open and competitive international trading context. Some of these obstacles are particular to the tourism industry, such as limits on currency allowances, entry visas and arrival/departure taxes on international travellers. The French government provided an example of such practices in 1983, when it set a limit upon how much money French tourists could take abroad, and again in 1986, when visas were introduced for visitors from certain OECD countries. Other barriers to liberalisation of trade in tourism services also affect other sectors. These include impediments on establishment and operation in certain national markets where foreign suppliers are discriminated against, as well as restrictions on the repatriation of company profits. An example of such an impediment is the recent requirement, in Canada, that travel agents and tour operators be *bona fide* residents of that country.

'Liberalisation' in this context means persuading national legislatures to relax or abolish such restrictions. To this end, in 1985, an *Inventory of Obstacles to International Tourism in the OECD Area* was published, and revised in 1991 (OECD, 1991). This was a catalogue of measures which the OECD considered not to fall in line with the basic principles of liberalisation of international tourism. The basic principle underlying the liberalisation of international tourism which the Inventory attempted to promote was 'market access'. **Market access** for tourism is a twofold concept.

1 The access by the residents of a country to foreign travel through the availability of funds and means of payment. It is expressed in the following OECD obligation for members: 'No restrictions shall be imposed by member countries on expenditure by residents for purposes of international tourism or other international travel.' Other questions connected with travellers' access and ease of travel addressed in the Inventory, were administrative formalities and controls (regarding documen-

tation, visas and passports) and duty-free imports and controls.

2 The opening up of market access for tourism enterprises. This implies the possibility of foreign businesses operating in a national market under conditions of open and fair competition with domestic firms. In the OECD context, this is granted through the right of establishment and investment contained in the organisation's Code of Liberalisation of Capital movements.

However, the Inventory's impact on removing obstacles to international tourism between member countries was limited, on the admission of the person responsible for drafting the document. In particular she laments the lack of strong political direction and objectives behind the Inventory, a well as the fact that it had no statutory authority:

> '. . . the major shortcoming is that the Inventory was elaborated on an empirical basis with a certain lack of political direction. And in certain cases, it was backed by a Decision-Recommendation which is an OECD instrument with no teeth.'
>
> *(Allard, 1995)*

TOURISM IN THE WIDER GLOBAL POLICY FRAMEWORK

GLOBAL ECONOMIC POLICY

General agreement on trade in services (GATS)

Although the OECD may be able to claim the credit for initially focusing attention on the issue of barriers to the liberalisation of international trade in tourism, most of these have since been dealt with by other legislators.

For Western Europe, many of these liberalisation issues fell within the competence of the European Union and were dealt with as part of the Single European Market legislation; others were similar to the principles enshrined in the Uruguay Round negotiations, which resulted in the **General Agreement on Tariffs and Trade (GATT)** and the **General Agreement on Trade in Services (GATS)** – the first multilateral legally-enforceable agreement covering trade and investment in the service industries, including tourism. The basic aim of the GATS agreement is similar to that of the GATT for goods:

> 'to expand world trade by liberalising markets and to put that liberalising process on a secure basis. The effect on trade in services, including tourism, is designed to be the reduction or elimination of barriers to, or other distortions of, international trade.'
>
> *(Edgell, 1995b)*

For tourism, the value of GATS is said to lie in its potential to propel travel and tourism internationally, by easing the flow of people, information and capital across borders. In particular, the GATS reduces restrictions on foreign investment and the transfer of funds across borders, supposedly giving investors and companies new confidence that, for example, once resources have been committed, key trading rules will not be shifted adversely. Thus, signatory countries (members) should enjoy full access to each others' markets for services and, once established, receive 'national treatment', i.e. the same treatment which domestic suppliers of services receive from their governments.

However, not everyone agrees with this optimistic vision of the forthcoming expansion of the travel and tourism industry following the increasing liberalisation which the GATS promises. In general terms, many of those involved in the global North-South debate are suspicious of the powerful industrialised countries of the North, who, they maintain, define the terms of world trade and are adept at using GATT to further their own interests, at the South's expense (Khor, 1994). By this token, they fear that GATS has the potential for exacerbating existing inequalities between rich and poor nations.

In particular, many have pointed out that GATS may aggravate the problems already being caused by foreign ownership and control of transport and accommodation facilities in developing countries. Clearly, the full implications of GATS have yet to be realised, but among the general optimism and euphoria, dissenting voices may be heard, and may yet grow louder (Plüss, 1994).

GLOBAL ENVIRONMENTAL POLICY

The Earth Summit and Agenda 21

Opinions differ on the overall success of the 1992 Earth Summit in Rio de Janeiro, but what may be most important is that the conference and all the preparations leading up to it happened at all. This was the first time that the vital link between environmental conservation and development had been placed on the global agenda, discussed and accepted on a worldwide scale.

By the end of the conference, most of the world's governments (including that of the UK) had committed themselves to a number of environmental protection treaties and sets of principles, including Agenda 21. **Agenda 21** is:

> '... a comprehensive programme of action providing a blueprint for securing the sustainable future of the planet, from now into the 21st century. It is the first document of its kind to achieve widespread international agreement, reflecting a global consensus and political commitment at the highest level.'
>
> *(WTTC/WTO, 1996)*

It is a non-statutory document negotiated by the representatives of the governments responsible for its implementation. However, although Agenda 21 designated national governments as having most of the responsibility for implementing the strategy; it was recognised that UN agencies, other inter-governmental and non-governmental organisations, the voluntary sector, business and industry, and the public at large had a role to play in the process – essentially a 'global partnership'.

The Agenda identifies three core tools which can be used by governments to achieve its objectives:

- 'Introduction of new, or strengthening of existing regulation, to ensure the protection of human health and the environment ...
- Use of free market mechanisms, by which the price of goods and services should increasingly reflect the environmental costs of resource inputs, manufacture, use, recycling, and disposal; ... these tools are identified as having considerable potential to bring about improvements in the areas of waste minimisation, water management and energy management ...
- Industry-led voluntary programmes which aim to ensure responsible and ethical management of products and processes from the point of view of health and safety and environmental aspects.' (*ibid*)

Very little reference was made during the conference to the interaction between tourism and the environment, despite the size and pace of growth of the industry on the global scale. But Agenda 21 touches upon tourism in two ways.

1 Tourism will be affected by the implementation of Agenda 21's programme of action, since, as is the case for all other industries, it can be altered by changes in the legal framework, polices and management practices under which it operates.
2 Tourism is specifically mentioned as an activity offering sustainable development potential to certain communities, particularly in fragile environments. For example, Chapter 11 advocates that governments 'promote and support the management of wildlife (and) ... ecotourism'; Chapter 17 states that 'coastal states should explore the scope for expanding recreation and tourist activities based on marine living resources'; Chapter 36 calls for countries to 'promote, as appropriate, environmentally sound leisure and tourism activities ... making suitable use of museums, heritage sites, zoos, botanical gardens, national parks and other protected areas'.

It is clear that the Agenda's emphasis, in respect of its tourism-related content, is on the potential of speciality, nature-oriented, and (by definition) low-capacity tourism to bring about environmental improvement.

But a more ambitious programme of action, with implications for all types of tourism, is set out by the WTTC and the WTO in their document 'Agenda 21 for the travel and tourism industry' (*ibid*). This identifies a number of tourism-related priority areas for action by governments, NTOs, representative trade organisations, and travel and tourism companies. The overall aim of these measures is (for the public sector):

'to establish systems and procedures to incorporate sustainable development considerations at the core of the decision-making process and to identify actions necessary to bring sustainable tourism development into being'; and (for companies): 'to establish systems and

procedures to incorporate suitable development issues as part of the core management function and to identify actions needed to bring sustainable tourism into being.'

(*ibid*)

The impact of Agenda 21 will be reviewed when the United Nations meets in 2005, to follow up the Rio process. Clearly, all of those involved in tourism, with its manifest dependence on environmental quality, have every reason to hope that, by then, some progress will have been made.

THE EUROPEAN POLICY FRAMEWORK

EUROPEAN TOURISM POLICY

EUROPEAN UNION (EU)

Tourism policies and guidelines for particular world regions and groups of trading nations are currently being developed. Particular emphasis is given here to the role of the **European Union (EU)** in this domain, due to its importance for tourism development in the UK.

As a supra-national organisation with statutory powers, the EU is the organisation which has the greatest potential to determine a specific policy framework for the tourism industry of its member countries. In practice, however, the EU's impact on tourism has been slight, and it has only relatively recently turned its attention to this sector.

Many authors mention the importance of domestic and international tourism for EU countries (Barnes and Barnes, 1993; Davidson, 1992; Fitzpatrick Associates, 1993; Hollier and Subremon, 1992). Of the world's top ten tourist destination countries, five are EU member states (France, Spain, Italy, the UK and Germany, in that order) and the EU accounts for approximately 40% of all international tourism arrivals. WTO estimates also show that the EU contains five of the ten most important tourism-

generating countries in terms of expenditure, in order (world ranking in parentheses): Germany (2), the UK (4), Italy (5), France (6), and the Netherlands (8) (Fitzpatrick Associates, 1993).

However, despite its importance, legislators and policy makers have been slow to direct their attention towards this sector, and there has never been a specific EU policy for tourism. One reason for this is suggested by Lickorish:

'The Commission has never accepted a policy for tourism, maintaining in its principle of "subsidiarity" that tourism is a matter for each member state, and that the Commission's intervention followed from other aspects of EU policy and was limited to a number of specific measures.'

(*Lickorish, 1991b*)

Other explanations are suggested by Forbes:

'The failure of the EU to get to grips with tourism at all until the early 1980s is undoubtedly in part a reflection of the low status given to tourism by the public sector in some member states, especially the more economically developed ones, and in part a result of the difficulty in identifying tourism.'

(*Forbes, 1994*)

Nevertheless, since the 1980s, EU administrators' and politicians' attention has been increasingly turned towards the tourism industry, and the number of tourism-related measures flowing out of Brussels has been steadily growing. This increase in involvement in tourism is explained by several economic and social factors.

Tourism's growing economic significance

EU expansion during the 1980s introduced a number of new member countries in which tourism is of major economic importance. With Greece joining in 1981, followed by Spain and Portugal in 1986, the relative importance of tourism to the EU economy as a whole suddenly increased. This coincided with a period of rapid expansion of tourism in other member states, including the five largest (France, Germany, Italy, Spain and the UK), each of which had between 1 and 1.5 million workers employed in tourism by the end of that decade. This expansion and apparent potential (at a time when many other sectors of economic activity in Europe were either experiencing difficulties or contracting) therefore attracted the attention of policy makers within the EU, for which economic growth and employment creation are major objectives. By 1995, the tourism sector of the EU accounted for 5.5% of EU GDP and almost 6% of total employment in terms of jobs directly linked to tourism products and activities (CEC, 1995).

Tourism's redistributive and regional development role

Since much of tourism's potential for economic development and job creation was being realised in regions which would otherwise have had difficulty in finding alternative sources of economic stimulus, this was consistent with another major EU objective – that of regional development. This added advantage of the tourism sector for the EU is emphasised by Akehurst *et al.*

> '[Tourism] also accounts for a high proportion of employment in the poorer countries of the EU, such as Spain, Ireland, Portugal and Greece, and so to some extent in the poorer regions of the higher income countries such as France, Italy and the UK.'
> *(Akehurst et al., 1993)*

Thus, tourism can have the effect of redistributing income within the EU, when tourists travel from the richer densely-populated industrial areas to the poorer, more sparsely-populated rural areas and the coast. In this respect, tourism has come to be regarded by the EU as a sector which offers great potential for helping it achieve its objective of increasing the level of economic activity and employment in the 'peripheral' regions.

> '[Tourism] is an industry which is located in many areas which the EC would like to see further developed, because of long-standing problems of poverty and high levels of unemployment. That is, it frequently works against the tide of development, which draws labour and investment towards the established centres for manufacturing industry and financial services.'
> *(Barnes and Barnes, 1993)*

Tourism as a factor in European integration

Since much tourist activity within Europe involves the movement of people across international borders, there are obvious social benefits to be reaped by the EU in terms of enhanced European integration through intra-EU tourism. Tourism has consequently come to be regarded as having a part to play in furthering the EU objective of promoting international understanding, and strengthening the EU citizens' sense of 'Union'. Barnes and Barnes recognised this characteristic of tourism and concluded that:

> '. . . while the rationale for EC intervention in tourism is essentially driven by economic considerations, the industry does contribute towards the integration of people in a much deeper sense than a number of other industries. It involves contact between people and cultures. This can assist understanding and create a stronger feeling of European identity and citizenship.'
> *(Barnes and Barnes, 1993)*

Tourism as a means of implementing sustainable development

Tourism's dependence on the quality of the environment means that much tourist activity in

EU countries fits into the objective laid down in Article 2 of the Treaty on European Union: to promote 'a harmonious and balanced development of economic activities, sustainable and non-inflationary growth respecting the environment.' The EU 1995 Green Paper on Tourism appears to consider the tourism sector's development as a useful experiment in sustainable development, from which lessons may be drawn and applied to other sectors.

> 'Tourism is a field of action ready-made for implementing sustainable development. In addition, the foreseeable growth of tourism and the pressure which it exerts, allied to an increased demand for quality on the part of tourists, means that such an approach can no longer be delayed ... This approach, which is essential and urgent for the tourist sector, could serve as an example for other activities, the future of which depends to an equal extent, but in a perhaps less directly perceptible way, on ensuring sustainable development.'
>
> *(CEC, 1995)*

As it has become evident that tourism has a role to play in helping the EU achieve many of its own objectives, the EU's decision-making institutions have developed their own structures for the discussion of issues relating to the industry. The European Parliament, whose role is to discuss proposed EU legislation, has its own Committee on Transport and Tourism. The European Commission is responsible for initiating EU policy and ensuring that EU rules are followed by member states. Its Economic and Social Committee also debates issues that relate to the tourism industry. In addition, since 1988, there have been regular meetings between member countries' Ministers of Tourism.

The Commission's 23 Directorates-General (DG) are the equivalent of national government ministries. Within DGXXIII (which has responsibility for Enterprise Policy, Tourism and Social Economy) is a small Tourism Unit. Its role is two-fold:

- to coordinate the efforts of other DGs as they affect tourism

- to coordinate the national efforts of EU member states in the field of tourism.

However, the modest means at the disposal of DGXXIII's Tourism Unit have reflected the low priority which the EU has traditionally given to tourism. The Unit has neither the authority nor the resources to devise a EU tourism policy – nor does it include responsibility for transport, an integral part of the tourism product.

Nevertheless, there have been a number of significant EU initiatives for tourism, beginning in 1982, when a set of proposals for coordinated action by member states was presented by the Commission to the Council of Ministers. These were designed to improve the effectiveness of the tourism industry, and the relevant issues identified were:

- the lengthening of the tourist season
- the preservation of Europe's architectural heritage
- the development of tourism in the less-favoured regions of the EU
- the promotion of social, cultural and rural tourism (Hollier and Subremon, 1990).

These same issues have reappeared throughout the 1980s and 1990s in other EU tourism-related initiatives. These initiatives are:

- the 1986 paper 'Community Action in the Field of Tourism'
- European Tourism Year, 1990
- the Community Action Plan to Assist Tourism 1992–95.

Taken together, these provide an insight into what form a future EU policy for tourism might take.

COMMUNITY ACTION IN THE FIELD OF TOURISM

In 1986, the first real move towards establishing an overall EU policy for tourism was made when the Commission published a paper entitled *Community Action in the field of Tourism* (Commission of the EC, 1986). Building on the general themes of the 1982 document, the 1986 paper concentrated on: facilitation, seasonal and geographical spread, better use of EU funding in tourism development, better information and protection for tourists, improved working conditions, provision of better information on the tourism industry, and the establishment of consultation and coordination between the Commission and member states. The paper's conclusions led the Council of Ministers to adopt a number of measures, including the implementation of a consultation and coordination procedure in tourism. This provided for the setting up of a Tourism Advisory Committee, composed of representatives from the member states and presided over by the European Commission, creating for the first time a formal framework for cooperation between EU countries.

Although this programme of initiatives was generally regarded as a step in the right direction, many in the industry itself were disappointed that there was still no official platform on which their views could be represented, a point emphasised by Lickorish:

> 'The absence of any reference to partnership with the trading sectors was a significant weakness. In the event, resources were scarce and progress restricted to a small number of limited initiatives. It was more a statement of broad long-term aims than a programme of effective action.'
>
> *(Lickorish, 1991b)*

EUROPEAN TOURISM YEAR

In 1988, the Tourism Advisory Committee held their first formal meeting and designated 1990 as **European Tourism Year (ETY)**. The ETY's objectives came close to resembling a broad tourism policy. They were:

> 'To stress the integrating role of tourism in working towards a single internal market, facilitating a greater knowledge of European lifestyles and cultures among citizens of member states, especially younger people' and 'To emphasise the economic and social importance of the sector, in regional policy and job creation and in other aspects.'
>
> *(Commission of the EC, 1990)*

Ministers agreed to initiate or to support a range of activities by the EU, the member states and private organisations involved in tourism. These activities were aimed particularly at achieving the ETY's objectives and at promoting intra-EU tourism and tourism from third countries, as well as a better distribution of tourism over time and place, with proper respect for the quality of the environment.

Some ECU 2.5 million was made available to support a range of activities involving information, service quality and promotion, in particular of products which could extend the season or which fell into favoured categories, such as rural tourism. A further ECU 2.5 million went towards supporting information campaigns, including competitions and prizes. Many authors have expressed the view that the sums of money made available were too modest and that consequently the overall impact of ETY was minimal. Akehurst questions its success and asks, for example, whether most EU citizens really became aware of alternative tourist destinations or the advantages of low-season tourism as a result of ETY (Akehurst, 1992). Barnes and Barnes described the ETY's funding as being:

> '. . . inadequate for the purpose for which it was intended . . . With a reliance on exhortation, and the lack of funding, it is no wonder that little was heard of the campaign outside the limited number of professionals working in the industry.'
>
> *(Barnes and Barnes, 1993)*

In its own assessment of ETY, the Commission maintains that its achievements were the improved exchange of information, and the development of closer links between national administrations, the Commission and trade associations. It claims that useful projects were put forward in the areas of rural, environmental and cultural tourism, and there were initiatives in the area of promoting tourism in relatively underdeveloped areas, such as urban tourism (CEC, 1991a).

Whatever the ETY's degree of success, the designation of 1990 as ETY can be seen as one further manifestation of a move towards a future

EU tourism policy. Indeed, the Commission it-self states:

> 'The effects of ETY should be prolonged long after 1990. It is a prime opportunity to consolidate and develop, in a long-term strategic framework, the Community's various activities in the field of tourism.'
>
> *(CEC, 1990)*

COMMUNITY ACTION PLAN TO ASSIST TOURISM

The EU's most important policy initiative yet in the area of tourism came in the form of a **Community Action Plan to Assist Tourism**, implemented on 1 January 1993 for a duration of three years. The Plan marked a significant step forward for tourism industry involvement in policy discussions at the EU level, since it was prepared in full consultation with representatives from the industry, meeting with the Tourism Advisory Committee. The European Tourism Action Group represented tourism operators, while the European Travel Commission submitted their own recommendations on policy and attended consultative meetings.

The resulting Plan acknowledged the importance of tourism in the EU, the need to take it into consideration in all EU policy making and the need to coordinate EU action in this field. It focused on two main priorities:

- strengthening the horizontal approach to tourism
- supporting specific measures in the field of tourism in the EU.

The European Parliament, in agreeing to the Plan, nevertheless insisted that the principle of subsidiarity be respected, so that the initiatives were taken at the local, regional, national or EU level, as appropriate.

The Plan's aim of strengthening the horizontal approach to tourism was seen as the key to better coordination and cooperation for the industry. Accordingly, it was agreed that the impact of all EU policies would be analysed during the various stages of policy making to ensure that greater account was taken of the impact of these policies on tourism. This would go hand-in-hand with better coordinating of national policies for tourism. Consultation procedures between the tourism industry and trade associations were formalised, with industry having direct links with the Tourism Advisory Committee. The horizontal approach had three other areas of action:

- improving knowledge about the tourism industry: developing EU tourism statistics, implementing studies and research into various aspects of the industry's development
- improving the seasonal and geographical distribution of tourism (e.g. improving the staggering of holidays)
- improving protection for the tourist as consumer – these measures came within the framework of EU consumer policy.

The Plan's proposals for specific measures to assist tourism in the EU included:

- initiatives for the development of rural, cultural, and social tourism – the development of new tourism products, in the interests of diversification and to get a higher proportion of the European population involved in one form or other of tourist activity
- improvement of the environmental features of tourism
- improvement of vocational training programmes for the tourism industry
- transnational measures – including cooperation between local governments and companies in border regions (the so-called 'Euroregions').

Giving the industry's reaction to these measures, Lickorish concludes,

> 'This Plan was welcome to industry representatives, as it responded in large part to their representations. But the official explanation that the programme focused on intervention in a number of specific and limited fields, and did not represent a policy for tourism was a disappointment, reflecting the continuing lack of priority and resources for the industry ... So far as it goes, [it] is

well planned. The assurance of full and continuing consultation and the recognition of the need for essential public–private sector partnership are particularly welcome and offer a firm foundation for future improvement in joint action.'

(Lickorish, 1991b)

Others have expressed disappointment at the Plan's lack of originality and lack of additional funding:

'Much of the Action Plan was simply restating ideas and initiatives that had been in place for some time ... It could be argued that such initiatives are just a token, given that the Community funding for these purposes is available via the Regional Development Fund, the Common Agricultural Policy, and via programmes like LEADER and FORCE.'

(Barnes and Barnes, 1993)

Another industry reaction, from the World Travel and Tourism Council, expresses similar reservations:

'The Tourism Action Plan is inadequately funded at ECU 6 million (US$6.7 million) per year. The results are actions which are too small and fragmented to maximise the industry's potential contribution to growth and job creation. While the measures are worthwhile, the Plan lacks the top level policy commitment and financial support to achieve them.'

(WTTC, 1995)

Regarding initiatives for the development of rural, cultural, environmental and social tourism, the Commission's Economic and Social Committee expressed its own reservations:

'There has not really been a structured policy in these areas. The projects supported, although agreeable, have been mostly on a small scale ... The question is arising more and more of whether enough thought has been given to the way in which money from the Structural Funds is to be used for tourism in accordance with declared objectives. The ESC fears that the aims set out in the Action Plan will, in practice, have little or no influence over decisions on Structural Fund projects. Here too, it seems, there is little talk of coordination.'

(Economic and Social Committee of the EC, 1994)

In fact, the principal value of both ETY and the Action Plan may not lie in the strengths and weaknesses of their individual measures and proposals, but in giving further prominence to tourism in the EU decision-making process and in further establishing tourism within the sphere of the EU's areas of activity. Both measures also provided a base for organising cooperation between member states and stimulating dialogue within the industry, as well as a platform for comparing ideas and experiences, building common projects and developing common strategies.

'The active participation of all the Member States in the actions tested as part of the [Community Action] plan has ... given a real indication of the advantages of transnational cooperation as a tool for tourism growth and European integration.'

(CEC, 1995, p. 20)

TOURISM IN THE WIDER EU POLICY FRAMEWORK

EU ENVIRONMENTAL POLICY

Policies for tourism and those for the environment are closely linked at EU level. DGXI, which has the main responsibility for developing the EU's environmental policy, has put forward a policy and action programme ('Towards Sustainability') to promote sustainable development. This proposes that environmental protection be integrated into other EU policies and identifies tourism as one of five sectors requiring special attention because of its impact and importance. Also in this capacity, the EU is involved as a contracting party to International Conventions aimed at regions particularly affected by tourism, such as the Barcelona Convention on the protection of the Mediterranean, and the Convention on the protection of the Alps (CEC, 1995).

However, EU environmental policies make their greatest impact on tourism when they are translated into mandatory laws. The great majority of EU environmental laws are in the form of Directives. Since the UK (in common with the other Member States) must implement Directives issued by the Council of Ministers by national legislation, the impact of the EU's environmental policy on all forms of economic activity (including tourism) in the UK is substantial.

> 'There can be no doubt that the EC has had a major impact on British environmental policy. Indeed, it is not a great exaggeration to say that much of the Government's policy has been dictated by EC directives.'
> *(Cullingworth and Nadin, 1994, p. 140)*

Two important EU measures serve as illustrations of the importance, for tourism, of the EU environmental policy:

- the 1985 Directive concerning the assessment of the environmental impact of projects
- EU norms for water cleanliness.

While the latter measure has become known to the general public through the 'Blue Flag' scheme which applies to coastal resorts, environmental assessment (EA) also plays an important part in the protection of the natural environment. EA, in the form of a highly systematic quantitative and qualitative review, is now mandatory in all EU countries for proposed large developments. Large tourism-related projects (such as airports, motorways and ports) are now subject to an EA before being granted final approval.

EU INTERNAL MARKET POLICY

The 1992 measures for establishing the internal market were designed to create a favourable environment for the growth of trade between EU member states. Intra-Community tourism stands to gain from the application of those measures, with the most obvious example being the removal of customs checks and formalities at the EU's internal frontiers. But progress is being made towards the completion of other aspects of the internal market which will modify the trading environment within which the tourism industry will operate: the free movement of workers, the right of establishment, the freedom to provide services, and the abolition of tax frontiers. All of these measures should simplify the cross-border establishment of tourist businesses and the freedom of movement of tourism employees throughout the EU, 'all of which will give substance to the idea of a transnational tourist industry and will increase the dynamism of the European tourist industry' (CEC, 1995).

EU TRANSPORT POLICY

The EU Common Transport policy stresses the establishment of a Community framework to ensure sustainable mobility through a global approach. This takes account of an improvement in infrastructures and more rational use of them, increased safety for users, and improved environmental protection. EU actions undertake to help establish and develop trans-European networks in the areas of transport.

Transport policies also have a very direct bearing on the development of tourism within the EU. For example, the deregulation of Europe's air transport which, as a key element of EU aviation transport policy, has potentially very significant consequences for the tourism industry in member states. Air links to the regions are expected to be particularly affected by deregulation, which may thus assist national governments who see the dispersal of tourism away from their respective capital cities as one of their objectives.

EU CONSUMER PROTECTION POLICY

The EU is well placed to legislate for the problems which can arise when consumers purchase a service such as a holiday in another member state. Action at EU level can overcome the complexities which arise when consumers are confronted with problems such as differing conditions applying to contracts, the difficulty of understanding foreign legal systems, and the absence of legal aid in other states.

Tourism has featured prominently in the EU's

Consumer Policy, with several important items of EU legislation being aimed at improving the legal position of the consumer of tourist products. Such legislation has had a significant impact on the legal context within which tourism businesses operate in EU member states. There have been a number of tourism-specific Directives on issues such as time-sharing, compensation for overbooking by the airlines, and the Directive on Package Travel which holds tour operators and travel agents responsible for any failure to deliver holiday packages exactly as described in the brochures, even if it is related to a service provided by a third party.

EU REGIONAL DEVELOPMENT POLICY

The most significant EU financial interventions in the field of tourism are provided by the EU's Structural and Cohesion Funds. These financial instruments are used in conjunction with the EU's Regional Development Policy to strengthen economic and social cohesion within the EU, and reduce disparities between the various regions in the Community. These disparities are considerable. At the end of the 1980s, the average income per capita of the EU's ten least favoured regions (mainly regions of Greece and Portugal) was less than one-third of the average income per head of the ten most prosperous regions. As economic and social cohesion are two of the pillars upon which the EU was built, the Structural and Cohesion Funds are key instruments in the process of promoting the development of the most disadvantaged regions.

There are two main Structural Funds from which the tourism industry particularly benefits:

- **European Regional Development Fund (ERDF)**, established in 1975 to promote economic activities and to finance infrastructural projects in disadvantaged regions
- **European Agricultural Guidance and Guarantee Fund (EAGGF)**, established in 1958, to contribute to the development of rural areas.

While the EAGGF has contributed to initiatives in favour of the development of rural tourism, by far the vast majority of EU financial interventions in the field of tourism have been met by the ERDF. These funds assist the tourism industry in two ways.

1 By helping disadvantaged regions develop their tourism potential: direct investment in tourism projects is used towards the construction of facilities such as marinas, conference centres and airports; and indirect investment in tourism, in the domains of transport infrastructure, telecommunications and environmental enhancement, (which also assist the development of the industry in such regions).
2 Regional assistance is also targeted on areas which are over-dependent on tourism and which may be suffering from its negative impacts. Here, funds are used, for example, to solve environmental problems or to diversify economic activities.

Structural Funds are assigned according to a system of six objectives. For example, for regional development, assistance is concentrated on regions experiencing some kind of difficulty, as defined by Objectives 1, 2 and 5(b):

- **Objective 1**: development and structural adjustment of regions whose development is lagging behind
- **Objective 2**: conversion of regions or parts of regions seriously affected by industrial decline
- **Objective 5(b)**: development of economic activities in rural areas, which creates jobs providing an alternative to employment in agriculture.

Tourism projects in certain regions of EU countries have benefited from these Structural Funds. During the period 1989–93, the tourism industry received between 2% and 20% (depending on the regions involved and objectives concerned) of the Community aid available from the Structural Funds (CEC, 1995).

The actual amount of direct assistance for tourism projects granted to EU member states, between 1989 and 1993, is shown in Figure 6.2.

While these sums amount to considerably more than the ECU 6 million allocated to the Tourism Action Programme, many commentators have been quick to point out that it is still

Country	Obj. 1 (1989–93)	Obj. 2 (1989–93)	Obj. 5 (1989–93)	Total
Greece	243.6			243.60
Spain	182.0		17.68	199.68
France	34.3		105.60	184.00
Ireland	188.6			188.60
Italy	786.0	24.7	51.20	861.90
Portugal	203.0			203.00
UK	46.2	173.9	5.80	225.90
Denmark		0.5		0.50
Germany		5.7		5.70
Netherlands		10.1	9.0	19.10
Belgium		12.9	4.40	17.30
Luxembourg			0.40	0.40
Total	**1683.7**	**271.9**	**194.08**	**2149.68**

Source: Commission of the European Communities

FIGURE 6.2 *Summary table of amounts set aside for tourism within the Community support framework (1989–93) [ECU million]*

derisory when compared to EU spending on other industries. Lickorish graphically demonstrates the disparity:

'The (tourism) industry's workforce, directly and indirectly, approaches – and in some countries exceeds those dependent on agriculture. Yet over 50% of EU funds are devoted to agriculture and less than 1% to tourism.'

(Lickorish, 1991b)

The UK qualifies for EU assistance under all three Objectives 1, 2 and 5(b), with tourism as a significant constituent. Until 1993, Northern Ireland was the UK's only Objective 1 region, but in that year the same status was given to Merseyside and to the Scottish Highlands and Islands. In Northern Ireland, some of the EU funding was specifically set aside to help the tourism industry's development through improved facilities and marketing. Following the drastic decline of its former manufacturing base, Northumbria is of one of the UK regions which

qualifies for EU assistance under Objective 2. In most of that region, up to 45% of the cost of eligible projects is available. Tourism was identified as a priority industry, and the Regional Tourist Board has been successful in attracting EU funds for promotion purposes. For example, the Northumbria conference and group travel initiative, Venue Points North, partnered by the Northumbria Tourist Board, received a £43,000 EU grant towards its revenue funding in 1993 (ETB, 1993).

Recently, application and implementation procedures for resources available through the Structural Funds have been rationalised, to increase their impact and their effectiveness. Lowyck and Wanhill (1992) note that one positive result of this reform has been to improve collaboration between the different levels of government, with real exchanges between the Commission and the other partners at national and, especially, regional level. They also maintain that another impact of the new system of allocation of the Structural Funds is the growth in importance of the regional tourism structures in some member states. Akehurst et al. remark upon this phenomenon in their discussion of tourism development funding:

'... in some countries, there are close links with the EC's financial structure – Ireland, Portugal, Italy and Spain derive a large part of the financial assistance they provide to tourism from the EU's ERDF, and the regional structure of their tourism policy is either already organised according to EU regions or is in the process of being developed to such regions. There is a large degree of overlap between tourism policy and regional policy in the poorer EU member states. Organisationally, there seems to be a shift to regional level ... with the national structure becoming less important (e.g. in Spain, Portugal and Italy). It appears that generally, the EU and individual EU regions are gaining in importance at the expense of national organisations.'

(Akehurst et al., 1993)

In the UK, applications for EU structural funds are coordinated through the regional offices. Tourism commonly features as one of the objectives, and Regional Tourist Boards are involved in drafting these applications as well as sifting individual project bids for the funds.

THE FUTURE OF THE EU TOURISM POLICY

What has been the result of over a decade of EU tourism-related initiatives? What remains to be done before a sound and effective framework for tourism planning and policy within the EU can be said to be established? Many commentators agree with Lickorish's opinion that tourism-specific measures undertaken to date amount to no more than: 'an *ad hoc* and piecemeal approach with a very limited budget and programme of activity, with little attempt to fit tourism into the major policies of the Community' (Lickorish, 1994, p. 155).

Consequently, there has been growing pressure from the European Parliament, most of the southern member states, and many European trade associations, for the EU to assume a much more important role in the field of tourism.

Their chief argument advanced for more EU power in this area is that, at present, DGXXIII has insufficient influence over and input into the policies of other DGs which affect tourism (such as those we have detailed previously under the wider policy framework). It is claimed that, as a consequence, the tourism industry is vulnerable to the unintended negative effects of measures which are drawn up by these other DGs, without due consideration of their potential impact on tourism. Since (as a multi-sectorial, horizontally-structured activity) tourism is affected by the policies of a large number of DGs, it is argued that there is a need for an overarching tourism policy with a long-term outlook, known to and respected by all other DGs.

The northern member states in general (with the exception of Ireland), and the UK and Germany in particular, are opposed to further powers being given to the EU in this area. Their argument is based either on a general opposition to intergovernmental intervention in any form, or on a reluctance to accept a special status for the tourism industry.

Akehurst supports these arguments against the EU intervening further in the tourism industry or regulating its activities, but does not rule out the need for an EU policy framework:

'Given that the tourist industry in Europe is a diverse mixture of private enterprises with public sector involvement, there is perhaps a need not for regulation but for a European sense of direction, of vision within the Council of Ministers supported by a well-briefed European Commission which understands the tourism phenomenon ... What is needed is a policy framework at Community level within which the tourism sector can prosper.'

(Akehurst, 1992)

In recent years, supporters of greater EU intervention in tourism have campaigned for a legal basis for further EU actions in this domain by including this in the Treaties which form the foundation of all EU legislation. The Treaty of Rome (the document which was signed by the original six countries who created the then European Community in 1957) made no specific mention of tourism, which was not an industry of major importance at that time. Since then, all EU actions concerning tourism (including the Tourism Action Plan) have been taken under a 'General Powers' section of the Treaty – the legal justification being that since EU nationals travelling abroad within the EU are considered to be 'recipients of services', tourism is covered by those Articles in the Treaty of Rome, concerning 'the free movement of persons, services, and capital'.

During the discussions leading to the Maastricht Treaty of 1991, the question arose as to whether tourism should be made a specific power or 'competence' of the EU. A tourism competence would raise the EU's actions in the domain of tourism to the same level of political legitimacy as its actions relating to transport and agriculture for example, which are other key EU competencies. Supporters of such a move argued that this was the key to political recognition for the tourism sector, and that, without this, the tourism industry would continue to be exposed to the negative effects of measures taken by other DGs. A tourism competence would also bring with it an increase in staff and financial resources for DGXXIII.

Although a tourism competence was eventually not included in the Maastricht Treaty, a formal commitment was made to re-examine the matter in 1996, when the Treaty was to be revised (Garland, 1995). Subsequently, those campaigning for tourism intervention to be given a legal basis, set their sights on the 1996 revision of the Maastricht Treaty at the **Inter-governmental Conference (IGC)**. In April 1995, a Green Paper on tourism (CEC, 1995), to form part of the discussions leading up to the IGC, was produced by DGXXIII. Garland sums up the arguments advanced by those opposing and those supporting a EU competence for tourism.

'The main arguments against a competence for tourism are: firstly that tourism is, and will remain, primarily a national, regional or local activity, rather than a European one

(the subsidiarity argument); and secondly, that under the General Powers provisions currently used, the EU can, and could continue to, get involved in any tourism matters which have a European dimension. The chief argument advanced for a competence is that at present DGXXIII has insufficient influence over and input into the policies of other DGs affecting tourism, and that a formal competence is the only way to give DGXXIII, a small low-budget unit, the desired influence.'

(Garland, 1995)

The Green Paper proposed the following four options and invited responses from representatives of the various sectors of the tourism industry:

1 A withdrawal from any EU level tourism activities, although tourism projects would continue to benefit from regional development and other funding.
2 A continuance of the status quo – that is, limited action without a formal competence.
3 Increased action, but still without a formal competence.
4 Increased action, but with a formal competence.

Most international professional tourism associations opted for Option 4, with supporters of this option including the European Tour Operators Association, Europarks, the World Travel and Tourism Council (WTTC), the Bureau International du Tourisme Social, and the Alliance Internationale de Tourisme. The WTTC's justification for their choice is that:

'... An EU role for travel and tourism, enshrined in the Treaty on European Union, would help further the Union's goals of growth, employment and competitiveness. At the same time, the Union would also reap the social benefits of enhanced European integration which travel and tourism can uniquely provide as an industry which almost by definition promotes international understanding and strengthens EU citizens' sense of 'Union'.

(WTTC, 1995)

Others, while supporting a tourism competence and the official EU tourism policy which this would entail, stipulated that this should not be interpreted as a wish for more regulatory measures for the tourism industry (Décision Tourisme, 1995).

As for the positions taken on this issue by the member states themselves, these were expressed at a European Tourism Forum held in Brussels in December 1995. Although all were in agreement as to the need for more coordination for tourism in the EU as well as to the need for a continuing role for the EU in this domain, there was no consensus as to what that role should be. Notably, no agreement was reached as to whether more EU staff and funds should be assigned to tourism matters or indeed whether there should be a tourism competence included in the future Treaty. The Options selected by the member states are shown in Figure 6.3.

The official UK response to the document stated that none of the four Options exactly reflected its position, but that it 'could not, under any circumstances, accept a Community competence in the domain of tourism or an increase in EU involvement in this sector'. The UK, it continued, saw no value in a EU policy for tourism, 'believing that the primary responsibility for tourism should be at the national and regional/local levels'.

The rationale which the EU itself gives for its own intervention in tourism matters is given in the same Green Paper. The themes which characterise this rationale are those of:

- conciliation between the sometimes competing aims of business interests, tourists themselves and environmentalists
- coordination.

	Option 1	Option 2	Option 3	Option 4	Other
Austria			●		
Belgium				●	
Denmark					●
Finland			●		
France					●
Germany		●			
Greece				●	
Ireland				●	
Italy				●	
Luxembourg			●[1]		
Netherlands		●			
Portugal			●[2]		
Spain			●[2]		
Sweden					●
UK		●			

[1] Luxembourg has stated that it will not oppose Option 4
[2] Spain and Portugal are likely to move towards Options 3 or 4 during the course of the negotiations

Source: Décision Tourisme, *No. 4, Feb. 1996*

FIGURE 6.3 *The Options selected by the member states*

Conciliation

According to the Green Paper, the EU (through its existing policies for enterprise, consumer protection and the environment) accords each of three poles (enterprise growth, tourist satisfaction, and the protection and renewal of heritage) equal standing with regard to an overall policy.

> '[The] overlap between private . . . and public . . . interests means that in some cases, conflicts have to be prevented and the seemingly divergent interests of groups involved with tourism reconciled (for example, consumer protection with growth of supply, or respect for the natural and cultural environment with creation of activities and jobs, etc).'
>
> *(CEC, 1995)*

As an example of how these conflicting interests are handled in different ways at the national level, the Green Paper draws attention to the divergence of approach between the tourist 'sender' countries (mainly in the north) and the receiver countries (mainly in the south).

> 'The former appear to give priority to the environmental problems linked to tourism, to respect of natural and cultural heritage and to the quality of tourism services, i.e. to demand requirements, while the latter – as a result of partially captive demand – appear to focus on the quantitative growth of private tourism services, sometimes at the expense of the public elements of supply (heritage, culture, protection of the tourist).'
>
> *(ibid., p. 18)*

A EU tourism policy, it is suggested, could serve as a point of reference for the reconciliation of such opposing viewpoints.

Coordination

The Green Paper argues that due to the cross-border nature of tourism (in terms of both tourist areas and tourist flows), a coordinating role is necessary and that such a role could be exercised more efficiently at EU level.

> 'In the field of tourism, more than in certain other areas, the Community could take practical steps to try out coordination methods. First of all, horizontally – since each of the three dimensions acting on the growth of tourism is . . . the focus for a specific Community policy – but also vertically, since several levels (local, regional, national, professional, etc) are involved in promoting or reacting to tourism. Effective mobilisation of the players involved could be achieved via a dual coordination of this kind.'
>
> *(CEC 1995)*

In conclusion:

> 'The value of a Union tourism policy would therefore be built on that which already exists and would move in two directions simultaneously: on the one hand it would ensure that proper consideration is given to the tourism dimension of Community policies with a possible impact on the growth of tourism and, on the other, it would focus on practical ways of combining the three poles of the tourism concept, i.e. on creating a convergence of the interests which have grown up at Community level . . . The acute need for coordination, growth and integrated management of the sector could, then, be met through the formulation – in agreement with the Member States and the professionals concerned – of EU guidelines which take account of the three complementary dimensions of tourism.'
>
> *(CEC, 1995)*

'PHILOXENIA' – A FIRST MULTIANNUAL PROGRAMME TO ASSIST EUROPEAN TOURISM

In 1996, the Commission submitted a proposal for the first Multiannual Programme to Assist Tourism 1997–2000. This sought to 'ensure continuity of Community action in this field whilst, at the same time, rationalising it and deepening it by taking greater account of European tourism as a phenomenon with a major economic and social impact'.

The proposal was made in the context of growing concern over Europe's declining market share of world tourism, with destinations such as those in South and Southeast Asia and the Americas becoming increasingly competitive, offering top quality infrastructure, facilities and service. The rationale behind the Philoxenia Programme of action is based on a number of quality and professionalism-related problems, caused by:

- complacency due to Europe's status as the predominant destination since the 1960s
- historically, a lack of recognition within government of the importance of the industry
- outdated facilities and poor infrastructure requiring wholescale regeneration of particular types of destination
- a diverse and highly fragmented industry, most of which are SMEs, often resulting in less coherent policy formation and ineffective coordination at many levels
- a large number of sub-sectors which have historically not worked together in the most effective manner
- over-concentration in terms of both the products offered and the destinations served, leading to standardisation of the product, over-development of certain areas and under-development of others
- limited use of strategic planning and tax development controls with consequent negative impacts on often fragile and built environments
- a short-term investment culture which has served to reduce the ability to plan tourism strategically in the longer term
- poor training provision and lack of an industry image (CEC, 1996).

The proposal claimed that the actions it contained all had a common denominator: they were not, or could not be, satisfactorily under-taken at the local, regional or national level. In addition, they aimed to make other Community measures which were relevant to tourism more cohesive.

In line with the Conciliation role which the EU has identified for itself (regarding its interventions in tourism), the document claims that the Philoxenia Programme responds to the needs of the tourist and the protection of the natural and cultural heritage. But the ultimate objective, however, was to stimulate the quality and competitiveness of European tourism, in order to contribute to growth and employment. The actions and objectives of the proposed programme are shown in Figure 6.4.

With its emphasis on 'partnership, cooperation, and consultation with the member states and the tourism industry', the Philoxenia Programme appears to have been developed according to the procedures suggested by Akehurst et al. (1993) in defining what they considered were the steps towards implementing a well-designed tourism policy for the EU. According to them, it would:

1 Identify and prioritise within the EU the policy problems.
2 Agree what needs to be done and what the EU is hoping to achieve.
3 Establish effective coordination and implementation of agreed programmes to solve the identified policy programmes.
4 Monitor and evaluate these programmes to determine policy performance.

These still provide useful criteria against which the implementation of any future EU policy for tourism may be measured.

Ultimate objective	Intermediate objectives	Immediate objectives	Actions
Stimulating quality and competitiveness of European tourism, in order to contribute to growth and employment	A Improving knowledge in the field of tourism	1 Developing tourism-related information 2 Pooling tourism information from other sources 3 Facilitating the assessment of Community measures affecting tourism	• European statistical system for tourism • surveys, studies and desk/field analysis • European research and documentation network on tourism • establishment of a legal and financial watch
	B Improving the legislative and financial environment for tourism	1 Reinforcing cooperation with Member States, the industry and other stakeholders	• organisation and follow up of regular meetings (technical/thematic meetings, round-tables, European fora)
	C Raising quality in European tourism	1 Promoting sustainable tourism	• local initiatives network • environmentally-friendly management systems • European Prize
		2 Removing obstacles to tourism development	• identification of obstacles and development of appropriate responses
	D Increasing the number of tourists from third countries	1 Promoting Europe as a tourist destination	• support for multiannual promotion campaigns

FIGURE 6.4 *Programme model*

Source: CEC (1996)

THE NATIONAL POLICY FRAMEWORK

NATIONAL TOURISM POLICIES

CENTRAL GOVERNMENTS AND NATIONAL TOURISM POLICY

The role of the state at the national level as landowner, as provider of infrastructure, and as beneficiary or victim of the positive and negative impacts of tourism, means that central governments are necessarily involved in determining the shape of tourism development within the territories under their control. The cross-sectoral nature of the industry also means that it is affected by a wide range of central government polices for areas such as the environment, education, and transport, as well as the macro-economic and fiscal policies of governments.

Governments can choose to adopt a more active, direct role for themselves, by providing a measure of leadership, direction and coordination specifically for the tourism industry. The diverse and fragmented nature of the tourism industry means that governments, if they choose to do so, can agree a unifying purpose for their countries' tourism businesses, and provide a framework and direction in which the different elements of the industry can move forward together. Referring to the 'diversity of the activities which collectively constitute the tourism industry', Wheatcroft emphasises this function of governments.

> 'All corporate planning must start from a precise definition of the purpose of the business or the "mission role" ... In a normal business organisation, this is something on which the board of directors and the owners can and must agree. The basic purpose of the tourism industry is, however, something which only governments can agree. And, if they do not, the tourism industry is likely to be left with some impossibly difficult decisions about its future course of development.'
>
> *(Wheatcroft, 1989)*

The most explicit manifestation of a government's stated purpose for tourism is its national tourism policy.

The extent of governmental intervention in tourism varies from country to country and the existence of published national tourism policy documents is by no means universal. In a survey of such documents, Baum notes that almost one in four of the countries responding to his questionnaire, reported having no published official national policy for tourism. He suggests that in countries where tourism has a long-standing history (in most cases, more developed countries), it is likely that the industry has evolved over this period of time without specific policy guidance. 'Where tourism, as an industry, has a rather shorter history, the guiding role of a formally articulated statement of policy and the existence of a specific ministry are likely to be deemed of greater importance' (Baum, 1994).

A simpler explanation may be that not all countries are equally interested in tourism. The level of government interest in this sector is likely to reflect, above all, the actual or potential importance of tourism within the economy. The governments of those countries in which the place of the tourism industry within the national economy is very limited – and likely to remain so – may be less motivated to draw up a policy for this sector.

Nevertheless, the growing importance of the tourism industry for many countries (developed and developing) means that increasingly there is a tendency for them to develop some form of national tourism policy. Lickorish emphasises this:

> 'In the developed countries, there is also a need for a tourism policy. Government must set out the parameters within which it wants to see tourism develop. It should guide the private sector by clearly indicating what type and volume of tourism is acceptable, and in which locations. Government should interact with levels of local government to encourage tourism in specific regions.'
>
> *(Lickorish, 1991a)*

POLICY ISSUES AND OBJECTIVES

The formulation of objectives for tourism policies at a national level inevitably reflects governments' wider political, economic, environmental and social priorities. Just as at the EU level, national governments' principal interest in tourism most often concerns the possibilities for using it to achieve their own wider objectives. Tourism policy objectives particularly tend to reflect governments' general economic objectives regarding factors such as economic growth, employment creation and balance of trade.

Moreover, as national priorities and circumstances change, so too do the objectives of tourism policies. Changes in these objectives are linked not only to changes in governments' general objectives for economic, social or environmental development on the national scale, but also to modifications in their own political philosophy. 'The degree of importance accorded to any one objective as well as the means chosen to implement it are ... a direct function of the overall economic climate and the ideology of the political party in power' (Joppe, 1989).

In the OECD's annual reports describing the national tourism policies of member countries, certain broad trends emerge, showing how the objectives of national tourism policies have evolved over the years. Reviewing these reports, Williams and Shaw provide the following analysis of how national tourism policies of OECD members have evolved over the years, in line with their changing priorities:

> 'Post 1945 tourism policies can be divided into three distinct phases: in the late 1940s and 1950s, there was a need to dismantle and streamline the many police, currency, health and customs regulations which were the legacy of a war and immediate post-war situation; in the 1960s, governments moved more into promotion as they became aware of the "dollar gap" and hence the need to increase their earnings of both dollars and any other hard currency; while, latterly, governments have become concerned with the problems of tourism supply and with the link between this and regional development.'
>
> *(Williams and Shaw, 1991)*

They add that by the 1970s and early 1980s, broader social and environmental issues had become dominant issues in the tourism policies, at least of northern Europe.

One of the earliest studies of different countries' tourism policy issues was undertaken by Airey in 1983. This showed the principal issues in the tourism policies of Belgium, France, the Federal Republic of Germany, Italy, the Netherlands and the UK between 1972 and 1982, by frequency of mention. These were, in descending order of priority: regional develop-

ment, seasonality, consumer protection, balance of payments, social tourism, rural/green tourism, and environmental protection (Airey, 1983).

However, regardless of the emphasis given to such worthy issues as seasonality and consumer protection in published policies, there is no doubt that the continuing preoccupation of national governments *vis à vis* their tourism industries is to reap the economic benefits it brings, particularly in terms of foreign revenue.

This is clearly demonstrated by Baum's more recent research survey into the determinants of national tourism policies, which widens the scope of the countries surveyed to include developing countries. He usefully categorises NTOs' replies to his survey by national economic criteria, dividing responses into three subgroups:

- **Group A** – those countries with a per capita income of less than US$1,000 (39% of total responses)
- **Group B** – those with a per capita income between US$1,000 and US$8,000 (18% of total responses)
- **Group C** – those with a per capita income greater than US$8,000 – which includes the UK (41% of total responses).

The survey generated average ratings for eight key objectives of national tourism policies, and these are shown in Figure 6.5 (Baum, 1994).

Determinant/factor	Ranking/average rating			
	Full sample	A	B	C
To generate foreign revenue/assist balance of payments	1/1.92	1/1.75	1/1.86	1/2.15
To provide employment nationally	2/2.66	2/2.58	2/2.71	2/2.69
To improve regional/local economy	3/3.10	3/2.86	3/3.00	3/3.45
To create awareness about country	4/3.78	5/4.13	5/3.83	4/3.54
To provide employment regionally/locally	5/3.79	4/3.82	4/3.80	5/3.77
To support environment/public conservation	6/5.00	7/6.00	7/5.50	6/4.77
To contribute to infrastructural development	7/5.11	6/4.69	6/4.86	8/6.80
To create international goodwill	8/5.65	7/6.00	7/5.50	7/5.50
Number of respondents	37[a]	16	7	13

Note:
a: One respondent unidentified according to group

Source: Baum (1994)

FIGURE 6.5 *Ranking of main determinants of national tourism policies*

It is clear that economic and employment-related factors were accorded overwhelming priority, both overall and within the three sub-groups. The generation of foreign exchange, the provision of employment and regional economic development were consistently the top three objectives mentioned.

These results are confirmed by Akehurst *at al.*, in their survey of national tourism policies of the member states of the EU. Once again, the economic focus of national tourism policies is significant in the prominence it is given by respondents. Figure 6.6 lists the rankings by country.

The highest average score (4.7) is received by the objective of 'Increasing the expenditure of foreign tourists', which gained almost twice as many maximum scores (10) as any other objective in the survey. The second highest ranking objective 'to improve product quality' is clearly linked with the first. These are followed in order of importance by two redistributive objectives 'to reduce seasonality' and 'to redistribute tourism' (geographically), as well as the objective of increasing the number of foreign tourists. The authors note that the redistributive objectives were ranked particularly highly by the southern European states, where demand for tourism is concentrated in a few congested coastal resorts during the July–September period. Nevertheless, it is worthy of note that, overall, respondents gave these redistributive objectives more prominence than two of the traditional economic objectives of increasing employment and increasing the size of the industry.

> 'Job creation seems to be a key objective in government policy towards tourism only in Ireland and Belgium, which have historically suffered from high rates of unemployment by EU standards, and in Germany.
> Elsewhere, it was ranked below other objectives, even though on a European-wide level tourism is a labour intensive sector.'
>
> *(Akehurst et al. 1993)*

Objectives serve essentially as principles, and must be translated into reality by a wide range of agencies and authorities. Among the most important of those authorities are the **National Tourism Organisations (NTO)**, which, as bodies funded wholly or partly by governments, are, throughout Western Europe, the most direct manifestations of the State's interest in tourism.

NATIONAL TOURISM ORGANISATIONS (NTO)

As major elements in the institutional framework for tourism in Western European countries, **National Tourism Organisations (NTOs)** (or National Tourism Offices, Administrations or Boards) are the primary instruments – and often producers – of their sponsoring governments' tourism policies.

In Baum's survey, 86% of responding countries reported the existence of a NTO, operating as a government agency with the aim of developing tourism in that country. 74% of all respondents reported 'Tourism policy development' as being one of their functions (rising to 78% for Group C countries only).

Responsibility for tourism and the operation of NTOs is held by a diversity of government departments. Baum's respondents from the most developed countries, indicated that almost half of these had placed tourism in economic and employment-related departments, reflecting their principal interest in tourism. Developing countries were found to be much more likely to have specific tourism ministries, or at least ministries including 'tourism' as part of a longer title (Baum, 1994).

As significant instruments for the implementation of their governments' tourism policies, NTOs provide an insight into those policies, through the range of activities included in their portfolios. These differ greatly from country to country, but certain activities are practically always undertaken:

- international and domestic marketing of the country as a whole
- the provision of tourist information
- the collection and analysis of tourism statistics.

In other words, the NTOs provide those services which the private sector itself is least likely to undertake on a national scale.

The value of overseas promotion speaks for it-

Country	Aggregate size and employment levels in the industry							Structure, quality and seasonality of the industry								
	[1] Increase industry size	[2] Create employ-ment	[3] Increase expenditure (a) Domestic	[3] (b) Foreign	[4] Increase numbers of tourists (a) Domestic	[4] (b) Foreign	[5] Diversi-fication to tourism	[6] Redis-tribute tourism	[7] Assist restruc-turing	[8] Improve product quality	[9] Reduce season-ality	[10] Provide expert advice	[11] Regulate industry	[12] Encourage joint initiatives	[13] Improve training and profession-alism	[14] Promote environ-mental tourism
Belgium (1)	4	5	2	3	3	4	2	3	3	5	3	2	4	2	3	5
(2)	5	2	3	5	4	5	0	1	1	5	3	2	3	4	2	3
Denmark	4	4	4	4	3	3	2	2	2	3	4	4	0	5	5	0
France (3)	4	1	1	5	1	5	2	5	2	4	5	4	2	5	2	2
Germany	0	5	0	5	0	5	0	3	0	4	2	3.5	0	1	2	4
Greece	2	2	4	5	0	0	1	4	0	3	4	2	4	3	3	3
Ireland	4	5	1	5	0	5	4	4	3	4	4	3	3	3	5	4
Italy	5	4	3	5	4	5	2	4	2	5	5	3	3	2	5	5
Luxembourg	5	2	1	4	1	4	4	4	1	3	5	4	3	5	3	2
Netherlands	3	3	5	5	4	4	3	4	1	4	4	3.5	1	5	2	3
Portugal	2	3	2	5	0	0	0	5	4	5	5	4	3	4	5	5
Spain	4	3	5	5	4	4	0	4	3	5	4	3	0	0	2	2
U.K.	3	4	0	5	0	5	0	4	0	4	4	4	0	3	3	2
Average	3.5	3.3	2.4	4.7	1.8	3.8	1.5	3.6	1.7	4.2	4.0	3.2	2.0	3.2	3.2	3.1
No. of maximum scores	3	3	2	10	0	8	0	2	0	5	4	0	0	4	4	3

(1) French department. (2) Flemish department. (3) Maison de la France.

FIGURE 6.6 Ranking of policy objectives – NTOs

Source: Akehurst et al. (1993)

self, with most countries vying with each other to increase the numbers and spending of their visitors from abroad. But the collection and analysis of tourism statistics also plays a vital role as an aid to effective tourism planning by the state and by tourism businesses. This importance of this essential public sector function was underlined by the authors of the annual OECD tourism report in 1989:

> 'The State's role in tourism will be increasingly judged on its ability to provide industry and other levels of government with the information they need to draw up their own investment and communications strategies ...'
>
> *(OECD, 1989)*

But these basic functions are only a fraction of the range of responsibilities with which governments can entrust their NTOs, if they choose to do so. The survey by Akehurst *et al.* showed that even within the fairly homogenous group of countries which comprise the EU, there are significant differences in the range of functions accorded by member states to their NTOs. The authors give this explanation for the differences:

> 'In general, it appears that NTOs tend to be stronger and have a wider remit in member states which:
> (a) have a comparatively high proportion of GDP generated by tourism;
> (b) have governments which are '*dirigiste*' rather than *laissez-faire* in their approach to economic management generally.'
>
> *(Akehurst et al. 1993)*

Within the EU, there are two main tendencies as follows.

- The national tourism policy of northern European states (such as Denmark, Germany, the Netherlands and Belgium) extends little beyond assistance with international marketing and the collection of tourism statistics through the NTO. In those countries with a liberal market-driven ethos, therefore, NTO activities are restricted to what might be regarded as the bare minimum functions.
- At the other end of the scale come the much more '*dirigiste*' Mediterranean states (such as Spain, Portugal, Greece and France), whose NTOs' activities extend in some cases to the management of certain aspects of the tourism industry (e.g. hotels – Spanish *paradores*, museums, and cultural centres) and to such interventionist actions as the compulsory inspecting, grading and licensing of hotels and restaurants, as well as regulating travel agents and tour operators.

It will be shown that the UK lies somewhere between these two groups in its approach.

The issue of the NTO's funding provides another distinguishing characteristic between them. Although all EU member states' NTOs receive the greater part of their funding through government grants, the majority of them also have non-governmental revenue sources:

- the sale of advertising space in promotional brochures
- membership subscriptions from private sector members
- contributions from the private sector towards specific promotional campaigns.

The Akehurst *et al.* survey showed the Netherlands to be the EU member state which raises the highest proportion of private finance (at 49%) to fund NTO initiatives. The Dutch government has a stated target of 50% private funding. The French government, by comparison, with 44% private funding for their NTO (Maison de la France) does not want its industry contribution to rise any higher, as it wishes to retain control of the strategy of MDLF. The British Tourist Authority (BTA) with 34% of its funding coming from the private sector, is seeking to increase this proportion by selling advisory and information services.

GOVERNMENT POLICIES FOR TOURISM TOWARDS THE 21ST CENTURY

What general direction are the national tourism polices of Western developed countries taking as the 20th century draws to an end? Governments of all countries operate in the context of global trends and developments, and all of their strategies and actions, including those in respect of tourism, have been evolving to keep pace with these changes.

The OECD 1996 report on the tourism policies of its member countries identifies the general global trends affecting tourism as: 'the difficult macroeconomic situation, environmental and security issues, emphasis on quality, increased competition between countries and the globalisation of the economy'. The same report goes on to identify the main developments in the national tourism policies of member countries. Cooperation and coordination emerge as major themes:

> 'The main objectives of policies are changing, influencing in turn the development and organisation of institutions. Tourism is becoming a complex and multidisciplinary activity. As a response, national tourism administrations increasingly build coordination between ministries into their strategies, in particular for transport, employment, the environment, culture and industry. Cooperation with regional and local authorities is also gaining ground and several countries have set up committees bringing together all partners to put forward regional and local policy initiatives.
>
> To formulate their strategies, governments are creating mechanisms for discussion and/or partnership with the private sector. Some member countries moreover have completely restructured the administration of tourism, partially privatising the units responsible for policy, marketing and promotion. Most countries now give representatives of the tourist industry more say (through advisory committees) whilst reserving the right to define tourism strategy. As far as promotion and marketing are concerned, the private sector is usually very closely involved and financial partnership is in place. However, full privatisation is rare.'
>
> *(OECD, 1996)*

TOURISM IN THE WIDER NATIONAL POLICY FRAMEWORK

Tourism policy (as expressed through the activities of NTOs and as laid down in the national policy documents) represents only one part of the overall picture of public-sector intervention in tourism, and not necessarily the most important. The State's power to legislate and regulate on a wide range of issues affecting tourism (from transport and the arts, to environmental issues and Sunday shop trading) gives it extensive scope to determine the shape of the tourism industry.

Pearce argues that 'while the activities of the NTOs may influence the path of tourist development directly, other more general or more indirect powers exercised by other central government agencies may also have a significant and perhaps greater impact' (Pearce, 1989). Indeed, many believe that governments, with their wide-ranging responsibilities, can even inadvertently undo or undermine their NTOs' marketing efforts, for example, by neglecting aspects which have an important impact on visitors' impressions of the destination. Even governments which are well-intentioned and well-disposed towards tourism can unintentionally put obstacles in the way of their tourism industry's success, as emphasised in *The Economist*'s analysis of Europe's tourism handicaps:

> 'Governments are trying to help ... Too bad that such efforts are undermined by poor policies in other areas of government. Sometimes the trouble is a bolshie immigration officer. Too often, a shabby airport and a bumpy road is a visitor's first and last view of a country ... Add poor signposting, parking and traffic jams around sites and it becomes clear that government-run infrastructure is also in much need of reform.'
>
> *(The Economist, 1995b)*

Two of the most important fields of general government policy affecting tourism are now considered: national economic and social policies. Other central government policies with relevance for tourism will be examined in the section of this chapter dealing with national tourism policy in the UK.

NATIONAL ECONOMIC POLICIES

One of the major impacts which governments have on the tourism industry arises from their power to influence the national economic environment within which any business must operate. In setting their macroeconomic policies, central governments exercise considerable powers over all businesses operating in their countries, including those in the tourism sector.

In line with their particular monetary and budgetary policies, governments regulate to support and stimulate the national economy. Supply-side and demand-side measures may be taken, and most of these will have some impact on tourism. An example of a possible measure, which can have significant consequences for national tourism, is the devaluation of a country's currency. Although rarely undertaken on behalf of the tourism industry alone, any devaluation has nevertheless a considerable positive impact on that industry by giving it a temporary competitive edge. Holidays in a country which has devalued its currency become less expensive (and therefore more attractive) for foreign visitors. Conversely, holidays abroad become more expensive for the residents of the country whose currency has been devalued and this may have a positive impact on domestic tourism.

The adjusting of interest rates is an example of a demand-side measure which has an impact on the level of tourist demand. Raising interest rates can have the effect of reducing the amount of disposable income available to homeowners with mortgages to repay; and money to pay for tourism, a non-essential activity, must come out of homeowners' residual income. By the same token, lowering interest rates brings down the cost of credit available to consumers and some of this may be used to purchase tourism products.

However, central governments' active involvement in tourism is also of interest, as it offers an insight into their attitude towards this sector and the objectives they hope to achieve through it. The essence of active involvement is the range of governments' supply-side and demand-side measures which discriminate in favour of the tourism sector.

One example of an active supply-side measure is governments' use of VAT as a fiscal incentive to the tourism industry. Member states are permitted by the EU to levy VAT at a rate lower than the standard rate for certain goods and services. At the beginning of the 1990s, nine of the then twelve EU member states had chosen to exercise this right for their hotel sectors (Hotrec, 1990). The effect of this simple measure was to reduce hotel tariffs in the countries concerned, making them more attractive to tourists. Such direct measures are often much more beneficial to the tourism industry of the country concerned than most systems involving government grants and subsidies, or subsidised loans. The revival of Ireland's tourism industry coincided with the decision of the Irish government to cut VAT rates on hotels from a standard (20%) to a reduced (10%) rate in 1983/84 (Akehurst *et al.*). Such measures may also bring benefits to the government itself, when there is evidence of a 'laffer curve' effect: lower tax rates may in certain cases generate higher tax revenues because of the expansion of the industry which a reduction in VAT rates can stimulate.

As part of their general economic policies, national governments may also intervene by offering a range of financial incentives. Such incentives are usually administered by State agencies. Wanhill (1994) lists the different types of incentives which governments use, and divides these into financial incentives and measures offering investment security.

- **Financial incentives** are designed to improve returns to capital so as to attract developers and investors. They may include measures which lead to reductions in capital costs (grants, 'soft' loans, equity participation, the provision of infrastructure, the provision of land on concessional terms, or tariff exemption on construction materials) and measures which lead to reductions in operating costs, to improve operating viability.

Measures which lead to reductions in operating costs include direct and indirect tax exemptions, labour or training subsidies, subsided tariffs on key inputs such as energy, or special depreciation allowances. For example, an idea for an interesting labour incentive was put forward in 1985 by the Trade and Industry Committee of the UK House of Commons, when it recommended that, on an experimental basis, the government should pay a grant of 30% towards the employment costs of tourist facilities remaining open for one month longer than the previous year. This incentive, never adopted, was aimed at extending the season, reflecting the employment creation objective which was a feature of the UK tourism policy of that time.

■ **Measures offering investment security** are measures which are developed to win investors' confidence. Tourism is very sensitive to the political environment and the economic climate, and therefore often regarded as high-risk in some countries by potential investors. Action to provide greater investment security may include such measures as guarantees against nationalisation, a reduction in administrative delays and simplified planning procedures.

The extent of any individual government's use of such incentives depends, as always, on its economic and political philosophy. Wanhill comments that 'The trend towards pure market-led economics in recent years has led to a clawback of state involvement and the questioning of incentives as mechanisms more likely to lead to market distortions.'

Within Europe, however, almost every government still continues to use some form of incentive, however diminished. Once again, it is the highly-interventionist governments of the Mediterranean states of Greece, Spain and Portugal which provide the greatest range of financial incentives to private enterprise in the tourism sector, even investing directly in that industry. France has occasionally assisted the infrastructural costs of specific tourism developments, for example in the Languedoc-Roussillon development and more recently in Disneyland, Paris.

In the UK, direct government financial support is channelled through a variety of agencies in the form of grants and subsidies. The role of these agencies will be examined later in this chapter.

NATIONAL SOCIAL POLICIES

National governments, as well as regulating economic activity, can also intervene to redistribute the wealth produced by that activity. In the case of tourism, the rationale behind such intervention arises from a consideration of the social and cultural importance of tourism for the individual. Hughes notes that some governments consider tourism as an example of 'merit goods', i.e. commodities which are regarded as being so important to the well-being of the individual that consumers should not be prevented from consuming them because of low income or ignorance (Hughes, 1984).

Governments can take a range of measures which, directly or indirectly, bring certain disadvantaged groups in society into the market of tourism (and which at the same time assist the tourism industry). Joppe describes the possibilities for such intervention:

'The government has a wide range of options at its disposal. The basic income can be fixed through minimum-wage legislation family and rent allowances, child benefits etc. can increase the basic income for many households; vacation funds or holiday vouchers, reduced cost of transportation or lodging, holiday villages subsidised by public funds, etc. are some of many possibilities to help people overcome the revenue barrier to vacations.'

(Joppe, 1989)

Some of these measures (e.g. minimum wage legislation, child benefits) represent passive involvement, not specific to the tourism industry, while others (e.g. holiday vouchers, vacation funds, subsidised tourism services) are examples of active involvement which specifically discriminates in favour of the tourism sector. The latter group of measures comprises the essence of social tourism, which, although practically non-existent in the UK (where tourism – unlike leisure – has always been regarded solely as a commercial activity) is widespread in Continental Europe. (See Richards, 1992 for a full discussion of this topic.)

The objective of social tourism policies is to 'allow the maximum number of people to go on holiday ... for the lowest possible daily cost' (Vellas and Bécherel, 1995). France, for example, uses an extensive system of Chèques-Vacances: holiday vouchers for low-income families. One million employees and their families benefited from this scheme in 1993, when FF1.285 billion (approx. £130 million) was paid out by the State. Since the Chèques-Vacances represent between 15% and 35% of the holiday budgets of their beneficiaries, the induced expenditure they generate for the tourism industry is four times the value of the vouchers distributed. The French government uses the Chèques-Vacances system to achieve its own objective of stimulating tourism development in specific areas, for example, by channelling such holiday-makers to rural areas which are in need of supplementary economic activity (METT, 1995)

UK NATIONAL TOURISM POLICY

GOVERNMENT OBJECTIVES

The path towards a formal government policy for tourism in the UK has been slow and circuitous.

Central government intervention in tourism over the years has been fairly sporadic, and overall the industry has received relatively little government attention, despite its economic importance. The situation is best summed up in the statement that 'in the UK, successive government policy on tourism has advanced little beyond regarding it generally as "a good thing".' (Shaw, Williams and Greenwood, 1987). More bluntly, Lord Clinton-Davis of Hackney, then Opposition Transport Spokesman in the House of Lords, stated in 1994 at the Tourism Society's Annual Conference, that tourism was treated as 'an appendage to government', dealt with by a variety of Government Departments, and presided over by a 'junior minister in the Department of Heritage'.

Direct government provision of facilities or of subsidies for tourism has been minimal, and there has been very little regulation aimed specifically at this sector. Traditionally, commentators have attributed this inaction to one or both of two factors:

- the belief (on the part of successive UK governments) that tourism was a lightweight industry of little significance
- governments' tacit acknowledgement that its own room for manoeuvre was severely limited, with the vast majority of the tourism industry being under the direct control of private enterprise.

In his detailed chronology of the politics of UK tourism, Richards (1995) demonstrates how the development of tourism policy can be linked to wider political, social and economic developments affecting the UK in the 20th century. He traces the gradual rise in UK government intervention in tourism from the 1930s, depicting the slow transition of the national administration of tourism from a non-statutory voluntary affair to becoming, by the end of the 1960s, an official part of the mechanism of the state.

Governments' primary interest in tourism in the UK has been to use it as means of achieving their own objectives, and these objectives have evolved throughout the years. Crawshaw is one of many authors to point out the:

'... changing attitude towards (UK) government intervention in tourism and changes in tourism policy ... Successive governments have viewed tourism in terms of the long term national objectives of economic growth, balance of payments, employment and regional balance.'

(Crawshaw, 1993)

In any case, the considerations which have led to public sector intervention in tourism in the UK have always been essentially economic in nature, with governments attempting to use tourism in order to achieve economic benefits. Demonstrating this, ministerial guidelines were issued in 1974, stressing tourism's role in both the UK's balance of payments and as an aid to promoting regional development. The introduction that year of Tourism Growth Points, concentrating financial assistance for tourism development in a number of economically-fragile areas of England, signalled an early recognition of tourism's potential to meet the government's regional policy objectives. However, during the 1980s, faced with substantial job losses through the restructuring of the UK's manufacturing industry, the government laid more emphasis on tourism's job creation potential, in common with many governments throughout Western Europe.

Richards (1995) notes that the re-creation of tourism as work served to boost government interest. The link between tourism and employment was consolidated by the publication of the report *Pleasure, Leisure and Jobs* (HMSO, 1985), which spelt out the employment creation potential of tourism, and the subsequent relocation of ministerial responsibility for tourism from the Department of Trade to the Department of Employment.

Further evidence of the new focus on employment creation is seen in the changing objectives of the ETB. By 1987, the primary objective had become: 'to maximise tourism's contribution to the economy through the creation of wealth and jobs'.

More recent objectives reflect ideological shifts in the wider political area, principally the 1990s emphasis on value-for-money and the cost effectiveness of government intervention in tourism:

'The change in policy emphasis is reflected in the objectives of the BTA after 1988. From 1988 onwards, objectives relating to the "provision and improvement of visitor amenities" and "complementing the work of the national tourist boards within Britain" were dropped. In their place, came references to ensuring that the BTA make "the most cost-effective use of resources in pursuing its objectives" and "stimulate the improvement of the quality of product"'

(ibid)

The most striking changes occurred in the use of language, however. Whereas the key phrases in objectives statements prior to 1988 were 'partnership', 'advising government', 'encouraging

provision', and 'encouraging support for the trade', by 1991 these had changed to acting where 'intervention will be effective', 'improving deficiencies' and identifying 'significant gaps unfilled by the market'. By 1994, the role of the BTA was characterised as being 'to deliver to our "shareholder" – the government on behalf of the taxpayer – and to our commercial partners the best possible return on their investment in BTA' (*ibid*).

NATIONAL TOURIST BOARDS

It is generally acknowledged that public sector support for tourism in the UK entered a new phase with the passing of the 1969 Development of Tourism Act. Shaw *et al.* (1991), for example, describe this development as 'the most significant legislation to date'.

The first two sections of the Act introduced the temporary provision of financial assistance for hotel development and gave government officials the right to inspect and grade hotels. Of these sections, the first resulted in an additional 55,000 bedrooms being added to the hotel stock, mainly in London; the second has never been fully implemented, successive governments preferring to accept the hotel industry's preference for a voluntary system of classification and grading.

The third section of the Act established four statutory boards – the **British Tourist Authority** (**BTA**), together with the three national boards – for England (**ETB**), Scotland (**STB**) and Wales (**WTB**). In Northern Ireland, a tourist board had been established much earlier through the Development of Tourism Act 1948. Under the Act, the BTA, ETB, STB and WTB were classified as Non-Departmental Public Bodies, which kept them at arm's length from the usual ministries of state.

The main functions of the tourist boards, as set out in the Act have changed very little since 1969. While the BTA promotes tourism to Britain in overseas countries and carries out research into trends in international tourism, the national tourist boards undertake a range of promotional activities directed at the UK domestic market and carry out statistical surveys. In addition to their primary role of marketing, Section 4 of the Act gave the boards a development function, with powers to guide and shape the provision and improvement of tourism facilities on the ground by offering financial assistance. Through the Section 4 grants scheme, the national boards distributed financial aid to encourage investment in tourism development. The ETB's power to award such tourism investment incentives was suspended in 1989. This followed a review of the operation of the ETB and BTA, which included looking at the cost-effectiveness of such funding at a time when grant aid to other industries had been stopped. The political argument for suspension was that tourism in England was now mature and no longer needed government support.

This reasoning is based on the 'infant industry' case for public subsidy, the explanation for the discontinuation being that in the case of tourism, the 'infant' had grown up. However, as Wanhill (1996) points out, this argument is difficult to substantiate, since the majority of tourism establishments in Britain are small in scale. Wanhill suggests that a better explanation can be found in the political climate of the time, which favoured a clawback of public expenditure and giving private markets a greater say in resource allocation, adding: 'In a product as complicated as "the tourist trip", this is somewhat simplistic when judged against the requirement to develop a balanced range of facilities to meet the demands of tourists in a sustainable way and the possibilities of market failure' (ibid).

Indeed, the government's argument for keeping investment incentives in Scotland and Wales was that these were peripheral areas where clear cases of market failure could be identified. However, following a 1992/93 tourism review, the Section 4 programme in Scotland was also suspended – although the STB's development activities were, in fact, simply transferred to other Non-departmental Public Bodies, Scottish Enterprise and the Highlands and Islands Enterprise networks, who were still empowered to assist the tourism industry through grant support. Section 4 assistance continues under its original form only in Wales.

Having created the tourist boards, successive governments have demonstrated their confusion as to how they might best be used. Since 1969, they have been the subject of no fewer than nine different reviews, which have focused mainly on efficiency issues and have resulted in a number of measures designed to cut costs, such as the merging of a number of services (e.g. finance, personnel, research, policy) common to the ETB and BTA. In addition to these minor organisational changes, the responsibility for sponsoring and overseeing the BTA and ETB has been passed around different government departments. The BTA and ETB were responsible to the Department of Trade and Industry until 1985, when they were placed under the authority of the Department of Employment. Responsibility for the BTA and ETB was once again moved in 1993, this time to the newly-created **Department of National Heritage (DNH)**, linking tourism with some of the key elements of the UK's appeal in this domain: its culture, heritage and sport.

There has been more stability for the other national tourist boards – the STB and WTB, who have always been responsible to their respective national Secretaries of State. Hughes attributes this long-standing separation of responsibility for tourism administration in the UK to 'nationalist feeling and the structure of government in the UK' and points out that the division of responsibilities has led to a disproportionate funding of the national tourist boards, due more to political pressure than to any overall strategic decision (Hughes, 1994). The structure of Britain's national tourist boards is shown in Figure 6.7.

The very existence of several national tourist boards (BTA, ETB, STB, WTB) has been a source of confusion for consumers and for those operating in the tourism industry in the UK and overseas, who have often been unclear as to which organisation should be addressed on what issues. In addition, since 1984, the STB has been allowed to promote itself directly in overseas markets, without using the BTA as an intermediary.

Given the confusion created by the present system, it is perhaps not surprising that there have been repeated demands from the industry

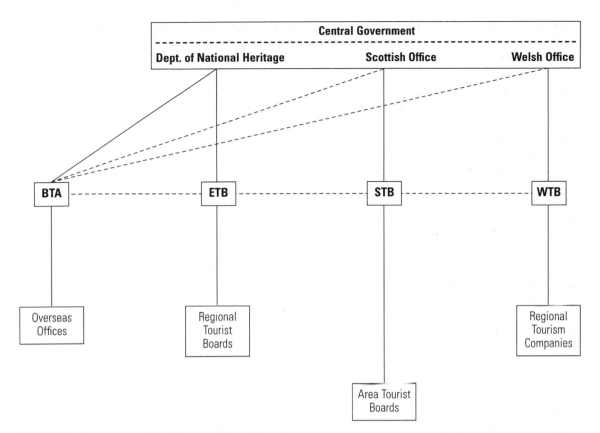

FIGURE 6.7 *The structure of Britain's national tourist boards*

for a supra-national tourism board for the UK to be created, with a single minister responsible for tourism (Crouch, 1993). However, any such move would be likely to meet with resistance from the Scottish and Welsh tourism boards and those operating in the tourism sectors in those countries. For while their respective Secretaries of State have consistently defended the STB's and WTB's level of funding, the political masters overseeing the work of the BTA and the ETB have often left them vulnerable to government economy measures. The role of the ETB has been diminished since 1989, as government policy has become one of devolving its marketing funds and initiatives to the English Regional Tourist Boards (see Chapter 7). As a result, the ETB's grant-in-aid support from the government had fallen to £10 million by 1995/96, or, as one commentator put it: less than the cost of one body scanner or bomber. This may be compared with the much more generous grant-in-aid available to each of the national tourist boards for Scotland and Wales, who, between them account for less than 10% of British tourism. Figure 6.8 highlights the growing disparity between ETB grant-in-aid, and the funding of the other national tourist boards.

Many commentators are of the opinion that this sharp fall in government resources for tourism was not wholly due to ideological reasons, and that the ETB and BTA themselves share part of the responsibility for it.

Year	BTA	ETB	STB	WTB	NITB
79/80	32.9	26.1	11.1	9.5	10.1
88/89	32.7	35.6	13.7	12.9	7.4
95/96	34.5	10.0	16.9	14.7	13.7

Source: Robinson (1995a)

FIGURE 6.8 *Government sponsorship for the tourist boards (£ million)*

'We are at the end of two decades of declining government support for tourism in England. For most of that period, the BTA considered itself to be competing with the ETB for its share of grant-in-aid, so annual reports and statistics would emphasise the up-side, the achievements, the growth, the success stories. These messages actually made it easier for the government to reduce its funding, in the cause of limiting public expenditure.'

(Robinson, 1995)

UK TOURISM POLICY

Despite the often ambiguous and wavering support given by the government to the national tourist boards, they play a more important role in the national tourism policy-making process than NTOs in countries where the governments take a more direct, active interest in tourism. When Shaw *et al.* (1991) expressed their view that 'Effective policy making in UK tourism is left to sub-state agencies which, in other fields, would only be charged with the task of policy implementation' they meant by 'sub-state agencies' primarily, the tourist boards. For Hughes, the reason for this lies in the wording of the 1969 Act, which:

'... created bodies which were, in effect, left to create policy; no policy guidelines were included in the Act ... This lack of central direction has added to the confusion at the level of the tourist boards, which have been able to devise their own separate responses to tourism.'

(Hughes, 1994)

UK governments, acting through the national tourist boards, have tended to react to opportunities and problems as they have arisen, instead of developing a long-term coherent strategy for tourism. Lickorish emphasises the disadvantage of this approach:

'Individual *ad hoc* responses to tourism opportunities and problems do not constitute a policy for tourism. Such responses might

merely provide short-term solutions to essentially long-term problems.'

(Lickorish, 1991a)

The tourist boards therefore, have been left to fill the policy vacuum; but without operational and statutory powers, the impact of their efforts has been limited. The BTA and the national tourist boards have produced a number of non-statutory 'strategy documents', which have taken the form of guidelines for future tourism development. These have been destined primarily for the tourism industry itself, but have also emphasised the need for partnership involving central and local government, the tourist boards and other public bodies. Typically, such documents describe tourism trends, the strengths and weaknesses of the country as a destination, and make forecasts of potential for the industry. They identify priorities and issues which may be reflected in regional and local strategies.

The basic aim of these strategy documents (as described in the foreword to one of the most recent) is 'to provide a framework for planning and decision taking by public and private sector organisations involved in tourism' (BTA, 1990). In an earlier strategy document, the contribution of the BTA to strategic planning by the tourism industry was expanded upon:

'The BTA cannot "order" the future development of British tourism. Many external factors will influence the future scale and pattern of demand. Even if these could be forecast accurately, many independent authorities and commercial organisations will make the decisions which determine whether the supply of facilities is properly matched to demand. Strategic planning in such circumstances is, therefore, a matter of providing a set of guidelines which, on the one hand, offer plausible and soundly-based forecasts of future demand potential and, on the other, give practical advice to encourage coordinated decisions to be taken by all sectors of the industry.'

(BTA, 1984)

A significant move towards a national tourism policy came in 1994, when the Department of

National Heritage (DNH) announced that it was to finally produce a 'programme of action' for tourism in the UK. Five main factors led to the upsurge in government interest in tourism:

- the commitment and close personal interest in tourism taken by the then Secretary of State for National Heritage, Stephen Dorrell
- the extent of the cuts in tourist boards' funding, which had begun to cause government concern
- the fact that Tom Pendry, who had assumed responsibility for tourism and sport in the then opposition Labour Party, had begun to work on a tourism strategy document
- the CBI's decision that it also had a role to play in guiding UK tourism policy, through its newly-established Tourism Action Group
- the fact that, in 1994, the Scottish and Wales Tourist Boards had both published their own strategic policy documents.

The prospect of a national tourism strategy was well received, not least by those in the industry itself. Writing on their behalf, Ken Robinson, chairman of the Tourism Society explained not only why such an initiative was required, but also why governments had, until then, been so slow to commit themselves to anything resembling a tourism policy:

> 'Industry leaders have continually advocated just such a plan to give clarity and purpose to the application of scarce funding, to be a focus for effort. There has for years been a great resistance in Government circles to a committed statement of tourism policy – as it carries with it the implication of commitment beyond the current year. Few in the industry would doubt the need for such an organised approach – in order that the potential of tourism can be realised. A policy would help build confidence, give some stability; a firmer basis on which to build a framework for action and coordination between government, tourist boards, local authorities and most important, the industry . . . in place of the destabilising switchback of constant and unexpected change.'
>
> *(Robinson, 1994)*

When *Tourism – Competing with the Best* was finally published on 1 March 1995 by the DNH, it was not launched as the grand strategic plan for the UK tourism industry which many had hoped for, but as a 'policy document' and a 'programme for action'. In the foreword, the Secretary of State admitted that:

> 'This programme is not a comprehensive strategy for the tourism industry. It is the beginning of a process of identifying some of the key issues for the industry with which Government can help, and undertaking some practical actions to address them. I hope that it will be the start of an evolving programme of policy development.'
>
> *(DNH, 1995)*

The document's main significance lay in its many departures from the usual statements made by the government concerning its own relationship to tourism. Although beginning with the customary assertion that 'Tourism in Britain is a success story', it went on to admit that the UK's inbound and domestic tourism performance had not matched that of its competitors and that there was considerable opportunity for improvement – in standards, systems, business performance and marketing.

There followed a statement of the traditional government view that the solution to the industry's problems is 'first and foremost a job for the industry itself'. But, despite referring repeatedly to this need for the industry to solve its own problems, the document also acknowledged that the:

> '. . . problems are compounded by the fragmentation of the industry . . . it is made up of businesses from many different sectors with large numbers of small operators. It is not easy for it to act in the concerted way necessary for it to compete successfully in world markets. The government seeks to address these problems.'
>
> *(ibid)*

However, most importantly of all, in a significant departure from the government's usual ambiguous and nebulous indications of commitment towards tourism, the document asserted that 'the government has a contribution to make through active sponsorship to help the tourism industry fulfil its potential'. Furthermore, as concrete proof, perhaps, of what active sponsorship could signify, the report marked a possible reversal of the well-established trend of cutting budgets for tourism promotion, in announcing the allocation of £2 million of additional funding for the promotion of London as a destination.

But *Tourism – Competing with the Best* also contained some disappointments for those operating in the tourism industry. The main one of these was the 'deliberately selective' nature of the document. The UK tourism 'product' was viewed almost entirely in terms of the hotel stock – its quality and value for money – with little of direct relevance to the other sectors of the industry, such as tourist attractions or other forms of accommodation. Neither was there any serious discussion of the role of the Regional Tourist Boards (RTBs) in England, or the planning and other activities undertaken by local authorities.

Nevertheless, on the whole, the document held out hope of a more constructive relationship between the UK government and tourism. In its concluding words, it read:

> 'This is the first step in an evolving policy of more effective [government] sponsorship. The role of government is to work in partnership, to identify our growth markets, constraints on growth and unexploited opportunities, and identify how the government can better help the industry through active sponsorship. The government is ideally placed to join in partnership with the industry to take an overview of constraints and opportunities, to catalyse action to address them, to do research and collect information of use to the industry as a whole, and to facilitate the exchange of good practice. It will continue to give the interests of tourism a high priority in its policy making, in areas that impact on the tourism infrastructure.'
>
> *(ibid)*

Tourism – Competing with the Best fell short of providing the grand strategic plan which many in the industry had wanted. But hopes in the industry itself were that it could turn out to be a long-awaited turning-point for tourism in the UK, heralding a new, sharper definition of the government's role. Finally, it took a General Election campaign to produce not one but *two* strategy documents, for tourism in the UK. The Labour Party's revised version of the 1969 Development of Tourism Act ('Breaking New Ground') was launched at the 1996 World Travel Market. The strategy included promoting more private and public sector partnerships, improving marketing of the UK, and improving the quality of the tourism product. In January 1997, the Conservative Party also produced a tourism strategy document. Time will tell to what extent these two strategies were simply electioneering devices, or whether they represent politicians' genuine allegiance to the tourism industry in the UK.

UK TOURISM IN THE WIDER NATIONAL POLICY FRAMEWORK

In the continuing absence of a formal tourism policy for the UK, the industry is nevertheless affected by a wide range of other government policies, as well as by legislation of a general nature. Although the vast majority of the UK government's legislation is not, of course, aimed specifically at the tourism industry, it nevertheless has considerable and often unexpected consequences for this sector. In recent years, there have been many examples of legislation which have had an impact on the experience of tourists in Britain. Among these are the liberalisation of Sunday shopping as well as the longer opening hours of pubs: Sunday opening and the introduction of children's certificates have strengthened the appeal of the British pub, one of the country's most distinctive attractions for overseas visitors.

There are, however, a number of other general areas of government activity which have a direct or indirect impact on tourism in the UK. For example, it is clear that tourism businesses must operate within the conditions which result from the government's macroeconomic policy.

They are directly affected by such factors as interest, inflation and foreign exchange rates. Similarly, UK governments' national transport policies represent another critical area for consideration, as a whole range of issues under this heading have a very direct bearing on how tourism develops in the UK: the promotion of high-speed rail links with the rest of Europe, via the Channel Tunnel; the provision of appropriate terminal facilities in London, and major regional centres; improvements to rail services generally; improvements to London Transport, and the provision of adequate coach parking in the capital.

Some other important policy areas affecting tourism development will now be considered.

ECONOMIC DEVELOPMENT

The government's national economic development policy also has a direct impact on businesses operating in certain areas of the country. As is the case for all sectors of industry, tourism businesses are able to benefit from the different forms of financial assistance made available through government departments and government agencies, as part of the national economic development policy.

The **Department of Trade and Industry (DTI)** uses public funds to assist businesses which operate within those parts of the country designated by it as 'Assisted Areas'. In those areas, grants are awarded to both manufacturing and service industries which are expanding or setting up. However, the job creation potential of the business in question is an important criterion for receiving such assistance, and there is a widespread impression that tourism is disadvantaged by the fact that 'many ministries and local authorities are still locked into the discredited theory that tourism is not a "real" industry – and does not create "real" jobs' (ETB, 1993). Despite all the publicity given (notably by the tourist boards) to tourism's ability to create jobs, it is felt by many in the industry that there is a strong manufacturing bias in the administration of the DTI grant scheme.

THE COUNTRYSIDE

Tourism is only one of the many economic activities based on the countryside, sharing (and in competition for) this valuable resource with the demands of the agriculture, fisheries, forestry and mineral extraction industries, among others.

The demand for public access to the British countryside has grown rapidly since the 1950s. Rising standards of living have brought with them increased car ownership and growing demands for recreation, which have increased the pressure on the countryside. Countryside planning and recreation management have accordingly grown in importance. These activities are undertaken through a proliferation of initiatives and designations, including the 'Areas of Outstanding Natural Beauty', 'Heritage Coasts', 'National Parks' and 'Rural Development Areas'.

The designations **Heritage Coast** and **Areas of Outstanding Natural Beauty (AONBs)** cover areas of great scenic beauty, most of which are key elements in the tourist appeal of the UK, including such areas as the Cotswolds, the White Cliffs of Dover and the Gower. Policies relating to their use for recreation and tourism are thus of considerable interest.

There are 45 AONBs currently designated in England and Wales, covering over 20,000 sq. km. These are the responsibility of the local authorities and the emphasis is on the conservation and enhancement of natural beauty, with recreation playing a secondary role. Scotland has 40 National Scenic Areas, a similar status to the AONBs.

There are three objectives which AONB designation seeks to achieve.

- the primary purpose of designation is to conserve and enhance natural beauty
- in pursuing this primary purpose, account is taken of the needs of agriculture, forestry, other rural industries and of the social and economic needs of local communities. Particular regard is paid to promoting sustainable forms of social and economic development which in themselves conserve and enhance the environment
- recreation is not an objective of designation, but the demand is met so far as this is consis-

tent with the conservation of natural beauty and the needs of agriculture, forestry and other uses.

There are currently 45 Heritage Coasts designated in England and Wales, while Scotland has 26 Preferred Coastal Conservation Zones. The objectives in both cases are to conserve their natural scenery and to facilitate and enhance their enjoyment by the public. The term 'Heritage coast' is a non-statutory designation based on recommendations by the Countryside Commission, who work in partnership with local authorities and other interested bodies to achieve policies designed to both conserve the quality of the coast and to facilitate the enjoyment of visitors.

Management plans have been drawn up for AONBs and Heritage Coasts, dealing with landscape and conservation issues as well as the management of tourism and recreation pressures. Such plans are usually drawn up by the constituent local authorities in consultation with other relevant interests (see North Pennines case study). Edwards (1987) describes the nature and extent of tourism's impacts on Heritage Coasts, as well as the range of management techniques employed to redress these.

Three central government agencies (the Countryside Commission, the ETB and the Rural Development Commission), together with the regional tourist boards, have taken the lead in publishing policies which promote sustainable tourism in the countryside. The results of this partnership can be seen in the many conferences, publications, case studies and examples of good practice disseminated by these agencies.

The **Rural Development Commission (RDC)** is the government's agency for economic and social development in rural England. It advises the government on issues pertaining to rural development and its prime concern is the well-being of the people who live and work in England's rural areas. In pursuit of its aim to stimulate job creation and the provision of essential services in the countryside, the RDC gives financial and advisory assistance to all types of businesses operating in certain disadvantaged rural areas of England – designated **Rural Development Areas**. Through its Rural

Development Programme, it offers two kinds of financial assistance: grants to help with the conversion of redundant farm buildings and soft loans. As in the case of the DTI, the job creation potential of any business project is one of the criteria taken into account when considering it for financial assistance. For example, Redundant Building Grants are not made available for self-catering or bed-and-breakfast accommodation, due to the limited job-creating potential of such businesses. Assistance on marketing, accounting, productivity and business management is also provided to businesses setting up in the Rural Development Areas, supported, in the case of tourism businesses, by the RDC's specialist Regional Tourism Consultants.

The RDC is committed to tourism (among other industries) as a tool for economic regeneration in rural areas. It recognises the rural tourism industry's potential for diversifying the economy of the countryside, and has declared itself in favour of tourism which:

- provides a wide range of job opportunities
- brings lasting social and economic benefits to rural areas
- improves or increases the range and access to local services
- respects the environment (RDC, 1992).

The **Countryside Commission (CoCo)** works to conserve and enhance the beauty of the English countryside and to help people enjoy it. The CoCo was created in 1968 when, as a result of the Countryside Act, it superseded the National Parks Commission. Although the main responsibility for **National Parks** lies with the local planning authorities, the CoCo is responsible nationally for the overall development of the National Parks of England (Wales has its own Countryside Council for Wales, and there are no National Parks in Scotland, where other terms are used to designate such areas).

Since considerable pressure, both from visitors and from developers seeking to provide services, is exerted on the National Parks, many of the joint efforts of the ETB, CoCo and RDC have been aimed at these areas of the countryside. The National Parks were created as a result of the 1949 National Parks and Access to the

Countryside Act, which established the National Parks Commission. From their inception, National Parks had a dual purpose:

- 'the preservation and enhancement of natural beauty
- encouraging the provision or improvement, for persons resorting to national parks, of facilities for the enjoyment thereof and for the enjoyment of the opportunities for open air recreation and the study of nature afforded thereby.'

(National Parks and Access to the Countryside Act 1949, Section 1)

There is inevitably some conflict between these two aims, and in 1991, a review panel set up by the Countryside Commission recommended that they be reformulated to give added weight to conservation.

As one of a range of practical initiatives relating to tourism in National Parks in England and Wales, the ETB, RDC and CoCo published in 1993 a guide to good practice on tourism in National Parks. The guide asserts that tourism is an important part of the life of National Parks, bringing a sense of refreshment and well-being to visitors while helping the rural economy through support for income and jobs. But it acknowledges that tourism can bring with it damage to the fabric and wildlife of the countryside.

'The future of tourism in the National Parks is ultimately dependent on their high quality natural environments. Where the natural beauty of the National Parks and tourism are in irreconcilable conflict, then the former must prevail.'

(ETB et al., 1993)

Regarding development, the guide states that:

'Appropriate facilities are needed to enable tourists to enjoy the National Parks. Its scale, in particular, must always be appropriate to the setting ... Proposals for development should always be tempered by the capacity of the immediate site and surrounding landscape to absorb visitors. Development can assist the purposes of conservation and recreation by, for example, bringing

sympathetic new uses to historical buildings and derelict sites and opening up new opportunities for quiet open air recreation.'

(ibid)

Development control in National Parks is the responsibility of the **National Park Authorities (NPAs)**. In addition to the normal Structure and Local Plans for their areas, each NPA is required to prepare a national park plan.

'The distinguishing feature of this is that it is concerned with management. In this it goes beyond the scope of development plans. In addition to policies, the plan spells out both short-term and long-term proposals and programmes for action to achieve the purposes for which the park was designated.'

(Cullingworth and Nadin, 1994)

The example of the Exmoor National Park Plan 1991–96 contains nearly 200 policies and actions, listing priorities for the five-year period under three headings: 'Conservation', 'Enjoyment', and the 'Park Community'. In addition, the plan looks ahead to the long-term vision of 'Exmoor in the 21st Century'.

WATERWAYS

Rivers, canals and reservoirs represent an important resource for recreation and tourism. They are used for boating, fishing and other forms of informal recreation such as visits to towing paths.

British Waterways (BW) is responsible for managing about 2,000 miles of the 3,700 miles of the UK's inland waterways and some 90 reservoirs. Although 350 miles of BW's waterways are designated for the carriage of freight, the rest are used mainly for cruising, fishing and other recreational purposes. BW estimates that some 130 million visits are made to its towing paths each year; 100,000 anglers fish regularly in their waterways; and 22,000 privately-owned powered-craft sail on them. Although most of BW's annual turnover is met from a Department of the Environment (DoE) grant, it is required by this department to run its affairs on a commercial basis as far as is practicable. As revenue from leisure and tourism constitutes 25% of BW's earned income, this makes a substantial financial contribution to the waterways' upkeep. But leisure and tourism are also seen by BW as fulfilling a social function – through the employment which they contribute to villages, towns and cities.

It is part of the role of BW to reconcile conflicts of interests concerning the use of waterways: notably that arising between their use for tourism and leisure, and the need to preserve and enhance their environmental quality.

BW regards involvement in the planning system as an effective way of expressing its position relative to the development and conservation of the waterways system and adjoining land. Its wish to be involved with local authorities in both policy formulation and in its implementation through the development control process is stated in its publication *British Waterways: the Waterway Environment and Development Plans* (BW, 1992). This aims to show local authorities and commercial developers how the competing interests of leisure, commercial development and environmental conservation can be reconciled and how development for leisure and tourism and other uses can be integrated and expressed in Structure and Local Plans. In this document, local authorities are requested to consult BW on all major planning applications adjacent to waterways.

In its more specific and detailed *Leisure and Tourism Strategy* (BW, 1994), BW describes its own role as that of 'the provider of a good quality infrastructure which offers an attractive environment in which leisure and tourism businesses can prosper'. BW's broad national policy guidelines are summarised in this document, to serve as a context for the Local Plans, which are the responsibility of individual waterway managers. Detailed policies are spelled out on boating, angling, visitor attractions, education and visitors' use of towpaths. Achieving a balance between the benefits of tourism and leisure development with those of conservation is a major theme of the strategy: 'We wish to share in the growth projected nationally for leisure and tourism, taking account of customer requirements and market opportunities but without

compromising our environmental and conservation aims' (*ibid*).

THE ENVIRONMENT

In the UK (as in many other countries), interest in regulating and protecting the environment is growing, with significant implications for the future development of tourism, and the political climate within which the tourism industry operates. Environmental politics has entered the UK political scene, with all political parties stating their concern for, and proposing programmes of action for, the protection of the natural and built environment.

In addition to the environmental measures which it is obliged, by EU law, to apply in the UK, central government has taken many initiatives of its own in recent years. In 1990, it published a White Paper on the environment, *This Common Inheritance*, which set out its targets and policies in various areas, and which was followed by annual reports identifying progress.

Following the Earth Summit in Rio, the UK government produced a national and sectoral strategy for the environment: *Sustainable Development – The UK Strategy*. This reviews the state of the environment and highlights the changes that may be required in different sectors of the economy if sustainability is to be realised. Leisure is one of the 14 sectors covered. The economic, social and environmental contribution of leisure activity is discussed, as are the problems that it can bring. A number of policy and management initiatives are highlighted together with the action that is required from government, statutory agencies, local authorities, the leisure industry and the general public. While this strategy adds little in the way of new thinking and evidence, it does reinforce the environmental argument and raise its priority. Other aspects of the report deal with issues such as energy, transport and waste, which may in time begin to impact on and constrain the operation of the tourism industry.

As well as these general, multisectoral policy statements on the environment, the UK government has published a number of reports on tourism and the environment in association with the national tourist boards. The most influential of these is the Government Task Force's 1991 report, *Tourism and the Environment: Maintaining the Balance*. This report defined sustainable tourism as a state of harmony between the needs of the visitor, the place and the host community, and provided the following guiding principles.

- The environment has an intrinsic value which outweighs its value as a tourist asset. Its enjoyment by future generations and its long-term survival must not be prejudiced by short-term considerations
- Tourism should be recognised as a positive activity, with the potential to benefit the community and the place as well as the visitor
- The relationship between tourism and the environment must be managed so that the environment is sustainable in the long term. Tourism must not be allowed to damage the resources, prejudice its future enjoyment, or bring unacceptable impacts
- Tourism activities and developments should respect the scale, nature and character of the place in which they are sited
- In any location, harmony must be sought between the needs of the visitor, the place, and the host community
- In a dynamic world, some change is inevitable and can often be beneficial. Adaptation to change, however, should not be at the expense of any of these principles
- The tourism industry, local authorities and environmental agencies all have a duty to respect the above principles, and to work together to achieve their practical realisation (ETB, 1991).

ARTS AND HERITAGE

The Department of National Heritage (DHN) as well as directly overseeing national tourism policy, is also responsible for a number of cultural activities which impinge on tourism, such as heritage, museums, sports, the arts and (through the funding possibilities it represents) the National Lottery. In Scotland and Wales, similar responsibilities are handled by the Scottish and Welsh Offices. However, much of the day-to-day responsibility for these areas is delegated to arms-length bodies and agencies such as the Arts Council, the Museums and Galleries Commission, and English Heritage.

English Heritage and its counterparts in Scotland and Wales (**Historic Scotland and CADW**) are responsible for protecting, and promoting enjoyment of, the nation's built heritage. The policies of these bodies impact on tourism in two main ways.

- They have in their guardianship (between them) just under 1,000 historic sites and properties open to the public and are responsible for promoting and interpreting them and organising events. These form an important part of the tourism infrastructure of the UK, including sites such as Stonehenge and Dover Castle.
- They are responsible for protecting and conserving historic buildings and sites through listing and scheduling. This gives them the authority to determine what can be done with the very large number of protected buildings, many of which are used for tourism-related purposes.

There are well over 2,000 museums and galleries in the UK and it is estimated that 80 million people visit them annually. Twenty 'national' museums, including the major museums in London, are directly funded by the DNH. These are significant visitor attractions in their own right, attracting a total of 24 million visits in 1994.

The **Museums and Galleries Commission (MGC)** advises the government on museum matters and is concerned with promoting museum and heritage interests and raising standards. It provides funding to seven area museum councils in England (those in Scotland and Wales being funded by the Scottish and Welsh Offices). An example of how this body can have an impact on tourism emerges from the MGC policy statement issued in 1994, *Towards a Government Policy for Museums*. This stresses the need to raise standards and secure funding and states that the priority should be to improve and maintain what already exists, as opposed to creating additional museums. Clearly, this policy has implications for tourism in areas where new museums are seen as a catalyst for tourism development projects.

Responsibility for promoting and supporting the living arts in England rests with the **Arts Council** (funded by the DNH), while Scotland and Wales have their own arts councils (funded through the Scottish and Welsh Offices). The Arts Council is responsible for supporting arts organisations and artists across the country. It has a number of regular clients, such as the Royal Opera House, which receive annual revenue funding. It also provides 90% of the funding for the Regional Arts Boards and distributes the arts' share of the National Lottery proceeds.

The policies and actions of all of the aforementioned organisations, and government departments, contribute significantly to the shaping of the national context within which tourism develops in the UK. Chapter 7 examines how tourism is planned and managed at the level of the individual destination, within this national policy context.

REFERENCES

Airey, D. (1983) 'European government approaches to tourism', in *Tourism Management*, vol 4, pp. 234–244.

Akehurst, G. (1992) 'European Community tourism policy' in Johnson, P. and Thomas, B. (eds) *Perspectives on Tourism Policy*, Mansell, London, pp. 215–231.

Akehurst, G.; Bland, N. and Nevin, M. (1993) 'Tourism policies in the European Community member states' in *International Journal of Hospitality Management*, vol 12, no. 1, pp. 33–66.

Allard, L. (1995) 'Obstacles to tourism trade and consumption abroad: the OECD experience', in *GATS Implications for Tourism*, World Tourism Organisation, Madrid.

Barnes, I. and Barnes, P. (1993) 'Tourism policy in the European Community' in Lavery, P. and Pompl, W. (eds) *Tourism in Europe – Structures and Developments*, CAB International.

Baum, T. (1994) 'The development and implementation of national tourism policies' in *Tourism Management*, 15(3), pp. 185–192.

BTA (1984) *Strategy for Growth 1984–1988*, British Tourist Authority, London.

BTA (1990) *Guidelines for Tourism to Britain 1991–1995*, British Tourist Authority, London.

Burns, B. (1994) 'Review of national and regional tourism planning, WTO' in *In Focus* (14), Tourism Concern, London.

BW (1992) *The Waterway Environment and Development Plans*, British Waterways.

BW (1994) *Leisure and Tourism Strategy*, British Waterways.

CBI (1985) *Paying Guests*, Confederation of British Industry.

CEC (1990) *1990, European Tourism Year*, Commission of the EC, Brussels.

CEC (1991a) *Community Action Plan to Assist Tourism*, Commission of the EC, Brussels.

CEC (1991b) *Guide to the Reform of the Community's Structural Funds*, Commission of the EC, Brussels.

CEC (1995) *The Role of the Union in the Field of Tourism*, Commission of the EC, Brussels.

CEC (1996) *Proposal for a Council Decision on a First Multiannual Programme to Assist European Tourism: 'Philoxenia'*, Commission of the EC, Brussels.

Cockerell, N. (1994) 'The changing role of international travel and tourism organisations', in *EIU Travel & Tourism Analyst* (5), Economist Intelligence Unit Limited, London.

Cooper, C. *et al.* (1993) *Tourism Principles and Practice*, Pitman, London.

Crawshaw, C. (1993) 'Tourism and the Environment' in *Town and Country Planning 1993 Summer School Proceedings*.

Crouch, S. (1993) 'How can the government best help the tourism industry: seminar proceedings' in *Tourism*, issue 79, The Tourism Society, London.

Cubbage, F. (1995) 'Finding a way through the maze: seminar proceedings' in *Tourism*, issue 84, The Tourism Society, London.

Davidson, R. (1992) *Tourism in Europe*, Pitman, London.

Décision Tourisme (1995) 'Le livre vert entre consultations et négotiations' in *Décision Tourisme*, no. 2, Dec. 1995, p. 29.

Décision Tourisme (1996) 'Grand débat et petit pas' in *Décision Tourisme*, no. 4, Dec. 1995, p. 29.

DNH (1995) *Tourism – Competing with the Best*, Department of National Heritage, London.

Dowling, R. (1993) 'An environmentally-based planning model for regional tourism development' in the *Journal of Sustainable Tourism*, 1(1), pp. 17–37.

Economic and Social Committee of the EC (1994) *Opinion on Tourism*, CEC, Brussels.

Economist, The (1995a) 'Faulty holiday towers' in *The Economist*, 29 July 1995, p. 15.

Economist, The (1995b) 'A place in the sun' in *The Economist*, 29 July 1995, p. 56.

Edgell, D.L. Sr (1995) 'New directions for world tourism' in *GATS Implications for Tourism*, World Tourism Organisation, Madrid.

Edwards, J.R. (1987) 'The UK Heritage coasts: an assessment of the ecological impacts of tourism' in *Annals of Tourism Research*, vol 14, pp. 71–87.

Elmore, R.F. (1987) 'Backward mapping: implementation research and policy decisions' in Williams, W. (ed) *Studying Implementation*, Chatham House, Chatham, NJ.

ETB (1991) *Tourism and the Environment – Maintaining the Balance*, English Tourist Board, London.

ETB (1993) 'Who can pull the public purse strings?' *Tourism Marketplace*, no. 95, English Tourist Board, London.

ETB *et al.* (1993) *Principles for Tourism in National Parks*, English Tourist Board, Countryside Commission, Rural Development Commission, London.

European Parliament (1991) 'Minutes of the proceedings of the sitting of 11 June 1991', CEC, Brussels.

Eurostat (1990) *Tourism in Europe: Trends 1989*, Office for Official Publications of the European Communities, Luxembourg.

Fitzpatrick Associates (1993) *Tourism in the European Community: the Impact of the Single Market*, Economist Intelligence Unit, London.

Forbes, A.H. (1994) 'Tourism and transport policy in the EU' in *Tourism: the State of the Art*, Seaton, A.V. *et al.* (eds), John Wiley and Sons, Chichester.

Frangialli, F. (1991) *La France dans le tourisme mondial*, Economica, Paris.

Garland, S. (1995) 'VAT Harmonisation, Distance Selling Directive and other EU Legislative Issues – an Update' in *Insights*, May 1995, English Tourist Board, London.

Getz, D. (1986) 'Models in tourism planning' in *Tourism Management*, March 1990, pp. 21–32.

Greenwood, J., Williams, A. and Shaw, G. (1990) 'Policy implementation and tourism in the UK' in *Tourism Management*, Mar. 1990.

Gunn, C.A. (1994a) 'The emergence of effective tourism planning and development' in *Tourism: The State of the Art*. Seaton, A.V. *et al.* (eds) John Wiley & Sons, Chichester.

Gunn, C.A. (1994b) *Tourism Planning – Basics Concepts Cases*, Taylor & Francis, Washington.

Hartley, K. and Hooper, N. (1993) 'Tourism Policy: Market Failure and Public Choice' in *Perspectives on Tourism Policy*, Johnson, P. and Thomas, B. (eds) Mansell.

Hollier, R. and Subremon, A (1992) *Le Tourisme dans la Communauté Européenne*, Presses Universitaires de France, Paris.

Holloway, C. (1989) *The Business of Tourism*, Pitman, London.

HOTREC (1990) *The 1992 Challenge for the Hotel, Restaurant and Cafe Industry*, HOTREC, Brussels.

Hughes, H.L. (1984) 'Government support for tourism in the UK: a different perspective' in *Tourism Management*, 5(1), 13–19.

Hughes, H.L. (1989) 'Resorts: a fragmented product in need of coalescence' in the *International Journal of Hospitality Management*, 8(1), pp. 15–17.

Human, B. (1994) 'Visitor management in the public planning policy context: a case study of Cambridge' in *The Journal of Sustainable Tourism*, Vol 2, no. 4.

Inskeep, E. (1991) *Tourism Planning: An integrated and sustainable development approach*, Van Nostrand Reinhold, New York.

Joppe, M. (1989) 'State tourism policy' in *Tourism Marketing and Management Handbook*, Witt, S. and Moutinho, L. (eds), Prentice Hall, Hemel Hempstead.

Khor, M. (1994) 'Developments and issues in the Uruguay Round of particular concern to developing countries' in *Third World Economics*, 1–31 May 1994.

Lickorish, L.J. (1991b) 'Developing a singe European tourism policy' in *Tourism Management*, 12(3), pp. 178–184.

Lickorish, L. (1994) *Developing Tourism Destinations – Policies and Perspectives*, Longman, London.

Lowyck, E. and Wanhill, S. (1992) 'Regional Development and Tourism within the European Community' in *Progress in Tourism, Recreation and Hospitality Management*, Cooper, C. and Lockwood, A. (eds) Belhaven, London.

METT (1995) *L'Administration du Tourisme*, Ministère de l'Equipement, des Transports et du Tourisme, Paris.

Murphy, P.E. (1985) *Tourism: A Community Approach*, Methuen, New York and London.

OECD (1989) *Tourism Policy and International Tourism in OECD Member Countries*, OECD, Paris.

OECD (1990) *Tourism Policy and International Tourism in OECD Member Countries*, OECD, Paris.

OECD (1991) *Inventory of Measures Perceived as Obstacles to International Tourism in the OECD Area*, OECD, Paris.

Pearce, D. (1989) *Tourist Development*, Longman, Harlow.

Plüss, C. (1994) *Liberalisierung des Tourismus: fragen zum Ausgang der Uruguay-Runde des GATT und seinen Auswirkungen auf Tourismus und Entwicklung*, Arbeitskreis Tourismus und Entwicklung, Basel.

RDC (1992) *Tourism in the Countryside*, Rural Development Commission.

Richards, G. (1992) 'European Social Tourism: Welfare or Investment' in *Proceedings of the 1992 Tourism in Europe Conference*, Centre for Trade and Tourism, Tyne and Wear.

Richards, G. (1995) 'Politics of national tourism policy in Britain' in *Leisure Studies*, 14, pp. 153–173.

Robinson, K. (1994) 'Politics, potential and policies' in *Tourism*, issue 83, The Tourism Society, London.

Robinson, K. (1995a) 'Judge them not by what they say but by what they do' in *Tourism*, issue 87, The Tourism Society, London.

Robinson, K. (1995b) 'Competing with the Best?' in *Leisure Management*, April 1995.

Shaw, G.; Greenwood, J. and Williams, A. (1991) 'The United Kingdom: market responses and public policy' in *Tourism and Economic Development: Western European Experiences*, Williams, A.M. and Shaw, G. (eds) Belhaven Press, London.

Shaw, G.; Williams, A. and Greenwood, J. (1987)

Public Policy and Tourism in England, Working Paper No. 3, Department of Geography, University of Exeter.

Simmons, D. (1994) 'Community participation in tourism planning' in *Tourism Management*, 15(2), pp. 98–108.

Tzoanos, G. (1991) *Formal opening speech at 'Tourism and Hospitality Management: established disciplines or 10-year wonders?'* Tourism Management/ University of Surrey conference, Guildford, 25 Sept. 1991.

Vellas, F. and Bécherel, L. (1995) *International Tourism*, Macmillan Press, Basingstoke.

Wanhill, S. (1994) 'The role of government incentives' in *Global Tourism: The Next Decade*, Theobald, W. (ed) Butterworth Heinemann, Oxford.

Wheatcroft, S. (1989) *Strategic planning for tourism: governmental view*, in Tourism Marketing and Management Handbook, Witt, S. and Moutinho, L. (eds), Prentice Hall, Hemel Hempstead.

Williams, A. and Shaw, G. (1991) 'Tourism policies in a changing economic environment' in *Tourism and Economic Development: Western European Experiences*, Williams, A.M. and Shaw, G. (eds) Belhaven Press, London.

WTO (1979) *A Study of the Role and Structure of NTOs*, World Tourism Organisation, Madrid.

WTO (1980) *Manila Declaation on World Tourism*, World Tourism Organisation, Madrid.

WTTC (1995) *European Union Travel & Tourism – Towards 1996 and Beyond*, World Travel & Tourism Council, Brussels.

WTTC/WTO (1996) *Agenda 21 for the travel and tourism industry: towards environmentally sustainable development*, World Travel & Tourism Council Brussels.

CHAPTER

7

Tourism planning at the destination level

INTRODUCTION

DESTINATION LEVEL PRIORITIES FOR PLANNING

In most countries, lower levels of government (such as regions, counties, districts and municipalities) have extensive powers to influence all kinds of development within their areas, including that of the tourism sector. They also provide much of the infrastructure upon which tourism depends, which adds to the considerable authority they have over how tourism is carried out at these levels. The tourism promotion undertaken at regional and local levels by the public sector, also increases its influence over the environment within which tourism businesses operate.

There are a number of important differences between national policies for tourism and those formulated and implemented at the lower levels of government. At the sub-national levels of government, tourism policies include a much greater emphasis on specific, practical action and local needs. At these levels, cooperation between agencies is often very effective and easier to put into action. Consultation with residents and local communities affected by tourism development is also more feasible when the spatial scale is smaller. Nevertheless, a rich diversity of different approaches to tourism planning and policy may be found within one country. Cooper *et al.* em-

phasise the variety of possible approaches to tourism planning at these levels:

'Regional and local tourism planning deals with specific issues which affect a sub-national area. They tend to be more detailed and specific than their national counterparts and can vary quite significantly from sub-national area to area. For example, there may be areas where tourism development is to be encouraged and others where specific types of tourism activity are actively discouraged.'

(Cooper et al., 1995)

Crawshaw goes further, underlining the differing objectives between the national and sub-national levels of government, and acknowledging the variance which may be found even within a single unit of local government:

'At the regional and local level, the long-term national objectives are not normally the primary concern. Regional and local authorities are concerned about the quality of life, employment and environment of their residents ... Even within the same region or county, various elements of government, whether political parties, departments or competing agencies, can have divergent tourism interests and policies.'

(Crawshaw, 1993)

THE IMPORTANCE OF PARTNERSHIP

One of the functions of tourism policies at the destination level is to attempt to reconcile the divergent interests of the different actors while, ideally at the same time, trying to work in harmony with the national tourism plan (where this exists) as far as local conditions will allow. Significant emphasis on partnership is therefore one of the distinguishing characteristics of tourism policies at this level. Van den Berg, in his study of urban tourism in Europe, makes this observation in commenting upon the highly fragmented nature of the tourism product as perceived from the local perspective:

> 'Tourist policy should reflect that complexity by taking into account the relations between the relevant elements of the private and public sectors ... Partnerships, public-public, as well as public-private, are eminently suitable to meet in practice the need for overall quality and integration ...'
>
> *(Van den Berg et al., 1994)*

Partnership is an idea which despite, or perhaps because of, its vagueness has come to enjoy increasing vogue in the 1990s. As Bailey (1995) puts it, in a discussion of regeneration policies: 'It may not be overstating the case to say that there is now a broad consensus among the main political parties and practitioners that claims that partnership is now the only basis on which successful regeneration can be achieved.'

Bailey discusses the development of partnerships as a response to the economic problems and shift of power from local to central government. Partnerships can be seen as arising from a number of interrelated factors:

- an attempt by local authorities (LAs) to redefine their role and regain influence in a restructured local state, in which their direct powers and control of finance have been severely curtailed
- a recognition of the fact that most of the investment required for regeneration must come from the private sector
- the practical problems which stem from the fragmentation of regeneration efforts amongst different agencies mean that coordination is needed, and partnership is a means of bringing that about.

Reviewing theories which seek to account for the rise of partnerships, Bailey follows Cox and Mair (1989) in arguing that partnerships can be seen as local growth coalitions which can arise when private sector companies and property owners are locally dependent – that is, have interests which are served by improvements in the locality, such as a better trained workforce or a better environment. Discussing the rationale of partnerships, he notes that they tend to rely heavily on promotional and marketing strategies, the identification of marketing opportunities, and the negotiation of strategies between the partners involved and other interests in the area.

These ideas of partnership have clear applicability to tourism. From the private-sector perspective, tourism firms can frequently be characterised as locally dependent – their well-being depends on destination resources which attract visitors, and small- and medium-sized enterprises in particular may be in no position to shift their investment. Since their interests are served by initiatives to improve the destination's physical or business environment, tourist firms can be motivated to join local growth coalitions.

Looking at things from a destination perspective, LAs require partnerships for effective destination management, whether focusing on dealing with visitor pressures or on tourism as part of a process of regeneration. There are three main reasons for this.

1 Destination development faces the problem that while most of the destination's resources are in the public domain, the finance required for development must come from the commercial sector (see Chapter 3), or be acquired from public agencies outside the destination, for example central government or the EU (see Chapter 6). In these circumstances, partnership is a means of gaining sufficient consensus to unlock private funds, and is now usually required to produce a convincing bid for public funds.

2 Tourism and leisure have a prominent role in promotion, marketing and the strategic oppor-

tunism which characterises 'entrepreneurial planning' (discussed later in this chapter). Places which are developing as tourism destinations will seek to use private-sector schemes as part of a more general marketing and promotional stance. Frequently, this involves not just an emphasis on the scheme itself (as a flagship example of development and thus an indicator of investment potential), but also an emphasis on how it has been achieved through partnership between the LA and the private sector – thus emphasising the place as 'investor friendly'.

3 Partnership is a necessary component of managing visitors in areas of tourism pressure – managing visitors in reality means managing the facilities and services they use. Since many of these are provided by the private sector, effective visitor management needs partnership between public and private sectors encompassing objectives, management mechanisms and funding.

Public-public partnerships are also important. LAs need to coordinate with: other tiers of government; other public agencies like Regional Tourist Boards; one another. The problem of coordination was one of the origins of the recent review of the two-tier system of local government in Britain. However, the outcome of the review in England and Wales is piecemeal change, with new unitary authorities in some areas and a continuation of the two-tier system in others (discussed further later in the chapter). Partnership and coordination will remain essential.

In this chapter, we begin with a discussion of the roles of two of the most important agents in the tourism planning process at the destination level – Local Authorities and Regional Tourist Boards (RTBs). The rest of the chapter examines the different types of planning and plans, which determine the shape of tourism at the destination.

ACTORS AT THE DESTINATION LEVEL IN UK TOURISM

LOCAL AUTHORITIES

At the regional and local level of government in the UK, the **local authorities (LAs)** exercise considerable power over the development of tourism within their areas. LAs are not only suppliers of part of the tourist product in the form of recreational facilities (e.g. parks, swimming pools) but are also involved, through their role as planning authorities with the overall development of their areas (Hughes, 1994). They can also play a vital role in promoting tourism to, and within, their areas by providing visitors with information, and by helping to pull together the efforts, and disparate elements, of the commercial tourist industry.

LA involvement in tourism development and promotion in the UK has a much longer history

than that of central government. It dates back to the development of spa towns and seaside resorts in the 19th century, when many LAs drew up and implemented ambitious plans for the construction of facilities, and managed extensive services for visitors. Wanhill describes how many resort towns developed in the Victorian era as a blend of municipal and individual entrepreneurialism. 'The local authorities invested in the promenades, piers, gardens and so on, while the private sector developed the revenue-earning activities which enhanced the income of the area and in turn increased property tax receipts for the authorities' (Wanhill, 1994).

In the 20th century, the influence of LAs over tourism has steadily grown. The Local Government Act (1948) empowered LAs to set up information and publicity services for tourism.

This was reinforced by the Local Government Act of 1972, giving LAs the power to encourage visitors to their area, to provide suitable facilities for them, and to work with other organisations to this end.

LAs in the UK have a range of responsibilities which can have a direct or indirect bearing upon the tourism that takes place in their localities. Bacon and Le Pelley (1993a) quote Byrne who lists these responsibilities, as shown in Figure 7.1.

The great diversity of these services and functions creates particular problems in fitting overall responsibility for tourism into existing departmental structures within LAs. Tourism impinges on several aspects of local government policy and operation, including recreation and the arts, planning and transport. As a consequence, local governments frequently leave responsibility for tourism split between several departments, often with no clear set of guidelines or corporate structure to provide strategic guidelines or set priorities (Bacon and Le Pelley, 1993b).

Tourism promotion and development functions may be undertaken by the staff of one, or several, of a whole range of LA departments. Where several LA departments share the responsibility for tourism, this can result in a serious lack of coordination of tourism-related policies. This can be the consequence of the (not uncommon) situation whereby, for example, the strategic development of tourism is located in the Economic Development Department, visitor research and statistics are the responsibility of the Planning Department, and tourism information and marketing come under Leisure Services. Such fragmentation is exacerbated by the fact that some roles are the responsibility of, and are undertaken at, district council level, while others are the remit of the county councils (Grant, Human and Le Pelley, 1996).

However, it would appear that as a distinct LA responsibility, tourism is now increasingly to be found in Leisure and Recreation Departments. In his survey of LAs, Richards (1992) noted that 28% of his respondents reported that tourism was a responsibility of their Leisure/Recreation departments. (It is also worthy of note that only 6% of LAs surveyed by Richards had a specific Tourism Department. These were mainly seaside resorts, other LAs perhaps not considering tourism important enough to warrant an entire department to itself.)

Tourism remains, however, a discretionary function of local government in the UK and tourism plans and strategies have no statutory power. The 1972 Local Government Act was an enabling piece of legislation, rather than one imposing a statutory requirement. It provided LAs with the possibility of undertaking a variety of tourism-related tasks, but LAs are under no obligation to do so. As a non-statutory function, tourism funding cannot be guaranteed and has to compete with other demands on a LA's discretionary budget.

This confusing and uncertain situation has led to many calls for tourism to be treated as a statutory function of local government with a clearly defined budget in its own right. (See Bacon and Le Pelley, 1993b and Bacon and Le Pelley, 1994, for a full discussion of this issue.)

As a result, despite their potential for influencing the development of tourism in their areas, LAs' involvement in tourism was, until recently, piecemeal and uneven over the country as a whole. Some authorities actively developed this sector, some remained indifferent, and others were antagonistic towards tourism development. Positive attitudes towards tourism tended to be limited to traditional seaside areas and to some spas and historic centres. However, the situation regarding LA support for tourism has been subject to a number of important changes in recent years. LAs' attitudes towards tourism have generally become much more positive, partly due to their recognition of both the economic significance of tourism and the importance of effective management, but also partly in response to a marked change in national government attitudes towards the role of LAs in tourism.

Prior to the 1980s, UK governments left LAs to develop tourism largely at will. Despite the 1948 and 1972 Acts of Parliament, there was little attempt on the part of central government actively to encourage LAs to get involved in tourism development and promotion. But, in the late 1960s and during the 1970s, a series of events focused more LA attention on the tourism devel-

District councils	County councils
Planning local plans planning applications conservation areas* historic buildings* country parks*	**Planning** structure plans conservation areas* historic buildings* country parks* national parks*
Recreation and arts parks and open spaces* support for the arts* swimming pools* museums/galleries* encouraging tourism*	**Recreation and arts** parks and open spaces* support for the arts* swimming pools* museums/galleries* encouraging tourism*
Building regulations	
Caravans site provision* site control/licensing	**Caravans** site provision*
Transport Districts may act as agents for counties to carry out certain delegated highway functions. Districts may claim right to maintain unclassified roads. footway lighting* off street car parking* footpaths/bridleways creation* footpaths/bridleways	**Transport** highways on street car parking traffic management public transport traffic regulation highway lighting off street car parking* footpaths/bridleways creation* signing, maintenance
Environmental services refuse collection litter control* public conveniences general environmental services (food hygiene, control of diseases and condition of shops, air/noise control) street cleaning markets and fairs	**Environmental** refuse disposal litter control*
Archives*	**Archaeology** **Archives***
Grants to voluntary bodies*	**Grants to voluntary bodies*** **Consumer protection** **trading standards, etc.**
Concessionary fares*	**Concessionary fares***
Economic development*	**Economic development***
Coastal protection	**Libraries**
Aerodromes*	**Aerodromes***

* Functions that can be carried by both county and district councils.

Source: Byrne 1987, quoted in Bacon and Le Pelley (1993a)

FIGURE 7.1 *Tourism related powers and duties of local authorities*

opment issue. In rural areas, the creation of the Countryside Commission and the need to formulate National Park Plans under the 1971 Town and Country Planning Act, highlighted tourism as a key factor in rural planning (Heeley, 1981). The new system of Structure and Local Plans created by the 1968 Town and Country Planning Act, reinforced county and district planning authorities' ability to influence the rate of new developments in all sectors, including tourism. The setting up of the English Regional Tourist Boards in the early 1970s also gave LAs the opportunity to further influence tourism development, through their membership of these organisations.

The first sign that national government was seeking to persuade all LAs to take a greater interest in tourism development came in the 1979 circular from the Department of the Environment (13/79, 1979) entitled *Local Government and the Development of Tourism*. This asked LAs to consider whether 'they should do more by the redeployment of resources to realise the full potential of tourism to create and sustain jobs and to produce income in their locality'. It also advised LAs to have regard to tourism in drawing up structure and local plans and to liaise with neighbouring authorities in tourism planning. However, as Richards and Wilkes point out, it was still left to individual LAs to 'have regard to the importance of tourism in their particular area in forming their policy'. Essentially, this allowed authorities indifferent or antagonistic to tourism development to continue ignoring tourism issues (Richards and Wilkes, 1990). Nevertheless, the number of LAs still indifferent to tourism development continued to shrink throughout the 1980s, as tourism's potential role in economic development was increasingly recognised. In particular, tourism's ability to create jobs was strongly emphasised in a flurry of reports from central government and government agencies, all proclaiming the optimistic vision of tourism as a potential source of new employment opportunities.

The Department of the Environment circular coincided with the publication of a report by the ETB entitled *Planning for Tourism*, which also urged LAs to take a more positive attitude towards tourism. This was followed in 1980 by another ETB publication, *Tourism in the Inner City*, which exhorted urban LAs to be more favourably disposed towards tourism-related developments.

In 1985, Lord Young's report on *Pleasure, Leisure and Jobs* (DoE, 1985) and a Confederation of British Industry report on tourism, *Paying Guests* (CBI, 1985) vaunted the positive impacts which tourism could have, particularly on employment. In the same year, the House of Commons Select Committee on Trade and Industry, in the report of its enquiry into UK tourism, emphasised the importance of the role of LAs in developing tourism, saying that 'the face the UK presents to the visitor is largely determined by local authorities'. But it is worthy of note that pressure on LAs to be more supportive of tourism development in their localities did not come from government sources alone. Three reports published between 1982 and 1984 by the Association of District Councils, emphasised the need for a more positive attitude towards this sector, mainly due to its potential for job creation (ADC, 1983, 1984).

Central government encouragement of LAs to take a more positive attitude towards tourism continued into the 1990s, repeating more or less the same themes. In October 1996, LAs were urged to make the most of the economic potential offered by tourism, with the publication of a Department of National Heritage (DNH) document entitled *Guidance to Successor Local Authorities on Tourism*. The five areas highlighted for particular attention were: planning policies relating to tourism; the management of tourist information centres; tourism's role in economic development and regeneration; effective tourism marketing; and LAs' enforcement of regulations (DNH 1996).

A useful profile of changing LA attitudes towards tourism, throughout the 1980s and into the 1990s, is provided by two surveys undertaken in 1983/4 and 1987/8, the results of which are described by Richards and Wilkes (1990), and by the 1991 UK Local Authority Tourism Survey (Richards, 1992).

Richards and Wilkes based their study on a comparison of two questionnaire surveys:

■ a 1984 survey of the extent of tourism involvement by non-metropolitan LAs in England, undertaken by the Association of District Councils (ADC, 1984)

■ a 1988 study conducted jointly by the Centre for Leisure and Tourism Studies at the Polytechnic of North London and Mid Sussex District Leisure Services.

Their study also analyses trends in other aspects of tourism activity over this period, including the number of staff employed, the presence of a tourism policy, and the political composition of the authorities concerned.

It shows that, during the 1980s, a considerable redeployment of resources in favour of the tourism sector took place among non-metropolitan LAs at a time when LA budgets were being restricted by central government.

There was an increase of over 40% in the number of authorities allocating specific budgets for tourism, rising from 55 (48% of the total number of authorities surveyed) to 79 (69% of the total). Total budget allocations doubled during the period 1983/4 to 1987/88 which, allowing for inflation, represented an increase of 70% in real terms. However, although this undoubtedly signals increased recognition of the importance of this sector over the country as a whole, an analysis of spending levels by geographical locations reveals that by far the most of the increase in actual spending came from 'traditional' tourism destinations (i.e. coastal authorities). These accounted for over 80% of total tourism budgets in 1987/88 and were responsible for the bulk of the absolute increase in expenditure since the 1983/4 survey. Nevertheless, it is significant that inland authorities (many of them non-traditional destinations) increased their tourism expenditure at a faster rate than their coastal counterparts, albeit from a much lower base (Richards and Wilks, 1990).

The marked increase in LA interest in tourism promotion and development during the 1980s, is indicated by several other factors highlighted by the Richards and Wilkes study. The total number of tourism staff employed by the authorities surveyed increased from 422 in 1983/4, to 545 in 1987/8; over the same period, the proportion of

those authorities running their own tourist information centres (TICs) rose from just over 50% to over 70%; and a still higher proportion (84%) published their own tourist information literature in 1988.

The 1990s were characterised by growing restrictions on LA spending, and there were early signs that the rapid expansion of tourism expenditure by LAs was over. Although their promotional expenditure on tourism at the beginning of the decade was estimated to be in the region of £30 million for the UK as a whole – a figure far outstripping the expenditure of the national and regional tourist boards – actual cutbacks on this form of spending in the 1990s were more widespread than the kind of expansion experienced in the previous decade (Richards, 1992). As a non-statutory area of provision, tourism was a natural victim of spending cuts, as financial pressure on LAs continued to mount. However, it is significant that such cuts were largely restricted to English LAs, with Scotland, Wales and Northern Ireland continuing to increase their promotional budgets (ibid).

Despite the downward pressure on their spending on tourism-related matters, LAs have emerged in their own right, in recent years, as effective agents of tourism development and marketing at the sub-national level in the UK. They are supported in this task by the regional and area tourist boards.

REGIONAL/AREA TOURIST BOARDS

Following the creation of the three national tourist boards of England, Scotland and Wales at the end of the 1960s, each set about forming its own regional structure for tourism marketing and development. In England, 12 Regional Tourist Boards (RTBs) were established, jointly funded by the ETB, LAs and contributions from the commercial sector. Working in liaison with these funding partners, the RTBs' principal objective is the marketing of their regions through a range of promotional activities, in the same way in which their Scottish and Welsh equivalents market their own local areas. In each case, however, the boards have a number of other responsibilities, which may include:

- producing a coordinated strategy for tourism within their regions
- representing the interests of the region at national level, and the interests of the tourist industry within the region
- encouraging the development of tourist amenities and facilities which meet the changing needs of the market.

Responsibilities under this last heading are assumed by the boards' Development Departments, whose activities are aimed at attracting new tourism development into their regions, through promoting expansion opportunities to developers such as hotel groups. In connection with this objective, the Development Departments administered the Section 4 grants scheme before the demise of this system (see page 148).

Since their respective inceptions, significant changes have occurred in the organisation of regional and area tourist boards in England, Scotland and Wales.

In Scotland, the 32 Area Tourist Boards set up in the early 1980s were amalgamated into a system of 14 statutory, but private sector-dominated, bodies which undertake a range of tourism marketing functions for the Scottish regions. Wales' original regional tourist boards were eventually privatised into three Tourism Companies.

Following the 1988 review of the ETB, resources were devolved from the ETB to the RTBs, giving them much more influence and autonomy (and, also, according to some commentators, leaving the ETB with so little in the way of resources that its ability to deliver its own statutory functions effectively, was seriously compromised). This increase in ETB funding to the regions (currently accounting for roughly 50% of the ETB's grant–in–aid) had a considerable impact, increasing their level of activity as well as their ability to generate additional support from partners (particularly the private sector) through growing numbers of commercial membership subscriptions.

Another role for the RTBs arose in the early 1990s, when the UK government established a greater regional element to government, through establishing its integrated Regional Government Offices (RGOs), bringing together the functions of the Departments of the Environment, Trade and Industry, Employment and Transport under a single director. The RTBs supply a valuable tourism perspective for the activities of the RGOs, where other agencies such as regional Arts Boards, Sports Councils and the Countryside Commission are also represented. Two areas of significance to tourism are the involvement of the RGOs in the administration of the Single Regeneration Budget and the applications for Structural Funds from the EU.

REGIONAL/AREA TOURIST BOARDS AND LOCAL AUTHORITIES

Given their common responsibilities and objectives, RTBs and LAs inevitably find themselves collaborating in the development and promotion of destination areas. Where the aims of both types of organisation coincide, such collaboration can be very productive, but this is by no means always the case, and relations between the RTBs and the LAs have occasionally been difficult. Indeed, in many ways, the increasing role of LAs in tourism promotion can be said to have undermined the effectiveness of RTBs (Robinson, 1996).

The fact that most LAs now have a Tourism Officer, a range of brochures and a preoccupation with the promotion of their area, combined with the fact that they are also the owner/operators of the TICs, means that they are in a very powerful position *vis à vis* their RTBs. Not all LAs have chosen to use that power cooperatively, and poor representation of some LAs on their RTBs by uninterested Councillors who do not liaise well, has been an impediment to the effectiveness of certain RTBs.

In terms of tourism strategy and policy, there is further scope for problems when LAs and RTBs differ in their objectives for tourism.

'Although RTBs must work with their LAs and cooperate with them in tourism planning, their aims may well be in conflict with those of the LAs. Therefore, the construction of a coordinated strategy for the promotion of tourism in the face of the diverse interests of LAs and RTBs is necessary, but is not an easy matter.'

(Gilbert and Tung, 1990)

There is a major distinction between the involvement in tourism of LAs and that of RTBs. Unlike the RTBs, whose aims are essentially promotional, the LAs bear wider responsibilities, including the protection of the environment and land-use planning. They may therefore be as concerned to reduce or stabilise tourism, as to develop it (particularly when, as can be the case in the popular tourist resorts or historic towns, local electors are opposed to increases in the numbers of tourists). The tourism-related objectives of some LAs may therefore differ considerably from those of the RTBs which cover their area. As Greenwood *et al.* (1990) observe: 'one obvious divergence is the greater priority attached by many LAs to conservation rather than to maximising the economic benefits of tourism'.

Nevertheless, despite the occasional resistance or indifference displayed by some LAs towards the local board covering their area, the boards have been relatively successful in enlisting LA support. This is demonstrated in the case of England by the fact that almost 9 out of 10 authorities are members of their RTB (Richards, 1992). The earlier survey of LAs had concluded that:

'authorities without RTB memberships generally had no tourism policy. Therefore, those authorities which have taken an interest in tourism development give a high level of support to RTBs.'

(Richard and Wilkes, 1990)

The high level of LA participation in RTB membership is undoubtedly related to the benefits that membership confers. When asked about the most important services provided to them by RTBs, LA members have in the past been most likely to cite marketing support, or advice and information, followed by TIC support (e.g. staff training) and research (Richards, 1992).

However, there is another important motivation for LAs becoming members of their local tourist board. As LAs have a major role to play in the implementing of RTB policies at local level, it is clearly in their interest to be part of the policy-making process. Their contributions to local tourist board funds entitle them to participation of this kind. LAs are usually represented on the boards' committees and sub-committees, where they join other parties with an interest in local tourism development and marketing, notably, representatives from the private sector (drawn from the boards' commercial members) and voluntary organisations (such as local heritage groups).

In addition to their collaboration at local tourist board committee level, RTBs, LAs, and the private and voluntary sector representatives have, in recent years, increasingly been entering into specific partnership ventures, through (for example) cooperative marketing programmes and joint support for TICs. More generally, the same partners have joined resources with others, including Urban Development Corporations and rural regeneration organisations, in a number of high-profile, action-oriented tourism programmes of the type we examine later in this chapter.

PLANNING AND MANAGING TOURISM AT THE DESTINATION LEVEL IN THE UK

DEVELOPMENT PLANNING AND ENTREPRENEURIAL PLANNING

Since the beginning of civilisation, the physical environment in which we live has been subject to a dynamic and continuous process of change brought about by human needs and activities. The land has been enclosed, cultivated, built upon and tunnelled through; while waterways and lakes have been bridged, dammed, diverted and drained. Industrialisation has changed the functioning, layout and appearance of our cities; while tourism has transformed the character of many coastal towns. Throughout history, moves have been made to regulate and control such changes for the common good. The result is that in most countries there is a system designed to guide and control the development and use of the built and natural environment 'in the public interest'. This is called 'development planning', or 'land-use' planning.

The critical importance of this form of planning was succinctly put by the Audit Commission in their 1992 report *Building in Quality* as follows:

> 'Decisions taken in the planning process have long-term consequences and are usually irreversible. Well-considered decisions can enhance and enrich the environment. Poor decisions will be endured long after the decision-takers have died.'
>
> *(Audit Commission, 1992)*

The development of tourism facilities and infrastructure is subject to a process of development planning, as is any other industry. So tourism development takes place within the context of the land-use planning system of the UK. Since 1947, a system of statutory development plans has provided LAs with a formal and legally-enforceable basis for guiding development in their areas. Most forms of development are subject to the prior approval of these LAs, who may grant or withhold planning permission on the basis of development planning policy and other relevant matters (known as 'material considerations'). Planning authorities have extensive powers of enforcement, including procedures which require anyone who carries out development without permission to 'undo' the development by returning the site to its former use (e.g. by demolishing a building erected without planning permission). In addition to these plans to guide and regulate development, post-war land-use planning has included a series of positive mechanisms to promote development in particular areas. These have varied over time, and with the

ideological stance of central government, but have always been concerned with managing the interface between public and private sectors in development. Initiatives have included: partnerships between public and private sectors in post-war reconstruction and city and town centre redevelopment; and single-purpose agencies for major projects, such as new Town Development Corporations and, more recently, Urban Development Corporations.

Broad agreement about the role and purpose of planning and of local government in managing and regulating development was established as part of the post-war consensus, and remained more or less intact for 30 years. However, by the mid 1970s that consensus was breaking down, and with it went the agreement about planning. The election of Mrs Thatcher's Conservative Party in 1979 saw a profound shift in perspective, which advocated the primacy and desirability of market processes, with a consequent preference for the private sector and distrust of the public sector. This inevitably had a significant effect on land-use planning which, as an arm of the public sector intervening in the operation of the private sector, was viewed with suspicion. As Rydin says:

> '... the twin elements of development planning and development control were restructured in line with a more market-oriented approach. Government advice on development control made it clear that a more "positive" approach to planning was to be adopted ... DoE Circular 14/85 established clearly that there was a presumption in favour of planning permission being granted unless planning objections could be sustained. And a series of Circulars ... stressed the need to take account of market forces.'
>
> *(Rydin, 1993)*

The importance of development plans was downgraded, and the importance of market forces emphasised. DoE Circular 16/84, for example, advised that planning permission could not be refused simply because the proposed development was contrary to the approved development plan.

On the face of it, this seems to show a clear reduction in the role of planning and a move in favour of market forces. However, in practice matters were more complicated, and in some areas planning control remained powerful. This was the result of two interlinked factors.

■ There was an upsurge of interest in the environment during the 1980s, embracing both rural areas and the natural environment, and heritage and conservation. This meant that there was strong public support for measures to protect the countryside and historic urban areas, and widespread opposition to allowing development to be determined by market forces

■ The 1980s saw the growth of NIMBY-ism ('Not In My Back Yard'), with well-organised residents' groups opposing development in commuter villages and urban conservation areas (Shucksmith, 1990, quoted Rydin, 1993). The strength of these pressures, and with them a requirement for effective planning, was hard for central government to resist.

The result was what Thornley (1991) describes as

'. . . a strong planning system operating in certain areas where conservation and environmental factors are considered important. Elsewhere the system has been much modified and weakened and market criteria are expected to dominate. There are also an increasing number of categories of development where previous planning controls have been removed altogether.'

(Thornley, 1991)

This division within the planning system has meant that policy on tourism has had distinct elements.

■ In rural areas and heritage towns and cities, the emphasis has been on strong **development planning**, regulating land use, seeking environmental protection and managing visitors to reduce their adverse impacts.

■ In many urban areas, tourism has played a leading role in new approaches to planning which have emerged from economic development and regeneration efforts in the 1980s. This approach (sometimes called **entrepreneurial planning**) works within the framework of development plans but relies for its effect on an ability to influence private-sector investment through marketing, promotion, subsidy and grants.

There is obviously overlap between the two approaches, and the distinction has perhaps become rather less sharp in the 1990s, when there has been some reassertion of the importance of land-use plans throughout the country (the reassertion of 'plan-led development'). In particular, implementing policies has increasingly come to rely on some form of partnership between the public- and private-sector agencies, whether the policy is to do with visitor management in National Parks and historic cities, or with regeneration initiatives in decaying metropolitan areas. Nonetheless, it is helpful to describe the two approaches separately, as we do below.

It is also worth noting two other themes which emerge from this brief discussion.

1 Planning is about managing the conflicting interests of different parties (e.g. developers and local residents, or defenders of the environment and promoters of economic development). It is political, in the sense that it requires decisions to be made which affect these different interests, and decisions on apparently similar developments may vary from place to place (and over time) as priorities change. For example, a city with high levels of unemployment will be likely to give very high priority to development which creates jobs, even if that results in damage to the natural environment. A prosperous town with low levels of unemployment may value the natural environment much more highly, and strongly resist any development which has adverse effects upon it.

2 Although LAs operate the planning system, they do so within a context which is set by central government, and which circumscribes their role and their policies. The policy a LA adopts on tourism (like any other development) depends both on its judgement of what

best serves the needs of its community, and on the scope for action permitted by central government. We elaborate these themes in the discussion that follows.

DEVELOPMENT PLANNING

In many countries, plans (or zoning schemes or ordinances) are complex and legally binding, with a clear hierarchical relationship between the plan and decisions on individual proposals; in addition, such plans are map based. In Britain, the system is one of flexibility. The administration of the system occurs predominantly at the local level. 'The two central elements [of the system] are the provision of indicative guidance through development plans and the control of development plans on a case-by-case basis through development control' (Rydin, 1993). Although the day-to-day operation of the system is the responsibility of local authorities in Britain, it is the Secretary of State who has overall responsibility for the operation of the system, and who sets out national policy and guidance within which the system must operate. Some would claim therefore that 'planning is an instrument for achieving in the land-use context whatever happen to be the political goals of the government of the day' (Alder, 1989).

Development plans 'are not prescriptive' (DoE PPG12, 1992). They are essentially policy documents, with maps and diagrams which are only illustrative, and they are only one of the factors to be taken into account in the determination of planning applications. Decisions are taken in the political arena with elected representatives (Councillors) responsible for the final decision. Development Plans are set within a context of **Planning Policy Guidance (PPGs)** and **Regional Policy Guidance (RPGs)**. RPGs set a policy context for the different regions of the country. PPGs are prepared by the Department of the Environment and provide advice and guidance on how particular policy issues should be dealt with. *PPG 21* which deals with tourism was issued in November 1992 and was the first planning guidance note ever produced specifically on tourism. The role of planning, according to this document, was to 'facilitate and encourage development and improvement in tourism provision, while tackling any adverse effects of existing tourist attractions and activity in a constructive and positive manner' (Paragraph 2.4). It emphasises that the overall objective is to achieve 'sustainable development' that serves the interests of both economic growth and the conservation of the environment. Recognition of the economic importance of tourism is, throughout the document, tempered by concern for environmental matters.

PPG 21 also identifies tourism as one of the key strategic topics which should be dealt with in Structure Plans (see below). There is specific encouragement to use tourism as an element in urban regeneration (see 'Entrepreneurial planning' below). Encouragement is also given in connection with the possible designation of **Action Areas** and **Simplified Planning Zones** as positive ways in which the planning system can assist the development of tourism. Also relevant are *PPG 13* and *PPG 6*, both of which stress the need to minimise car movements, a preference for locating major traffic generators in town centres, and the need for developments to be accessible by a range of means of transport. Tourism and leisure developments will clearly be significantly affected by all of this guidance.

Prior to the reorganisation of local government which began in April 1996, there were three main types of development plan in England and Wales (a different system applied in Scotland), designed for a two-tier system of local government.

- **Structure Plans** (which are county-wide and prepared by County Councils) provide a broad framework for development planning, with a 15-year horizon. Their role is:
  - to provide the strategic policy framework for planning and control at the local level
  - to ensure that the provision for development is realistic and consistent with national and regional policy
  - to secure consistency between local plans for neighbouring areas.
- **Local Plans** (which are district-wide and prepared by District/Borough Councils or

National Park Authorities) must be in general conformity with the Structure Plan. They set out more detailed policies and site-specific proposals for the development and use of land, and should guide most day-to-day planning decisions. In general, they have a 10-year horizon.

- **Unitary Development Plans (UDPs)** are prepared in single-tier 'unitary' authorities. Such authorities were first established in 1985 when the Government's abolition of the Metropolitan County Councils and the GLC created a single-tier system of government in large urban areas. UDPs essentially combine Structure and Local Plans in one document. As *PPG 12* puts it:

'Part 1 is analogous to the structure plan in non-metropolitan areas ... The broad development and land-use strategy in Part I provides a framework for the authority's detailed proposals in Part II, which is analogous to the local plan in non-metropolitan areas ... The proposals in Part II must be in general conformity with Part I.'
(PPG 12)

The process of local government reorganisation is complicating this picture considerably. The reorganisation which has emerged is piecemeal. While in some areas the two-tier system will be replaced by a single unitary authority, in others the two-tier structure remains. There has been no wholesale abolition of the upper tier of counties, so in many cases new unitary authorities (which take over county functions for their area) are geographically located within counties which elsewhere have continuing administrative functions. So far as planning is concerned, five of the new unitary authorities (Isle of Wight, Halton, Herefordshire, Thurrock and Warrington) will prepare UDPs, while the rest will prepare Joint Structure Plans, usually with the remainder of the county of which they form a geographical part. Unitary authorities will also prepare district-wide Local Plans. The new system will come into being gradually as the new Unitary District Councils are established – currently scheduled to be in three tranches in April 1996, 1997, and 1998.

In the UK, most forms of development are subject to the prior approval of the local planning authority, who may give or withhold planning permission, although their decision making is circumscribed by central government influence. LAs must take account of national policies (expressed, for example in PPGs) – the Secretary of State sets procedural rules and can intervene in the process of plan-making or 'call in' planning applicants. In addition, applicants can appeal to the Secretary of State against a refusal of planning permission, and the Secretary's decisions set precedents for similar applications in the future. In reaching their decision, authorities are required to take account of the development plan and any other material considerations, and there is a presumption in favour of granting permission unless there are clear reasons to show a proposal is harmful.

The term 'development' when used in this context has been statutorily defined as 'the carrying out of building, engineering, mining or other operations in, on, over, or under land, or the making of any material change in the use of any buildings or other land' (Town and Country Planning Act, 1990, s 55).

There are two parts to this definition.

1 The first concerns activities which physically change the environment, e.g. through the building of a new marina, caravan site or hotel complex in a town. Clearly, such developments can have a major impact on the town's economy, as well as implications for its appearance and factors such as traffic, noise and waste disposal, but these effects will not fall within the commercial considerations of developers. The role of development planning and control is to ensure that careful consideration is given to proposed developments, including their siting, scale, and visual impact, their economic, social and community impacts, and their overall effect on the character of a place. For example, holiday villages such as those belonging to the Center Parcs chain usually receive planning permission because:

- they are carefully sited to minimise impact on the natural environment and on the local roads from the traffic they generate

■ they generate significant numbers of jobs
■ they are of high quality design using local materials for construction
■ they are screened by woods.

But, by contrast, many communities object to coastal caravan parks in their vicinity since they create few jobs and have a series of adverse environmental impacts, of which their effect on the landscape is the most noticeable. In such cases, planning permission may be refused or given subject to a number of conditions (e.g. limiting the number of pitches or the period of the year during which the caravan park may operate). Some types of development fall within the class of 'permitted development' and do not require an application for planning permission, even though they can have a significant effect on the environment, e.g. many agricultural buildings.

2 The second half of the above definition of 'development' is concerned with a change in the *use* of a piece of land or building, rather than its physical development. To qualify as development, any change in use has to be 'substantial', for example, the change from a private residence to a hotel (as opposed to the taking in of lodgers or 'bed-and-breakfast' guests in what remains primarily a family home). Such substantial changes of use can have effects as great as actual physical development. For example, the change from house to hotel will create jobs, but generate more traffic, cause noise or congestion, affect the character of the area and result in a loss of housing. Again, the decision to give or withhold planning permission will depend on an assessment of the overall effects of the proposed development. However, the power of local planning authorities to limit changes in the use of buildings is circumscribed by the fact that many types of proposed changes do not constitute development and so avoid the need to obtain planning permission. This can have particular relevance for tourism. For example, no planning permission is necessary for the conversion of cottages into second homes or for turning a local bakery into a souvenir shop, however much local people

might wish to prevent such changes. In addition, minor forms of development (such as extensions to dwelling houses or alterations to other types of building) may not need planning permission unless they take place in a specially-protected area such as a Conservation Area.

It can be seen that much development planning is regulatory in nature, but more positively, its principal value lies in the fact that it can influence and guide development according to the objectives set by policy makers for the destination. Well-considered planning decisions based on effective development plans can shape the destination in terms of matters such as: the type of development on a prime site; the location of facilities; type and location of accommodation; traffic management; and the overall character, design and appearance of the place. Accordingly, through the actions of its locally-elected representatives, the community has the opportunity to influence the type of tourism which takes place in its area of residence. In addition, the system can secure advantages and improvements from particular developments. For example, conditions can be attached to planning permissions to control or restrict uses (e.g. opening hours) and to limit future development. Legal agreements (known as 'Section 106 agreements') can be attached to planning permissions so that community facilities or benefits are provided as part of the development. In Plymouth, for example, Sainsburys obtained planning permission for a superstore with an agreement to provide facilities including a TIC, a bird-watching hide, a static art feature, a park-and-ride facility, and a contribution of £1 million to infrastructure on a nearby industrial site (Mole, 1996).

Significant strengthening of the positive features of the planning system apparently arrived with the publication of the *Environment White Paper* in 1990 and the passing of the Planning and Compensation Act in 1991, which retrospectively introduced a new section, Section 54A, into the 1990 Town and Country Planning Act. Section 54A appeared to give more weight to the development plan in the determination of applications. It states: 'Where in making any determination under Planning acts, regard is to be had to the development plan, the determination shall be in accordance with the plan unless material considerations indicate otherwise.'

There has been much debate about the significance of Section 54A since its introduction. The government suggests that we now have a plan-led system and that the weight accorded to the development plan is far greater than it was. Kaye (1992) argued that this had some important consequences:

(a) Planning decision-making is firmly based at Local Authority level, and the Government is committed to keeping down the number of appeals.

(b) As part of the same philosophy, the Development Plan   Structure Plan, Local Plan or Unitary Plan as the case may be – takes on a new importance ...

(c) Environmental considerations are playing an increasingly dominant role in the consideration of all types of development.

(d) A new enforcement regime is now settling into place, giving Local Authorities new powers and greatly increasing the penalties for non-compliance.'

(Kaye, 1992)

This perhaps overstates the case. The legal position is little changed as other material considerations need only 'indicate otherwise' for decisions to be made, quite legitimately, which do not accord with the plan.

'The new commitment towards development planning is to be welcomed but appears to be too constrained by central government policy in both policy formulation and policy implementation ... Decision makers are starting to realise that the newly found status of the development plan as a means of determining applications is off-set by numerous checks and balances imposed by the DoE, one of which is referring to the contents of national policy documents.'

(Tewdr-Jones, 1994)

'Court rulings suggest that the increased weight to be given to the plan will be limited [because] rigid policies are discouraged by DoE intervention in the plan making process. Circumstances change and plans get out of date, ... there is scope for discretion in interpreting policies and in deciding which of two or more conflicting policies should take precedence.'

(Edmundson, 1993)

In practice, it seems that more weight is being given to development plans in appeal decisions. This will undoubtedly influence LAs in their determination of planning applications, and to that extent there has been a shift toward a plan-led system; however, government influence remains very considerable. In any event, plans can only lead development when there is development pressure. In a flat market, or in areas where developers do not wish to invest, plans alone will not secure development, however desirable (see 'Entrepreneurial planning' below).

Clearly, there is considerable scope for tension between those with the power to grant or withhold planning permission, the planning authorities; and those wishing to construct new developments, the developers and operators. Within the context of the tourism sector, such tensions were summed up by Chris Evans, chairing a joint Tourism Society/Royal Town Planning Institute meeting in 1993. He mentioned 'the real or imaginary problems applicants face when dealing with the planners', on the one hand, and, on the other, the view that 'planners frequently fail to fully appreciate the needs and aspirations of the leisure developer and the role which leisure can play in the economic and social fabric of the community'. This latter point of view includes the perception that leisure and tourism do not create 'real' jobs. Tourism developers complain that LAs with this attitude are more favourable towards planning applications from the manufacturing or retail sectors, for example (Kaye, 1993). Chris Evans is in fact referring to two different sources of conflict, and it is worth unpicking them.

- **'Real' problems** arise because there is a real conflict. Tourism developers (like other developers) have interests which, quite legitimately, diverge from those of the wider community, as represented by the planning authority. Developers are concerned primarily with the commercial success of their development; planners are concerned with its broader effect on the area in which it will take place. One function of the planning process is to mediate these conflicts and to seek resolution through a process of negotiation. This may be achieved through conditions attached to permissions, or through an agreement. However, there will be circumstances in which a development, though desirable from a developer's point of view, is undesirable from the community's, and permission will be refused.

- **Imaginary problems** can arise because of misunderstanding by either or both sides — about the nature of developments, and their costs and benefits (the perception that tourism jobs are not 'real' jobs is an example that we discussed in Chapter 5). Misunderstandings can be resolved by the parties making deliberate attempts to understand one another better. The various forms of partnership discussed in this book and illustrated in the case studies are one means of achieving this. Working towards consensus on objectives and policy means that imaginary problems can be done away with, and real problems or conflicts revealed (see case study C, Cambridge). In addition, the tourism and leisure industry needs to involve itself in the development planning process. As Kaye (1992) says, they should:

'Be aware of and take an active role in the preparation of Development Plans. This does not simply mean checking that your pet project has an allocation in the Plan, but, perhaps more important, that the written policies applicable throughout the Plan's area are appropriately worded in a way which will ensure a positive response on all tourism-related developments.'

(Kaye, 1992)

but should also bear in mind that:

'Environmental factors will play an ever-increasing role in the consideration of all future developments. The fact that a development is intended to meet tourist needs does not mean that planning policies to protect the environment will not apply or that they will be applied any less rigorously.'

(Kaye, 1992)

ENTREPRENEURIAL PLANNING

Development planning controls and guides development and, by doing so, can act positively to make the most of a destination's potential, and protect and enhance its resources. However, development planning is heavily reliant on private-sector action for its effects, and without pressure for development, its scope is limited. In many areas of the UK in the 1980s and 1990s, there has been little or no development pressure and planning has therefore sought to *create* products and projects to achieve regeneration. In this section we discuss the evolution of planning for urban regeneration. We argue that a new approach to planning is emerging which seeks to combine private-sector requirements with a greater sense of public purpose: **entrepreneurial planning**. The potential of tourism and leisure in regeneration has helped shape this approach. Partnership between public and private sectors has been a key element, and this links entrepreneurial planning with specific tourism initiatives such as TDAPs and LATIs, examined later in this chapter.

During the 1980s, planning in many urban areas in the UK was preoccupied with securing economic regeneration and with adapting to the requirements of the Conservative government's 'enterprise culture' (Deakins and Edwards, 1993). The focus on economic regeneration resulted from economic changes (described in Chapter 5) which led to the widespread loss of traditional industries with consequent dereliction, unemployment and stagnation. The 'enterprise culture' arose from the government's ideological commitment to market solutions as means of organising and achieving economic development. So far as planning was concerned, there were three interlinked elements which had the effect of downgrading the role of planning and elevating that of market forces:

- **Centralisation** – LAs lost planning powers to new agencies established by central government (such as Urban Development orporations), or saw them reduced by government initiatives (such as Enterprise Zones). In addition, central government reduced the scope for local initiative by taking control of LA finance. Total expenditure was capped, and spending under particular budget heads was prescribed. In the most extreme case, it dealt with opposition from the Greater London Council and Metropolitan County Councils by abolishing them.
- **Fragmentation** – not only were powers to organise and carry out redevelopment initiatives dispersed to the new Quangos, but new central government programmes originated from different departments, and were often small scale and applied to small geographic areas. In these circumstances, there were problems of coordination, and of establishing coherent area strategies.
- **Private-sector leadership** – public policies were designed to encourage and facilitate investment by the private sector, and also to give the private sector a leading role in formulating policy. In Stewart's words there were a 'a range of initiatives ... which by-pass the local political process of planning' (Stewart, 1994). In addition, some commentators believe that there was a related element of hegemonic change involved, in the face of evidence that the Thatcher values of enterprise and initiative were actually taken up by local government staff. In many cases, there was a change in attitude from regulation to entrepreneurship.

The result was that in contrast to earlier years, the approach to regeneration, particularly in urban areas, was based much less on direct development by the public sector and much more on levering in private-sector investment by subsidies, land provision and confidence building strategies (see Rydin, 1993). Tourism and leisure activities were often central to initiatives to attract private investment and change the image of an area (see Chapter 5). The stress was primarily on property-led economic development,

with an assumption that economic success would deliver broader environmental and social benefits. Planning became strongly oriented toward processes which could influence the behaviour of private investors, and so developed a concern for the construction of effective public-private partnerships.

Harvey (1989) sets these changes in a wider context, in a review of trends in urban governance in USA and Europe (quoted in Bailey, 1995).

> 'First, the new entrepreneurialism has, as its centrepiece, the notion of "public-private partnership" in which a traditional local boosterism is integrated with the use of local governmental powers to try and attract external sources of funding, new investments or new employment sources. ... Secondly, the activity of the public-private partnership is entrepreneurial precisely because it is speculative in execution and design and therefore dogged by all the difficulties and dangers that attach to speculative as opposed to rationally planned and coordinated development.'
>
> *(Harvey, 1989)*

By the late 1980s, some of the problems of relying on private-sector led development were becoming apparent. The disintegration of the UK property market meant that even with grants and subsidies, it was increasingly difficult to secure private-sector investment, and the credibility of property-led regeneration was damaged with the collapse of Olympia and York, the developers of the Canary Wharf project in London's Docklands. At the same time, it became clear that there was little evidence that where development was successful, benefits were 'trickling down' to local people (Thornley, 1991). From the private sector point-of-view, in a weak market, developers became more concerned to secure the certainty that clearer planning strategies could provide. From central government's standpoint, there was a return to a greater acceptance of plan-led development as a means of dealing with the conflict between developers and increasingly-effective advocates of protection of the environment (*ibid*). Planning was required to balance the needs of development with protecting the natural and built environment (*PPG 1*, para.4). However despite this increased role for planning, concern with the requirements of the private sector remains dominant. '... Finance is controlled by central government who are able to ... ensure ... that a private-sector led strategy is adopted, even though local authorities have apparent freedom' (Thornley, 1991).

Stoker and Young (1993) argue that although the private sector still has a central role, in the 1990s there is a move to a more holistic approach to analysing and tackling the problems of an area. This approach to renewal can be characterised as developing a business plan approach to area development (an approach which tries to combine long-term vision, from a community point of view, with the requirements of the private sector). In this way, a greater concern with longer range planning has begun to return. As David Taylor, former Chief Executive of English Partnerships (a government Quango) said:

> 'The view of the public sector at central government level is that the private sector is free of bureaucracy and can spend money when and where it likes. In fact, business plans and long-term thinking are integral to the private sector. This needs to be mirrored in the public sector. We must rehabilitate the concept of "think ahead".'
>
> *(Taylor, 1995)*

Stoker and Young have described this emerging approach to regeneration as entrepreneurial planning. It is an approach within which tourism and leisure have important roles to play. Stoker and Young see entrepreneurial planning stemming from approaches devised in the 1980s to regenerate and attract investment to rundown areas. It means understanding the requirements of the private sector so as to create a market and lever private investment into these rundown areas. These may be within generally prosperous cities (e.g. Bristol Docks, where the Arnolfini and Watershed arts complexes played a crucial role), or within cities coping with major economic change (e.g. Little Germany in the Bradford case study), or in smaller towns. However, entrepre-

neurial planning is not simply about economic development; it seeks also to 'accommodate a wider social regeneration approach targeted more explicitly at local needs and local problems' (Stoker and Young, 1993). Crucially, this view of regeneration requires more than investment in property and the physical environment. It sees area revival coming from a mixture of investment, with measures to address local needs and recreate vitality and life in an area. This means that tourism and leisure can have a central role to play, through their potential to attract people at all times of the day and to generate fun and festivity.

Stoker and Young describe entrepreneurial planning in terms of 'flagship projects and schemes on big vacant sites' with a five-stage approach, requiring five key implementation tasks.

The five stages are:

1 **Securing access to the site**: dealing with problems of land ownership which are blocking redevelopment.
2 **Land renewal**: carrying out remediation works and providing infrastructure so that the site is ready for redevelopment.
3 **Public-sector investment projects**: schemes carried out by the public sector to signal the area's potential and the LAs commitment, and thus generate confidence.
4 **Initiating private-sector investment**: for example, through promoting development briefs or packages, perhaps including grant assistance.
5 **Implementing private-sector schemes**: carrying out the projects prepared in the previous stage and dealing with problems and amendments.

Stoker and Young identify five implementation tasks (which they term the five Ss) which must be undertaken if renewal is to be achieved:

■ **sites** – effort should be focused on the sites with greatest potential, where limited public-sector investments can stimulate or create a market (e.g. the regeneration of Covent Garden in the 1970s)
■ **strategy** – a framework for development is needed to promote confidence and guide de-

velopment, but it must incorporate private-sector perceptions about market potential, and should focus on implementation and the tasks for the different agencies involved

- subsidies – affect the private sector's calculation of the viability of investment and a package of loans and grants can be assembled from a variety of sources
- spotlights – publicity, and telling a story about the success of the development process increases confidence and provides free marketing, thus promoting further investment
- skills – entrepreneurial planners need the skills to develop effective partnerships with the private sector, including a clear understanding of private-sector objectives and perspectives.

Tourism and leisure activities can be crucial to this process. It is interesting that although Stoker and Young are not writing from a tourism perspective, six of the nine specific developments they quote to illustrate the entrepreneurial planning process are tourism or leisure schemes (pages 39–42). The reasons are clear, and derive from the potential of tourism as a regeneration catalyst which we discussed in Chapter 5. Tourism can be involved at the most crucial stages of the process.

- It can assist **land renewal** by providing potential uses for derelict historic buildings; museums or galleries are common **public-sector investment projects** which can help build confidence.
- As a growth industry with links to other activities, tourism or leisure uses can be a vital component in development packages designed to **initiate private investment**. The high visibility of such projects, and their potential to attract widespread interest makes them important in **strategies** to promote developer confidence and an obvious target for **spotlights**. Since many projects will involve the arts or sport, they may attract specific **subsidies** which can be added to regeneration funding.
- Finally, some '*skills*' required for entrepreneurial planning (such as marketing) may be well developed among those working in tourism and leisure.

Entrepreneurial planning seeks to achieve regeneration through a process which combines public objectives and private sector requirements, and inherent in this approach is the idea of partnership between public sector agencies and between the private sector and the public.

DESTINATION PLANS AND STRATEGIES

LOCAL AUTHORITY TOURISM STRATEGIES

LA tourism strategies and policies vary considerably in their scope, content and level of detail. Some are based on detailed research and analysis, highlighting specific action and initiatives. Others are simply general statements of council policy and intentions towards tourism. However, a well-researched and realistic tourism strategy or policy can be a very effective tool in developing tourism at a particular destination, to the advantage of residents, the environment and the tourism industry itself.

In his UK Local Authority Tourism Survey, Richards noted that over two-thirds of the authorities surveyed had a specific tourism policy and that there were signs that this proportion was set to increase, as 5% of respondents indicated that their authority was in the process of adopting a policy. Almost 60% of those LAs with a policy had adopted it between 1987 and 1990 – a figure which may partly be explained by the requirement for tourism to be considered in Structure Plans and Unitary Development Plans, as well as by the increasing economic importance of tourism. In general, those authorities which did not have a specific tourism policy tended to attract few tourists, had low promotion budgets and few tourism staff. Those authorities with larger visitor numbers, which did not have a specific tourism policy, tended to subsume tourism as part of a wider economic development or leisure strategy (Richards, 1992).

Many useful insights into the formulation and content of LAs' strategies for tourism are provided by J. Long's (1994) study based on a survey of tourism officers. Three of Long's comments regarding the formulation of tourism strategies by the authorities he surveyed are of particular interest.

1 First, concerning the issue of actual responsibility for producing the tourism strategy within the LA, Long comments that 'although the work of many hands, these British strategies have more commonly been produced by Leisure Services Departments than by Planning Departments'. This distinguishes LA tourism strategies from the type of plans so far considered in this chapter, which tend to be in the domain of Planning Departments/Economic Development Departments.

2 Second, referring to the consultation process leading up to the production of the strategies he states that:

'... greatest emphasis was given to the role of the Department and external consultation (both cited by just over a third). Rather fewer mentioned internal consultation and inter-departmental working parties. Some had had the luxury of using consultants either to produce a strategy or to do background work for it.'

3 Finally, regarding research:

'... while 15% indicated that research had been done to support the formulation of the strategy, it later became clear when analysing the strategies that rather more had had to rely on national data to make their case. This is a dangerous ploy because, while it may be useful in terms of advocacy in producing an upbeat manifesto for tourism, it does seem rather spurious to apply national statistics to some areas with as yet minimal levels of tourism ...'

(Long, 1994)

The survey identified the three principal reasons which LA tourism officers gave for the production of a strategy:

- to draw different parts of the authority together in common purpose (especially important in those authorities that do not have a Tourism Department) – or sometimes to provide the basis for restructuring
- to provide a manifesto for tourism (especially in those authorities where the role of tourism was not established) which could assist the search for funds
- to help to ensure effective coordinated action in pursuit of agreed goals.

Long favourably compares the strategies included in his survey with the strategic plans reviewed in a similar survey undertaken in Australia (Dredge and Moore, 1992), which were 'rooted in the traditions of land-use planning', whereas

'... the British strategies ... were more wide-reaching, notably also encompassing organisation and administration, promotion, information and development. Indeed, at their best, they seem to be rather closer to what Dredge and Moore have in mind as being desirable.'

(J. Long, 1994)

The various strategies reviewed by Long were distinguished by the extent to which they were characterised by one of the following objectives:

- development of the product
  - through improving infrastructure (roads, signs, etc.)
  - through enhancing the attractions of the area
  - through changing/improving the accommodation base
- promotion of the destination
- management of tourism to protect the environment or interests of local residents
- organisation/administration of tourism in the local area.

These objectives closely reflect those identified by Richards in his survey. Development of the tourism product (in Richards' terminology, improving visitor facilities) is clearly linked to increasing visitor numbers and expenditure. The relative importance of these economic objectives is shown in the ranking accorded to them by the local authorities surveyed by Richards, in Figure 7.2.

In the Richards and Long surveys, marketing and promotion featured significantly as objectives, as did concern for the environmental aspects of the destination.

Policy objective	Rank
Improve visitor facilities	1
Increase visitor spend	2
Generate employment	3
Promote the area	3
Tourism marketing	5
Increase visitor numbers	6
Conservation	7
Encourage development	8
Provide tourist information	9
Links with other organisations	10

Source: adapted from Richards, 1992

FIGURE 7.2 *Tourism policy objectives*

'The policy priorities ... seem to encapsulate the problem of balancing contradictory pressures. The primary aims are to develop visitor facilities and to increase visitor spending, but these development activities are closely followed by a desire to conserve the basic tourism resource.'

(Richards, 1992)

Another useful distinguishing factor identified by Long was his respondents' definition of good practice in their authority's tourism efforts.

'The nature of good practice varied in part as a result of the different roles and relationships respondents saw for the public and private sector. A simple distinction can be made between those who saw their role as one that would establish the conditions that would allow the private sector to operate profitably, and those who were concerned to encourage the private sector to get involved in meeting desirable goals in keeping with the resort or destination. Yet others saw the role of the LA as that of honest broker, balancing the competing interests.'

(J. Long, 1994)

The themes most commonly cited by tourism officers as constituting good practice in their authorities are identified in Figure 7.3.

Partnerships clearly emerge as an important theme. Whether for the purposes of development or for promotion, partnership arrange-

Partnership – with private sector
– with other agencies
– with other local authorities
Single integrated department
Involve local people – through consultation
– as tourists
Make publications and TICs pay for themselves
Aggressive promotion
Quality information readily available
Enhancing attractions base/link attractions
Promotion of special events
Develop sustainable tourism/protect the environment
Make sure the staff are in a post with an appropriate budget
Use a consultant for specialist expertise
Training programmes for staff

Source: J. Long (1994)

FIGURE 7.3 *Local authority good practice in addressing tourism*

ments with adjoining authorities, individual companies and other agencies have enabled LAs to undertake tourism-related activities much more effectively than they could have done alone. Long gives the example of one LA which was involved with eleven other bodes in one promotional initiative, with over twenty in another, and with nine others in a TDAP (Tourism Development Action Programme).

(However, it is worthy of note that while most LA tourism officers appear convinced of the importance of partnerships and external consultation, only a small minority were found to regularly engage the local population through consultation. And even where there was some effort made to communicate with local people, the emphasis was less on implementing a 'community tourism' approach than on encouraging them to be tourists in their own backyards, and trying to make sure that provision for tourists would also benefit local residents, through the staging of special events such as festivals and sports occasions, for example.)

Long identifies his own examples of good practice from the LA strategies included in his survey. Apart from emphasising the importance of monitoring the form and quality of the actual product, which was acknowledged by practically all of his respondents, Long highlights the following positive qualities of the LA strategies reviewed.

- **Clarity of aims**: LAs should be quite clear about why they are going to be involved in the development and promotion of tourism. In the better strategies, the various components were linked back to the original aims.
- **Tourists as real people**: LAs should start from the perspective of the tourist. Some, like Edinburgh, incorporated interviews with (potential) tourists in the formulation of the strategy. Others, like Fylde, identified the need to solicit the views of tourists to guide future developments.
- **Tourist needs and local needs**: some strategies specifically seek to address the resentment that can occur if residents feel that 'their' money is being spent for the benefit of others. This was done in five principal ways:
  - by ensuring that new facilities or events will be as desirable to local people as to visitors
  - by encouraging local people to be tourists in their area and to take pride in it
  - by adopting tactics to level out the peaks of visiting, to lessen the problems caused by excessive demands
  - by engaging local residents in debates about the most appropriate kind of development
  - by ensuring that tourism activities are self-financing and not a burden to tax payers (not an option open to all)
- **Targets and review**: strategies' stated objectives should not just be pious hopes. In order to make sure that the various objectives are achieved, it is necessary to establish a set of targets that can provide the basis for regular review. Long cites the example of the strategy produced by Fylde, which includes stated targets (immediate, year one, year two, and beyond). He adds that it is probably important that such targets should not just be quantitative, but have a qualitative dimension as well.

LA tourism policies and strategies are an important element in several of the case studies in this book; Cambridge and Winchester, in particular, provide examples of many of the issues discussed in this section.

LOCAL AGENDA 21 STRATEGIES

In response to Agenda 21 agreed at the 1992 Earth Summit in Rio, many LAs are developing Local Agenda 21 strategies for their areas. These are non-statutory, but they cover a wide range of environmental issues including sustainable development, conservation, waste management and pollution. Implementation of these measures will affect the environment within which the tourism industry operates and will also affect LA policies and attitudes toward tourism development.

It is too early yet to say what the full impact of these measures will be. A 1994/95 survey of LAs revealed that 71% of respondents were committed to participating in the Local Agenda 21 programme and 24% claimed that sustainable development principles were incorporated into their tourism and visitor strategies (LGMB, 1995).

LOCAL TOURISM PARTNERSHIP INITIATIVES

In the 1980s, tourism planning at the destination level in the UK was characterised by a change in emphasis, with growing recognition that tourism plans require the participation of a variety of actors and interests for their successful execution. There was also a growing impatience with detailed and comprehensive tourism studies that are long on analysis, but short on practical action. The trend therefore moved towards shorter and more action-orientated programmes, often addressed to or involving a wider cross section of interests.

Such local tourism partnerships between the public and the private sectors were pioneered by the ETB from 1982 onwards and became widely established throughout the UK, with substantial funding being channelled through them. In his analysis of partnership organisations as an approach to local tourism development, P. Long notes that:

'references to partnerships between public and private sectors in the development, marketing and management of tourism in local areas are now commonplace in reports and strategies produced by LAs, RTBs and other organisations with an interest in tourism.'

(P. Long, 1994)

As our earlier discussion shows, partnership approaches have not been restricted to tourism. They are also prevalent in local economic development in general and in urban regeneration. Within the tourism sector, Turner (1992) regards the proliferation of partnership arrangements partly as a result of the prevailing politicoeconomic situation (with central government directing LAs to act as 'enablers' and not 'providers' of services) and partly as a result of restrictions on local government spending. From the perspective of the private sector, he provides another reason:

'On the private sector side, anticipated difficulties in achieving the desired rate of return from tourism developments, particularly from innovative schemes, has led private enterprises to look to local authorities either to contribute to capital costs or to offer favourable rental terms (where they are the landowners) in recognition of the wider economic benefits of new developments. There has, additionally, been a realisation that there needs to be a pooling of resources in what is a very fragmented industry in order to compete with spending on the promotion of overseas holidays. There is also a recognition, within both public and private sectors, that for many of the complex infrastructure problems which confront tourist areas, a simple solution is insufficient, or such a solution requires a partnership between the institutions which make up the local community.'

(Turner, 1992)

Organisational arrangements for local tourism partnership initiatives sponsored by the ETB during the 1980s were known as **Tourism Development Action Programmes** (TDAPs),
which were replaced in 1990 by their successor **Local Area Tourism Initiatives (LATIs).** Between 1984 and 1990, 20 different areas within England were designated as TDAPs by the ETB, in consultation with local interests. (See Bradford and North Pennines case studies.)

Long (1994) lists the following characteristics shared by TDAPs and LATIs:

- They seek collaboration and cooperation between a wide range of public and private sector organisations located in, or having an interest in, their areas' tourism.
- They are action-oriented, with the programme emphasis on implementing initiatives rather than on prolonged and detailed research and strategy formulation.
- They are comprehensive and integrated in approach, encompassing the range of interrelated aspects which affect tourism in the programme area. Consequently, they normally include development, marketing, information and environmental advisory and training initiatives.
- They are corporate in approach and involve objectives and work programmes which are shared both among and within organisations. This is particularly important when tourism-related activities are the functions of several different LA departments and where the programme area transcends administrative boundaries.
- They are short-term programmes with a limited duration, usually three years, with the aim of establishing sufficient momentum for progress to be sustained in the longer term, based on local resources.

LATIs have been initiated in a wide variety of settings, from urban districts, such as the London boroughs of Greenwich and Islington, Leeds Waterfront, and Manchester's Castlefield district, to coastal resorts and rural areas, such as the Peak District and the Forest of Dean. The partners in all LATIs are:

- the LA, or several LAs within the LATI area
- local private sector operators and associations (such as Chambers of Commerce and travel associations)

- the relevant RTBs
- the ETB.

Other organisations directly involved vary between each LATI, but have included:

- National Park authorities
- urban development corporations, and economic development and enterprise agencies (themselves partnership organisations)
- local community groups and associations, e.g. civic societies, parish councils.

Formal organisational arrangements for TDAP/LATI administration and management have generally involved a Steering Group comprising representatives from partner organisations and a Working Group (or groups) responsible for programme implementation. Such programmes have few direct employees, but rather involve staff on secondments from partnership organisations or personnel allocated to partnership responsibilities as part of their jobs with partner organisations. All have a project manager to act as a coordinator/facilitator of action. 'Nevertheless, [LATIs] can be considered as organisations in their own right, with their own identity, management and objectives, albeit with a high degree of dependency on the sponsoring partners and with a possibly limited life span' (P. Long, 1994).

VISITOR MANAGEMENT PLANS

Visitor management is a comparatively new discipline, developed in response to the growing concern about the environmental and social impacts of tourism and the wish to maximise the benefits of tourism for the destination – as such, **Visitor Management Plans (VMPs)** have a vital part to play in achieving sustainability for tourist destinations. Human distinguishes VMPs from earlier plans and strategies:

'During the 1980s, tourism strategies and development plans were viewed almost as a panacea for unemployment by LAs who heeded advice to take advantage of the economic benefits of the industry. In the more environmentally-aware 1990s, VMPs are the order of the day.'

(Human, 1994)

In 1991, the UK Government Tourism and Environment Task Force (coordinated by the ETB, and involving a wide range of industry and local authority representatives) developed a definition of visitor management. Defined as 'an ongoing process to reconcile the potentially competing needs of the visitor, the place and the host community', the visitor management process was depicted by the diagram shown in Figure 7.4.

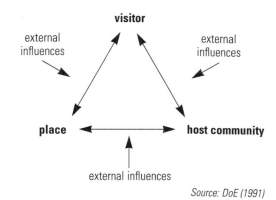

Source: DoE (1991)

FIGURE 7.4 *The visitor management process*

The aim of visitor management is to achieve a harmony between the three concerns represented in the diagram, taking into account the following considerations:

- the inter-relationship between the physical environment/residents/visitors
- the need to balance the requirements/demands of each group
- external factors – which are often beyond the control of the destination – these may be factors such as national/EU legislation, or physical or financial constraints.

Visitor management is sometimes regarded simply as finding a solution to vehicular and pedestrian congestion, but its advocates believe that in the true meaning of the term, it is much more than this. It is an approach which destinations can use in order to 'integrate visitor activity within the long-term planning and day-to-day management of a town/city and to maximise the benefit of tourism, including its contribution to town viability and vitality' (McNamara, 1996, cites Grant). In preparing VMPs, tourism is considered *in relationship to the functioning of the destination as a whole.*

The term 'visitor management' itself is ambiguous, as it is not the activities of the visitors themselves which are being managed, but the destination's services and facilities. Visitors are not under the direct control of the destination's managers (LAs, for the most part), but many services and facilities are, and these can be managed to 'control' visitors' activities indirectly through suggestion and persuasion.

Furthermore, if visitor activity is accepted as an integral part of the destination's functioning, then 'visitor management' is too narrow a term to describe the more global and integrated approach to the management of tourism which recognises the overlap between visitors' activities and those of other user groups (e.g. shoppers, commuters, residents). For these reasons, many commentators and practitioners consider that the term 'destination management' better encapsulates the reality behind these types of strategy.

The English Historic Towns Forum report *Getting it Right* (EHTF, 1994) lists the possible benefits which successful visitor management can bring to the destination:

- enhancing the visitor experience
- enhancing the town's reputation as a destination to visit
- creating a quality environment in which to live and work
- maximising the economic opportunities of tourism
- minimising the associated impact, particularly on local people
- encouraging more profitable overnight stays
- encouraging off-season visits to extend the length of the season and to reduce peak season pressure
- reducing wear and tear at sensitive sites
- identifying the necessary capital and maintenance costs for town centre management
- strengthening a local sense of civic pride.

Elsewhere Grant (1996) adds three more benefits of visitor management:

- contributing to the vitality of the town – especially in the evenings
- supporting existing facilities and encouraging new facilities that will benefit residents and visitors alike (e.g. retail, sports, arts, leisure facilities)
- encouraging and creating a demand for the conservation of specific heritage facets, as well as contributing to the costs of this conservation.

To translate these benefits and objectives into action, an integrated approach involving most or all of the following elements is generally used:

- an analysis of visitor activity, is volume and value
- an appraisal of tourism in the town, in order to establish priorities and direction
- identification of likely future trends and changes
- an analysis of host communities' views on visitors
- the identification of specific assets and problems; along with objectives, programmes and targets to tackle them
- the quantification and sources of funding required
- the identification of organisations and departments whose involvement to develop and implement the plan is needed
- the identification of local residents' needs and gaining their commitment to the plan'.

A typical VMP, therefore, encompasses the destination's marketing plan as well as various aspects of the development of the product, including: interpretation and signage, transport policy and traffic, visitor services (e.g. toilets, guides etc.), attractions (including shopping) and conservation and environmental improvements.

Regarding the organisational arrangements for the actual delivery and implementation of VMPs, strategic intervention by a range of key partners working together towards a common aim is called for. These partners will typically include a wide range of LA departments, directly or indirectly concerned with tourism, private-sector representatives (e.g. Chambers of Commerce, traders' associations), conservation groups (e.g. Civic trusts), as well as residents' representatives.

Within urban destinations, many aspects of visitor management (VM) are closely related to wider Town Centre Management (TCM) issues.

TCM has been developed in response to the range of growing problems facing traditional town centres as they came under increasing pressure from several directions. Grant, Human and Le Pelley (1995) describe the typical process by which the quality of town centre environments can deteriorate. One significant cause of the decline of major centres is competition from alternative, out-of-town shopping. Key retailers move out to the new locations and other shops close as total trade falls in a spiral of decline. In some cases, high unemployment reduces spending and with it, the viability and vitality of the town centre. Another issue is the decline in residential accommodation in some town centres, which means there is less evening activity and a lack of a sense of ownership. A reduction in the powers and financial base of LAs, and indeed of civic pride, have compounded these pressures.

They add that not all town centres are in decline and that some, on the contrary, are victims of their own success, suffering from the pressures of excess demand with consequent pedestrian and traffic congestion. Tourism is often a major contributor to this pressure. The problem of congestion is compounded by the fact that in historic towns, environmental considerations may restrict the potential to expand the infrastructure to meet increasing demands from visitors, shoppers and residents.

The consequences of these problems, if they are allowed to develop without any form of strategic intervention, are a poorer environment, reduced services and a fall in viability and vitality. One response has been the growth of TCM schemes. There were over 100 such schemes in operation in the UK in 1995 (Grant, Human and Le Pelley, 1995).

TCM is 'a comprehensive programme by public authorities, private sector interests and voluntary organisations, which aims to improve the standards of facilities, environment, con-venience and safety in town centres'. Its goals, according to the Association of Town Centre Management, are:

- to achieve a competitive edge
- to improve the management of the public realm
- to satisfy the aspirations of all town centre users.

The emphasis is on creating a *partnership*, a *shared vision*, and *direct action* to achieve improvements. Typically, schemes develop strategies around: the environment, access, security, promotion and retailing vitality. Practical projects include: business development and skills training; paving schemes and control of fly-posting; closed-circuit TV; tackling aggressive begging; access for people with disabilities; and advance information on car parking.

The main benefits of effective TCM have been described as follows:

- it emphasises the uniqueness of the place, builds consensus, partnership and civic pride, and encourages return visits
- it attracts development, encourages private sector investment and support, and encourages joint operator initiatives, such as quality staff training.

(ibid)

There is a clear overlap between tourism concerns and those of TCM. Visitors use many of the same facilities as local people (for example, car parks, public toilets and litter bins), and quality of life is as important to the visitor as it is to residents. The town centre of many destinations is the focus for services and facilities enjoyed by tourists, and there is an important dynamic between tourists and town centres. Shops, pubs, restaurants, museums, parks and gardens, theatres and nightclubs are among the many attractions which bring visitors into town and city centres. Those visitors can make an important contribution to keeping these centres lively and animated, particularly in the evening. For their part, tourists can get more satisfaction out of visiting a well-managed centre, which may encourage a higher level of spending and repeat visits. Effective TCM also manages visitors in ways that help to reduce the problems affecting town centres, e.g. cutting congestion by encouraging the use of park–and–ride schemes.

The tourism industry itself reaps distinct advantages from TCM (see case study C, Cambridge and case study D, Winchester for examples of how tourism has been successfully integrated into TCM programmes):

- it integrates tourism with other town centre functions as a mainstream feature
- it improves the general image of the town, giving a practical marketing advantage
- better communications between the tourism industry, other sectors and the public can provide a chance to address visitor/host/environmental issues
- TCM, which has high political and commercial credibility, helps to put visitor management on the agenda
- the practical approach of TCM encourages cross departmental/authority working at LA

level, which is also a requirement of visitor management
- it is cost effective; the concerns of TCM and visitor management overlap, and a great deal can be achieved without duplicating research, staff, liaison and investment.

Finally, there is a definite complementarity between plans for TCM and the other types of plan we have examined in this chapter:

'There is a vital role for VMPs, tourism and economic development strategies and Local (land-use and transport) Plans to complement and work with TCM to ensure that the full benefits of tourism are achieved with a minimum negative impact on the immediate environment and local communities. TCM will often provide the enabling mechanism to meet, in part, the objectives of these other structures by implementing practical projects.'

(ibid)

CONCLUSION

No single plan, policy or strategy of the types examined in this chapter can provide destinations with either a panacea for tourism-related problems, or a get–rich–quick key to instant prosperity through tourism. Because of the great variety of destinations concerned, the very wide range of measures necessary, and the vast number of different areas of responsibility which come into play, no single scheme can tackle all the issues. There is therefore no off–the–peg package which will guarantee all destinations success through tourism. It is necessary for all of the actors involved to respond creatively to the needs of each individual destination, using an integrated package of the type of measures discussed in this book: statutory and non–statutory plans, development planning and entrepreneurial planning, local authority tourism strategies, local

tourism partnership initiatives and visitor management plans. For maximum effectiveness, a multi-disciplinary, partnership approach is required, and the measures agreed upon should be, to as great an extent as possible, compatible with the wider policy context described in Chapter 6.

The following detailed case studies have been chosen to demonstrate the variety of challenges facing individual tourism destinations, and the range of types of intervention which have been used to meet them. They include examples of rural, historic and heritage, and non-traditional destinations. The problems with which the destinations are grappling range from managing apparently inexorable increases in visitor numbers, to using tourism to help reconfigure and regenerate a local economy, where traditional industries have declined. We have not included a case study of a resort, since our intention has been to focus on a wider range of destinations, and resorts are frequently examined in other literature.

In each case study, we describe the destination's location, tourism history and identify the issues involved. The key themes each case study illustrates are identified at the outset. We examine the policies which have been developed, and assess their effects. Finally, we draw conclusions.

REFERENCES

ADC (1983) *Direct Job Creation: Leisure and Tourism, Current Practice Paper*, Association of District Councils.

ADC (1984) *Survey of District Councils' Involvement in Tourism, Best Practice Paper no. 9*, Association of District Councils.

Alder, J. (1989) *Development Control*, 2nd edn. Sweet and Maxwell.

Audit Commission (1992) *Building in Quality: A Study of Development Control*, HMSO, London.

Bacon, M. and Le Pelley, B. (1993a) 'Local government reorganisation – tourism's chance or peril?' in *Insights*, English Tourist Board, London.

Bacon, M. and Le Pelley, B. (1993b) 'District Councils and the economic benefits of tourism' in *Insights*, English Tourist Board, London.

Bacon, M. and Le Pelley, B. (1994) 'Should tourism be a statutory LA function?' in *Insights* (November), English Tourist Board, London.

Bailey, N. (1995) *Partnership Agencies in British Urban Policy*, UCL Press, London.

Cooper, C. *et al.* (1993) *Tourism Principles and Practice*, Pitman.

Crawshaw, C. (1993) 'Tourism and the Environment', in *Town and Country Planning 1993 Summer School Proceedings*.

Cullingworth, J.B. and Nadin, V. (1994) *Town and Country Planning in Britain*, Routledge, London.

Deakins, N. and Edwards, J. (1993) *The Enterprise Culture and the Inner City*, Routledge, London.

DNH (1996) *Guidance to successor local authorities on tourism*, Department of National Heritage, London.

DOE (1985) *Pleasure, Leisure and Jobs: the Business of Tourism*, HMSO.

DoE (1992) *PPG 21 Tourism*, HMSO.

Dredge, D. and Moore, S. (1992) 'A methodology for the integration of tourism in town planning', in *The Journal of Tourism Studies*, 3(1).

Edmundson, T. (1993) 'Public demands right to say where control shoe pinches' in *Planning*, Nov 26, 1993.

EHTF (1994) *Getting it Right: A Guide to Visitor Management in Historic Towns*, The English Historic Towns Forum.

ETB (1991) *Tourism and the Environment – Maintaining the Balance*, English Tourist Board, London.

Gilbert, D. and Tung, L. (1990) 'Public organisations and rural planning in England and Wales', in *Tourism Management*, June 1990.

Grant, M. (1996) *Presentation to Tourism Society seminar: Working together for visitor management*, Cambridge.

Grant, M.; Human, B. and Le Pelley, B. (1995) 'Tourism and town centre management' in *Insights* (July), English Tourist Board, London.

Grant, M.; Human, B. and Le Pelley, B. (1996) 'Visitor management: whose role is it anyway?' in *Insights* (March), English Tourist Board, London.

Greenwood, J. (1993) 'Business interest groups in tourism governance', in *Tourism Management*, 14(5), pp. 335–348.

Heeley, J. (1981) 'Planning for tourism in Britain' in *Town Planning Review*, 52, pp. 61–79.

Hughes, H.L. (1994) 'Tourism and government: a subset of leisure policy?' in *Tourism: The State of the Art*, Seaton, A.V. *et al.* (eds), John Wiley and Sons, Chichester.

Human, B. (1994) 'Visitor management in the public planning policy context: a case-study of Cambridge' in *The Journal of Sustainable Tourism*, Vol 2: 4 pp. 221–231.

Kaye, T. (1992) 'Planning and tourism development' in *Tourism*, (75), Tourism Society.

Kaye, T. (1993) 'Leisure, tourism and the planning maze' in *Tourism* (78), Tourism Society.

LGMB (1995) *Local Agenda 21 Survey*, Local Government Management Board.

Long, J. (1994) 'Local authority tourism strategies – A British appraisal' in *The Journal of Tourism Studies*, vol. 5, no. 2.

Long, P. (1994) 'Perspectives on partnership organisations as an approach to local tourism development' in *Tourism: The State of the Art*, Seaton, A.V. *et al*. (eds), John Wiley and Sons, Chichester.

McNamara, K. (1996) 'Working together for visitor management in towns' in *Tourism* (89), Tourism Society, London.

Mole, D. (1996) 'Planning gain after the Tesco case in *Journal of Planning Law*, March, 1996, pp. 183–193.

Rydin, Y. (1993) *The British Planning System: an Introduction*, Macmillan, London.

Stewart, J. (1994) 'Between Whitehall and Town Hall: the realignment of urban regeneration policy in England', *Policy and Politics*, 22, 2.

Stoker, G. and Young, S. (1993) *Cities in the 1990s*, Longman, Harlow.

Taylor, D. (1995) *Planning Week*, 8 June.

Tewdr-Jones, M. (1994) 'Policy implications of the Plan-led System' in *Journal of Planning Law*.

Thornley, A. (1991) *Urban planning under Thatcherism: the challenge of the market*, (2nd ed.), Routledge, London.

Turner, G. (1992) 'Public/Private sector partnership – panacea or passing phase?' in *Insight*, March, ETB, London.

Van den Berg, L., Van der Borg, J. and Van der Meer, J. (1994) *Urban Tourism*, Erasmus University, Rotterdam.

A Bradford

THEMES

- tourism, regeneration and sources of new employment
- tourism, marketing and image

- the role of the local authority in tourism development

LOCATION AND BACKGROUND

A 1971 guidebook described Bradford as follows:

'From all directions roads drop down to the centre of the city, and here at the heart of the wool market is industrial scenery that may not attract but cannot fail to impress. A city born of the industrial revolution, from the flamboyant architecture of the Wool Exchange to the unplanned labyrinth of streets burrowing between tiers of terraced houses.'

(*AA Illustrated Guide to Britain, 1971*)

Twenty-five years later this description remains accurate, with one exception – Bradford now clearly attracts. The intervening period has seen significant economic change in the city and its environs. This has brought about an era in which the Metropolitan Council has fostered economic diversification and more specifically developed an urban and rural tourism market; born, for the most part, out of the city's industrial legacy, its history and its location.

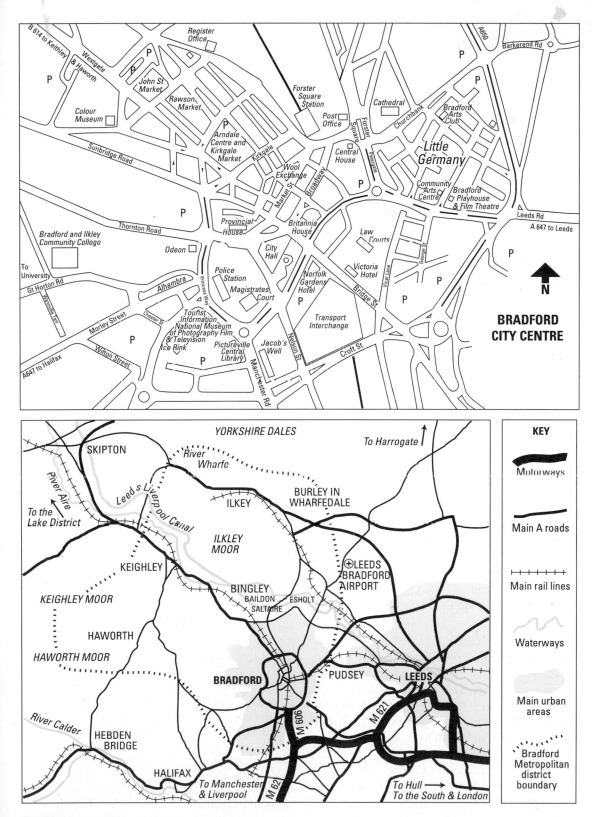

FIGURE A.1 *Maps of Bradford (city centre and district)*

Bradford Metropolitan District (143 square miles) is located within West Yorkshire and lies at the heart of the trans-Pennine region which runs from Hull on the east coast to Liverpool on the west. The city is considered by some worthy of the description, 'city in the countryside' because it stretches into rural Yorkshire, adjacent to the Yorkshire Dales National Park (Bradford EDU, 1995). Only about one-third of the district is built up (including the city and adjoining settlements), with the remaining 100 square miles being undeveloped. With so much open countryside and wild unspoilt moors less than ten minutes from the city centre, the rural backdrop for the city provides some of the most attractive landscape of the region.

The city itself has good communication links, being directly served by the M606 (a spur of the M62), from which the M1 and M6 motorways are easily accessible. Two rail stations provide Intercity links throughout the UK, and connections by air can be found at the Leeds/Bradford Airport which lies seven miles to the north: it operates both domestic and international flights to destinations such as Heathrow, Edinburgh, Glasgow, Amsterdam, Brussels and Paris. Within the district itself modern transportation is supplemented by the use of the Leeds–Liverpool canal, which supports a limited Waterbus service and is popular with leisure boaters.

The present population of the city and the surrounding built-up areas is estimated at 480,000, a total that has remained relatively stable over the last ten years. Since the early 19th century, Bradford has expanded and grown with successive waves of immigrants from different parts of the world (Bradford UPD, 1993), and currently some 12% of the population has New Commonwealth origins (principally Asian). The growth in the Asian community means that in the 1990s seven out of ten people in the inner city area are Asian, and Bradford boasts 1,400 Asian businesses (Parajia, 1994). It is this growth in ethnicity that contributes greatly to Bradford's cultural diversity and richness.

As recently as the 1970s Bradford's economic base was dominated by its traditional industries of textiles and (to a lesser extent) engineering, which had emerged during the 19th century. However, they had been declining since the 1950s as a result of structural changes in the global economy as well as periods of recession. By 1985 it was estimated that there were 48,000 fewer jobs than 20 years previously (Bradford TDAP, 1985), and unemployment at its peak in May 1985 reached 15.7% in the Bradford TTWA (Bradford E & E, 1985) with parts of the city having a rate as high as 25% (Page, 1986). Gains made in the service sector were not enough to compensate for the massive loss of jobs in traditional industries.

Bradford's problems of industrial decline were compounded at the start of the 1980s by a poor image and by the comparative successes of its neighbouring city Leeds. Leeds, facing similar problems of a decline in traditional industries, had managed to become the major regional business and retail centre of the Yorkshire and Humberside region, and subsequently laid a claim to being the second city of the North after Manchester. Ultimately Bradford tended to lose out in the face of competition from Leeds. It was felt that Bradford's economic decline was reinforced by the comparative successes of neighbouring cities: 'investors were reluctant to commit money to what they believed was a grimy backward, industrial area' which was 'making the headlines on a daily basis as television documentaries reported on high levels of social deprivation and the Yorkshire Ripper stalked the streets' (Bradford EDU, 1995).

In fact, Page (1986) looking back to the late 1970s and early '80s, doubted that the image of the city and the broader area had ever been worse. Diversification of the economy was crucial, and the crux of the problem was the city's image. As a prerequisite to attracting investment, its image had to change.

HISTORY OF INVOLVEMENT WITH TOURISM

In 1979, in the face of this adversity, Bradford City Council (then under Conservative control) formed a working party to propose a new industrial strategy, and the strategy that emerged considered the potential for promoting tourism. It was at this point that tourism, previously never associated with urban Bradford, began to feature on the economic agenda.

Prior to the 1980s, nobody had ever linked Bradford with leisure tourism, and consequently its experience in the industry was minimal, although as a major city it inevitably saw a significant number of business travellers. The exceptions were the rural areas of Haworth (home of the Brontës) and Ilkley which had significant numbers of visitors − however, prior to 1974 they were not, by definition, visitors to Bradford, since it was only in 1974 that these areas became part of the new Bradford Metropolitan District. In addition, most of these tourists were day visitors, passing through enroute to traditional destinations like Stratford and York, and did not stay overnight. They were not therefore seen as 'true tourists' (Page, 1986).

Before the tourism initiative was launched in 1980, the Council's **Economic Development Unit (EDU)** had investigated tourism potential. The main findings were as follows (Fenn, 1984).

- There was a supply of 550 bed spaces in three- and four-star hotels and a similar supply of bed spaces in quality smaller hotels. More significant, occupancy rates were highest from Monday to Thursday, with the hotels almost empty on Friday, Saturday and Sunday. As a result, city-centre hotels offered very attractive weekend rates, content to recoup a modest profit by basing charges on marginal costs. These occupancy patterns tied up conveniently with a national growth in the short-stay holiday market − primarily those aged over 40 who were willing to pay around £50 (1980 prices) for such a holiday.
- Bradford was not without its renowned attractions. The district included: the village of Haworth; the nearby Keighley and Worth Valley railway (film location for 'The Railway Children', 'A Woman of Substance' and 'The Adventures of Sherlock Holmes'); a superb Victorian industrial heritage including Saltaire (a Victorian model community which took 20 years to build and was the inspiration of the philanthropist Titus Salt); the picturesque town of Ilkley (Roman settlement and spa town); and Esholt, the location of the popular television soap 'Emmerdale Farm'. These were established and unique selling points with which to lure the travel trade.

On this basis, a product was developed. The city could not compete directly with traditional and well-established inland destinations, such as York or Harrogate, and the target market was most likely to be for short, themed weekend-trips.

In 1980, the intention of the council to launch Bradford into the leisure tourism market was not only treated with much scepticism but was considered as one of the best jokes circulating in the travel trade and press. As events transpired, the disbelief that a 'dirty, backward industrial northern city' could contemplate a move into such a market, represented a key stage in the development of the city's tourism drive. The scepticism raised the city's profile and its marketing team sought, with some tenacity, to use the publicity to their advantage. As recalled by Eddie Fenn, the then marketing manager, they invited the first person who booked a holiday to Bradford for a free preview of his holiday. Media interest was all but guaranteed, with the council laying on a full range of added attractions, including a red carpet at the railway station, plus a full-scale brass band, a welcome from the Lord Mayor, lunch in City Hall, guided tours and even a giant stick of Bradford rock (Fenn, 1984). It had the desired effect. The launch was featured on every national radio and television programme, including Radio 1, ITN and BBC News. In addition, it was reported in all national morning newspapers (with the exception of the *Financial Times*), and was extensively covered in a wide range of consumer and travel trade magazines. The council estimated that the free publicity generated would have cost in excess of £250,000 (*ibid*).

The publicity brought a 'deluge of enquiry coupons'(*ibid*) taken from Bradford holiday advertisements, leading ultimately to the sale of 2,000 holidays direct to the public. Far more importantly, this turn of events convinced the travel trade that Bradford had tourism potential and that they could sell holidays as a profitable operation. From 1980, tourist and visitor numbers increased, and in response the tourism products that Bradford offered grew in number and variety. Its success was such that in 1983 it was awarded the Sir Mark Henig Award by the English Tourist Board as England's fastest growing tourist destination.

During the 1980s, the council consolidated the leisure tourism industry that had emerged, but it also endeavoured to capitalise on business tourism and conferences, which has now become its main priority. In 1995, as a result of council re-organisation and budget constraints, the tourism budget and tourism staff were axed, and tourism development ceased to be a separately-identified council activity. One result is that Bradford is no longer represented by the council at trade exhibitions, such as the World Travel Market, and tourism in the city is no longer actively promoted by the council, although many of its attractions continue promotion and marketing. However, the 'Bradford Conference Desk', set up and partly funded with European resources, was safeguarded and continues to act as a liaison between conference organisers and all the facilities and the services in the area. Bradford Conference Desk assists in a variety of ways, ranging from venue selection and pre- and post-convention tours, to supplying tourist information and arranging social and partners' programmes. In this respect, business tourism is still a key element to the activities of the council and its marketing divisions. We explore the changing role of the council in tourism development in later sections.

DIMENSIONS OF TOURISM

Bradford lacks comprehensive, accurate and consistent information about its visitors and their characteristics. Despite the importance accorded to the development of tourism in the 1980s, Bradford (unlike its neighbour Calderdale) did not carry out much research into its visitor profile (EDU, 1995b). Getting a sense of the dimensions of tourism in the city therefore means assembling and interpreting a variety of data from various sources. There is little consistency and the estimates derived must be treated with considerable caution. It is especially difficult to obtain information about the origins and characteristics of visitors and how these have changed over time. Our discussions, however, do give some quantified indications of how tourism has developed.

Bradford was launched as a leisure destination with two principal packages: 'In the Steps of the Brontë's and 'Industrial Heritage' were both based on distinctive elements of the district, and aimed principally at the adult rather than the family market (Page, 1986). These early council-backed packages were a proven success, with the sale of 2,000 packages in 1981–82, 15,000 packages in 1982–83, and 25,000 packages in 1983–84 (Buckley and De Witt, 1985). From this foothold in the short-stay market, the range of themed short-breaks was expanded to include: Mill Shopping; TV Themes; Bradford Entertains; Psychic Sightseeing; Flavours of Asia (experiencing local cultures, food, dress and lifestyles); Artlovers' Bradford; and Photographic Weekends. The most popular periods proved to be between March and June, and between September and November, reflecting that, as anticipated, the city was attractive as a short-stay destination outside the peak season.

Although some estimate of short-break visitor numbers for the earlier years can be derived from the sale of council-backed packages, there are no continuous data on short-break visitors and/or day visitors. The vast majority of visits do seem to be day trips (Guy, 1984), and one estimate suggests that the city currently attracts six million national and international visitors annually (Herrier, 1992), though the basis of this estimate remains elusive. An earlier estimate by the council does give a breakdown of the different types of visitor: in 1983, total visitors were estimated to be 260,000; of which 104,000 (40%) were local visitors (from the immediate Bradford sub-region), 142,800 were day-trip visitors (55%), and 13,200 (5%) were overnight stays. It is unwise to compare these figures since their basis cannot be determined, and there is a great scope for confusion over definitions such as 'local' or 'day' visitors. A crude direct comparison suggests a phenomenal 23-fold increase in tourist numbers in the space of 12 years; this seems unlikely.

One way of filling this information gap is through inferring changes in visitor numbers by using information on occupancy of accommodation and on visits to attractions. In 1995 there were some 2,270 bedrooms in the metropolitan district – with a further supply of 1,600 bedrooms when one considers the contribution of the University and Colleges in Bradford during vacations. Out of the 2,270, 1,800 bedrooms are within one mile of the city centre, and 1,400 bedrooms have en-suite facilities (Bradford EDU, 1995). Yorkshire and Humberside Tourist Board data now detail room and bed-occupancy figures, and these are combined in Figure A.2 with early figures provided by BMDC and the English Tourist Board.

The average figures for both bed and room occupancy figures have fluctuated over the years, generally mirroring national trends. There has been no significant increase in the number of hotel bed spaces, and there has not been a major and systematic rise in occupancy rates. It is therefore reasonable to infer that the most significant increase in visitation has come from local or day visitors, rather than from people staying overnight (though short breaks may have grown).

Occupancy %	1981	1985	1990	1991	1992	1993	1994
Bed							
Bradford	48	60	41	38	39	36	40
National			46	41	38	39	43
Room							
Bradford			65	55	57	55	60
National			57	51	48	48	52

Source: Bradford City Council YHTB, and English Tourist Board

FIGURE A.2 *Bed and room occupancy rates*

Figure A.3 shows attendances at the main attractions. It is clear that the number of attractions is growing, they are becoming more diverse, and that visitor numbers are increasing (although the major reason for the leap in numbers in 1993 is the inclusion for the first time of estimates of visitors at several major attractions, which have long existed and long been popular). In 1994, a total of almost five million visits were made to these attractions. This does not equate to visitor numbers, since visitors frequently visit more than one attraction, and some attractions attract repeat visits. On the other hand, the figures do *not* include a significant number of smaller attractions, or indeed the annual Bradford Festival, which it is claimed has over 400 associated events and an attendance of over 500,000 (NMPFT, 1994). A significant number of visits will be by city residents and day visitors from the sub-region, but since no comprehensive visitor survey has ever been undertaken, there is no basis on which the proportions can be estimated. The growth in the number of attractions is in itself one way of tracking the growth in tourism, however, and we take up the point later on.

On the basis of this information, we can tentatively represent Bradford's current position on the tourism product portfolio and tourism dominance grids as shown in Figures A.4 and A.5. This is a considerable change from the pre-1980 position, when tourism would have been placed firmly in the lower right-hand corner of the dominance grid.

Attraction	1986	1987	1988	1989	1990	1991	1992	1993	1994	Totals	Average
Transport Museum	25,000	20,000	24,470	13,500	13,500	12,000	18,000			125,970	17,996
Manor House	30,806	25,510	21,415	24,962	29,904	35,579	35,089			203,265	29,038
East Riddlesden Hall	24,000	30,000	42,500	18,558	36,700	40,000	40,000	37,000	34,923	303,681	33,742
Bolling Hall	39,275	38,066	36,848	39,894	45,492	40,889	39,113	38,200	37,908	355,685	39,521
Industrial Museum	63,887	60,221	66,963	58,855	62,899	82,007	164,721	158,107	170,000	887,660	98,629
Cliffe Castle	92,969	76,114	87,385	84,695	89,456	110,679	103,440	92,846	99,739	837,323	93,036
Cartwright Hall	89,008	94,134	96,053	152,567	116,281	115,116	95,653	87,612	90,477	936,901	104,100
Keighley & Worth Valley Railway	144,766	150,000	168,515	162,474	156,000	155,582	137,000	141,000	141,028	1,356,365	150,707
Brontë Parsonage	176,963	186,060	212,545	199,412	197,050	159,630	119,907	113,754	101,900	1,307,591	163,449
National Museum of Photography, Film and TV	667,329	702,680	824,811	736,444	738,374	712,624	784,814	853,784	737,098	6,757,958	750,884
Colour Museum	8,000	24,054	25,212	18,411	16,287	18,209	16,735	15,020	15,355	157,283	17,476
Sooty's Wonderful World/Furever Feline (as from 10/94)		20,751		25,274	26,673	30,630	32,000	38,000	21,026	194,327	27,761
Bracken Hall							28,505			28,505	28,505
1853 Gallery					156,000	208,000	260,000	350,000	500,000	1,474,000	294,800
Yorks Car Collection							24,567	27,500	24,000	76,067	25,356
Haworth Village								1,000,000	1,000,000	2,000,000	1,000,000
Esholt – 'Emmerdale' (estimated)								750,000	750,000	1,500,000	750,000
Ilkley, The Moor and Cow & Half Rocks (estimated)								500,000	555,000	1,055,000	527,500
Five Rise Locks (estimated)								505,000	505,000	1,010,000	505,000
Bradford Cathedral								200,000	202,200	402,200	201,100
Transperience (new 1995)											
Totals	1,362,003	1,427,590	1,606,717	1,535,019	1,684,116	1,561,315	1,899,544	4,907,823	4,985,654	20,969,781	2,329,976

Figures 1986–92 (Tourism Development Status Report, 1993)
Figures 1993–94 (EDU, 1995)

	growth	day visits		
Market			short breaks	business
	decline			long stay
		high		low
			Share	

FIGURE A.4 *Tourism product portfolio: Bradford*

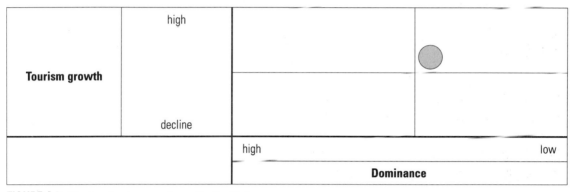

FIGURE A.5 *Tourism dominance and growth: Bradford*

TOURISM IMPACTS

Assessment of impacts cannot be unambiguous because of the lack of clear data on visitors and their behaviour, because of the subjective nature of some impacts, and because the distribution of positive and negative impacts between different areas and groups is complex.

ECONOMIC IMPACTS

By 1993, it was estimated that Bradford's tourism and conference industry was worth £64 million annually (EDU, 1993), although the calculation is not qualified in any way, and details of spending by different types of visitor are not available. However, it is possible to draw on spending patterns in the West Yorkshire region to try and qualify the Bradford figure. In 1994, tourism spending in West Yorkshire totalled £276 million: (£210 million from UK residents, £66 million from overseas visitors). Forty-eight per cent of this total is accounted for by the city of Leeds (YHTB 1994 and personal communication). Assuming that there was no significant variation between 1993 and 1994, this would mean that Bradford accounted for a little under half of the £133 million spent in West Yorkshire apart from Leeds. This is credible, although the county also includes Calderdale, Kirklees and a number of other popular visitor attractions.

The increase in visitation has undoubtedly increased employment, but the effects are very difficult to quantify. The number of jobs created by visitor spending cannot be estimated since the necessary surveys have not been carried out. It is possible to infer some information on tourism employment from information about jobs in tourism-related industries. Figure A.6 summarises information extracted by the EDU (EDU, 1993) from the 1989 Census of Employment.

Group description	Persons
Restaurants, snack bars, cafés	1 848
Public houses/bars	3 719
Night clubs/licensed	1 017
Hotel trade	1 133
Other tourist/short-stay accommodation	6
Libraries, museums, art galleries	346
Sport recreational services	2 278
Total	**10 347**

FIGURE A.6 *Tourism-related employment*

Figure A.6 shows that employment in tourism-related industries stood at over 10,000. However, this is obviously not an accurate estimate of employment in tourism.

■ In some ways it exaggerates tourism employment. While in some of these industries (like hotels) most of the turnover, and thus employment, is attributable to tourism, in others, local people will account for a substantial element of turnover (e.g. local people use pubs). However, there are reasonably reliable estimates (at the national level) of the proportion of total employment in each category which is directly attributable to tourism (Morrell, 1985). When these ratios are applied, we can estimate a total of some 4,400 jobs *directly* attributable to tourism.

■ The figures also underestimate the jobs attributable to tourism, since no account is taken of the extent to which tourism supports jobs in other industries (e.g. retailing), nor of jobs created in non-tourism industries as a result of an improvement in the city's image.

A further means of estimating economic impacts is by looking at the developments which appear to be attributable to the growth of tourism in the city. It is clear that the city's tourism infrastructure has expanded considerably since its 1980 entry into the market. Numerous new attractions have been established.

For example, the National Museum of Photography, Film & Television (NMPFT) which opened in 1983 was born out of a partnership between the Science Museum and the City Council. In the mid to late 1970s, the National Museum of Science and Industry was looking for somewhere outside London to locate the NMPFT. The timing roughly coincided with Bradford's consideration of the possibilities of tourism. At the same time, in the centre of Bradford, a vacant theatre was available (it had originally been built by the council as a replacement for one lost as a result of redevelopment, but was never occupied). This coincidence of events, and the commitment to tourism that the council showed, was key to influencing the decision of the NMPFT to locate in Bradford. The council put £1.8 million into the building's conversion and refurbishment (of which £0.5 million was EC funding) and the Science Museum took over all establishment and revenue costs (NMPFT, 1994).

Other attractions followed the establishment of the NMPFT, and the renovation of the Alhambra at the heart of the city's 'West End' is now seen as one of Britain's best preserved Edwardian Theatres (Bradford EDU, 1995). There followed the Colour Museum, the Industrial Museum and the Victorian and Edwardian paintings and multicultural exhibitions at Cartwright Hall. Most notable, however, has been the purchase and conversion of Salts Mill and most recently the opening of Transperience (West Yorkshire Transport Discovery Park) in July 1995. Salts Mill was purchased by local entrepreneur Jonathan Silver and now provides offices, shop, and a diner; however the main attraction is the huge '1853 Art Gallery' displaying original works by David Hockney. Attempts were also made to generate tourism benefits for existing city businesses. For example, the 'Curry Trail' encouraged visitors to sample some of the city's Asian restaurants.

Growth in the tourism market was not immediately translated into substantial new hotel development, although there is evidence of pressure on the existing accommodation stock. A recent study argued that there had been little growth in the supply of hotel accommodation; that there were high levels of frustrated demand (with midweek corporate demand exceeding supply on 25% of available nights in the district); that no four-star accommodation was available other than in the city centre itself; and that a lack of suitable accommodation was hampering the area's ability to tap into the conference and tour market (Bradford Enterprise Services, nd). Indeed, during the period January 1991 to June 1992, the EDUs Conference Marketing Team were unable to place 33 events, owing to a lack of suitable accommodation, representing an estimated minimum loss of £1 million in hotel revenues. (Bradford EDU, 1993). However, by 1993, the EDU identified £9.5 million investment in hotels in the previous two years, and the start of work on a new 125-bed hotel out of town: EuroCam Estate. Subsequently the EDU and RGA forged a partnership: 'The Hotel Development Initiative', aiming to 'stimulate the expansion and improvement of hotel supply in the Bradford District' by identifying and marketing potential hotel-development sites (Bradford EDU, nd).

While this account demonstrates that there has been a considerable amount of tourist-related development, it provides no direct evidence of what would have happened in its absence. Would sites have lain idle or been used for some other purpose? However, given the depressed state of the city economy during much of the 1980s and the wide availability of development sites, its seems reasonable to conclude that most or all of the tourist development was additional to other potential activity, rather than a displacement of it.

ENVIRONMENTAL AND SOCIAL IMPACTS

Tourism has been one of the factors behind the environmental improvements that have taken place in the city centre. Design improvements in the central area, the development of the West End for entertainment and leisure, and the refur-bishment of historic buildings in areas such as Little Germany, were all encouraged by the drive to make the city attractive to visitors – although that was far from being the sole motivation.

Large cities are generally less affected than other destinations by the adverse impacts that tourism can cause. They are more robust than areas of countryside, and absorb visitors comparatively easily, and tourism is less dominant than in resorts. Tourism is usually just one contributor to problems like traffic congestion and litter, but may attract a disproportionate share of the blame. In Bradford's case this is illustrated by a 'catalogue of gloom amid tourist boom' compiled by the local paper in 1991, which voiced concerns that the thousands of visitors to the district's rural, cultural and heritage attractions were bringing problems the city could do without. It pointed to traffic congestion, poor parking facilities, litter and land erosion, increased housing costs, and lack of job security for the thousands involved in the local tourist trade (*Telegraph and Argus*, 6 December 1991).

Problems are most acute outside the city centre and urban areas, in rural settlements. Esholt, a small village used as a location for the 'Emmerdale Farm' TV soap opera, has attracted large numbers of visitors and caused predictable disturbance to the local residents. Villagers' concerns centred on coach trips – it was alleged that up to 40 coaches a day would enter the village during the summer months, bringing half a million people to a place without a single public lavatory. Litter, traffic, noise and invasion of privacy were among significant problems raised (quoted *Telegraph and Argus*, 1 December 1986).

Haworth is perhaps the best illustration of the problems of increasing visitation. Attracting over one million visitors annually (see Figure A.3), it is clearly one of Bradford's most famous assets, with visitors from all walks of life making the trip to the literary shrine of the Brontë sisters, including an increasing number from Japan (Steel, 1991). Some village concerns have centred on the environmental and social effects, with the sheer number of visitors causing congestion in the narrow village main street and surrounding roads, and with tourist shops allegedly driving out local shops. The local neighbourhood forum blamed the council for exacerbating the situation through its tourist promotion and urged 'for goodness sake, stop telling people to come here' (*Keighley News*, 28 February 1992). However, traders' concern centred not on too many visitors, but their short stay. It was argued that lack of parking meant that visitors treated the village as a 'whistle-stop' on a longer tour, and spent little – the result, it was said, was vacant shops (*Telegraph and Argus*, October 1994).

The council has acknowledged these problems:

> 'The promotion of tourism has brought a number of benefits to the district in the past decade. However some of this work may be undone by the growing problems of tourism management faced by local communities'.
>
> *(Steel, 1991)*

A report discussing potential problems highlighted the problems tourism could cause:

- local communities damaged through local shops being forced out in favour of tourist shops and by increased housing costs
- environmental problems such as traffic congestion and litter – it pointed out that 'these "externalities" are seldom costed and are often concentrated at specific localities'
- jobs in tourism are often poorly paid, insecure, non-unionised with poor conditions
- although a substantial amount of tourism-related expenditure is generated in the district, an unknown (but probably high proportion) 'leaks' out in the form of profits to be spent outside the area (e.g. to head offices and in the importation of food and services).

The report concluded that 'all of these problems are present in the district according to anecdotal evidence' (*ibid*). It proposed that a survey should be carried out by consultants and funded by the council in conjunction with the ETB and local partners. However, this proposal was not implemented, and without such information it is difficult to assess the balance between adverse and beneficial impacts, and the extent to which tourism development enjoys local support.

ISSUES AND PROBLEMS

The initial thrust of tourism promotion in Bradford had two parallel strands.

- The need to market the city and improve the image of the area from an apparently grimy industrial backwater, to one that could successfully compete with other West Yorkshire towns and cities in attracting inward investment.
- The need to diversify an economy which had seen considerable contraction of employment in staple industries (such as textiles and engineering), and which had experienced high rates of unemployment.

Our review thus far suggests that three sets of issues must be considered:

- how have benefits and costs from tourism development been distributed?
- how far has the image of the city been changed as a result of the tourism initiatives?
- what role has the council played in leading and guiding development?

We return to these issues in the final section of this case study.

POLICIES AND PLANS

ORGANISATION AND MANAGEMENT OF TOURISM

The policy framework for tourism derives from Bradford's statutory policies in land-use plans, its economic development strategies, and formal but non-statutory policies, such as the Tourism Development Action Plan. Regional Planning Guidance and the policies of the Yorkshire and Humberside Tourist Board also have an influence. However, formal policies are not necessarily the most significant. The unit charged with realising a 'new' Bradford was the purposely formed **Economic Development Unit (EDU)** which was created by Bradford Council in 1979, and was the first of its kind in the UK. Its brief was to create new employment opportunities by encouraging new company formation, the expansion of indigenous industries and the attraction of inward investment.

The original structure of the EDU is shown in Figure A.7. It had a strong marketing element and this drove forward the tourism initiative. The initiative was pioneering, innovative and something of a gamble. The £100,000 funding the EDU received to develop the city's tourism potential was seen as risk funding. Without results, the funding would not be renewed in subsequent years. It was the EDU (or, more specifically, the innovative members of the Marketing and Promotions Team), that carried out the initial research, established the market, gained publicity, and thus initially played the greatest role in developing tourism. The approach could be described as strategic opportunism, or an aspect of 'entrepreneurial planning' (see Chapter 7). Formal and, particularly, statutory policies followed from rather than created the initiative, as we demonstrate next.

LAND-USE PLANNING

When tourism came onto the agenda in 1979–80, the strategic plan that provided the planning framework for the city and county was the **West Yorkshire Structure Plan** (adopted 1980). It contained limited land-use policies in respect of tourism. Within the Employment and Economy chapter there was only one significant tourism policy: this concerned supporting the promotion of business tourism in the main centres of West Yorkshire, and encouraging leisure tourism wherever appropriate, in cooperation with the Yorkshire & Humberside Tourist Board (Policy CC7). In 1984, four years after the tourism marketing campaign had begun, the first alteration of the Structure Plan incorporated a policy seeking to encourage the development of hotels (Policy E14).

Local Plan policy covering the Metropolitan District did not emerge until the late 1980s. The statutory adopted plan, the **Bradford City Centre Local Plan** (1988), then recognised that tourism was a growth industry for the city, but no specific (pro-active or restrictive) policies were included in the plan, perhaps surprising given the momentum that tourism had achieved by 1988. However, the supporting text recognised that the 1980s was a period of challenge in which new roles needed to be developed in Bradford and that one such role was tourism (para. 2.10, p. 6); growth was envisaged in hotels, entertainment and attractions, and the importance of the architectural heritage as a base for tourism was recognised (para. 2.8, p. 5).

The City Centre Local Plan was accompanied by three non-adopted local plans covering the wider area of Bradford: the **Greater Bradford Local Plan**, **Lower Airedale Local Plan**, and

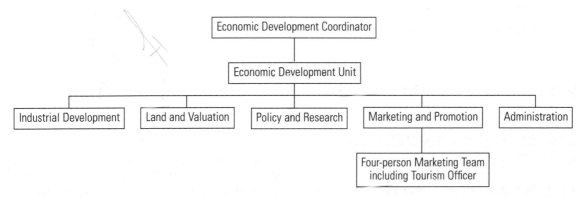

FIGURE A.7 *Organisation of the Economic Development Unit*

the **Upper Airedale Local Plan** (all subject to Inspectors' report in 1989–90). Little specific attention is paid to tourism in any of them. The Upper and Lower Airedale Plans incorporate the Pennines, with the former covering Haworth, and the need for control of tourism is acknowledged. The philosophy of both plans is very similar, seeking a balance between the promotion of tourism and other activities with the need to respect the conservation of the area (Policies UA/EN22/24 and LA/EN21/23).

Superseding all these plans, is the emerging Bradford **Unitary Development Plan (UDP)**, which comprises both district-wide policies and proposals which offer guidance and policies specific to each of Bradford's constituencies (Bradford North, South and West; Keighley; Shipley). Regional Planning Guidance for Yorkshire and Humberside, which provides a context for the UDP, is positive, arguing that leisure and tourism will 'increase substantially' in the 10 years it covers (to 2006), and suggesting that attracting visitors 'in the close season' may be a possible market (DoE, 1995). The UDP recognises that tourism-related industries are generating an increasing level of employment for the district's residents and generating income for the area. Tourism is not dealt with separately, but by two policies in the economy and employment chapter and one policy in the retailing chapter. The former policies are aimed at encouraging tourism development in urban and rural areas, which maximises the use of existing buildings and respects the locality while satisfying infrastructure requirements. The latter policy provides for retail development associated with tourism in rural areas. Reference to tourism in the constituency reports is largely restricted to a few site allocations (e.g. the West Yorkshire Transport Museum in Bradford South). However, area-based initiatives aimed at supporting tourism development are identified in three reports: Shipley (Saltaire), Keighley, and Bradford West (city centre). In addition, town and landscape character are safeguarded through a series of environmental protection polices.

It is clear that in the last 15 years, land-use planning guidance has contributed little to the development of tourism in the district. Statutory plans have neither played a significant proactive role (forward planning), nor a notably restrictive role (through development control).

TOURISM PLANS AND INFORMAL STRATEGIES

One reason for the modest role of statutory land-use planning was that policy was developed through other means. The Bradford **Tourism Development Action Plan (TDAP)**, proposed in January 1985, published in June and launched at the end of 1985, was a key policy document implemented over a period of 12 months. The TDAP attempted to tackle the major obstacles in the way of Bradford's tourism development, in order to assist in creating a more stable tourism industry.

It was a policy document that emphasised the need to attract more private investment and commercial interest in Bradford, thus building on the investment of public funds that had already taken place. In effect, it offered a tourism strategy which aimed selectively to increase the tourism infrastructure of Bradford, broaden its tourism base and appeal, and increase its number of visitors. The ultimate aim was to use tourism as a way of creating jobs and local prosperity (BTA/ETB, 1985).

The strategy had five objectives, and focused on:

- exploiting the conference and exhibition market
- improving the visitor experience of the city centre
- expanding the accommodation base
- developing a major new attraction
- broadening the marketing perspective.

The TDAP produced notable successes, with the marketing and development of Little Germany (initiated through TDAP) exceeding all expectations. Between the beginning of 1986 and the middle of 1988, £10 million of investment was achieved in the area, with 10 schemes completed, 10 schemes underway and 13 others proposed. Such schemes included hotel accommodation, wine bars, art galleries, manufacturing and services industries and general environmental improvements and car parks (Davies, 1988).

The Yorkshire and Humberside Tourist Board is responsible for the non-statutory tourism framework guiding tourism in the region. In 1988, it identified itself as the fundamental agency which has encouraged tourism in the region as a whole for 20 years, and considered itself as the 'catalyst for tourism in the regions' (YHTB, 1988). The thrust of its guidance issued in 1988 was partnership, as the title 'Working Together' suggests. In collaboration with local authorities, the commercial sector, government departments, the voluntary sector and the English Tourist Board, the Board hoped to implement its own strategy which hinged on 'Product Development and Effective Marketing'. The significance of this strategy, and indeed its successor 'Partnership in Quality' (1994–98), for Bradford is difficult to measure, since it represents advice on tourism development throughout the region over a five-year period, and thus detailed advice to specific destinations is inappropriate. It is not clear how far it has been integrated with policies in Bradford.

Since 1990, the council has produced an economic development strategy annually. The strategies are required to specify the broad aims and objectives of economic development in the Bradford District and list specific proposals for the relevant financial year. Comparison of the strategies allows shifts in priorities to be identified. The strategy for 1991–92 stressed the aim of the council was to build on the cultural, heritage and leisure assets of the district in order to provide a resource that would benefit the people of Bradford, and by attracting visitors make a positive contribution to the local economy (EDU, 1990). This was subsequently reflected in the funding given to various projects: for example funds were allocated to the Industrial Museum, to support the proposed relocation of part of the Victoria & Albert Museum, and to Tourist Information Centres. However, the strategy for 1995–96 lacked any commitment to tourism apart from a brief mention of the Conference Desk. Thus, budgeting for tourism has ceased at a time when emerging Regional Planning Guidance and the Regional Tourist Board strategy suggest that the significant opportunities offered by tourism be explored. It seems that the council's budget priorities have changed or that it considers tourism to be self-sustaining and thus no longer in need of council marketing and promotion. We explore this issue in the following section.

The most recent plan produced that touches upon tourism development is that of '**Vision into Action**' developed by Bradford City Centre Steering Group which comprises members from the public, private and voluntary sectors (June 1995). This forms part of a **City Centre Management** initiative and, in 1995, a £4 million bid was submitted to the EU to transform the centre, to help renovate the city for its centenary year in 1997 (including the creation of a 'Centenary Square'), and match the city's progress as a significant tourist destination.

The plan details the future of the principal activities within the centre, but also identifies six specific quarters in the city and their future: City Hall Precinct, The West End, Exchange Quarter, Forster Square, City Centre Shopping – Old Bradford, and Merchants' Quarter. The plan tackles the future and the management of the city centre in much greater detail than the Unitary Development Plan. It aims (uncontroversially) to promote the city as an attractive place to work, shop and visit, and seeks to promote investment and development in the quarters (BCCSG, 1995). Tourism would be among the beneficiaries, and specific emphasis is given to tourism development in the Merchants' Quarter and Little Germany. The integration between this plan and existing policies is not clear, and a significant part of its role appears to be as a means of generating consensus and commitment between the range of public- and private-sector agencies involved.

CONCLUSION

It is nearly 17 years since, in the face of significant adversity, the City Council accepted a new industrial strategy, the objectives of which were to:

- change Bradford's image
- assist existing firms
- attract new firms
- promote tourism. (Page, 1986)

What has been achieved? Assessment is made difficult by the lack of clear, consistent and quantified information, but we can make some assessment of how the city has developed as a destination and of the role of the council.

1 DEVELOPMENT OF TOURISM

There can be no doubt that the city has developed significantly as a tourism destination. Despite measurement problems, it is clear that leisure tourism grew rapidly from a low base in the early 1980s, and that growth seems to have continued though at a slower pace. It is important not to underestimate this achievement. The potential of tourism in former industrial areas has now become conventional wisdom, but in 1980 these were new types of destination, and Bradford's ideas and initiatives were truly pioneering. As Bramwell puts it:

> 'Bradford was the first British old city to put substantial resources into marketing itself as a tourist destination, using short-break packages to attract leisure visitors. This marketing has been largely conducted by the public sector, being organised within the City Council's EDU. This work began in 1980, and their tourism marketing activities have been acclaimed as both innovative for an industrial city and also successful in attracting visitors and improving the city's image.'
>
> *Bramwell (1994)*

Subsequently, there has been significant investment in new attractions and there is now some evidence of an increasing demand for, and willingness to invest in, the accommodation sector. Reasonably credible estimates suggest that visitor spending is around £60 million a year, and this will support a substantial number of jobs – but in the absence of information on spending patterns and local multipliers, estimating the actual number of jobs supported can be little more than guesswork. There have been the usual concerns about the quality of tourism jobs, but since 1980 there has been a general convergence between tourism and non-tourism employment, as insecurity and contract working have become more widespread. The development of attractions provides benefits to city residents as well as visitors, and provides direct economic benefits, since it retains resident spending that might otherwise have gone to competing cities – most obviously, Leeds.

The distribution of costs and benefits has been uneven. In the city centre, tourism has helped promote environmental improvement and create jobs and has been generally beneficial. However, the villages of Haworth and Esholt, which were important elements in marketing campaigns, have suffered from their increase in visitation. This is unsurprising. Cities generally can absorb visitors effectively, while small settlements are much more vulnerable. Thinking in terms of tourism dominance: while Bradford as a whole has low tourism dominance, dominance in the villages is high and the problems of effective management are correspondingly greater – the problems have not yet been overcome.

2 TOURISM AND IMAGE

Improving the city's image was an explicit part of Bradford's tourism initiative. It was felt that the city had a poor image – as old-fashioned, grimy, unpleasant – and that this was deterring the investment required to build new industries and create new jobs at a time of rapid economic change. Achieving the desired outcome, a more prosperous economy, meant creating a more positive image, which would then lead to more investment. Tourism was seen as a key element in image change through showing visitors what the city had to offer, and by providing a means of positive promotion in the media.

As the innovator in promoting tourism to industrial cities, Bradford was rewarded by a great deal of media coverage. It is clear that one consequence was an increase in visitation to the city. There is no direct evidence about how visitors' images of the city were changed by their visit, although the assumption is that they were improved. This certainly appears to be the case in Sheffield, where tourism and leisure have also been used as part of a strategy to reconfigure the city economy after major job losses in traditional industries. A detailed survey of visitors in 1992 showed that over half of first-time visitors said that their image had changed as a result of their visit, and of these, four out of five had a more positive image (Bramwell and Laws, 1993).

Again, no evidence is available on the difficult question of whether the tourism initiatives succeeded in influencing investment decisions. One piece of indirect evidence though, is that Bradford's initiative was quickly followed by many other industrial cities. The belief that tourism can bring image improvement and investment has become widespread.

3 THE ROLE OF THE COUNCIL

The route that the city took in its industrial strategy was far from conventional, and represents an interesting example of an 'entrepreneurial planning' approach. It was the local authority, not the commercial sector, which developed a new (and at the time very surprising and enterprising) product. As the then marketing manager acknowledged, the city had:

> '... to a large degree been opportunist. By being the first northern industrial city to package a product and launch it into the market with a degree of budgetary clout Bradford has "stolen a march" on its potential competitors. By doing so it has gone some way along the path towards developing a new local industry in tourism'.
> *(Fenn, 1985)*

It is possible to identify three principal stages in the development of Bradford's tourism industry and in the council's role. These can be loosely defined as opportunism in the late 1970s and early 1980s, consolidation in the mid and late 1980s, and disengagement in the 1990s.

The council's initial involvement was led by its EDU, and was both opportunistic and novel. It was marketing-led, intended to raise the city's profile and attract visitors while affecting its image through media attention. While the council created the initiative and the concept of themed breaks, involvement with the private sector was a key factor. The local authority knew it could not attempt to act as a travel agent and sell its own holiday package, and instead it forged links with independent tour operators to sell holidays in Bradford. The breaks themselves were sold and run by the tour operators and by some hotels. The EDU looked to local companies to bid for council backing and the result was an official Bradford operator, Enterprise Travel, which received free publicity through the council's own tourism drive. The initial confidence of local tour operators stimulated interest from others, and by 1986 over 50 tour operators incorporated Bradford in their brochures (Page, 1986). Looking back, the council's Marketing and Tourism Officer saw the local authority role at that time as being to originate the creative concept and assure the promotion and publicity (personal communication, 1995). This approach meant that action was running ahead of formal policy, and formal and statutory policies followed rather than led developments – with the exception of the 1979 industrial strategy from which the whole initiative derived.

The initial success of the tourism promotion of the early 1980s was based in part on its novelty, and subsequently the council sought to consolidate this success by expanding the tourism product portfolio and improving tourism services. It realised that marketing and promoting selected elements of the district sold holidays, but did not firmly establish the city as a tourist destination. Attempts to consolidate achievements and maintain growth centred around the production of a set of policies for tourism through the TDAP in 1985, which proposed moving into new markets, such as conferences, developing new attractions and increasing the accommodation base. The emphasis continued to be on partnership between public-sector agencies (the local authority and the ETB) and between the public and private sectors. The TDAP sought to encourage private-sector investment in target areas like Little Germany, and there were also attempts to increase the benefits visitation brought local businesses, through initiatives like the 'Curry Trail'.

In the 1990s, the council has substantially disengaged from taking a proactive role in specifically tourism development. The role of the Economic Development Unit shifted, to place less emphasis on marketing for tourism and more on general marketing for economic investment and development (Bramwell, 1994), and so far as tourism is concerned, the focus has been on greater attention on the conference industry. Since 1995, there has been no separately-identified tourism function within the council, nor is there a specific tourism budget, although the Conference Desk continues to provide and coordinate information for conference organisers. Tourism policy is included in statutory land-use plans within the wider context of area and economic development.

This disengagement by the council seems, in part, to be the result of tourism issues becoming incorporated in broader initiatives, such as City Centre Management which involve the local authority and other private- and public-sector partners. This might be seen as the result of the 'entrepreneurial planning' approach, which characterised tourism from the start, being incorporated into the mainstream, so that the need for a specific set of tourism activities is lessened. There is also a view that sufficient progress has been made for tourism development to be sustained by mainly private-sector action. The council has continued to support specific initiatives, such as a proposed National Superdrome (which sought but failed to gain National Lottery funding), and the West End redevelopments.

Whether the council's' disengagement is the correct strategy remains to be seen. Although it could be interpreted as an acknowledgement that the city is becoming a self-sustaining destination, it does seem a surprising decision in the light of the continued emphasis placed on tourism by neighbouring cities such as Leeds and Sheffield. It is unfortunate that the lack of good quality information on tourism trends and impacts means that judging the effectiveness of council action and the consequences of withdrawal is extremely difficult. The danger is clearly that momentum will be lost – a concern expressed in the local press in 1995, in an article headlined 'Our lost window of opportunity'. This article questioned the logic of Bradford Council (having pioneered tourism in northern industrial cities) being without a Tourism Officer at a time when art and culture were playing an increasing role (*Telegraph & Argus*, 2 March 1995).

REFERENCES

AA (1971) *Illustrated Guide to Britain*, Drive Publications.

BCCSG (1995) *Vision into Action*, Bradford City Centre Steering Group.

Bradford City Council (1988) *Bradford City Centre Local Plan*, Bradford MC.

Bradford City Council (1989) *Lower Airedale Local Plan*, Bradford MC.

Bradford City Council (1989) *Upper Airedale Local Plan*, Bradford MC.

Bradford City Council (1989) *Greater Bradford Local Plan*, Bradford MC.

Bradford Economic Development Unit (1990) *Draft Employment Strategy*, Bradford Metropolitan Council.

Bradford Economic Development Unit (1993) *Economic Development Annual Report 1992/93*, Bradford Metropolitan Council.

Bradford Economic Development Unit (1993b) *Tourism Status Report*, Bradford Metropolitan Council.

Bradford Economic Development Unit (1995) *The Bradford Disk*, Bradford Metropolitan Council.

Bradford Enterprise Services (nd) *Bradford – a unique opportunity for hotel development*. Bradford MDC.

Bradford Economic Development Unit (nd) Bradford Hotel Development Initative – Promoting Hotel Development. Bradford MDC.

Bradford Metropolitan Council (1985) *Tourism Development Action Plan*, Bradford MC.

Bradford Metropolitan Council (1987) *Tourism Development in the Bradford District*, Bradford MC.

Bradford Metropolitan Council (1993) *Draft Unitary Development Plan Part 1, 2*, Bradford MC.

Bramwell, B. and Rawding, I. (1994) 'Tourism Marketing Organisation in Industrial Cities', *Tourism Management* 15, 6, pp. 425–434.

Bramwell, B. and Laws, D. (1993) *Sheffield Visitors 1992*, Sheffield Visitor and Conference Bureau.

British Tourist Authority/English Tourist Board (1985) *Bradford Tourism Development Action Programme*, BTA/ETB.

Buckley, J. and de Witt, S. (1985) 'Tourism in Difficult Areas' *Tourism Management Journal*.

DoE (1995) *Regional Planning Guidance: Yorkshire and Humberside Consultation Draft*, Department of the Environment.

Fenn, E. (1984) *Marketing Strategy and Economic Overview*, Bradford Economic Development Unit.

Fenn, E. (1986) 'The Bradford Submission Local Government Tourist Authority of the Year Award', Bradford Economic Development Unit.

Guy, J. (1984) 'Alhambra complex, Bradford: Application for ERDF assistance. Supplementary Information', Yorkshire and Humberside Regional Tourist Board.

Kerrier, A. (1992) 'Urban and Rural Tourism: a case study of Bradford and Cornwall', Local Government Policy Making.

Morrell, B. (1985) *Employment in Tourism*, British Tourist Authority, London.

NMPFT (1994) Background Information, National Museum of Photography, Film and Television.

Page, I. (1986) 'Tourism Promotion in Bradford' *The Planner:* TCPSS Proceedings, February, pp. 72–75.

Parajia, A. (1994) 'Bradford and the Flavours of Asia', in *Tourism in Focus*, Winter, 14.

Steel, J. (1991) *Proposal for Tourism Management Strategy*, report to Economic Strategy Sub-Committee, Community and Environmental Services Committee, City of Bradford.

West Yorkshire Metropolitan County Council (1980) *West Yorkshire County Structure Plan*, West Yorkshire MCC.

West Yorkshire Metropolitan County Council (1984) *West Yorkshire County Structure Plan: 1st Alteration*, West Yorkshire MCC.

YHTB (1988) *Working Together: into the Nineties*, Yorkshire and Humberside Tourist Board.

YHTB (1994) *Tourism Strategy 1994–98: Partnership in Quality*, Yorkshire and Humberside Tourist Board.

B  *Dover*

THEMES

- using tourism to diversify the local economy in order to compensate for anticipated job losses due to wider developments
- synergy between tourism and the retail sector
- the importance of partnership arrangements to achieve objectives
- the importance of attracting external funding to achieve objectives.

LOCATION AND BACKGROUND

Dover District is one of the six districts of East Kent in South East England, some 60 miles south-east of London, to which it is joined by the A2 road. Its population is mainly centred on the towns of Dover, Deal and Sandwich. The town of Dover itself is the busiest ferry port in Europe, due to its gateway position at the closest point of the UK to continental Europe.

By virtue of its location, the Dover area reflects in its landscape and heritage the history of England from its earliest beginnings. In the past, most of those wishing to come to Britain have passed through this area, either peacefully or by invasion. As a result, a great many relics, monuments, castles and items of historic interest are to be found there. Some of the most interesting date from the Roman period, the Norman era, the Napoleonic phase and the World Wars: from the Roman Painted House in Dover, the Guildhall in Sandwich and the Victorian South Foreland Lighthouse, to the castles at Dover, Deal, Richborough and Walmer. But the Dover area's best-known attractions are undoubtedly its famous white chalk cliffs, which are the first and last view of England for those travelling by ferry, and which were immortalised in the wartime song by Vera Lynn.

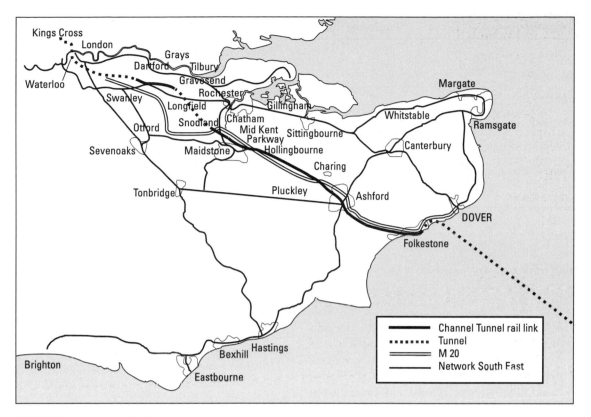

FIGURE B.1 *South East England*

Built by Henry II 800 years ago on the White Cliffs, Dover Castle dominates the town itself and is now the most popular attraction of the district's built heritage. In common with Sandwich and Deal, the town of Dover also has a rich urban heritage, much of which has been carefully safeguarded.

However, Dover also bears the scars of history. Most recently, Second World War damage to the town of Dover meant that much of it was rebuilt during the 1950s, often in a somewhat haphazard manner, leaving parts of the urban landscape with a rather rundown and inconsistent image. This was exacerbated by changes in the structure of the shipping industry which led to parts of the docks in Dover falling into disuse during the 1980s.

ECONOMY

In the past, much of the economic life in the district traditionally focused on the Port of Dover and the transport companies operating from there to the continent. A 1989 survey of employment sectors in the Dover area demonstrated the importance of transport for the local employment market as shown in Figure B.2.

By the early 1990s, however, two important challenges for the local economy were on the horizon for the years lying immediately ahead: the opening of the Channel Tunnel (originally set for 1993) and the proposed Ministry of Defence cutbacks following the end of the Cold War and the collapse of the Berlin Wall in 1989.

Industrial division	Employees (1989)
Primary	1 900
Manufacturing	5 300
Construction	5 300
Distribution, hotels/catering, repairs	6 000
Transport/communication	11 600
Banking, finance, insurance	2 100
Other services	11 000
Total	**43 200**

Source: DDC Tourism Business Plan 1992/93

FIGURE B.2 *Employment sectors in the Dover area (1989)*

- **Channel Tunnel**: confirmation of the challenge facing Dover as a result of the opening of the Channel Tunnel, was provided by the Kent Impact Study in 1991. This predicted that the opening of the Channel Tunnel could increase the number of unemployed within Dover District by up to 6,000 people by the mid 1990s, bringing with it a local unemployment level of around 20% to 25% and the very severe decline of the area. One year later than scheduled, the Channel Tunnel opened for business in 1994, in direct competition with the ferries using the Port of Dover. Since then cut-throat competition between the ferry companies and the Channel Tunnel has continued to fuel local anxieties over the possibility of rationalisation in the ferry industry and the potentially disastrous effects this could have on the local economy.
- **Ministry of Defence cutbacks**: these cutbacks directly affected the Dover area, which included several garrison towns. The military and naval presence in the area provided direct employment for the civilian populations of these towns, as well as indirect benefits for local hotels and shops. The cuts included the closure of the Old Park Barracks which employed 250 people (military and civilians), and the loss of the Royal Marines School of Music in Deal, which employed 80 civilians and around 150 Royal Marines or Navy personnel. By 1996, both of these properties had closed.

By the end of the 1980s, the local authority, **Dover District Council (DDC)** had recognised that if the worst effects of these two problems were to be avoided, action needed to be taken. However, at that time, there were no funds available nor even the recognition of the potential problems by either central government or Kent County Council. As a result, DDC realised that it would have to act on its own to start addressing these issues on a local basis.

In anticipation of the severe adverse effects which the opening of the Channel Tunnel and the Ministry of Defence cutbacks would have on Dover's employment patterns, DDC's policy became one of **diversifying** the local economy: away from port-related and defence-related activities, to other forms of commerce and industry with more promising job-creation potential.

The council, through its **Tourism Unit** and **Economic Development Unit**, which were created in 1991, adopted a two-pronged strategy to promote the economic development and diversification of the industry base of Dover District:

- economic development and diversification of the industrial base
- development of the tourism industry.

DIVERSIFICATION OF THE INDUSTRIAL BASE

The council's main objective under this heading is: 'To work with others to implement sustainable economic development activities which create and safeguard employment while maintaining the quality of the environment' (*DDC Economic Development Strategy*, 1996/97).

A key element of the council's approach was to identify suitable land for industrial development. Through the land-use planning process, some 70 hectares of land alongside the A2 road in the Whitfield suburb of Dover town were designated for this purpose. This became the site of the White Cliffs Business Park, the district's flagship initiative to strengthen the economic base of the Dover area by attracting new industries or relocating indigenous companies. In addition, the Old Park and Royal Marines Deal site became available for development.

Before undertaking marketing campaigns to find potentially mobile companies and attract them to Dover District, the council's Economic Development Unit priority has been to prepare the sites for occupation.

TOURISM

BACKGROUND

Tourism in the DDC area, prior to the council's decision to develop this activity, was mostly focused on the port and the transport needs of people crossing the Channel. However, of the 14 million people a year using the port facilities at the end of the 1980s, only a very small proportion actually spent any time in the area. Most passed straight through, heading inland to other, more established destinations in Kent, or directly to London and beyond.

Nevertheless, a number of guesthouses and bed-and-breakfast establishments satisfying the demand for mostly one-night accommodation had developed in the town of Dover. This 'stopover' characteristic of tourism in Dover in the past may account for the mixed quality of hotels and restaurants which prevailed there at the beginning of the 1990s.

> 'Certain [hotel] establishments pride themselves on careful control of quality and providing a welcome and thereby achieve a high level of repeat business. On the other hand, the one-night stay element in Dover has encouraged the notion that repeat business did not have a high priority. The catering and restaurant sector has also been of a rather mixed quality. The lack of a big city in the area has meant that a local market to support good quality eating places does not exist and has led to a strong seasonal aspect in the provision of food and drink.'
>
> (*DDC Tourism Business Plan, 1992/93*)

In Deal, the hotel provision was on a rather limited basis, providing accommodation for people visiting friends and relatives in the area. In Sandwich, there was one hotel catering mainly for business visitors and golfers visiting the nearby Links. Another important market was created by the area's military connections, which generated a certain amount of business from visiting relatives of army, airforce and navy personnel.

However, it was clear to those responsible for drawing up DDC's tourism strategy that although the quality of Dover District's stock of accommodation and catering establishments may have been uneven, the natural and historic built environment represented one of the area's greatest tourism assets. But while some of these assets were already attracting visitors, others remained relatively unknown outside the immediate area, such as the undulating and unspoilt countryside and picturesque villages of the hinterland.

The marketing of Dover as a tourist destination faced an additional challenge – two events of the 1980s had left the area with a somewhat tarnished image: the Zeebrugge disaster and the bitter P&O ferry strike. The impact of these events on Dover's image had to be reversed in order to further develop the area as a successful tourist destination.

DDC'S TOURISM REGENERATION POLICY

WHITE CLIFFS COUNTRY

The main DDC policy objective for tourism is: 'To work to realise the potential of tourism in creating economic activity and jobs (including self-employment) and help to make the district a vibrant place to work, live and visit.' (*DDC Economic Development Strategy*, 1996/97).

The strategy to achieve this objective is implemented by the council's Tourism Unit, which undertakes a range of marketing and development activities to raise awareness of the area in order to stimulate tourism and provide tangible backing to the local commercial sector. The **White Cliffs Country (WCC)** brand name for marketing the area was developed to incorporate the resorts of Dover, Deal and Sandwich and remains a vital element in the council's tourism policy.

The aim of WCC is to position itself as a product primarily aiming at the day-visitor target market and at the market for short stays. The message transmitted through the council's annual advertising campaign may be summed up as follows: 'White Cliffs Country: a pleasant, accessible area of countryside with a wide choice of inexpensive accommodation, offering the benefits of child and adult entertainment with the added bonus of a day's trip to France.'

PLANS AND POLICIES

DDC's tourism strategy is determined and implemented according to a number of policy vehicles as follows.

- **Dover District Local Plan**: this provides an official background to the authority's policies over a 5–10 year period. It determines the land-use elements of the tourism strategy, for example, by identifying land suitable for the development of tourist attractions.
- **DDC Tourism and Economic Development Committee's annual Economic Development Strategy**: this annual report sets objectives and explains the activities that

DDC intends carrying out in the year ahead in order to enhance the attractiveness of the district as a business and tourist location. Such a document is required by the 1989 Local Government and Housing Act, which places a statutory duty on all local authorities intending to carry out any economic development activities to publish details of these before the start of the financial year, and to consult with a range of organisations on these activities. Contained in that strategy document are the objectives of the Tourism and Economic Development Committee which determine the annual activities of both the Economic Development Unit and the Tourism Unit.

- **DDC Tourism Business Plan**: this annual plan provides a framework for specific action for the Tourism Unit. It includes the council's analysis of current tourism trends, as well as an indication of how the local tourism industry is performing. Its purpose is to determine priorities in the fields of marketing and product development in the White Cliffs Country during the following financial year, in line with the council's financial resources. It reviews what was achieved from the previous year's Plan and develops specific targets, measures and actions to achieve the general objectives set out in the Tourism and Economic Development Committee's strategy.

THE POLICY PROCESS

The direction and content of the district's strategy for tourism are agreed in consultation with a number of relevant local organisations, including:

- White Cliffs Dover Hotel and Guest House Group
- Dover Guest House Association
- Chambers of Trade/Commerce in Dover, Deal and Sandwich
- neighbouring local authorities and Kent County Council
- South East England Tourist Board
- White Cliffs Country Tourism Association.

In this way, care is taken to ensure that the strategy is relevant and realistic but also that it is compatible with tourism-related strategies at other administrative levels.

Recognising the need for an effective strategy to be based on up-to-date and reliable research, DDC makes budgetary provision for professional market research. Recent work includes the White Cliffs Country Visitor Survey (Surrey Research Group, 1995), Le Tour Impact Study (Surrey Research Group, 1994), White Cliffs Experience Re-development Needs (Continental Research, 1994). Other relevant research includes the Dover area hotel occupancy returns (DDC), as well as research documents by Kent County Council and the South East England Tourist Board.

TOURISM DEVELOPMENT ACTIVITIES

The work undertaken by DDC's Tourism Unit falls into a number of programme areas:

- marketing
- arts and events
- tourism development
- partnership initiatives
- attractions and museums.

Within the first five years of DDC's Tourism Regeneration Policy, considerable progress was made under a number of headings. These include the following examples.

Tourist attractions

With a large number of vacant shop premises in the centre of Dover at the end of the 1980s, there had been an urgent need for a solution which could improve the retail sector of the town. DDC decided to build a visitor attraction of national importance which would bring a significant number of visitors into the centre of the town and, as a result, make it easier to attract new commercial organisations there. Thus the White Cliffs Experience was created in 1991, just off Dover's Market Square. The cost of the visitor attraction was £14 million, most of which came from DDC's capital reserves. (A few years later, European funding may have been another possibility; but the policy was to develop the White Cliffs Experience quickly – in time for the opening of the Channel Tunnel – and European funding was not available at that time.)

The attraction was built on an important archaeological site which, in the past, had had a number of plans for retail and commercial development but which, because of Dover's limited catchment area, had not taken place.

The attraction's main focus is based on two eras of local significance: the Roman invasion and the Second World War. Using a combination of audiovisual techniques, archaeological restoration and historical reconstruction, visitors are able to 'witness' the Roman invasion of 55BC and discover the important archaeological remains of Classis Britannica. Similar techniques are used to reconstruct a typical Dover street in the throes of the Second World War. The 'street' features a cinema, pub, bakery and a post office, each one with a video monitor installed, showing interviews with local residents who recount their wartime experiences.

The White Cliffs Experience in its first year exceeded all expectations. During the first financial year, it was expected to have 150,000 visitors, but in fact achieved almost 235,000. This meant that an additional £1.5 million was spent locally by visitors who would not have otherwise come to Dover in that year. It has won a number of national awards including the ETB's England for Excellence Award as Visitor Attraction of the Year.

Tourism development

The White Cliffs themselves, including spectacular walks along Langdon Cliffs and St Margarets as well as the Shakespeare Cliff area, were improved and opened up to the public with new facilities under the stewardship of the White Cliffs Countryside Project. Measures were also taken to encourage people to enjoy the countryside and villages of the area, including the promotion of cycling and horse riding as well as walking and visiting village churches. In order to create a Historical Villages Trail, a network of interpretation panels was developed. The urban heritage of Dover, Deal and Sandwich was highlighted and made more accessible to visitors through the development of trails and a network of history panels with accompanying literature.

Accommodation

As a means of tackling the problem of the un-even quality of hotels and guesthouses in the WCC area, the local authority pursued a policy of only officially recognising those establishments which had had themselves classified using the ETB system. This means, for example, that council-run Tourist Information Centres will only assist establishments which have been classi-fied. By 1996, the Tourism Unit was able to re-port that:

> 'The Council's policy of encouraging all accommodation to join the ETB Crown Classification system has been implemented. The target of 60 premises with a score of 1+ crowns has been achieved'.
>
> *(DDC Tourism Action Plan, 1996/97)*

Events

By 1992, a number of high-profile events were already in place for the years ahead, promising to put WCC to the forefront of public attention: the 1993 British Open Golf Championship at Sandwich; the 1993 2,000th anniversary of the Roman Claudian invasion of Britain; and the 1994 and 1995 commemorations of the 50th an-niversary of the liberation of Nazi-occupied Europe and VE Day. In 1994, the Tour de France cycle race came to Britain for the first time since 1974, creating worldwide media at-tention for Dover, which was the race's point of entry to the UK.

Partnership initiatives

Many of the activities undertaken by the Tourism Unit take the form of joint initiatives with local organisations and private-sector companies with an interest in the area's marketing and develop-ment as a tourist destination. DDC works in col-laboration with the private sector and other agencies not only to launch joint marketing pro-motions but also to develop the local tourism product. Its principal partners are as follows.

- **Discover East Kent Consortium and East Kent Initiative.** DDC lobbying led to the setting up, in 1989–90, of the English Tourist Board seed-funded **East Kent Local Area Tourism Initiative (LATI)**, to help Kent shed the 'corridor county' image and to entice the flow of Channel Tunnel and cross-Channel ferry users to spend more time ex-ploring its heritage and other tourist attractions. The LAI later evolved into the **Discover East Kent Consortium**, whose role it is to coordinate public-private-sector tourism initiatives in the area. The Discover East Kent Consortium is in turn the tourism arm of the **East Kent Initiative (EKI)**, in the formation of which DDC was instrumen-tal. The EKI itself is a public-private-sector task force consisting of:
  - the six District Councils in East Kent.
  - Kent County Council.
  - representatives from four central govern-ment departments (Transport, Trade and Industry, Environment, and Employment).
  - Kent TEC.
  - the private sector including Eurotunnel, Dover Harbour Board, P&O and British Telecom.

  Its aim (to tackle challenges brought about as a result of the Single European Market and the opening of the Channel Tunnel) is entirely com-patible with that of DDC's economic develop-ment objectives.
- **White Cliffs Countryside Project**: DDC is a key player in this joint agency which is en-trusted with the stewardship of the coastal landscape of the area.
- **South East England Tourist Board**: DDC plays an active role in this Regional Tourist Board, in order to gain maximum benefit for the District from regional and national (ETB) tourism initiatives aimed at the tourism devel-opment and marketing of the region.
- **White Cliffs Country Tourism Associa-ation (WCCTA)**: DDC was instrumental in establishing in 1990 this local tourism forum which includes all major tourism operators, including: hoteliers, Dover Harbour Board and cross-Channel transport operators. The value of such a private-sector-led forum is that it can (and does) issue good practice awards and set up promotions. The WCCTA has, in fact, been regarded as a model local

tourism association, and the DDC Tourism Manager was invited to Italy and Hungary in 1995 to describe how it was set up.

- **English Heritage**: Dover Castle is an English Heritage property. DDC works with this government agency to extend the potential of the castle and increase annual visitor numbers.
- **Dover District Chamber of Commerce and Industry and Dover Harbour Board**: DDC collaborates with the Chamber of Commerce in industrial and tourism-related matters. An example of a joint venture between the two organisations is provided by the opening of the new Dover Cruise Ship Terminal. This was inaugurated in 1996 by Dover Harbour Board, as part of the Board's plan to redevelop the Western Docks area of Dover. Over 100 ship arrivals were expected for 1996, a major benefit for Dover. In order to make the most of the opportunity presented by cruise ships visiting Dover, DDC and the Chamber of Commerce launched a joint programme of marketing and welcoming support for the new cruise terminal, providing a meet-and-greet service for passengers, as well as brochures and displays to tempt them to visit the town, its shops and attractions.
- **European partners**: DDC understands the need to set up partnerships with other destinations on the French side of the Channel, since there is a growing alliance of interests as cross-Channel travel becomes more widespread. Reciprocal marketing with French partners is one example of this form of co-operation. On the tourism development side, DDC has made joint submissions with Calais and Boulogne for funding from the EUs Interreg scheme for frontier regions.

TOURISM NOW

By 1995, after a six year drive to promote its assets as a destination and to develop the appeal of the area, the White Cliffs Country of DDC had become 'a well-established location within the South East of England for transit day visits, short stays, longer stays' (*DDC Tourism Business Plan*,

1995/96). An insight into tourism in White Cliffs Country is given in the following figures.

VISITOR PROFILE

One of the results of the tourism strategy has been to rejuvenate the visitor profile of the area. When the first visitors' survey in the Dover, Deal and Sandwich area was conducted in 1989, one third of the visitors were in the over 60 years age group and 28% were comprised of family groups. By 1995, only 5% of visitors were over 60 and almost 60% of visitors came to the area in family groups, typically in the ABC1 social category. More than 8 in 10 visitors in the 1995 sample were below the age of 46 (although the venue of this survey which has a strong appeal for younger visitors, Dover Castle, most certainly influenced the results). In part, the area's added appeal for the family market may be attributed to the opening of the White Cliffs Experience and the WCC promotional campaign using the 'Sid the Seagull' character as a mascot.

VISITOR NUMBERS

In 1995, a total of 60% of visitors were from the UK, and almost half of these were from the southern counties of England, as shown in Figure B.3.

Concerning overseas visitors, the USA and Canada and northern European countries were the main markets in 1995, as in previous years (see Figure B.4).

The previous visitor survey, undertaken in 1993, pointed out that, due to its gateway role, WCC receives a much higher share of the UK's overseas visitors than the national average for destinations outside London: 22% as opposed to around 15–20% on average (1993, WCC Visitors' Survey, Surrey Research Group). The geographical position of WCC also explains the relatively high proportion of visitors who arrive by sea: 7% of all those surveyed in 1995. However, road transport remains the main means of getting to the area: 75% of visitors came by car in 1995.

The total number of visitors to White Cliffs Country is shown in Figure B.5 (page 218).

As the figures indicate, there was a small fall in

Where UK visitors are from	Number of respondents	Percentage of UK visitors	Percentage of total sample
Kent	95	31	19
Home Counties	93	31	19
South/South West	43	14	9
Midlands	25	8	5
East	13	4	3
North	13	4	3
North East	6	2	1
North West	6	2	1
Scotland	6	2	1
Northern Ireland	1	–	–
Wales	1	–	–
Total	**302**		

Source: 1995 WCC Visitors Survey, *Surrey Research Group*

FIGURE B.3 *Origins of UK visitors*

1995 in the number of visitors compared to two years previously. However, in 1993, the British Open Golf Championship in Sandwich had brought many visitors to the area (and contributed an estimated £2,220,000 to the economy of East Kent – 1993 WCC Visitors' Survey). However, the overall picture is one of visitor numbers stabilising, after a five-year period of impressive growth.

DAY-TRIPPERS

Most visitors (60%) came on day trips. Regarding the distance travelled by day-trippers to reach the destination area, it is a characteristic of WCC that, on average, its day visitors travel from fairly far afield to get there, much further than the national average for day trips. Only 25% of respondents in the ETB 'Out for the day' study of day visitors to destinations in England (ETB *Insights*, Sept 1994) travelled more than 50 miles to reach their day-trip destination, while 56% of WCC's day visitors travel over 50 miles to get there. This may be explained by the location of WCC, 50 to 100 miles from the Home Counties and London, and a gateway to the UK from the continent (1995 WCC Visitors' Survey).

STAYING VISITORS

In 1995, 56% of foreign visitors to WCC were found to be staying there overnight, as opposed to only 40% of UK visitors. For all staying visitors, the average number of nights spent in the area was 6 nights. This rose to 7.27 nights for overseas visitors, compared to 5.02 nights for domestic visitors. Nearly one quarter of overseas visitors (23%) stayed more than 7 nights compared with 14% of UK visitors. Clearly, overseas visitors bring more economic benefits to the area, since a greater percentage of them stay in the area and for a longer length of stay than UK visitors.

VISITOR SATISFACTION

Visitor surveys of WCC visitors consistently report a high level of satisfaction among visitors, and this is reflected in the high level of repeat

Where overseas visitors are from	Number of respondents	Percentage of overseas visitors	Percentage of total sample
USA	44	22	9
Germany	34	17	7
The Netherlands	23	12	5
France	18	9	4
Belgium	11	6	2
Italy	10	5	2
Australia	10	5	2
Japan	10	5	2
Spain	7	4	1
Canada	5	3	1
Norway	4	2	1
Finland	3	2	1
Austria	2	1	–
China	2	2	–
New Zealand	2	1	–
Portugal	2	1	–
South Africa	2	1	–
Sweden	2	1	–
Switzerland	2	1	–
Czech Republic	1	1	–
Ireland	1	1	–
Korea	1	1	–
Poland	1	1	–
Turkey	1	1	–
Total	**198**		

Source: 1995 WCC Visitors Survey, *Surrey Research Group*

FIGURE B.4 *Origins of overseas visitors*

visitors to the area. In the case of UK visitors, 1995 research showed that 61% of these had already visited the area (1995 WCC Visitors Survey, Surrey Research Group). This figure is all the more impressive when the strong competition for day-trippers in Kent is taken into account. WCC is in competition with well-known destinations such as Canterbury, Rochester,

Year	Total number of visitors
1989	540 000
1990	616 000
1991	730 000
1993	755 000
1995	730 000

Source: 1995 WCC Visitors Survey, *Surrey Research Group*

FIGURE B.5 *Total number of visitors*

Estimated sectors	Number employed
Port and infrastructure	4 000
Ferries, shipping	4 000
Transport	2 000
Hotels	2 000
Catering	3 000
Services	4 000

Source: DDC Tourism Business Plan *1995/96 DDC–EKI*

FIGURE B.6 *Employment in tourism-related activities*

Folkestone, Margate and Leeds Castle for the day-tripper market.

TOURISM-RELATED EMPLOYMENT

The number of people employed in tourism-related activities in the Dover District is now approximately 19,000 – shown divided up by sector in Figure B.6.

VALUE OF TOURISM TO THE LOCAL ECONOMY

In all, the value of tourism to the local economy was estimated at £40 million for 1995 (DDC Tourism Business Plan, 1995/96 – source: South East England Tourist Board). The sum was divided up as shown in Figure B.7.

One significant difference between the proportions shown in Figure B.7 and the results of the 'Out for the day' ETB survey concerns the amount spent on shopping. WCC falls significantly below the national average of 22%, indicating the still relatively underdeveloped state of the area's commercial sector of WCC.

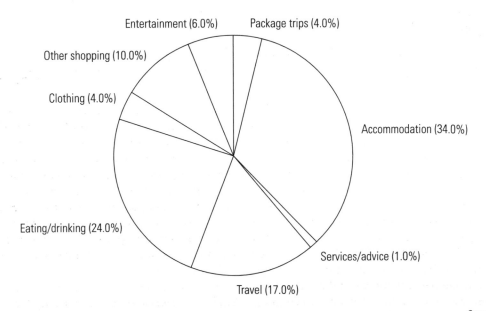

Entertainment (6.0%)
Package trips (4.0%)
Other shopping (10.0%)
Clothing (4.0%)
Accommodation (34.0%)
Eating/drinking (24.0%)
Services/advice (1.0%)
Travel (17.0%)

Source: SEETB

FIGURE B.7 *Tourism income – value of tourism in the district*

MOTIVATIONS

The problem posed by the weakness of WCC as a shopping destination re-emerges in the survey of the main motivations given by tourists or visiting WCC in 1995. These were as follows:

- the countryside: 41%
- history: 34%
- major attractions/events: 30%
- VFR: 17%
- Channel crossing: 15%
- shopping: 12%
- other: 14%

Source: DDC Economic Development Strategy 1996/97

(Figures are for non-residents only, and do not add up to 100% because respondents mentioned more than one reason.)

The 12% rating for shopping is well below the average rate for day trips in England (as shown by the ETB 'Out for the day' study, which identified shopping as a major motivator for day trips). The weakness of WCC's shopping product is a significant disadvantage for the area, as the DDC Tourism Business Plan for 1995/96 highlights.

ACCOMMODATION

In 1995, the most popular locations for accommodation in WCC were found to be Dover and Deal. However, a significant proportion of staying visitors stayed in other towns in Kent, outside the immediate WCC area, notably in Canterbury.

The survey demonstrated that, in spite of anxieties about the effects of the Channel Tunnel, the market share of hotels in the area remained stable. The guesthouse sector also performed well in 1995, apparently at the expense of the self-catering and VFR sectors. Occupancy levels of all sectors of commercial accommodation remained stable between 1993 and 1995, as compared to national trends (see Figure B.8).

The foregoing profile of tourism in Dover highlights the place of tourism in the local economy and shows current trends within the industry itself. Using our **tourism product portfolio** and **tourism dominance and growth** grids, this information may be represented as shown in Figures B.9 and B.10.

EXTERNAL FUNDING PROGRAMMES

The Tourism and Economic Development Sections of DDC are funded essentially through the council's revenue expenditure, which made £1.5 million available for this purpose in 1996.

However, in carrying forward the various elements of its Tourism and Economic Development strategy, the local authority aims to attract the maximum of funding from sources outside the district, as well as from private-sector sources. Thus, an important objective of the Tourism and Economic Development Committee is 'to maximise external and private sector financial investment in the delivery of economic development objectives'.

In pursuit of this aim, much time and energy is invested by council officers in competing for funds made available by the '... increasing proliferation of European, Government, Kent TEC and Kent County Council targeted programmes which require lobbying, bidding, joint actions, implementation or detailed justification' (DDC Economic Development Strategy, 1995/96).

Priority is given to seeking funds at the national and European level, as stated in the DDC Economic Development Strategy 1995/96:

'DDC works with Kent County Council's European Unit and other District Councils to ensure increased levels of EU Funding to

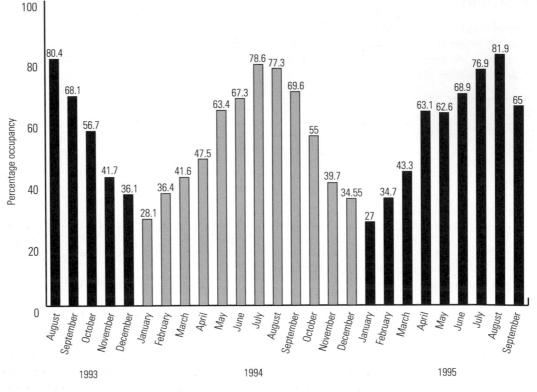

Source: 1995 WCC Visitors Survey, Surrey Research Group

FIGURE B.8 *Hotels and guesthouses occupancy rates (1993–95)*

		day visits		business tourism
Market	growth	staying visits		
				VFR
	decline			Channel crossing
		high		low
			Share	

FIGURE B.9 *Tourism product portfolio: Dover*

projects of direct benefit to the District. Achieving this objective, and that of obtaining funds from submissions to the Single Regeneration Budget of the Government Office of the South East, are priorities.'

(DDC Economic Development Strategy, 1995/96)

NATIONAL SOURCES OF FINANCE

GOVERNMENT OFFICE OF THE SOUTH EAST AND THE DEPARTMENT OF TRADE AND INDUSTRY

DDC is supported in its bids for these sources of central government development funding by the

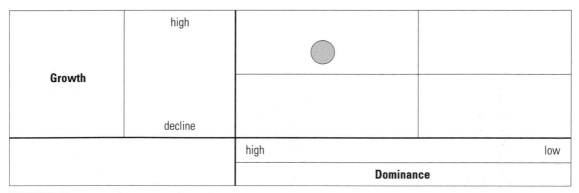

FIGURE B.10 *Tourism dominance and growth: Dover*

East Kent Initiative (EKI) (see page 214), which is based in Dover. The EKI orchestrated in 1993 a successful bid to have parts of East Kent awarded **Assisted Area** status, leading to the sub-region receiving funding from the DTI to help create new jobs in the area. However, no tourism-related schemes were successful in their bids for funding. The most likely project – a hotel at Dover Castle – was dropped.

Resources from the UK central government's Single Regeneration Budget, which are distributed via the GOSE have also been obtained for DDC through the efforts of its Economic Development Unit, but once again, not directly for tourism development. A successful submission for substantial funds for infrastructure for the White Cliffs Business Park led in 1995 to an award of £2.58 million, to be used over three years. These funds were to be principally used for the construction of infrastructure, workspace and starter workshops at the White Cliffs Business Park.

RURAL DEVELOPMENT COMMISSION

The granting by the **Rural Development Commission (RDC)** of Rural Development Area status to fourteen wards in the district means that much of the rural area of the district is available for RDC grant funding for a range of social and economic initiatives, including tourism development. 1995 saw the preparation, by DDC, of a Rural Development Strategy and a three-year Action Programme for Sandwich, in order to access resources from the £1 million Rural Challenge funding offered by the RDC in the form of a national competition. However, despite reaching the national final, the DDC's bid was unsuccessful.

THE NATIONAL LOTTERY AND MILLENNIUM FUND

Another source of funding is the National Lottery and Millennium Fund, which has a bearing on tourism. DDC, keen to see the development of cycle routes and other forms of trails which will encourage new visitors to the area, are contributing towards the development of local cycle routes with SUSTRANS (Sustainable Transport Systems, a national charity founded to promote cycle routes) which won £43 million from the Millennium Fund to develop the National Cycle Network.

Another potential source of funding is the DDC bid for the National Lottery's 'Celebration of the Coast' marketing scheme (the answer was expected by the end of 1996).

EUROPEAN UNION SOURCES OF FINANCE

DDC's geographical position as well as the specific problems facing the local economy make it eligible for the following EU awards.

INTERREG I AND II

By 1994, EU funding via its Interreg I

Transfrontier European Programme had brought funds amounting to around £1,300,000 to DDC. Most of the funds were spent on an environmental improvement programme around Dover and Deal (e.g. on seafront improvements) indirectly benefiting the tourism industry through the better image thus created for these towns.

In 1996, Interreg II bids were being sought for the £14 million identified for the UK from those funds. Along with all other district councils in Kent, DDC made an application for a share of this sum. The DDC proposals were:

- more environmental improvements
- a joint programme of research and development between DDC and the Ville de Calais
- a Sandwich Bay/Oye Plage joint scheme
- a joint programme of interpretation and promotion involving 15 historic towns in Kent, Belgian Flanders and the Nord Pas de Calais (Historic Towns Association)
- a number of joint cultural projects (Cross Channel Arts Association).

KONVER

Konver is the EU funding programme to assist those areas directly affected by demilitarisation. In 1996, DDC applied for about £½ million, to be spent on developing tourist attractions, in particular in renovating and expanding the White Cliffs Experience.

The principal external funding sources relevant to tourism development in the WCC area are shown schematically in Figure B.11.

National source	DDC designation	Purpose	DDC examples
RDC	Rural Development Areas (14 wards)	Rural development	St Augustines Trail, along Stour valley
Single Regeneration Budget 1	–	Economic regeneration	White Cliffs and Old Park Business Park infrastructure
DTI	Intermediate Assisted Area	Grants to assist company expansions	550 jobs created in two years
National Lottery and Millennium Fund	–	Arts, heritage and sports projects	'Celebration of the Coast' competition, cycle routes

EU source	DDC designation	Purpose	DDC examples
Interreg I and II	Transfrontier regions	Cross-border cooperation	Environmental improvements
EU Structural Funds	Objective 2	Combat the effects of industrial decline	General infrastructure
Konver programme	Demilitarised areas	Compensate for the withdrawal of defence industries	Renovation of White Cliffs Experience and Bronze Age Boat Museum

FIGURE B.11 *External funding sources for tourism and economic development*

CONCLUSION

1 DOVER DISTRICT IS USING TOURISM STRATEGICALLY IN THE REGENERATION OF THE LOCAL ECONOMY

The district was in danger of being a victim of circumstances beyond its control: the opening of the Channel Tunnel and cuts in defence. Tourism was selected as one part of the strategy to diversify the local economy and reduce its dependence on the ferry companies and local garrisons. DDC's tourism-related activities have given a boost to local tourism, attracting new markets and considerably improving the tourism product. This has happened in conjunction with the council's Economic Development activities, which are complementary to those of the Tourism Unit, being mainly concerned with industrial development: attracting new businesses to the district and assisting indigenous companies with, for example, training and grants advice. Nevertheless, elements such as environmental and infrastructural improvements are relevant to both aspects of the council's two-pronged strategy to develop the local economy.

2 THE PARTNERSHIP APPROACH IS VITAL

DDC itself directly owns and controls very little of the tourism product (which is a collection of disparate small- and medium-sized businesses, from guesthouses and hotels to gift shops and street theatre groups). Partnership is essential not only to ensure that the council's tourism policy is based in reality, but also to carry out the implementation of that policy in an effective way. As long as local operators in the industry see encouraging results arising from local authority activities (for example, in the form of improving occupancy rates), they will have an incentive to cooperate with DDC and support its interventions.

3 THERE IS A MARKED SYMBIOSIS BETWEEN TOURISM AND SHOPPING

One of DDC's aims in developing tourism in the area was to provide tangible backing to the local commercial sector by attracting a new pool of potential customers. However, although new customers are visiting the area, shopping opportunities for them are not increasing quickly enough to keep up with the potential demand. There is evidence from the visitors' surveys that the limitations of the local shopping product may be beginning to act as a disincentive to visit WCC.

Destinations can obtain more economic benefits from tourism when strong linkages exist between the tourism sector and other local economic activities. DDC realises that unless the district succeeds in attracting sufficient shops to form the 'critical mass' of shopping opportunities which will act as an attraction in itself for visitors, the area will not be maximising the potential financial benefits to itself from tourism. By 1996, there were hopeful signs that shopping outlets could be developed in the Western Docks area within two years. (However, the council had already rejected a proposed factory shopping centre at White Cliffs Business Park, because of the adverse effect it would have on the town centre.)

4 EXTERNAL FUNDING IS A KEY ELEMENT OF THE REGENERATION STRATEGY

As public funds for local authority activities have become an ever-scarcer commodity, devices for their fairer distribution have been sought, in the attempt to ensure that limited funds are spent most effectively. Local authorities find themselves increasingly in competition with each other and with other organisations, as they bid for funds on offer from the EU, as well as national government and government agencies. The complex and time-consuming preparation and submission of bids is correspondingly a growing necessity for local authorities, with little in the way of internal financial resources upon which they can draw.

The criteria for success in the competition for

external funding often seem weighted against the tourism industry, which is still too often perceived as less deserving of financial assistance than 'real' industries such as manufacturing. As a result much of the benefit to tourism from such schemes is indirect, for example, through the carrying out of environmental and infrastructural improvement.

As always, where external funds are involved, the question arises as to whether DDC's policies and strategies for tourism are plan-led or fund-led. In other words, does the existence of external sources of finance sometimes have too much impact on the council's activities? This would be the case if the Tourism Unit, hungry for funds, was tempted to set its strategy in line with external funding available for projects, rather than by independently and objectively identifying the projects most relevant to the tourism development of the area and pursuing them. Or are projects which stand a chance of being financed, even partially, from sources outside the district, simply a better bet than others for which, although more laudable, there is no local or external funding available?

REFERENCES

DDC (1992) *Tourism Business Plan 1992/3*, Dover District Council.

DDC (1994) *Tourism Business Plan 1994/5*, Dover District Council.

DDC (1995) *Tourism Business Plan 1995/6*, Dover District Council.

DDC (1995) *Economic Development Strategy 1995/6*, Dover District Council.

DDC (1996) *Tourism Action Plan 1996/97*, Dover District Council.

DDC (1996) *Economic Development Strategy 1996/97*, Dover District Council.

KCC (1990) *Kent Strategic Tourism Framework 1990–1994*, Kent County Council.

Surrey Research Group (1996) *1995 White Cliffs Country Visitors Survey*, for DDC.

C Cambridge

THEMES

- positive visitor management
- tourism, land-use and transport planning linkages

- partnership approaches to policy.

LOCATION AND BACKGROUND

Cambridge is a historic city with a 1991 population of around 106,000. It came into existence as a crossing point for the River Cam and its historic core is built around the river. The city lies some 50 miles northeast of London with which it has good rail and motorway links. There are motorway standard connections to the A1(M), and the expanding Stansted airport is close by.

Although its origins can be traced to pre-Roman times, the historic growth of the city is most closely linked to the development of the University. Peterhouse, the first college, was founded in 1384, and subsequent foundations saw the city develop as a centre of scholarship. The University has given the city its particular physical character, and a strong and memorable image that is world famous: the colleges, The Backs, punting on the river. It has a wealth of historic buildings confined within a tight historic core, largely defined by the River Cam and medieval street pattern. There are 1,411 listed buildings, most of which are associated with the University and some of which are very well known, for example, King's College Chapel. The college buildings and gardens provide a distinctive mixture of buildings and green space. The colleges are private institutions, but they have historically had strongly public elements, and the life of the city and the University are in-

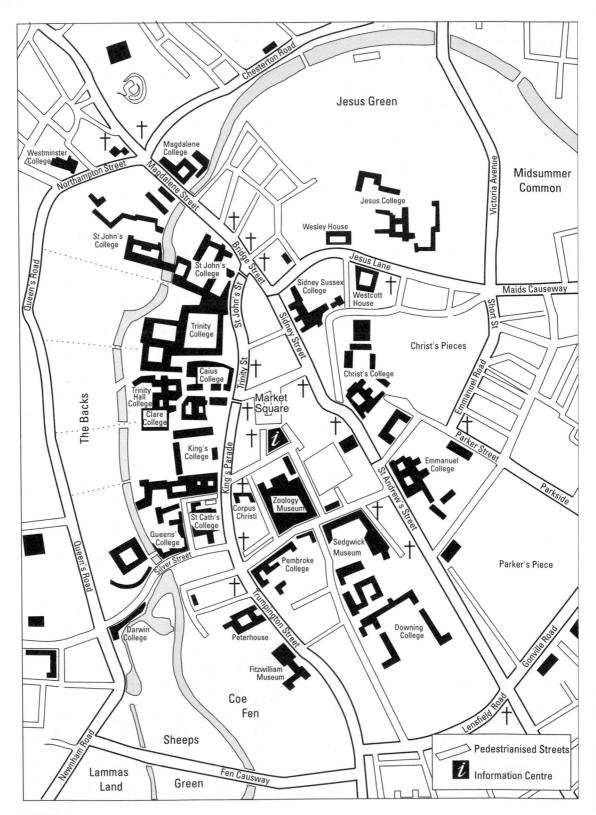

FIGURE C.1 *Map of Cambridge city centre*

tertwined. The colleges have generally been open and freely accessible to local people and to visitors, and they are integral to the city's fabric. They have traditionally been used as part of pedestrian routes through the city centre and across the river, and, in practice formed semi-public spaces. As major landowners, the colleges continue to play an influential part in the city's development.

The need to protect the historic core of the city means that opportunities for new developments in the centre are extremely limited. In addition, the city's boundary and green belt are tightly drawn around the existing built-up area so that the opportunities elsewhere in the city are also very constrained. The area within South Cambridgeshire DC adjacent to and surrounding the city has been the main location for developments dispersed from the city itself.

The city's economy is dominated by service industries, which account for almost 75% of employment. As Figure C.2 shows, public services are the dominant employers; these include the University of Cambridge and Anglia Polytechnic University, hospitals and health services, as well as local government and central government agencies. Cambridge's role as a sub-regional service centre is reflected in the substantial number of jobs in retailing and other distributive

industries. While there are some significant manufacturing employers (such as Marshall's Engineering, Cambridge University Press and Phillips), manufacturing accounts for only 14% of jobs.

The city is strongly-represented in high technology and research and development; these have spun off from or are supported by academic activities. Business services have developed to support the high technology sector and in response to Cambridge's growing role as a service centre for the sub-region. The positive image of the city, together with a large concentration of highly qualified labour, have made it a favoured location for such activities. Tourism is not separately identified in the employment count, but is estimated to support some 6,500 jobs in the city and in South Cambridgeshire (Cambridge City Council, 1995b).

Overall, fast growing industries are strongly represented in the Cambridge economy, and as a result there was growth in jobs of 3% per year during the 1980s. The main motor was the high technology research and development sector – this currently includes some 600 firms and 19,000 jobs in the city and the surrounding area (where most new growth is taking place). Growth slowed or halted in the early 1990s, but has resumed since 1994 (Cambridge City Council, 1995). The city's role as a sub-regional centre has continued to develop, and retail floorspace increased by an estimated 500,000 square feet in the last ten years (Human, 1995).

The strength of the local economy has a number of implications.

1 Unemployment has been relatively low: unemployment in the city has been consistently below the national average, although the difference has been small during the 1990s; unemployment in the wider area represented by the Cambridge Travel to Work Area; (TTWA) has been lower still. In January 1995, unemployment in the city was 7.8% and in the TTWA 4.5%, compared to a national average of 8.3% (Cambridge City council, 1995). There is, however, a notable duality in the labour market. While comparatively high pay, high skill, secure employment

Industrial order	Number	%
0 Agriculture	140	0.2
1 Energy	290	0.4
2 Chemicals/minerals	510	0.7
3 Metals/engineering	6 000	7.9
4 Other manufacturing	3 480	4.6
5 Construction	3 000	3.9
6 Distribution	14 610	19.2
7 Transport/telecommunications	3 910	5.1
8 Business services	9 700	12.8
9 National/local government	34 300	45.2
Total	**75 940**	**100.0**

Source: Cambridge City Council Economic Development Strategy 1995/96

FIGURE C.2 *Employment estimates for main industrial orders, Cambridge City, 1991*

is available in the high technology and many service sectors, other industries (including much of retailing and tourism) are characterised by low pay, insecure employment and unsocial hours.

2 The number of jobs in the city has grown faster than the resident workforce, so there were over 9,000 more commuters in the early 1990s than there had been in 1981. The inevitable result has been a worsening of congestion and traffic problems that have been further exacerbated by the city's growth as a sub-regional centre.

3 The growth of the local economy has increased pressure for development — both directly for commercial uses, and indirectly for housing.

In summary, Cambridge is a historic city with a unique and highly-valued built heritage, a renowned centre of scholarship and education, and a centre for dynamic economic growth, and this gives rise to a series of pressures and problems as well as benefits. Tourism is a significant element in the economy, and contributes to both the problems and benefits.

HISTORY OF INVOLVEMENT WITH TOURISM

Tourism has been an element of the city throughout its history. The first guidebook was published in 1748, and by the end of the 19th century, *Pall Mall Magazine* described Cambridge as a 'happy hunting ground for tourists'. Visitation continued to increase in the 20th century, but it has been the rapid and sustained growth since the 1960s that has highlighted the benefits and problems of tourism. In 1994, Cambridge had some 3.4 million visitors, making it one of Britain's most popular tourist destinations. Visitor numbers have more than doubled since the mid 1970s, and there is continuing pressure for further growth. It has been estimated that visitation could reach 4.2 million by 2001 (Cambridge City Council, 1995). The rapid growth of tourism inevitably gave rise to concerns that management was required. The most important initial event in developing policies for visitor management was the publication of *Tourism in Cambridge* by the City Council in 1978 (Human, 1994).

DIMENSIONS OF TOURISM

In common with other destinations, Cambridge has real difficulties in assembling accurate information about the number and characteristics of its visitors. Regular and comprehensive information on all types of visitation is difficult, time-consuming and costly to collect; so destinations rely on estimates based on periodic sample surveys. While this inevitably means that data must be treated with caution, and some types of visitor may be systematically undercounted, it allows most significant trends to be identified. Cambridge bases most of its estimates on sample surveys, and monitoring of visitors and enquirers at the Tourist Information Centre. Unless otherwise stated, the information that follows derives from the City Council's sample surveys, and relates to the period 1993–95. It includes day visitors, and students visiting for short language courses (university students are excluded).

VISITOR ORIGINS

Looking at all visitors to the historic centre, visitation is more or less equally-divided between UK and overseas tourists. It is notable, however, that around one in five visitors is a local resident – someone who lives in the city or the surrounding area. This is a reflection of Cambridge's role as a local retail and service centre. If these resident visitors are excluded, then the importance of overseas visitors is much greater. Almost two-thirds of visitors are from overseas, and there are almost as many visitors from mainland Europe as from the UK.

Origin	% (rounded)	
	All	**Excl. residents**[1]
Cambridge/South Cambs	21	*
Rest of UK	30	38
Total UK	**51**	**38**
Mainland Europe	28	36
North America	11	14
Australasia	5	6
Asia	2	3
South America	1	1
Africa	1	1
Rest of world	1	1
Total overseas	**49**	**62**

[1] 'Residents' are residents of Cambridge and South Cambridgeshire.
Source: Cambridge City Council

FIGURE C.3 *Visitor origins, Cambridge historic centre*

Three out of four non-resident visitors gave sightseeing or holiday as the reason for their visit (Figure C.4). Business tourism (which could be taken to include conferences and courses) was mentioned by one visitor in seven, while one in ten mentioned shopping. Some visitors mention more than one reason for their visit, for example the possibility of combining sightseeing with some shopping is part of the city's attraction.

SEASONALITY AND LENGTH OF STAY

Reflecting the importance of holidays and sightseeing, there is strong seasonality in visitation, and 40–50% of visitation takes place in July, August and September, though the extent of seasonality has been reduced since the 1970s (Cambridge City Council, 1990). This change

Reason[1]	% (rounded)
Sightseeing	50
Holiday	28
Shopping	11
Visiting friends/relatives	8
Business	6
Language course	5
Conference	3
Other	10

[1] Multiple answers accepted.
Source: Cambridge City Council, 1993–95

FIGURE C.4 *Reason for visit – non-residents*

reflects the general growth in short-break and other off-peak visits, but has probably been assisted by policy initiatives (discussed later).

Most visitors come for a day visit only, and do not stay long – the average length of visit is five hours (Figure C.5). Cambridge is easily accessible from London, and offers a convenient day out or stopover as part of a longer tour. Many visitors arrive in groups, and the numbers involved can be substantial. A survey in 1992 estimated that in peak season up to 1,000 youth-group/language-student visitors per day could arrive by coach (Cambridge City Council, 1992). A coach survey in 1994 (again in peak season) found that almost 2,600 tour coach passengers arrived on Saturday, and over 1,600 in midweek.

Those visitors who do spend the night in the city stay for a short time – one or two nights is the norm. Visitors staying for over two weeks probably include a substantial number of students attending language courses. It is estimated that up to 20,000 students attend language courses every year – two-thirds of them during the summer. The average length of stay is three weeks in the summer and six weeks in the rest of the year (EFL Services Ltd, 1992).

MEANS OF TRAVEL

Two-thirds of visitors to Cambridge arrive by private transport: car and tour coach (Figure C.6). Rather less than one-third arrive by public transport: train or service bus. There seems to have

Period	%
1 day or less	66
2 days	22
1 week	4
2 weeks	3
1 month or more	5

Source: Cambridge City Council, 1993–95

FIGURE C.5 *Length of stay*

Mode	% (rounded)
Car	55
Train	16
Service bus	15
Tour coach	10
Cycle	1
Other	3

Source: Cambridge City Council, 1993–95

FIGURE C.6 *Means of travel*

been some reduction in the proportion of visitors arriving by car since the early 1980s, though available data is difficult to interpret precisely.

VISITORS' LIKES AND DISLIKES

The colleges and their open spaces and gardens are overwhelmingly the most popular attraction for visitors, although the river and The Backs, and churches, museums, galleries and other historic buildings are also important (Figure C.7). All these attractions are concentrated in the com-

paratively small area of the historic centre. Although they constitute the major attraction to tourists, they are not designed or intended as tourist attractions, and this contradiction lies at the heart of some of the problems of management in the destination. Comparatively few features are disliked, but the most significant relate to the congestion which large numbers of visitors and other users can create in the small historic centre.

The position of tourism in Cambridge can be summarised in the tourism product portfolio and tourism dominance grids (see Figures C.8 and C.9).

Most liked features[1]	%
Colleges and buildings	40
Atmosphere	11
Shopping	7
People	6
Parks and gardens	4
River and punting	4
Scenery	4

Most disliked features[1]	%
Traffic, parking, streets	15
Crowds and tourists	6
Signposting	3
Expensive	3
Public transport	2
People	2
Dirty and noisy	2

[1] Multiple answers accepted.

Source: Cambridge City Council, 1993–95

FIGURE C.7 *Visitors' main likes and dislikes*

		growth	day visits			
					local leisure	business tourism
Market					short breaks	
						long holidays
		decline				
			high			low
			Share			

FIGURE C.8 *Tourism product portfolio: Cambridge*

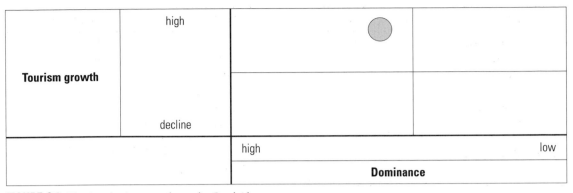

FIGURE C.9 *Tourism dominance and growth: Cambridge*

TOURISM IMPACTS

The impacts of tourism, both positive and negative, cannot be stated unambiguously. Ambiguity and imprecision arises for two main reasons.

- Many impacts have strong subjective elements, and will be perceived differently by different people and in different circumstances. Noise is an obvious example: one person's lively evening with a group of friends can be someone else's intolerable disturbance by rowdy youths.
- Many impacts are inherently difficult to estimate and to quantify, so that assessment and comparison depend on judgement.

ECONOMIC IMPACTS

Tourism plays an important but by no means dominant role in the city economy. Visitor spending in 1994 was estimated to be £195 million. This spending was estimated to support 5,010 jobs in the city and a further 1,640 in South Cambridgeshire – 6,550 in all, or some 6% of total jobs in the area (Cambridge City Council, 1995c). However, visitors spending has grown at only a quarter of the rate of growth in visitor numbers.

The impacts of visitor spending depend on the amount and incidence, leakages from the city economy, and the types of jobs created. The amount of spending depends on visitor numbers and the type of visitor. Spending is greatest when visitors stay overnight and when those stays are in serviced accommodation. The information available for Cambridge confirms this pattern. Estimates of spending by British visitors to Cambridge who stayed for at least one night are available for 1980–84, and are derived from a special analysis of the British Home Tourism Survey (Cambridge City Council, 1988).

The greatest spending is generated by visitors

Purpose of trip	£s (1984 prices)
All holidays	27.9
Visiting friends/relatives	10.6
Business/conference	48.4
Other	33.4
Accommodation used	
Hotel/guest house	61.8
Friends/relations	17.8
Rental accommodation	29.4
Touring caravan/camping	19.3
Static caravan	28.2
Other	19.9
Average spend per trip	**28.5**

Source: Cambridge City Council, 1988

FIGURE C.10 *Average visitor spending per trip (1980–84)*

who are on business or attending conferences, and by visitors who are staying in hotels or guesthouses (many of whom are of course business visitors – see Figure C.10). A particular sector of the market not covered in these estimates is spending by students on English language courses. A survey in 1992 estimated that the annual value of the EFL market to Cambridge was £19.2 million, of which £5.6 million was spent on accommodation (mostly with host families, thus boosting some local households' incomes), and £5.6 million was general spending on shopping, eating, drinking and entertainment (EFL Ltd, 1992).

Not all visitor spending will be retained in the city, since leakages occur as goods produced elsewhere are purchased and when profits are channelled to firms based elsewhere. No estimates of leakages from the local economy are available, although a comparatively high incidence of locally-based enterprises in the accommodation and service sectors should mean that retention will be relatively high.

Jobs created or supported by this visitor spending will be predominantly in the hospitality, catering and retailing sectors; such jobs are frequently low skill, temporary, seasonal or part-time, and offer lower wages than other sectors. The low quality of many of these jobs is reflected in their high turnover (Cambridge City Council, 1995). There are positive features, however. Cambridge's buoyant high technology and business and public-service sector generates mainly high skill jobs requiring well-trained and educated workers. The manufacturing sector (which provided a source of semi- and unskilled work) has declined since 1981. In that context, there is value in tourism as a source of jobs for workers who lack education or appropriate skills. Indeed, by increasing competition for low skill labour, it might bid up wages or improve working conditions. Tourism also provides useful opportunities and sources of income for local small business, for example, in accommodation, restaurants or taxis (Segal Quince Wicksteed, 1989).

Tourism has wider economic benefits through its effects on the image of the city, though these effects are impossible to quantify. Cambridge is involved in global competition as a centre of excellence in education and scholarship, research and high technology industry. Tourism contributes to maintaining its profile internationally, and reinforcing its positive image worldwide. By so doing, it provides advantages to the University and companies already located in the area, and makes it easier for the city to attract high-quality new companies. (Human 1994; Segal Quince Wicksteed, 1989).

However, visitation also creates costs.

1 Most obvious are the effects of congestion. Congestion is discussed in environmental terms later on, but we should note that it imposes real economic costs through delays experienced by businesses and workers.

2 Visitation contributes to pressures for development, or to the change of use of existing buildings. This may contribute to bidding up costs and rents, and may result in the displacement of uses serving local people in favour of those serving tourists. So far, displacement in the retail sector seems to have been limited, perhaps because the city's role as a sub-regional centre has maintained strong demand for retail premises serving non-tourist markets (Human, 1995). However, attempts to add to the stock of accommodation have put further pressure on the housing market. Conversion of houses into visitor accommodation reduces the residential stock accessible to local people, and there were 109 applications for changes of use from housing to guesthouses or bed-and-breakfast in the period of 1979–89.

3 There are the direct costs to the local authority of providing services for tourists. The direct cost of tourism services in 1994–95 was £331,000 or £2.91 per resident (Cambridge City Council, 1995c). There are additional revenue costs incurred by the council in street cleaning and emptying litter bins, environmental health and traffic management work. Other services such as police and doctors also bear additional costs. Coping with tourists may also require capital expenditure, for example on traffic management schemes, or provision of facilities such as toilets (£168,000 was spent on new lavatories for visitors in 1987) (Human, 1994). Under the current sys-

tem of local authority funding, the city does not benefit from additional commercial activity through enhanced business rate income, although staying and day visitors are taken into account in the calculation of the Standard Spending Assessment and Revenue Support Grant.

ENVIRONMENTAL IMPACTS

Congestion affects the physical environment and the experience of visitors and residents alike. In the heart of the city, the streets and the colleges can become heavily congested with pedestrians. A survey in 1987 showed that, in peak season, tourists accounted for between 30% and 50% of pedestrians in some streets in the historic centre (Human, 1994). On the roads, 55% of visitors arrive by car and a further 10% by tourist coach (see Figure C.6). The additional car-borne traffic has a disproportionate effect, since the highway network is already overloaded and congested, and often heavily used by bicycles as well as motor vehicles. On peak Saturdays, 64 tour coaches carrying around 2,600 passengers have been recorded (Cambridge City Council, 1995). They contribute to congestion on the roads in general, and particularly in the vicinity of the coach drop-off points. Cars and coaches have adverse environmental effects: through the pollution and noise they create, the danger they represent to pedestrians and cyclists, and their visual intrusion in the historic centre. The need to provide parking for cars and coaches adds to development pressures on scarce sites, and can cause noise and visual intrusion in the immediate area.

The scale of visitation in the historic centre can result in damage to the physical fabric, with wear and tear to buildings, green spaces and even paving. Inexperienced punters can damage the banks of the Cam; the fabric of historic buildings can be literally worn away by visitors walking around them or touching decorative carving; and heavy pedestrian traffic erodes the grass. This damage is the inevitable result of large numbers of people, rather than the consequence of bad behaviour. At the least, it gives rise to the costs of restoration which must be met by the council,

the colleges or other agencies which have few means to recover the expense – although charging by colleges is one means. At worst, the result is irreparable damage to historic buildings.

Large numbers of visitors, especially concentrated in small areas, can also cause noise, disturbance and litter. Noise from visitors in the streets or in colleges can last all day and well into the night, ruining the peace expected by residents or those studying. The problem is particularly acute for the colleges, since large numbers of visitors, even in well-organised parties, can cause considerable disturbance that conflicts with their educational purpose. Traffic congestion, overcrowding, wear and tear, and pollution were the most frequently-mentioned problems in a recent public consultation on tourism in the city (Cambridge City Council, 1995b).

Again, different types of visitors have different impacts. Day visitors' arrivals, departures and time in the city are all clustered into peak hours, whereas staying tourists spread the visitor load across the day and make less use of cars and coaches at peak times. In Cambridge, language-school students are widely seen as causing particular problems, including noise, obstruction of pavements, domination of particular open spaces (notably Parker's Piece) and dangerous cycling (EFL Services Ltd, 1992). This accords with perceptions in other historic cities popular for language tuition (such as Canterbury) and is at least in part a result of the students' high visibility, and the fact that they have free time out and about in the city. Conference delegates, on the other hand, are perceived to have far fewer adverse impacts. They spend much of their time in meetings, and when out and about in the city are largely indistinguishable from residents and workers.

SOCIAL, CULTURAL AND COMMUNITY IMPACTS

Tourists can improve local services when their spending contributes to activities which would otherwise not be viable, or extends the range of services available to residents. Recent consultation confirmed that tourists help sustain the rich variety of artistic and cultural events and entertainments, and the wide range of shops and restaurants in Cambridge, to the benefit of workers, residents and students (Cambridge City Council, 1995b).

More generally, visitors can create a more cosmopolitan atmosphere and promote contact between cultures. But there can be severe disadvantages to the host community from large scale and intense tourism. The growth of tourism has contributed to, but is not the sole cause of, a change in Cambridge's character. It is:

'. . . no longer a peaceful East Anglia market-cum-university town . . . Shops and market stalls cater for the sometimes tawdry tastes of

tourists and the University's historic crest is reduced to a sweatshirt emblem.'

(Human, 1994)

The pressures caused by tourists can disturb long-standing elements of the local way of life. For example, closing colleges to keep out visitors also affects residents, who have traditionally used them as part of pedestrian routes through the city. In the recent public consultation on tourism (Cambridge City Council, 1995b), problems of conflicts between residents and tourist, the changing character of some local shops (especially in the centre), and the loss of Cambridge's original character were mentioned, although these were not seen as the most important problems.

ISSUES AND PROBLEMS

Tourism in Cambridge follows a pattern familiar to other historic towns and cities, in that it generates a mix of beneficial and adverse impacts. While there are substantial economic benefits, these are offset by serious costs which are largely environmental and social or cultural. Evaluating the outcome of these costs and benefits (the net benefit of tourism) is difficult, since there is no wholly objective means of evaluation. This arises from two factors.

■ The impacts of tourism are not evenly distributed and people's opinions of the impacts will depend on the mix they have experienced. For example, some parties experience adverse impacts but do not share in positive impacts (e.g. a local resident who is not involved in the tourist industry, but is affected by noise and congestion).

■ Different people have different objectives, and thus different perspectives on the same situation. The colleges are an obvious example. They are private educational institutions devoted to learning, and that requires, among other things, reasonable peace and quiet. From the point of view of visitors and of Cambridge's tourist industry they are the city's main attraction, and that requires access.

Reconciling these differing views is not easy. As the council's strategy review in 1990 put it:

'. . . it is clear that there is still a wide gulf between the colleges and the commercial sector as to the perceived benefits and disbenefits of tourism . . . it should be recognised that the main area of shared interest, especially on environmental matters, is between the Council and the colleges.'

(Cambridge City Council, 1990)

Impacts derive both from the overall volume of visitation and its nature (since different types of tourist generate different mixes of impact). At one end of the scale is the business visitor. Business tourists usually stay overnight, and generate substantial economic benefits through their spending; they often travel outside the peak season, have few adverse impacts, and (if satisfied with their stay) promote a positive image of the city – perhaps among key decision makers (Davidson, 1994). At the opposite end of the scale is the day visitor in a poorly organised party, who arrives by coach, spends a few hours in the historic centre looking at the most popular sights and eating the packed lunch they brought with them. Such visitation incurs costs but generates few benefits. This means that managing visitor profiles and their behaviour while in the city is as important as managing numbers. At the same time, the difference in perception between visitors and residents should not be exaggerated. As Figure C.7 shows, visitors themselves identified traffic, crowds and tourists as the least-liked features of the city.

Three overlapping sets of issues are suggested by the review of impacts.

■ **Development pressures** in a city which is also experiencing considerable development pressure because of its other economic roles, and in which tourism is a significant but not dominant part of the economy.
■ **Congestion, noise and disturbance** especially in the historic centre, the colleges, and on roads.
■ **Visitor numbers and behaviour** including the types of visitor, and their length of stay.

We will now consider the ways in which these issues are being tackled.

POLICIES AND PLANS

ORGANISATION AND MANAGEMENT OF TOURISM

Management of tourism involves a number of public- and private-sector agencies. Like all destinations, Cambridge is affected by the context set at the EU and national government levels. This section discusses the key players in the city.

■ **The City Council** has the lead responsibility for the management of tourism, but views the industry within a wider context. It is responsible for the city and to its electorate, and must look at tourism in the context of the city as a whole. It sees itself as 'the arbitrator between conflicting interests, striving to achieve an acceptable balance' (Cambridge City Council, 1990). Council policy for tourism is set out both in its statutory Local Plan, which is confined to land-use matters, and in broader non-statutory policies. Its policy must be set in the context of those of Cambridgeshire County Council and the adjoining South Cambridgeshire District Council. The council's direct powers and resources are limited, so successful policy requires collaboration with other public- and private-sector agencies, and its roles as enabler and coordinator are central.
■ **The East Anglia Tourist Board** is responsible for tourism and tourism marketing in the region, and has an important role in formulating and implementing tourism policy.
■ **The colleges** are significant both as the main attraction for visitors and as powerful interests within the city. The colleges are private educational institutions devoted to learning. They 'recognise the economic advantages of tourism ... nevertheless maintain strongly that they are in the education not the tourism business' (Cambridge City Council, 1990). Although they have traditionally offered open access to visitors, their priority is academic study, not visitor satisfaction, and as private institutions they can control or exclude access. They have a variety of historic powers dating from their foundations, and are major landowners in the city and the surrounding areas. This means that they can have considerable influence on development.
■ **The commercial sector** includes retailers, the hospitality industry, other local businesses, and language schools (which as stated, host some 20,000 students per year). Since tourists are the basis of its business, it will tend to favour increases in numbers and to stress the benefits of visitation, though 'commercial operators recognise that problems do occur' (Cambridge City Council, 1990). However, we must remember that the commercial sector includes a diverse range of firms and individuals: some are wholly reliant on tourism

(e.g. hotels and language schools), while others see tourists as just one part of their market (e.g. most retailers and restaurants). Equally, different firms will be serving different and perhaps incompatible segments of the market, so there may be differing priorities and there is potential for conflict. Any new or modified provision for tourism will depend heavily on investment and actions from the commercial sector.

■ **Local residents and non–tourism industries** are affected by the costs imposed by tourism, but do not participate directly in most of the benefits it generates (apart from residents working in tourism). This means they are more likely to be ambivalent about the continuing development of tourism.

TOURISM POLICY

As the previous sections have shown, tourism is fragmented, affecting and affected by a range of different participants with different views and influences. Whatever the substantive elements of policy, a key element is to achieve sufficient consensus for coordinated action. The City Council has the lead role in tourism policy, but requires support from other agencies to be effective. In its 1990 review of strategy, the council considered the range of attitudes it might take towards tourism, ranging from promotion to actively discouraging visitors. It concluded that it should play an active role in management, but that strategy would be ineffective unless it could attract some support from all participants in the industry. This section considers policy objectives and the policy framework, and then considers three initiatives designed to tackle the issues identified in the earlier review of impacts.

OBJECTIVES OF POLICY

The City Council now has four policy objectives on tourism:

1 To conserve (protect and enhance) the local life, beauty and character of Cambridge and the surrounding area

2 To ensure a satisfying and enjoyable experience for visitors to Cambridge

3 To support a prosperous local tourism industry which can contribute significant long-term and widespread benefits to the local economy and local residents

4 To ensure reinvestment by the industry in the infrastructure on which tourism depends, including conservation of the environment.
(Cambridge Tourism Strategy Review, 1995)

These are to be achieved by a strategic approach with six elements:

1 Emphasis on the inherent attractions of Cambridge as a historic town centre for learning, culture and the arts

2 Aim for excellence in services

3 Control the growth in total number of visitors to Cambridge

4 Manage tourism to minimise environmental pressures and reduce congestion

5 Ensure Cambridge is a centre where visitors stay and from which they visit the surrounding area and East Anglia

6 Spread the benefits of tourism geographically and socially.
(Cambridge Tourism Strategy Review, 1995)

The emphasis is thus on managing and controlling the overall growth of tourism, and attempting to influence the visitor profile to reduce costs and maximise benefits to the city.

POLICY MECHANISMS

The main policy vehicles are:

■ **Cambridge Local Plan** (Cambridge Council, 1994) – which has statutory force, and deals with the land-use elements of policy. It is set within the general context of EU and national government guidance. At regional level it is set within the framework of **RPG 6 – Regional Planning Guidance for East Anglia** (DoE, 1991), and sub-regionally, Cambridgeshire County Council's **Structure Plan** (CCC, 1989).

■ **Council Tourism Strategies** – these cover non land-use policies, including: marketing, visitor services, information, managing coaches and visitor management (including measures to affect the visitor profile). The key elements of policy were set out in *Cambridge Tourism − The Way Ahead* (Cambridge City Council, 1990), which formed the basis for the **Tourism 2000** initiative. Tourism 2000 was established in 1992 and brought together representatives of all the major participants in the industry, including: the local authorities, the Tourist Board, the colleges, language schools, hospitality industry, transport industry and the Chamber of Commerce. The intention was to gain consensus for a long-term strategy for tourism and then implement it − this collaborative approach was an important feature of the policy mechanism. Although the initiative succeeded in gaining support from all participants for the policy objectives set out above, the implementation of policy measures has now been subsumed within the **City Centre Management** initiative (discussed below).

A new Tourism Strategy was devised in 1995 (Cambridge City Council, 1995c). The process of review involved extensive consultation with industry participants and local residents to identify perceived problems and discuss policy approaches. The revised strategy echoes many polices introduced in *Cambridge − the Way Ahead*, but places increased emphasis on the spatial and temporal dispersal of visitors, minimising environmental pressures, stabilising visitor numbers and encouraging staying visitors. The Tourism Strategy establishes clear and explicit targets for achieving its objectives (e.g. the target for the proportion of visitors arriving by car in 2000/2001 is 50% against the existing proportion of 55%). The Tourism Strategy also includes a detailed Action Plan for the implementation of policy, with timing, costs and responsibilities identified.

In addition it should be noted that there is overlap between policies for tourism and other policy areas. Tourism is recognised as important in the County's **Economic Development Strategy and Programme** (CCC, 1992) which emphasises the need to promote the rest of the county to tourists, and in the city's **Employment Development Strategy** (CCC, 1993). It plays a significant part in the Local Agenda 21 initiative currently being developed.

TOURISM INITIATIVES

The following initiatives illustrate the ways in which policy can be used to tackle the issues we have identified and to meet the objectives we have discussed.

DEVELOPMENT AND LAND USE

The main Local Plan policies affecting tourism are set out in its Chapter 9 'Higher and Further Education', Chapter 12 'Tourism', and Chapter 14 'Transport', although many other elements of the plan are relevant to the industry and the quality of the visitor experience. The Local Plan uses control of development to influence the numbers and types of visitor to the city, and to influence their behaviour. Only policies directly related to land use can form part of the statutory plan (other elements of visitor management are discussed later).

There are four main areas of policy.

1 The plan aims to meet the objective of increasing the number of longer-stay visitors by providing more overnight accommodation. The danger of increasing overnight accommodation is that it will be provided through the conversion of parts of the existing housing stock to guesthouses and small hotels, thus increasing pressure on a limited amount of residential accommodation, and having adverse effects on residents. The Local Plan seeks to balance these pressures. Hotels in suitable locations are supported and a number of sites are identified (Policy TO1), but the change of use of private houses to guesthouses is controlled on the basis of size and location (Polices TO2, TO3, TO4, TO5). Small bed-and-breakfast businesses within family homes are however encouraged, and planning permission is not required for the use of not more than two rooms as guest bedrooms. These policies are

reinforced and underlined by the new Tourism Strategy.

2 In line with the objectives of emphasising Cambridge's individuality and character, and avoiding creating new demands for visits, major new attractions drawing additional visitors will be resisted (Policy TO10). Some additional attractions that complement the nature of the city and which can be located away from areas of greatest congestion could play a positive role in managing visitors and improving the quality of their experience, but new tourist magnets that would simply bring in additional visitors would only add to existing problems. The council is especially anxious to resist 'theme park' or 'heritage experience' attractions, such as the Jorvik Centre (York) or Canterbury Tales Experience. However, a major heritage centre on the edge of the city, linked to park-and-ride provision, is now being considered (Tourism Strategy TS7, 1995).

3 Policy aims to change the visitor profile by influencing the purpose of visits. The city's cultural and historic qualities, and its strong association with scholarship has made it an attractive location for conferences and business tourism, and for a variety of specialist schools (e.g. tutorial colleges, secretarial and language schools). The plan aims to encourage conference and business tourism, seen as having a generally positive impact; and to restrict severely the expansion of specialist schools which are seen as having serious negative impacts. Developments that facilitate conferences are supported in the plan, subject to the location, scale and design of new facilities (Policy HE9). The Local Plan controls specialist-schools' development very strictly, preventing the development of new establishments (Policy HE13) or the expansion of existing schools (Policies HE14, HE15).

4 The Local Plan seeks to minimise congestion caused by tourist vehicles, especially in the city centre. In addition to a series of policies designed to control car use in general, and to promote rail travel, it seeks to develop park-and-ride sites as terminals for tourist coaches (Policies TR9, 10). Coach-borne visitors would arrive at the park-and-ride sites which should be provided with a range of facilities, including information, toilets and refreshments. Tourist coaches would remain at the site, and visitors would travel on to the centre in shuttle buses or would walk. No specific sites for such facilities are identified in the plan. However, during consultation on the review of tourism strategy in 1995, the possibility of a major facility near the M11 was raised. At its most ambitious, this could include interpretation and exhibition facilities, and might mean some visitors did not even come into the city centre (Cambridge City Council, 1995b)

POSITIVE VISITOR MANAGEMENT

Visitor management is designed to influence both the number and type of visitors coming to the city and their behaviour once they have arrived. Specifically, it seeks to encourage the 'target visitor' – those for whom [the city] is a deliberate and preferred choice of destination' (Draft Local Plan, 1992) – and to deal with the major problems of congestion in the historic centre.

Marketing is used to influence visitors prior to arrival, in line with objectives of emphasising the distinctive nature of the city and of encouraging longer stays. Council marketing is selective, with limited advertising in the trade press and no general advertising in the consumer press; and directive, in that it promotes alternatives to the most famous attractions (e.g. churches within the city, or other nearby destinations such as Ely). The East Anglian Tourist Board supports this strategy, and underplays Cambridge in its promotion of the region. Marketing focuses on attracting overseas visitors from northern Europe, North America and Australasia; domestic visitors on short breaks; and business visitors; and on promoting the city as a year-round destination (Tourism Strategy TS1, 2). A conference venue service and accommodation booking service encourage business tourism and overnight stays.

Once visitors arrive in the city, the emphasis is on positive measures to deal with congestion and nuisance. Since 1990, there have been attempts to disperse visitors away from the colleges and historic buildings along The Backs that are currently their main focus. Five additional focal points elsewhere in the historic centre have been identified. They consist of clusters of colleges and other historic buildings or open spaces in areas that have potential to absorb more visitors. Dispersal is encouraged through information provided at the Tourist Information Centre (TIC), with the use of guides, signposting, and information panels. These help visitors to orient themselves and encourage them to seek out comparatively unfamiliar attractions.

However, the most positive means of managing visitors and reducing their adverse impact in the most popular places is through the linked initiatives of the **College Pass** scheme, **charging** by some of the most popular colleges, and the introduction of **Courtesy Couriers**, funded by the City Council. These initiatives have been designed to reduce congestion and nuisance at the colleges, and to encourage parties to use the services of a guide.

The College Pass scheme is intended to restrict and control large parties of visitors to colleges. It was introduced in 1985 and requires all parties of 10 or more people who wish to visit a college to pre-book with the TIC. Parties without a pass are refused admission by the colleges. The maximum size of party is twenty, each must be accompanied by a Blue Badge Guide, and there are quotas for the number of parties which may visit (alternative tours are available if the quota is full). Visitors clearly need to be made aware of the College Pass scheme and may need help to use it. Courtesy Couriers were introduced in 1985, primarily to reinforce the scheme.

Courtesy Couriers are part of the TIC service, and their main task is to meet incoming tour parties at the main coach set-down point. They are briefed each day and have details of all pre-booked groups, who will be met by their guide. If a group arrives without a College Pass, the Courtesy Courier can contact the TIC (via walkie-talkie) and attempt to arrange a guide and College Pass for them. Should a group without a College Pass be determined to visit the colleges, the Courtesy Courier can warn the TIC which

can inform the colleges so they can act. Courtesy Couriers can also relay to guides messages from the TIC about parties that have been delayed. Couriers are present in the most popular areas of the centre, and provide information and advice to individual visitors as well as parties. Four are on duty, and the service operates between 09.00 and 14.30 hours every day from the beginning of April to early October.

The Pass Scheme and Courtesy Couriers have made visits to the colleges by groups more orderly and controlled, but do not in themselves reduce the pressure for visitation – individuals or small groups are unaffected, for example. Two further actions have been taken.

1 Most colleges now close to visitors altogether between mid-April and mid-June when undergraduates are studying for examinations and the problem of disturbance is most acute. While clearly effective, closure for the whole season would be unacceptable, and temporary closure increases pressure during the times when the colleges are open.

2 Some colleges have experimented with charging as a means of managing visitor numbers. Currently five colleges (Queens', St John's, King's, Trinity and Clare) levy charges. All are in the most heavily visited part of the city. Charging is possible since the colleges are private institutions, and the initiative is comparable with the introduction of charges at some cathedrals. Charging has several potential advantages compared to closures and passes. It is flexible – charges can be set to restrict visitation to a chosen target level, or to encourage visits at some times and discourage them at others. The scheme can be made self-funding, some of the income can be used to provide information or services for visitors, and other income generated can be used to defray the costs of visitation, such as increased maintenance to counter wear and tear. Finally, reduced congestion improves the experience of those who do visit.

There are however potential disadvantages to charging. While charging for tourist attractions is the norm, there may be public resistance to paying an entrance fee when entrance has previously been free. However, no significant dislike of charging has been recorded in visitor surveys (see Figure C.7). Alternatively, having paid the entrance fee, visitors may feel they have gained rights, which could give rise to a further need for control. Charging may be seen as unfair to people on low incomes. An uncoordinated scheme might simply transfer problems from one college to another. In addition, there is a particular problem in Cambridge: colleges are part of the city fabric and local residents have been used to ready access, to enjoy the buildings and gardens and to use them as part of the pedestrian routes through the city.

The schemes have been designed to reduce any disadvantages. Key elements are:
- charges are made only between mid–March and early October
- free admission is available to local residents (who may obtain a pass), students at the University and Anglia Polytechnic University, children under 12, unemployed people and holders of a City Council Leisure Card
- charging times are set so that those people walking to and from work are unaffected
- reduced charges are made to groups with a Blue Badge Guide under the College Pass scheme
- visitors are given a leaflet about the colleges.

The scheme appears to have been effective in reducing visitor numbers – for example, visitors to St John's 'were reduced by 58% during the charging period in 1992' (Human, 1994) – and further improving management of visitors. The colleges regard the experiment as a success, and the way that the scheme has been introduced seems to have avoided the potential problems, and it has been generally accepted without difficulty.

PARTNERSHIP IN TOURISM POLICY

The fragmentation of the tourism industry means that while the City Council has a lead role, co-ordination and consensus are at the heart of effective policy. Coordination and consensus require both appropriate policy mechanisms and processes. A series of mechanisms have been established to help coordinate tourism policies and actions. They deal with the interaction between different participants in tourism and the overlap between tourism and other policy areas.

The **Cambridgeshire Tourism Officers' Group** comprises the officers from the county and all districts in Cambridgeshire and the East Anglia Tourist Board. It coordinates public policy, development and marketing initiatives, and involves representatives of other tourism interests as necessary (Human, 1994).

The **Cambridge Tourism Group** is made up of representatives of the main tourism interests in the city, including the council. It seeks to achieve the agreed objectives of tourism policy by identifying common ground between tourism interests, reconciling conflicts, and promoting liaison. It has around a dozen members, who are treated as equal contributors, and who canvass the views of and represent all the interest in their sector (TWLG, 1994). The Cambridge Tourism Group was formed in 1994 to replace the **Tourism Liaison Working Group** that had existed since 1980. That group was large, with over 40 members, lacked clear aims, and was perceived to be dominated by the council. The new Tourism Group represents a much more focused approach to partnership.

Tourism 2000 was established in 1992, and intended both to gain consensus on tourism policy objectives, and to help achieve them through a visitor management project. Consensus on objectives was achieved, but the project was not implemented, largely as a result of unwillingness on the part of the private sector to commit funds to supplement the public money available. However, since 1993, the possibilities of **City Centre Management (CCM)** have been discussed, and in 1995 a CCM project was established. Since most of the visitor management issues focus on the centre, and many city centre issues involve tourism, the Tourism 2000 initiative has been subsumed within CCM.

CCM revolves round a Steering Group of 24 representatives: eight from local authorities, five from the hospitality industry, five from retailers, four from residents and students and two from the colleges and the University. Management is the responsibility of a City Centre Manager who is accountable to the Steering Group, which in turn is accountable to the City Council's Environment Committee. The initiative is funded by the public and private sectors, initially in the ratio 2:1. CCM is intended to provide a unifying vision for the centre, recognising the diversity of users and their requirements, and to coordinate initiatives (Cambridge City Council, 1994b). From a tourism perspective, it represents recognition by participants in the industry that visitor management is not only necessary, but must be integrated with other policies.

Building consensus depends on process as well as formal organisational structures, and a participative and inclusive approach has been taken to policy making. Participation is a statutory requirement in the Local Plan process, but it has also been introduced into other areas of policy. Tourism 2000 included consultation with a wide range of interests. The council initiated CCM with a forum attended by 60 representatives of a wide range of interests, to identify key issues and most appropriate structures. The recent review of tourism strategy has included a structured consultation meeting with representatives from a wide range of organisations in the tourism industry, the colleges and the University, and local residents. This approach has been successful in developing greater consensus among potentially conflicting interests, and in creating wider ownership of policies.

CONCLUSION

1 CAMBRIDGE IS DEALING WITH THE PROBLEMS OF SUCCESS

The city has a buoyant local economy based around higher education and research, high technology industry, and retailing and services. Tourism enriches but can also conflict with these activities. Tourists, shoppers, managers and workers in high-tech industry and public services, and students and scholars are all competing for access to the same resources: the attractive environment of a compact historic city. Policy has to balance these conflicting demands and ensure that development pressures do not erode the very environment which all seek to enjoy.

A possible reaction in these circumstances would be to adopt highly restrictive policies towards tourism on the grounds that it generates costs out of proportion to its benefits, and that the local economy has other sources of growth. The City Council has rejected this approach, partly because of the positive features of tourism, and partly because such a policy is probably unworkable – the local authority lacks the powers to reduce visitation significantly. Instead, policy has been aimed at maximising the benefits of tourism to the city and its residents, while minimising the costs. This has involved restrictions (e.g. on some forms of development) and positive action (e.g. in managing visitors).

2 PERCEPTIONS OF IMPACT VARY AND COMMON OBJECTIVES ARE HARD TO ACHIEVE

It is difficult to gain a common view of the nature and significance of the various impacts tourism has, because of the different perspectives of the parties involved. Glasson (1994) puts the point helpfully in a discussion of Oxford. In many ways the conflicts can be seen in terms of different definitions of 'tourism carrying capacity'. While the city may not have reached its 'economic carrying capacity' ('the limit beyond which the quality of the visitor's experience falls dramatically, and visitors decide to go elsewhere') it may be at or near its social carrying capacity ('the number of visitors ... [it] can absorb without hindrance of other social and economic functions'). Capacity can be thought of at the city level, or for smaller areas such as the historic centre, or parts of the centre. Even at the comparatively small scale of the city centre, some areas may be at social or environmental capacity, while others still have capacity to spare.

In general, the commercial sector will think in terms of 'economic carrying capacity', since many commercial operators will benefit financially so long as visitor numbers continue to increase. Residents, the colleges, non-tourist businesses and the council, on the other hand, will be concerned with 'social carrying capacity', which will be exceeded before full 'economic carrying capacity' is reached. Tour coaches are a very visible example. They generate additional visitation, by the least desirable visitors (day-trippers who spend little), add to congestion and are visually intrusive. Though profitable to the operators, coach excursions impose significant costs on the city. These differing perceptions of the same issue (how many visitors can the city accommodate?) mean that it is difficult to gain agreement even about the nature of the problem, and the objectives which policy should address. Promoting dialogue between the parties and seeking consensus over objectives is a key element of effective policy. Dialogue does not mean that all conflict can be done away with; it does mean, however, that 'imaginary problems', based on misunderstanding, can be removed and effort focused on 'real problems' (see Chapter 7).

3 TOURISM MANAGEMENT DEPENDS ON PARTNERSHIP AND A MIX OF POLICIES

While the City Council can play a leading and enabling role, it lacks the powers and resources to manage tourism alone. Policy requires action by other local authorities, other agencies such as the Tourist Board, the commercial sector, and the colleges and the University. Effectiveness depends on the following

- A consensus-building approach to policy making, so that maximum agreement on objectives is achieved, and ownership of policy is shared among all parties. The approaches to the tourism policy review and to City Centre

Management were specifically designed to achieve this.
- Coordination of the actions of all participants in the industry, in pursuit of agreed objectives. 'Unilateral decisions [in the corporate and private sectors] have the power to frustrate visitor management' (Human, 1994).
- Integration of different areas of public policy, for example, between different local authorities' land-use plans, or between the city's Local Plan and visitor management initiatives.

However, consensus-building and partnership can only go so far, since the parties involved have different interests, and there are 'real' problems if these conflict. Policy aims to influence the tourism product portfolio so that it confers greater benefits on the city. This means encouraging some products (such as business tourism) and discouraging others. Although maximum agreement between all those involved in tourism is sought as a basis for effective policy, it is inevitable that the development of some tourism products will be controlled or halted in the wider interest. Examples include restrictions on the conversion of existing housing, on the development of language schools, and on parking and dropping off by coaches.

4 THE COLLEGES HAVE A KEY MANAGEMENT ROLE

As private institutions which constitute the major tourist attractions, the colleges are in a powerful position. While the council cannot significantly affect the number of visitors to the city, the colleges could, in principle, close to visitors entirely. This obviously allows colleges to regulate admission, but it also provides leverage for a broader range of policies. The College Pass and Courtesy Courier schemes have shown that managing access to the colleges as attractions is possible, and can have benefits which go beyond the colleges themselves. The schemes have regulated the level of visitation to the colleges and made it more orderly, but by requiring groups to use Blue Badge Guides and Courtesy Couriers they have also encouraged more effective management of visitors throughout the historic centre. The council now intends to investigate linking coach restrictions to the provision of College Passes (Policy TS16).

5 FUNDING OF TOURISM MANAGEMENT IS PROBLEMATIC

Successful tourism management increases benefits – yet it is difficult for public authorities to capture a share of those benefits to fund management initiatives. College charging and Courtesy Couriers are cases in point. Both have proved effective in improving visitor management and reducing adverse impacts. However, while the colleges are, as private institutions, charging admission, and are able to recoup the cost of the scheme, there is no means for the council to recover the costs of providing Courtesy Couriers. The result is that although Courtesy Couriers have been successful and more are needed, they cannot be provided. Despite revenue raising initiatives, the net costs of the tourism service in 1995 was some £300,000. These problems would be alleviated if there were some means of the council sharing in the revenues generated by tourism.

REFERENCES

CCC (1988) *British Visitors to Cambridge 1980–84*, Cambridge City Council.

CCC (1990) *Tourism – the way ahead*, Cambridge City Council.

CCC (1992) *Language Students/Youth Groups Day Visitors to Cambridge*, Cambridge City Council.

CCC (1992) *Draft Local Plan*, Cambridge City Council.

CCC (1993) *Tourism 2000 – Action Plan*, Cambridge City Council.

CCC (1994) *Coach Survey 1994*, Cambridge City Council,

CCC (1994b) *City Centre Management: Report to Environment Committee 20.09.94*, Cambridge City Council.

CCC (1995) *Economic Development Strategy 1995/96*, Cambridge City Council.

CCC (1995b) *Tourism Strategy Group: Report of Consultation*, Cambridge City Council.

CCC (1995c) *Cambridge Tourism Strategy Review*, Cambridge City Council.

EFL Services Ltd (1992) *English Language Students in Cambridge*, EFL Services Ltd.

Glasson, J. (1994) 'Oxford – a heritage city under pressure' in *Tourism Management*, 15, 2, 1994.

Human, B. (1994) *Tourism in Cambridge: impact, planning and management*, CCC.

Human, B. (1995) 'Visitor management in the public planning context: a case study of Cambridge' in *Journal of Sustainable Tourism* (2, 4. pp. 221–230).

Segal Quince Wicksteed Ltd (1989) *Cambridge Tourism Review*, Segal Quince Wicksteed Ltd.

D Winchester

THEMES

- the impact of development plans and other strategies on shaping tourism at the destination
- the range of local authority services which impinge on visitor management issues

- the impact of external factors and external developments on managing visitors and the tourism-related environment.

LOCATION AND BACKGROUND

'An exceeding pleasant town, enriched with a beautiful cathedral and surrounded by a fresh-looking country.'

(Keats, 1819)

At the age of 23, the English Romantic poet John Keats stayed in Winchester during the late summer and early autumn of 1819, and described the city in the lines quoted above. It was on Sunday 19 September, after his daily walk through the cathedral close and Water Meadows on the way to St Cross, that Keats wrote his ode 'To Autumn': 'Season of mists and mellow fruitfulness . . .'

The area between Winchester cathedral and St Cross has changed little since Keats' visit, retaining many of the characteristics described by the poet in a letter to his brother George. The medieval buildings are still 'mixed up with trees'; the waters of the River Itchen still 'most beauti-

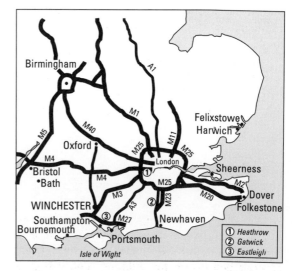

FIGURE D.1 *Map showing Winchester*

Winchester's famous cathedral was consecrated. It was to become the site of many events marking England's tumultuous history. In the Middle Ages, the cathedral tower collapsed seven years after Wicked King Rufus was buried below it. During the Reformation, Henry VIII's commissioners destroyed St Swithun's shrine in the Cathedral as the city's three monastic institutions were dissolved. At the end of the Civil War, Roundhead troops ransacked the Cathedral itself.

In Georgian times, Winchester prospered with shops, trade and the growth of the professions, establishing the character of the city as we now know it.

Modern Winchester is one of the premier tourist attractions in the county of Hampshire, due to its outstanding heritage and accessible location. It is situated on the M3, 65 miles from London and 12 miles inland from the south-coast port of Southampton. Also accessible by rail, Winchester is a 55-minute train journey from London.

The city enjoys a vibrant commercial life, due as much to the activities of its residents as to its visitors. The compact nature of this city of 34,000 inhabitants means that most residential housing is in, or close to, the centre. This provides a substantial local shopping population which supports Winchester's varied stock of retail units, including department stores, speciality shops, banks and building societies. Winchester is also an established and attractive office location. The unemployment rate is low and, if car ownership is an indicator of affluence, it is worthy of note that Winchester has the highest rate in the country.

fully clear'; and mists rise from the river in the early mornings and late afternoons of autumn.

But the history of Winchester begins long before. In 450BC, the first settlement was founded when a Celtic tribe made what is now known as St Catherine's Hill their home. Four hundred years later, the Romans built the walled city 'Venta Belgarum' on the same site. This became an important regional town, but was disintegrated after the Romans' departure in 400AD.

Winchester was restored after the Dark Ages by King Alfred the Great, King of Wessex, who drove back the invading Danes and made the city his capital of Saxon England. In 1093,

TOURISM

In 1840, the new railway brought the first day visitors to Winchester in substantial numbers. From then on, the city was to become a major day-visit destination for millions. The desire to visit the Cathedral of world renown was only one of their motivations for visiting the city, whose history had endowed it with many other unique attractions.

Throughout the centuries, Winchester had been a 'royal playground' where Britain's kings and queens willingly rested from their state duties, and socialised with bishops and eminent artists. These illustrious visitors left their mark on the city's architectural heritage, its monuments, parks and gardens. The most visited sites connected with Winchester's royal and ecclesiastical past include: the Great Hall, the only remaining visible part of the castle built by Henry III, which houses the famous Arthurian Round Table; Wolvesey Castle, once the chief residence of the Bishops of Winchester; Cheyney Court, formerly the Bishop's Court House.

To these may be added the attractions based on the city's military traditions, notably the five museums telling the history of the famous regiments based in and around Winchester. Finally, the city's literary and educational heritage also provides a number of popular attractions: John Keats' lodgings; the house where Jane Austen lived her last days and died; and Winchester College, the oldest school in England, founded in 1382 by William of Wakeham.

Tourism in Winchester today is a thriving industry, worth approximately £53 million annually to the district. It employs in excess of 2,900 people directly and many more indirectly in shops, cafés, etc. Tourism was of considerable importance to the local economy during the recession of the early and mid 1990s, growing at a rate of approximately 6% per annum (WCC, 1995).

The 1994 Winchester Visitor Survey estimated that more than 1.7 million people visited the city and district that year, an increase of almost 250,000 compared with 1992. This growth in visitor numbers was largely accounted for by the increase in the number of day visitors from home: from 520,000 in 1992 to 920,000 two years later. This increase partly reflected the success of events such as 'Le Tour' in attracting visitors to Winchester from surrounding areas. The number of visitors staying overnight in Winchester remained relatively constant between 1992 and 1994 at around 290,000, although there was an increase in the proportion of those staying in hotel accommodation.

Average daily expenditure by visitors to the district increased significantly over 1992 levels, but generally remained slightly lower than the UK average. The increases in the average expenditure of visitors and in the volume of higher spending groups (such as visitors staying in hotels), account for the overall growth in the value of tourism in Winchester district from £33 million in 1992 to almost £53 million in 1994.

Concerning the general profile of visitors, there were few changes between 1994 and the patterns identified in previous years: only 15% of groups included children; two-thirds of visitors were aged 45 or over; and more than 70% were in the ABC1 socioeconomic groups. The proportion of staying visitors who came from overseas was 34%; and 29% of the day visitors on holiday were from overseas. The average length of stay in Winchester was 3.35 nights, compared with 4.03 nights in 1992 – due to the increase in the number of day visitors. However, average spend per stay rose in that period, from £78 per head to £106, an increase of over 35%.

Almost three-quarters of visitors travelled to Winchester by car – 93% found it 'very' or 'quite easy' to find a parking space. (However, when complaints were made, parking was one of the issues which came up most frequently.)

In 1994, opinion scores were generally slightly lower than in previous years. All aspects of shopping in the city scored well, as did the district's countryside and scenery, but visitors complained about a lack of things to do in the evening and the availability and cleanliness of the public toilets. The Cathedral was the aspect that visitors to Winchester particularly liked. Traffic congestion, the one-way system and car parking caused the biggest negative reaction (WCC, 1994). This information may be represented in terms of the 'tourism product portfolio' and 'tourism dominance' grids as shown in Figures D.2 and D.3.

	growth	day visits		business tourism
Market				staying visits
	decline			
		high		low
		Share		

FIGURE D.2 *Tourism product portfolio: Winchester*

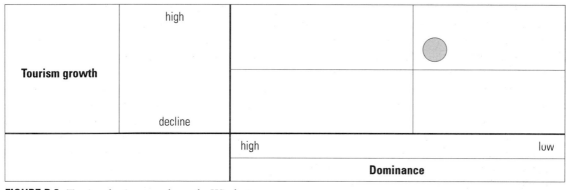

	high		
Tourism growth			
	decline		
		high	luw
		Dominance	

FIGURE D.3 *Tourism dominance and growth: Winchester*

VISITOR MANAGEMENT

In common with many other historic towns, Winchester faces difficulties and opportunities which arise from the particular volume and profile of its visitors and their behaviour. Increasingly, attention has been focused on ways of managing the environment and influencing visitor behaviour in order to reap the maximum benefits from tourist activity, and to minimise its negative impacts.

As the local authority with the responsibility for Winchester, Winchester City Council (WCC) necessarily plays a major role in intervening to manage tourists' impacts on the city and district. By 1995, all of the council's actions with implications for tourism were set out in a **Visitor Management Plan (VMP)**, the development of which we shall now examine.

Many important WCC initiatives with bearing on **visitor management (VM)** pre-date the development of the VMP itself. A shining example is provided by Winchester's park-and-ride service, located outside the city centre, just off Junction 10 of the M3. For £1, visitors can park their cars in the large car park and travel free to the city and around it all day on the fast and frequent park-and-ride buses. By providing a cheap and convenient alternative to parking in the city centre, the park-and-ride service clearly has a major impact on controlling the flow of traffic in and around Winchester, and thus represents a major element in the city's VM strategy.

However, the council services with the greatest potential for taking a direct role in the city's VM are its specialist tourism services.

In 1978, Winchester City Council established its first **Marketing and Tourism Division** within its Leisure Department. WCC Tourism Services now comprise four independent but inter-related tourism units, each of which plays a distinct role in VM. Each has its own 'business plan' of activities designed to achieve the policy and relevant key objectives of the Council's Tourism Strategy. The four units in WCC Tourism Services are as follows.

MARKETING UNIT

Marketing through promotion and the provision of information plays a vital role in the VM of the city and district. It makes an early impression on visitors, helps shape their perceptions and attitudes, and guides how they use the city and countryside. The Marketing Unit designs, produces and distributes a range of informative literature, including attractive leaflets describing themed walks and trails, such as the 'Sunset Walk' and 'Keats Walk'. Trails in themselves are a major mechanism for effective VM, helping avoid congestion at sensitive spots and adding to visitor enjoyment.

To ensure the efficacy of these promotional and information production activities, the Marketing Unit researches and analyses visitor profiles including their spending, behaviour and opinions, as a basis for tourism policies. The unit also develops and activates quality standard initiatives and training programmes, such as Welcome Host, a customer relations skills initiative.

TOURIST INFORMATION CENTRE (TIC)

Whereas the Marketing Unit is concerned with influencing the future visitor, the TIC provides 'on the ground' VM when the visitors arrive in Winchester. Approximately 250,000 visitors use the facilities every year and the TIC responds to over 19,000 telephone and 7,000 postal enquiries annually – this volume accounts for approximately 30% of visitors to the city in any one year, (WCC, 1995).

The advice and assistance these people receive has a large bearing on their perceptions and attitudes towards the host community and environment, their movements within the area and the length of time they stay. Thus, the TIC plays an important role in channelling the flow of visitors through Winchester. For example, the range of visitor services available from the TIC includes standard and tailor-made guided tours which 'control' large group movements.

GUILDHALL CONFERENCE OPERATIONS

Winchester's Guildhall plays many roles within the community, not least of which is its ability, as a conference centre, to attract very high-spending conference groups into the area. The income generated benefits retailers, hoteliers, bed-and-breakfast establishments, and helps to reduce the overall cost to the local tax-payer of the provision of tourism services; the community also use the Guildhall itself for concerts, exhibitions, etc.

In VM terms, the Guildhall provides the opportunity to:

- attract high-spending, long-stay groups
- plan and control their stay and place large groups of people within either a confined area or disperse them throughout the city and district
- coordinate their movements (sightseeing, tours, etc.) to achieve maximum economic return with minimum disruption to the community
- provide directional tourism information to known delegates before arrival.

SPECIAL EVENTS AND LIAISON UNIT

The role of this unit is to develop and/or coordinate events and activities which benefit both the local community and the visitor (one group usually being reliant upon the other for the event to take place). Examples of such events include one-off events such as the D-Day celebrations and the visit to Winchester of 'Le Tour', as well as major annual events such as the Hat Fair, Britain's longest-running festival of street theatre, and the Southern Cathedrals Festival, which alternates between Salisbury, Chichester and Winchester.

This unit, by linking tourism to the 'arts', thus attracts visitors to the area, to the benefit of the visitors themselves, local groups developing cultural programmes reliant upon visitor patronage, and the various suppliers of tourism services in and around Winchester.

CONTEXTUAL PLANS AND POLICIES

Visitor management in Winchester takes place within the context of a number of statutory and non-statutory plans and policies operating at city, county, region, national and international levels. Some of these plans are exclusively concerned with tourism, while others only impact upon visitor-related issues in an indirect way. Some of the most important non-tourism plans affecting the shape and nature of the tourism which takes place in Winchester are the various land-use

plans as well as those dealing with economic development and urban generation. These, together with tourism-specific plans are shown in diagrammatic form in Figure D.4. The diagram could, of course, be extended to include relevant plans at the regional, national and international levels, but we restrict ourselves here to those which most specifically impact upon Winchester's tourism.

The most important tourism-related elements

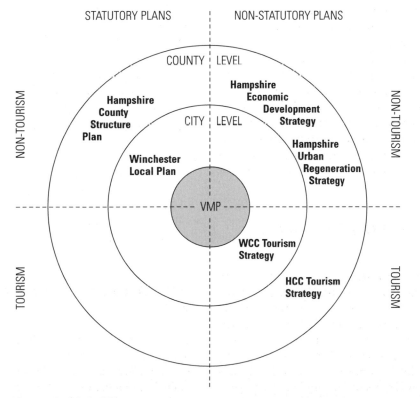

FIGURE D.4 *Development plans for Winchester*

of each of these plans will now be examined, emphasising linkages between the different plans: how certain policies are complemented and reinforced (or not, as the case may be) by policies in other documents.

STATUTORY PLANS

HAMPSHIRE COUNTY STRUCTURE PLAN – DEPOSITED MAY 1991; ADOPTED NOVEMBER 1993

The framework of policies within the Hampshire County Structure Plan provides a flexible setting to respond to the changing demands of tourism in the area and also, where appropriate, to take advantage of private sector initiatives. The tourism-related policy areas covered are as follows.

- **Urban Tourism Development (Policy R1):** a positive policy in terms of its encouragement of the utilisation of existent redundant or under-used land and buildings for tourist facilities. The policy becomes specific in relation to the industrial nature of Southern Hampshire (Portsmouth/Southampton), referring to 'built-up areas – including docks surplus to naval or port requirements' (an allusion to one of the county's unique selling points – its naval history and the revitalisation of redundant docks as tourist attractions).
- **Rural Tourism Development and Heritage Protection (Policy R2/R3):** policies to restrict future obtrusive recreational development in rural areas (R2); enabling the preservation and possible improvement of the county's acknowledged historic, landscape, archaeological and nature conservation values (R3). Despite the restrictive nature of Policy R2, it does hold some scope for the provision of low-key facilities that enhance the landscape and utilise redundant land as a means of rural economic diversification.
- **Improvement of Hotel, Conference and Serviced Accommodation (Policy R4).**
- **Caravans and Camping (Policy R5):** a

presumption against additional sites on the coast, in the Southern Hampshire Green Belt and in areas of landscape, nature conservation or archaeological interest.

WINCHESTER LOCAL PLAN: DEPOSITED AUGUST 1994

Much of Winchester Local Plan's 'recreation and tourism' chapter deals with the provision of various forms of recreational open space, such as playing fields and children's play areas, as well as the provision of recreational space for new housing development. However, a number of the policies are more directly tourism-related. These include policies to improve the county's footpath, bridleway and cycleway networks; to allow the development of stables, horse-riding schools and/or riding centres, subject to certain environmental controls; and a policy setting out the conditions under which golf courses and associated buildings may be developed, with particular encouragement being given to more 'pay as you play' courses, which have less of an impact on the environment.

Other policies are complemented by policies in the Hampshire County Structure Plan, (described previously) and include the following.

- **Tourist facilities in settlements (Policy RT12):** a standard policy encouraging the development of facilities and accommodation to suit all visitor types, on condition that these meet a number of stipulations concerning layout, access, size and appearance. This policy is complemented by Policy R1 of the Hampshire County Structure Plan.
- **Rural tourism development (Policy RT13):** a policy encouraging the conversion or change of use of existing buildings to small-scale tourism-related facilities, such as holiday accommodation; provided that the proposal retains the building's character and the quality of the environment. This policy is strengthened by Policy R2 in the Hampshire County Structure Plan.
- **Camping and caravaning (Policy RT14):** a restrictive policy (that compliments Policy R5) setting out areas where sites would *not* be

acceptable (e.g. Strategic Gaps and the East Hampshire AONB). However, the policy also states that there may be opportunities for small sites to be developed elsewhere in the Winchester Local Plan area, with regard to both countryside and environment policies.

Finally, Winchester Local Plan contains two tourism-related policies which are not reinforced by Hampshire County Structure Plan policies:

- **Permanent tourist accommodation (Policy RT15):** a negative policy which deems permanent holiday accommodation (such as chalets or mobile homes) less acceptable than touring sites, as the accommodation tends to be present all year round and intrusion into the landscape is therefore greater.
- **Mutual support (Policy RT16):** a restrictive policy requiring that the development of any new tourist and leisure facilities should be viable in their own right and should not require other development (such as housing or business uses) to ensure viability.

NON-STATUTORY PLANS

HAMPSHIRE ECONOMIC DEVELOPMENT STRATEGY: 1995–96

Increasing the benefits of tourism and leisure is identified as one of the six main objectives of economic development in the county. To carry forward this policy, five 'Action Areas' are identified:

1 Planning and infrastructure
2 Business support
3 Trade, investment, tourism and leisure
4 People and jobs
5 Hampshire in Europe

There are clear implications from all of these action areas for tourism, but Action Areas 3 and 5 are the most directly relevant.

Action Area 3: Trade, investment, tourism & leisure (Ec Strat PP13/14)

If successful, Hampshire Economic Development Strategy stands to have favourable conse-

quences for business tourism in the county as a whole; marketing of the area to new investment, creating a business-friendly attitude and establishing international links feature prominently throughout the policy. Actioning these policy aims comes in a variety of techniques for marketing the county to inward investors. More directly tourist-based actions include:

- the support of cultural, sporting and arts events which focus media attention on the area
- promoting the historic, cultural and artistic image, aided by capital grants and such marketing initiatives as 'Arts Marketing Hampshire'
- maintenance of overseas representation of Hampshire as a tourist destination.

Action Area 5: Hampshire in Europe (Ec Strat PP16)

Although not exclusively aimed at improving tourism, the improvement of inter-regional relations and the raising of Hampshire's profile throughout the EU clearly strengthen the measures taken under Action Area 3. Tourism objectives are particularly complemented by the following actions:

- inter-regional partnerships (e.g. with Lower Normandy and North Brabant)
- active membership of inter-regional groupings (e.g. Atlantic Arc)
- bidding for European funding programmes.

HAMPSHIRE URBAN REGENERATION STRATEGY: OCTOBER 1989

Hampshire's regeneration programme with its £¾ million annual budget, is primarily a conservation and restoration tool, with obvious indirect implications for tourism within the county. Although it does not identify tourism specifically as a main objective, it does imply that heritage restoration in the major urban centres will be to the benefit of visitors as well as residents. Similarly, the programme of support for arts facilities (such as the restoration of the Theatre Royal in Portsmouth) will also have implications for that city's tourism.

HAMPSHIRE COUNTY COUNCIL TOURISM STRATEGY 1995

Hampshire CC is only one of many parties with an interest in tourism in the county. In addition to commercial enterprises there is the Southern Tourist Board (which is a Regional Tourist Board with responsibility for tourism promotion and development over five counties); and there are the 13 district councils, Hampshire TEC and the Hampshire Economic Partnership (which has a tourism sub-group). The CC therefore sees its role as concentrating on 'issues of strategic importance, developing initiatives which cross administrative boundaries and pursuing new areas of opportunity as yet unexploited'. Its Tourism Strategy is the key policy instrument in this area of activity.

The Tourism Strategy starts from the proposition that Hampshire as a region is an ideal area where economic and cultural strategies can meet. This is why both the tourism and economic strategies were produced simultaneously.

The Tourism Strategy's overall objective is to obtain an economic advantage for the county by adopting policies that will, over time, expand the economic contribution made by Hampshire's tourist industry. This will be achieved by utilising its cultural heritage and arts provision and, in the process, enhance the quality of life enjoyed by local people. In order to realise the benefits and secure a sustainable industry, five priority areas have been identified for future action as follows:

- **Protecting and enhancing the environment** – maintain the quality and character of Hampshire, which are, in terms of tourism, its greatest asset. There is a need to identify ways of reducing the impact of visitor pressure in sensitive areas, to manage tourism more effectively and to show how tourism can make a positive contribution towards enhancing the environment.
- **Increasing economic benefits** – the aim is to attract not greater numbers but more higher spending sectors (such as the overseas, business and short break visitor). At the same time, visitors should be encouraged to stay longer and to make a return visit.
- **Raising the profile of Hampshire as a tourist destination** – currently, Hampshire's marketing is fragmented and under-resourced. The aim is to seek ways of channelling more resources into marketing and using these resources to raise the awareness of Hampshire's strengths.
- **Improving and strengthening the product** – visitors are becoming more discerning and sophisticated. In order to be continually attractive, there is a need to invest in existing accommodation and attractions, raise standards, improve customer care and identify new opportunities for development.
- **Effective use of resources** – currently many organisations and businesses are involved in tourism in Hampshire, and this has in the past led to duplication and wasted effort. Ensuring better coordination and cooperation will channel resources where they can have most impact. Additional funding can also be sought from EU and national sources.

Hampshire County Council's Tourism Strategy ends with a detailed Action Plan, setting out 30 measures which have been designed to achieve the objectives we have just discussed.

WINCHESTER CITY COUNCIL TOURISM STRATEGY 1992–95

This document, WCC's first Tourism Strategy, highlights priorities and opportunities for tourism in the Winchester District. It was implemented through the council's activities and programmes over the three year period leading up to 1995. The WCC Tourism Strategy recognised the need for a proactive approach to tourism in the city and district, against a background composed of three important elements:

- general financial constraints
- the recession and its effects on the private sector's ability to contribute to tourism's development
- general political reluctance on the part of the City Council to place tourism, a non-statutory function, high on its agenda.

The overall objective is 'to develop tourism in the Winchester district in order to support and improve the local economy, and to manage this development in such a way as to protect and enhance the quality of life for local residents.' The guiding principles behind this are described in the WCC Tourism Strategy as follows:

1 The historic fabric and, so far as possible, ambience of Winchester should be safeguarded so as to ensure its long term preservation for future generations to enjoy

2 The needs and interests of the local community should be protected and visitor activities considered and harmonised with them

3 Winchester is an important part of the nation's heritage, and visitors have a right to enjoy and share the benefits of this heritage with the Winchester community

4 Regard should be paid to the wide range of activities in Winchester, not just as a place to visit, but as a place to live and work and as a substantial regional centre in its own right

5 In planning for visitors, the wide range and variety of organisations and individuals involved in tourism should be recognised and coordinated

6 Any visitor management programme should aim to maximise the benefits to the local community and local economy, while minimising the pressures caused by visitors.

In order to achieve the overall objective, the WCC Tourism Strategy divides objectives under three headings: 'Positioning', 'Processes' and 'Product'(see Figure D.5).

Positioning	Processes	Product
Place greater emphasis on the proactive long-term development of tourism within the district, for maximum economic and employment return	Work with other divisions, members and local community groups to develop a Visitor Management Plan by 1995	Work in conjunction with the Planning Department and hotel developers in securing the development of at least one new hotel (3/4 star category) within the city, thus increasing bedspace capacity and generating increased spending within the local economy
Enhance and improve communication and organisation systems with the private sector	Investigate and seek to introduce a Quality Initiative within the district which assists the tourism sectors in meeting the expectations of visitors	Repackage all existing promotional materials to increase visitors' perception of Winchester District as a long-stay base, and promote aggressively
Focus primary marketing attention on the development of the long-stay visitor programme	Develop and make available to all groups, database and visitor demographic information systems, to allow for proactive development and investment in tourism within the district	Develop mini-packages within (a) Winchester City, (b) Winchester District, reflecting visitors' requirements while allowing for a degree of control over visitor movements and obtaining maximum revenue from visitor spending
Develop information/educational devices to assist in improving visitors' appreciation of Winchester's heritage and expectations of their behaviour	Develop Tourist Information services, to ensure that units are strategically placed to manage future visitor growth effectively	Develop Winchester City as high quality long-stay conference location attracting both domestic and international visitors
Restructure the Marketing and Tourism Division	Investigate and seek to develop common marketing goals and objectives between the public and private sectors in the promotion of Winchester District	
	Develop internal management information systems which provide accurate statistics for future decision making and assist the process of the management of change to a more commercial base	

FIGURE D.5 *WCC's Tourism Strategy (1992–95)*

By 1995, most of the elements of the WCC Tourism Strategy were comfortably in place, in particular the following achievements:

- the effective marketing to target markets producing maximum return to the local economy, i.e. longer-staying visitors and business tourists
- the effective managing of visitors by the Tourist Information Centre
- the provision of a high-quality conference operation based at the city's Guildhall, capable of attracting very high spending groups into the area
- the development of a Special Events and Liaison function, collaborating with various organisations involved in (or contributing to) the district's tourism effort (e.g. tourist attractions, community sectors, arts and cultural organisations).
- greater political support for tourism, which is

now seen as a cornerstone of Winchester's Economic Development Strategy.

The vast majority of these objectives and the specific achievements which followed from them reflect the exclusively 'tourism-focused' approach of the strategy, which was mainly concerned with *growth* in the number of visitors and their spending. As the WCC Head of Tourism was later to remark, 'the focus of this intervention has been fairly narrow, however, concentrating on primary tourism suppliers and organisers'. (Wyatt, 1996). This approach is represented in diagrammatic form in Figure D.6.

However, an important element in *widening* the scope of the council's intervention in tourism-related issues in Winchester still remained to be addressed by the end of the strategy's period – the Visitor Management Plan.

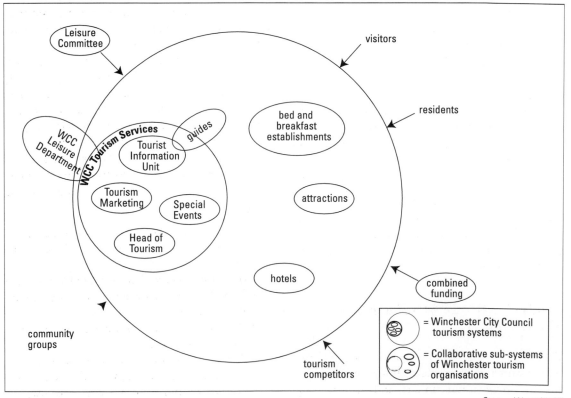

FIGURE D.6 *Marketing and tourism organisation as a system*

Source: Wyatt (1996)

WINCHESTER VISITOR MANAGEMENT PLAN

An important objective of Winchester City Council's Tourism Strategy was the development of a specific VMP for Winchester.

Because of the scale of the undertaking and because the council provided most of Winchester's tourism infrastructure, it was decided that WCC was best placed to take the lead in developing and coordinating the VMP. The starting point of the VMP development process was an internal appraisal of how WCC already managed visitors and the visitor-related environment through its various operations and activities.

Accordingly, as the first part of the process, an audit of the practices of all council departments whose work has an impact on visitors was undertaken. The departments involved were:

- Tourism Marketing
- Conference Operations (Guildhall)
- Tourism Information Services
- Special Events
- Traffic and Engineering
- Planning and Conservation
- Environmental Services

Each department identified:

- its key practices and objectives regarding VM
- any VM initiatives being planned in the future
- where responsibility for VM lay within the department
- strengths and weaknesses of current practices.

The roles of Winchester's four Tourism Services units on VM were described on pages 248–9 in this book. The VM-related responsibilities and policies of the other relevant departments were identified as follows.

TRAFFIC AND ENGINEERING DEPARTMENT

The Engineering Department's work is concerned primarily with maintaining and improving the built environment and in ensuring people's freedom and ability to get about.

Key responsibilities which relate to visitors and tourism are:

- pedestrianisation
- road signs
- pedestrian signs
- traffic management
- parking
- road maintenance
- road improvements
- traffic calming
- street lighting
- river maintenance.

Generally, the requirements of all road users are considered when proposals are made, and the engineers use their professional judgement to assess whether consultation with special interests is necessary. The Planning Department, the Preservation Trust and the Winchester Chamber of Commerce are regular consultees. The Leisure (Tourism) Department is consulted from time to time on matters such as special events, signing or updating maps.

The Transportation Policies for Winchester were reassessed in the mid-1990s in a joint study with the County Council. The proposals, known as the Winchester Movement and Access Plan, were designed to reduce people's dependence on the motor car and to reduce the adverse effects of the motor car on Winchester. This will be achieved by providing better opportunities to use alternatives of cycling, walking and public transport.

- access for cars to the centre will be restrained because no new roads or car parks are proposed
- parking on-street will be restricted to residents only and more pedestrian and traffic-calmed areas are proposed
- cyclists will benefit from new dedicated cycle routes and cycle parks
- pedestrians will enjoy a more pleasant environment with reduced traffic and more pedestrian crossings and pedestrian zones
- the park-and-ride service will be developed

and extended to provide a cheap, convenient alternative to parking in the town centre.

These policies were established in recognition of the needs of business, commerce, residents, conservationists, tourism etc., and seek to strike a balance in these conflicting requirements.

PLANNING AND CONSERVATION DEPARTMENT

The built environment (the villages, towns and buildings of the district) forms a major attraction for the visitor. At the same time, tourism expenditure is vitally important to assist with the ongoing maintenance and upkeep of the many historic buildings. Without tourists, the financial burdens would fall to a much greater extent on to local residents and businesses.

Supporting tourism is therefore 'good business' in terms of the City Council's planning and conservation policies.

The City Council already has vigorous policies and standards which aim to protect individual buildings, to conserve important areas and to protect the open countryside. There are many Listed Buildings throughout the district as well as nearly 40 Conservation Areas.

Recent visitor-related projects which have received strong backing from the planners include:

- the hotel at Marwell Zoo
- the Winchester Cathedral Visitors' Centre
- a number of individual initiatives to create visitor accommodation in the rural areas
- a strong shopfront and sign policy in Conservation Areas to enhance their attractiveness for visitors.

Current projects include:

- grant assistance and expert advice in support of the upgrading of the Southgate Hotel in Winchester
- a major input into the formation and development of detailed regeneration plans for the Peninsula Barracks in Winchester – including enhanced settings for the existing military museums and the opening up to the general public of the whole of this historic site

- positive backing and support for the opening and further development of the park-and-ride scheme in Winchester.

Accommodating new development will always be more difficult in a district such as Winchester. Planning policies designed to control excessive development and to preserve historic settlements and countryside will also affect new tourism-related schemes. However, as it is now quite clear that tourism makes a major economic contribution to the well-being and wealth of the district, the planning service works with prospective developers to create acceptable schemes wherever this is possible.

ENVIRONMENTAL SERVICES

Residents and visitors alike benefit from a clean and litter-free environment which helps make Winchester an attractive place in which to live and an enjoyable place to visit.

Enhancing the local environment by maintaining a good quality Street Cleansing and Litter Control service is therefore a major objective of this department. It has as a related objective the fostering of a positive change in attitude amongst local residents and visitors towards reducing litter.

The provision of public conveniences is another service supplied by the City Council, for shoppers and visitors alike. Most conveniences have facilities for disabled people and, wherever possible, remain open 24 hours a day.

In collecting the information from this exercise, it became apparent that the council already had fairly well-defined VM systems in place, although they were not always called or recognised as such. But what had never been produced before was one document setting out all of the council departments' work which has a visitor focus or which impacts upon the visitor in some way. The conclusions arising from this exercise were summarised in an internally-circulated draft VMP (WCC, 1995), as follows.

MAJOR STRENGTHS

1 All key departments recognise the importance of visitors to the local economy and the responsibility of the role the departments play in helping to achieve harmony between visitor/host/community/environment.

2 Clear transportation policies exist (Winchester Movement and Access Plan) which seek to protect the environment.

3 Vigorous planning policies and standards exist to protect individual buildings, conserve important and sensitive areas, and protect open countryside.

4 Well-defined objectives and operations exist to ensure effective street cleaning and litter control standards.

5 Dedicated tourism and marketing infrastructure exists providing visitor research and analysis, targeted promotion, 'on the ground' VM in Winchester City and strong links with district community and tourism suppliers.

6 A number of forums exist with outside bodies which permit regular consultation of plans which affect both host community and visitors.

7 Despite revenue budget restrictions, a number of positive VM initiatives have been activated in the past year (e.g. park-and-ride, Shopmobility, Welcome Host, etc.).

8 The council's 1995/6 Strategic Plan focuses heavily on protection of the environment and developing transportation policies to support this.

MAJOR WEAKNESSES

1 VM is not currently a corporate function or identified as a strategic priority in its own right. It is a cross-departmental discipline and requires a controlling vehicle if it is to be truly effective.

2 Inter-departmental communication regarding VM tends to be informal and *ad hoc*. As a result, there tends to be a lack of awareness of the expertise that exists within the authority which would, if harnessed in a more formal way, create a very powerful vehicle to manage and add value to VM medium- and long term-development.

3 The district has only one Tourist Information Centre, based in Winchester, with no effective way of managing or maximising economic benefits of visitors arriving in the district villages and towns of Bishops Waltham, Alresford or Wickam. Consideration should be given to developing a district infrastructure of TICs.

4 With no capital budgets operative, little has been done to create, improve, upgrade or change physical approaches to the district or base facilities such as toilets, etc. Existing facilities, while functional, are old and do not lend themselves to projecting a welcoming and quality image.

The draft VMP also identified a number of external factors which it was necessary to take into account in formulating the strategy (these are represented in Figure D.7).

In addition to these external factors, an assessment was made of various concerns, conflicts and tensions present within the environment and community of the destination.

■ The **environmental factors** included the acknowledgement that car-borne and day visitors were increasing, while the number of staying visitors which the city was capable of accommodating was close to its maximum. This latter factor was explained by the fact that bed-space capacity was static in Winchester, for two reasons: land-use issues and the reluctance of developers to invest capital. As demand for overnight accommodation was rising, anecdotal evidence suggested that saturation point lay only a few years ahead. In addition, another important environmental factor noted was that any large increase in the volume of visitors would reduce the attractiveness of the product and potentially harm the fabric of the city.

■ **Anti-social behaviour** was another concern highlighted in the draft VMP. The fact that the city is a target for 'vagrants and rough sleepers' who regard visitors as a source of 'rich pickings' makes the product less attractive. Similarly, the city's nightlife is dominated by pubs and youth, which staying visitors can find intimidating. There is a lack

Sociological	Technological
Pace and stress of modern life: leading to people placing a higher priority on leisure and short breaks Increase in middle-aged and older-age groups, with high disposable income – the typical Winchester visitor Increased mobility, greater access Greater awareness and interest in culture and heritage Greater consumer choice, increased competition for disposable income	Rapid changes in computer technology will create new demands in information, marketing, distribution and service delivery Customer expectations for sophisticated products and hi-tech 'added-value' will increase
Economic	**Political**
Lingering recessional pressures and lack of 'feel-good' factor will constrain visitor spending In continuing to maximise tourism income, greater bedspace capacity will be required	Tourism remains a non-statutory function of local government. Public-sector spending is static or reducing – hence greater reliance on commercial development or revenue streams to support tourism infrastructure Central government continues to reduce funding to English Tourist Board, thus putting greater onus on local marketing operations to fill the gap

FIGURE D.7 *External factors with an impact on visitor management*

of alternative evening activities or cultural events.

Other issues identified included:

- **a budget conflict** between the maintenance of visitors, and the provision of facilities and services to residents
- **potential conflict between visitors and residents** competing for use of facilities and amenities
- **the need to provide additional signing, street furniture and information points** which, unless handled sensitively, could impair the environment which attracts visitors
- **the main beneficiaries from tourism spending** are not typically those who are required to meet the infrastructure and maintenance costs incurred.

Taking into account all of these strengths, weaknesses, external factors, concerns and possible conflicts of interest, as well as the results of the 1994 Visitor Survey, a series of recommendations for future action was made in a draft VMP document which was circulated to the local authority's Chief Officers and Tourism Working Group Members for comment and additions.

This document included the VMP's proposed objectives:

1 To maximise the economic benefits of tourism to the district in support of the broader strategy of economic development in Winchester District
2 To work with the private sector to maintain and improve the competitive position of Winchester district as a quality tourism destination all year round
3 To encourage a more coordinated and professional approach to the marketing, development and management of the industry
4 To achieve a higher recognised tourism profile for the Winchester District at local, regional and international levels
5 To support the careful visitor management of the area and develop sustainable tourism in the district.

RECOMMENDATIONS

In the light of the consultation exercise and the 1994 Visitor Survey results, the draft VMP identifies the need for a number of actions, including the following:

- a corporate communication system to ensure that VM issues are considered on a regular ongoing basis
- A special Working Group to develop an action plan to deal with three specific issues:
  - extending the TIC infrastructure to cover the whole district
  - upgrading physical approaches to the district and city
  - upgrading toilet facilities
- more bedspaces/hotels in the city and district
- the development of evening activities, to encourage more staying visitors and to change the 'drinking' and unsafe image of Winchester by night
- the development of an alternative marketing approach to attract younger age groups, as well as overseas visitors
- the development of upper city trails to complement trails such as the 'Sunset Walk' and 'Keats Walk' designed for the lower end of the city
- the development of district trails to enhance visitor movement within the district and encourage tourists to visit key attractions outside the city of Winchester.

By 1996, many of these recommendations had either been achieved or were under review by the various council services. Notably, a corporate communication system was in place, to ensure that VM issues were considered on a regular ongoing basis, through the mechanism of an inter-departmental officer group. Only issues requiring substantial budget commitments – such as the extension of the TIC network – had failed to move forward.

FROM VISITOR MANAGEMENT TO TOWN CENTRE MANAGEMENT

In 1996, Winchester City Council began to place greater emphasis on the forming of partnerships and alliances with the private sector, in particular through the establishing of a public sector/private sector **Town Centre Management Group (TCMG)** with a remit 'to develop a strategy and key initiatives to improve Winchester city centre as place to live, work and visit' (Wyatt, 1996).

The TCMG was established partly in response to certain developments which were perceived as potential threats to Winchester's future as a thriving, bustling and prosperous centre. The **Winchester City Centre Management Business Plan** (TCMG, 1996) describes these threats as follows:

- small retailers of essential goods have largely vanished
- empty shop and office properties have existed for longer than anyone would want

- nearby town shopping centres are investing in themselves to attract customers – within 20 miles' radius, we have Basingstoke, Eastleigh, Southampton and Portsmouth
- motoring to and through the city, and parking, are perceived to be difficult
- anti-social behaviour by a few is inhibiting the city showing itself off to the best advantage
- out-of-city shopping centres at Hedge End and Winnall, and also at Lakeside, Bristol and Bicester, have sprung up within reachable motoring distances, offering an easy parking and shopping experience.

The TCMG's Mission Statement, therefore, is: 'to make Winchester the preferred place to shop, work, live and visit'.

Within the council itself, the Marketing and Tourism Division was identified as being best placed to support this group, due to its already extensive interface with the private sector and because many of its planned VMP initiatives were convergent with the goals of the TCMG.

Figure D.8 provides a diagrammatic view of the new enlarged system within which the Marketing and Tourism Division undertakes its new role in supporting the TCMG.

As a result of the TCMG development, the Marketing and Tourism Division therefore finds itself in the position of having to extend its borders of network organisation, diverting resources to support the new initiatives, while continuing to lead in the field of tourism marketing and public-sector tourism service provision. Apart from the internal organisational changes which this necessitates, the move towards wider town centre management responsibilities also affects the four WCC Tourism Units' work both qualitatively and quantitatively. The network of collaborators has been enlarged from being predominantly composed of suppliers of tourism services (e.g. accommodation, attractions, guides), to include other actors whose work impinges upon town centre management issues (e.g. retailers, community groups, police).

The ethos of the Tourism Units' working environment has also been changed by their involvement with the TCMG. Regarding this, one perceived problem to be overcome at the organisational level was the need for the WCC tourism staff to be able to adapt to working even more closely with their private-sector partners and collaborators in the TCMG. As the Head of Tourism put it: 'A new culture will need to be established which recognises that traditional public-sector values cannot be applied to the dynamics of the new (TCMG) system' (Wyatt, 1996).

However, early signs of public-sector/private-sector collaboration through the TCMG look promising. One example which has been widely hailed as a success is the joint Tourism Marketing Unit/TCMG initiative in producing the *Winchester Days to Treasure* leaflet. This attractive map and guide to Winchester was produced using substantial private-sector financial

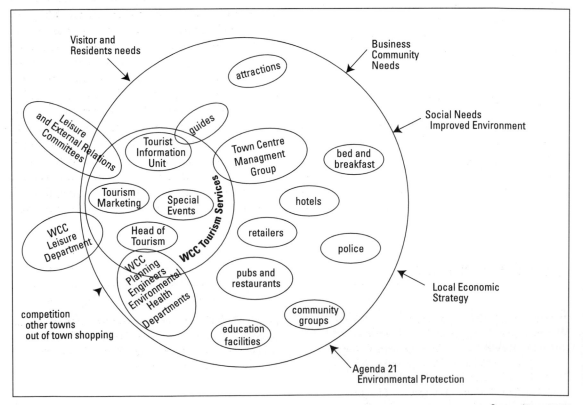

FIGURE D.8 *Marketing visitor management network*

Source: Wyatt (1996)

support from the attractions, shops and hotels featured in the leaflet.

Most important of all, however, may be the fact that the production of this leaflet has successfully established a pattern of future public-sector/private-sector cooperation for the tourism element of Winchester's nascent town centre management initiative.

CONCLUSION

1 TOURISM PLANNING IN WINCHESTER TAKES PLACE WITHIN A MULTILAYERED PUBLIC POLICY CONTEXT

Winchester's VMP is part of a dynamic process of planning and policy making at several different spatial levels. Only city-level and county-level plans and strategies were specified in this case study, but the matrix extends to the regional level, national level and international level. Statutory Development Plans play an important role in shaping tourism at the destination, by specifying what type of development is permitted, and where one of the objectives of the VMP is to develop sustainable tourism in the district, this is supported by all of the other plans mentioned at the county and city levels.

2 RESEARCH IS VITAL

The WCC Tourism Division makes extensive use of research and analysis to encourage greater understanding and support from politicians, retailers and other groups of importance to tourism, through the role they play in providing the product. Well-researched facts and figures are particularly necessary tools when support from ratepayers and elected members is tenuous.

A major element in the WCC tourism-research programme is the biennial Visitor Survey, providing quantitative and qualitative information on the profile of Winchester's visitors, which is indispensable in the planning and management of tourism at the destination.

3 A COLLABORATIVE AND FLEXIBLE APPROACH TO VM IS NECESSARY

With many council departments and private-sector operators being involved in providing services which are used by visitors (as well as by local residents, businesses and shoppers), VM must take place through a system of networks, partnerships and alliances. A single organisation is incapable of working effectively to deal with all of the aspects affecting VM. However, the Tourism Services in Winchester are well-placed to coordinate and animate the VM system, by acting as facilitator and leader. Latterly, the development of the TCMG has given the Tourism Services a new extended role in managing change, through supporting and influencing this wider initiative.

REFERENCES

TCMG (1996) *Making Winchester First: Winchester City Centre Management Business Plan 1996/7* (draft), Town Centre Management Group.

WCC (1994) *Winchester Visitor Survey 1994*, Winchester City Council.

WCC (1995) *A Visitor Management Plan for Winchester District*, Winchester City Council.

Wyatt, C. (1996) *Report on Organisational Development Requirements within the Marketing and Tourism Division of Winchester City Council*, Winchester City Council (internal report).

The North Pennines

THEMES

- the partnership approach to solving conflict
- designations and public-sector intervention
- sources of funding.

LOCATION AND BACKGROUND

'This country, though politically distributed among three counties, is one and the same in all its characteristic features. From it flow the Tyne, the Wear and the Tees and many branches which fall into these rivers. Along the banks of these and several other smaller streams which fall into them are dales or valleys, cultivated near the banks and for a short distance up the sides of the hills, but soon cultivation and enclosure cease, and beyond them the dark fells, covered with peat and moss and heath; and between one vale and another is a wide extent of high moorland, extending sometimes for a dozen miles. In these upland tracts are no inhabited homes but thousands of black-faced sheep are scattered over them; and there breed the grouse which attract the sportsmen at the proper season of the year to this country'.

(Royal Commission into Children's Employment in the Mines, Mitchell, W.R., 1842)

This description of the North Pennines in 1842 might equally have been written in the late 20th century, so little has the landscape of this area changed in over 150 years.

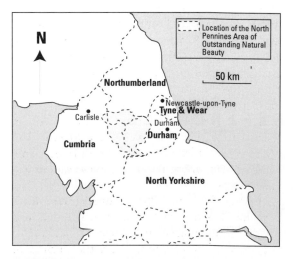

FIGURE E.1 *Map showing the North Pennines*

The North Pennines is one of the remotest regions of upland England. It is an area covering over 2,000 square kilometres situated to the south of Hadrian's Wall, between the well-known tourism landscapes of the Lake District, the Yorkshire Dales and the Northumberland National Parks. Although it has a less widely-established identity than these neighbouring regions, the North Pennines area has its own distinctive characteristics, notably its high uninhabited heather moorlands, intersected by green settled dales. A haven for wild birds and plants, it includes within its boundaries many nationally important nature reserves and conservation areas.

In the 18th and 19th centuries, the North Pennines was one of the most productive lead and zinc mining areas in Europe and an area of considerable immigration. With the decline of the extraction industries in the late 19th century, as a result of competition from abroad and exhaustion of the mines, the North Pennines area was left with a relatively large population in what would normally have been high marginal hill-farming country.

Now, the North Pennines is one of the most sparsely populated areas of its size in England, with approximately 12,000 inhabitants, less than half the population it had in 1861 when 27,000 people lived there. The area is characterised by small widely-separated settlements, between which there are wide expanses of open country. The majority of the population live in the North Pennine dales, where settlements include small towns such as Alston (the highest market town in England) and Allendale Town, together with relatively compact villages, isolated hamlets and a wide scatter of individual farmhouses.

The moorland areas of the North Pennines together total 77,094 hectares, which is equivalent to 38% of the land in the North Pennines – the moorland comprises about 24% of the total area of heather moorland in England and Wales.

Geographically remote, the North Pennines is crossed by few roads, the major routes being the A686 (Haydon Bridge to Penrith), A689 (Brampton to Bishop Auckland), and A66 (Scotch Corner to Penrith). Following the closure of the Alston to Haltwhistle line in 1976, there are now no links to the main railway network. Road-based public transport services in the North Pennines are generally better than for many rural areas, but still only offer a basic service; communities which are not on the main road network have poor access to public transport. As a result, access to private transport is a necessity within most of the area and levels of car ownership are correspondingly high (NP AONB, 1995).

The beautiful dales scenery is a major draw for visitors to the area. Its rivers, reservoirs and moorlands accommodate a variety of outdoor activities including fishing, sailing, bird watching and grouse shooting. But, scattered in the hills, are a number of other attractions of which the following are examples:

- the Killhope Lead Mining Centre, where former workings have been restored as a visitor centre, attracts over 40,000 visitors a year
- England's highest narrow gauge railway, the South Tynedale, which runs from Alston, attracts over 25,000 visitors annually
- High Force, England's largest waterfall is in the area
- the Weardale Museum at Ireshopeburn includes recreated scenes from the 1870s.

In addition to these, the Pennine Way passes through the outskirts of Alston and there is an extensive network of Public Rights of Way. Accommodation is largely in the form of small hotels and bed-and-breakfast establishments, the latter being increasingly found in the farm sector.

The North Pennines area straddles a region covered by three county councils and includes parts of six different district councils. The administrative centres for these counties and districts lie well outside the area itself.

ECONOMY

As well as being a beautiful environment, the North Pennines is also a place of work for thousands of people.

Unemployment is a major problem. The proportion of local people out of work stands at 13% – well above the national average (NP AONB, 1995). The area suffers from pockets of high unemployment, but in addition there is the problem of general underemployment throughout the North Pennines. Employment surveys of the area indicate the relatively high dependence on part-time labour in the North Pennines. There is a 'long established practice in the North Pennines of individuals holding a number of part-time jobs in small-scale business enterprises, often too small to offer full-time employment' (Heap and Wylie, 1992).

The economy is based largely on agriculture, which accounts for 25% of all employment.

Over 90% of the North Pennines is farmed and there are approximately, 1,700 farm units in the North Pennines area. Livestock farming is the dominant agricultural activity, with an estimated 900,000 sheep and 100,000 cattle. Economic circumstances have led to a decline in mid-sized family farming units, with an increase in both the very small and large businesses. These changes have resulted in some contraction in agricultural employment at the same time as an intensification of agricultural production (NP AONB, 1995). Nevertheless, there has been no real decrease in the farming population, which, on the whole, appears to be very resilient.

The viability of many upland farms in the North Pennines has been long dependent on other sources of income. In 1995, over 45% of the region's farms were still classified as part time. Work in the lead mines provided essential support for many of the small holdings during past centuries. In modern times, diversification has been widely seen as a way of stabilising incomes for farmers. Many of the diversification methods already used in the region are tourism-related, including: camping and bunkhouse barns, bed-and-breakfast and self-catering accommodation, farmhouse holidays, craft industries, and horse riding.

Shooting is another source of income for the North Pennines, which includes 39 separate units of heather moorland, at least 90% of which are used for shooting purposes. The income brought into the area from shooting revenue is considerable, in direct terms equalling approximately £1,100,000 per year. Much of this income is ploughed back into the local economy, not only through the maintenance of the estates but also through the provision of employment for beaters and other, often casual, labour. The local tourist industry is also supported, (NP AONB, 1995).

Remnants of the area's extraction industries remain, with several active workings for a variety of stone and mineral reserves, as a number of small privately-owned companies continue to mine for coal within the Alston and South Tyne areas. Nevertheless, the decrease in the mining sector this century has been dramatic.

The economic and social difficulties facing North Pennine communities are recognised by a variety of designations qualifying the area for assistance. Three **Rural Development Areas** (Cumbria, Northumberland and West Durham) encompass the area, enabling the North Pennines to qualify for grant aid incentives to support economic and social initiatives.

The North Pennines is also covered by European Union **Less Favoured Area** status, which enables special support to be offered to farming. Within the area, Cumbria, Northumberland and Teesdale have secured Objective 5b status through which EU assistance may be given for rural regeneration. The other districts have Objective 2 status, which qualifies the area for EU support for economic initiatives.

INVOLVEMENT IN TOURISM

The first major public-sector intervention in North Pennines tourism came in the mid 1970s, when it was identified as a **Tourism Growth Point (TGP)** by the English Tourist Board. This was the first coordinated attempt to stimulate tourism in the area and it brought some extra financial resources for small-scale tourist facilities. Although a few tourism-related projects benefited considerably from this designation (notably the South Tynedale Railway), progress was fragmented and slow, mainly due to the lack of a local project officer with specific responsibility for the TGP measures.

In the 1980s, as a continuation of the TGP project, the **North Pennines Tourism Consultative Group** was set up, composed of representatives from government agencies and local authorities. The Group's activities were severely limited by its lack of resources, and it suffered from the same problem as the TGP – namely the lack of an officer with a full-time, exclusive, commitment to its activities. However, one of its most significant actions was the commissioning (from consultants Roger Tym & Partners) of a report on tourism in the North Pennines. Known as the Tym report (Tym, 1988), it gave a profile of tourism activity in the area and set out a suggested short-term (three to five years) plan of action to improve the tourism product and its marketing, to increase the number of visitors, to create more jobs, and to ensure that any developments proposed were consistent with the environmental objectives of those responsible for this aspect of the area.

PROBLEMS AND OPPORTUNITIES

The publication in 1988 of the Tym report *Tourism in the North Pennines* coincided with, and was linked to, a major event in the area: the official confirmation of the North Pennines as an **Area of Outstanding Natural Beauty (AONB)**. This designation (awarded by the **Countryside Commission (CoCo)** in order to conserve and enhance the flora, fauna and geological and physiographical features of the area) was the latest in a series of designations recognising the particular characteristics of the North Pennines region. It had already been awarded **Conservation Area** status for many of its towns and villages, as well as special designations for certain areas with particular nature conservation value or scientific interest. Many local people and several of the local authorities regarded AONB status as one designation too many.

In the area, many people had been of the opinion that the AONB status would aggravate the North Pennines' economic problems. They feared that the AONB status would impose further restraints on economic recovery in an area already subject to a plethora of development restrictions arising from the other conservation designations. In 1978, when the original AONB designation order was submitted to the Secretary of State, it was opposed by some of the area's local authorities and other local interests who feared that designation would fossilise an already decaying rural economy, and stifle development and the creation of new jobs.

After many years of local resistance to AONB designation, a Public Inquiry was held in 1985 to consider the issues. At this inquiry, the CoCo and the Rural Development Commission (RDC) argued that AONB designation need not in itself prevent development and could effectively bring tangible, economic benefits to the local community through the creation of jobs in conservation, recreation and tourism. A joint approach was proposed, which would encompass the aims of both the CoCo (to conserve the countryside and encompass public enjoyment, access and understanding of it) and the RDC (to

promote and assist the economic and social well-being of rural communities). AONB designation was granted, with both government commissions thereafter collaborating on a programme of initiatives designed to benefit both the environment and rural development. The vast majority of those measures were tourism-related.

Both commissions' participation in the North Pennines Tourism Consultative Group represented part of their joint approach to the development of tourism in the area. Their key concern was to demonstrate that economic development through tourism could go hand-in-hand with conservation. While tourism was regarded as an important key to the economic development of the area, it was recognised that careful management was vital in order to preserve the vital assets of the North Pennines.

> 'Tourists and visitors make an essential contribution to the local economy, but also cause some problems. Trespass, intensive recreational pursuits and lack of care may cause damage and destruction to farming, grouse moor and management interests. Disturbance to wildlife and damage to natural habitats and historic sites may also occur in areas which are subject to high visitor pressures ... If not well managed, tourism could have a serious effect on the countryside, destroying the peace, quiet and beauty which people come to enjoy. In such a fragile natural environment, the promotion of tourist activity must direct people to areas which are robust or can be managed to avoid damage to the natural resource. Fragile moorland, particularly in the highest and wettest areas, is particularly vulnerable to pressure from walkers and other problems such as disturbance to stock can occur through ignorance on the part of the visitor.'
>
> *(NP AONB, 1995)*

The Tym report found the tourism industry in the area to be relatively underdeveloped in comparison with many other rural areas. It proposed a number of ideas for the marketing and development of North Pennines tourism, including the important recommendation that the Group should pursue the establishment of a **Tourism Development Action Programme (TDAP)**. The rationale behind this idea was that it would result in English Tourist Board (ETB) support and financial contributions to guide future tourism development in the area. The Group's bid to the ETB was successful and in 1990, a three-year TDAP in the North Pennines came into being, with funding partners including the ETB, the CoCo, the RDC and the relevant local authorities.

NORTH PENNINES TOURISM PARTNERSHIP

With so many local authorities and government agencies sharing responsibility for the North Pennines area and given the nature of the area itself, the partners recognised that in order for the TDAP to be effective, close collaboration and local involvement were critical. Accordingly, in 1990, the **North Pennines Tourism Partnership (NPTP)** was created as 'a Partnership to help strengthen the rural economy and care for the countryside in the North Pennines'. Unlike its predecessors, the NPTP included a significant number of private-sector and voluntary-sector representatives. Its membership is as shown below.

A full-time NPTP Manager was appointed and an office base was set up in Alston.

The NPTP's objectives are mainly concerned with strengthening rural tourism. They are as follows:

- to increase awareness of the North Pennines as an area and a visitor destination by coordinating appropriate marketing opportunities
- to increase the range of active and informal countryside activities and promote these activities
- to improve existing attractions and provide quality small-to-medium-scale attractions based on the area's heritage and attributes
- to improve the quality and standards of existing accommodation and encourage modest expansion in key market sectors
- to promote the development of rural arts and crafts
- to help conserve the character of the landscape and heritage, and enhance the appearance of the area's towns and villages
- to develop community and private-sector support for tourism
- to improve business advice and training for the local tourism industry.

Membership of the North Pennines Tourism Partnership

Government agencies
English Tourist Board (represented through the Cumbria and Northumbria Regional Tourist Boards)
Countryside Commission
Rural Development Commission

Local authorities
Cumbria County Council
Durham County Council
Northumberland County Council
Eden District Council
Tynedale District Council
Wear Valley District Council
Teesdale District Council

Representatives from the private sector
Including representation from the farming community

Representatives from the voluntary sector
Including the North Pennines Heritage Trust

Parish councils
A representative from each county

A key concern of the agencies contributing to the NPTP was to show that economic development through tourism could go hand-in-hand with conservation. Its objectives reflect this development/conservation approach. The NPTP sought, from the outset, to follow the guiding principles of the Government Task Force:

> 'The Partnership has developed consciously along the lines of the guiding principles from the *Maintaining the Balance* 1991 ETB/Department of Employment report highlighting the importance of linking the visitor, the place and the host community, and also along the principle of being research-based. The issue of promoting sustainable development based on the intrinsic qualities of the area is paramount in all the Partnership's work.'
>
> *(NPTP, 1994)*

In addition, the NPTP's objectives follow closely the guidance on the development of environmentally-sensitive tourism presented in the joint ETB, CoCo, RDC strategy document, *Principles for Tourism in the Countryside*.

ORGANISATION

The NPTP began with a full-time manager and a part time secretary/assistant. For the first five and a half years of its existence, its line management was through the Cumbria Tourist Board who acted as treasurer. This role was taken over by Durham County Council in 1996. A management group of officers from the national agencies is responsible for the supervision of the financial aspect of the NPTP.

A NPTP Committee meets twice a year to oversee the general work programme of the project. This includes councillors from the seven local authorities, and representatives of the national funding agencies, the NFU, and the North Pennines Heritage Trust (a local voluntary conservation society). There are seven private-sector representatives, drawn from the North Pennines Tourism Association (a trade body representing tourism business interests). In addition, the committee includes representatives

from parish councils – one representative per county.

Detailed work programmes are executed through the development and marketing working groups. These meet regularly and draw other expertise in to help. Partners contribute to different elements of the work and it is the role of the NPTP Manager to ensure that momentum is kept up and work programmes delivered.

FUNDING

The NPTP is essentially public-sector funded. After the expiry of ETB funding through the TDAP, the other partners voted to continue their funding on a year-on-year basis. For 1994/95, the sources of income were as follows:

- **core income**: £42,000 (RDC 20%, CoCo 28%, counties 33%, districts 18%)
- **additional project income**: £19,000.

Expenditure is divided into salaries and administration (44%), and projects (56%).

EU FUNDS

In 1995, the awarding of 5(b) status to many parts of the North Pennines, made possible the offer of funding from the European Regional Development Fund (ERDF). Many new marketing and development projects were financed from this source, with matching funding from the local authorities' contributions to the NPTP. In addition, two new staff members were employed, partly funded by ERDF funds.

Under the EU 'LEADER' initiative for rural regions in difficulty, the North Pennines became eligible in 1995 for £1.5 million in funding over a five-year period.

By the Spring of 1996, as the NPTP entered its sixth year, core funding for 1996/97 had already been pledged from the three county councils, four district councils and the Countryside Commission.

INITIATIVES

The Tym report provided an initial marketing plan for the NPTP, but the practical initiatives have primarily come forward through the working groups. The initial emphasis was on image building, marketing and training and advisory work, to create awareness of the area and confidence among tourism businesses. To these initiatives was later added the NPTP's interpretative and conservation work.

As the NPTP aims to play the role of catalyst, its emphasis has been on enabling and communication rather than direct activity. It has left the individual businesses involved to implement specific measures.

A 1995 report for the CoCo and other government agencies (CoCo, 1995) identified the following as the NPTP's most important achievements.

MARKETING

The methods of marketing the North Pennines posed a challenge for the NPTP. The rapid expansion of the volume of tourists in the area was not the objective. Rather, slow, sustainable growth was desired, and this underlies all of the NPTP's approach to marketing.

Part of that approach was to get others to promote awareness of the area as a special destination through their own marketing. Key elements in this strategy were the logo (see Figure E.2) and the slogan: 'England's Last Wilderness'.

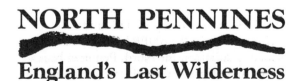

FIGURE E.2 *North Pennines logo*

Print and promotion were undertaken in a low key way, for two reasons:

- to avoid duplication with the tourism marketing being undertaken by the Regional Tourist Boards and local authorities

- because local tourism businesses in the area are too small to support glossy print publications.

Two print items were produced to generate awareness: a small colour flyer for operators to use freely in mailings, and a simple single-colour list of accommodation in the North Pennines area.

The NPTP also experimented with direct advertising, but after an advertising campaign in the *Radio Times* led to only a low level of response, the NPTP's main marketing emphasis switched to press work, distribution, direct mail and working through tourism officers. As an example of this approach, a themed short-breaks campaign in 1994 called 'Blustery Breaks' generated £100,000 worth of media coverage (although actual visitor numbers were limited).

The addition of EU funding enabled the NPTP to undertake some overseas marketing targeting Northern Europe, particularly Holland and Germany – two countries with a strong market for holidays based on the outdoors and the countryside, and with good transport communications with the North of England.

COUNTRYSIDE ACTIVITIES AND ATTRACTIONS

The NPTP's role under this heading has also been an enabling one, bringing different actors together in order to improve the activity and attractions aspect of the North Pennines tourism product. For example, the area's outdoor activity centres were brought together, and links were created between them and local authority countryside staff. Local authority countryside staff have also been encouraged to work with accommodation providers on the provision of information on walking.

ARTS AND CRAFTS

The development of the area's rural arts and crafts (for cultural as well as economic reasons) has been a priority for the NPTP. Craft enterprises have been helped with marketing through coordination of exhibition work and the creation of the 'North Pennines Produce Trail' centred on a map-based leaflet. The process has enabled some small craft enterprises to be identified and to have access to business and marketing advice.

CONSERVATION WORK

The NPTP has worked with local people to prepare an 'Interpretation Strategy' in order to increase visitor understanding and appreciation of the area: this has been adopted in the North Pennines Management Plan. Interpretation on the ground has been taken forward through community groups in specific villages, and includes the development of visitor centres at Stanhope, Bowlees, Killhope and Allenheads, as well as more widespread and low-key provision such as self-guided walks leaflets. A longer-term 'Local Interpretative Plans' project, putting together interpretive strategies for individual towns and villages began in 1995, using European Regional Development Fund (ERDF) finance.

The North Pennines Heritage Trust oversees the majority of the conservation schemes in the area. The approval of 5(b) status for the North Pennines created a new potential source of funding for environmental enhancement and conservation schemes, which tend to be capital intensive in nature.

Action has been taken to raise the environmental consciousness of local operators. This has included a North Pennines Green Tourism Award Scheme which invites local people to come up with their own ideas for 'greening' – these have been publicised.

INFRASTRUCTURE

The results of an early 1990s study of the possibility of placing strategic tourist information points in shops, pubs, hotels and post offices of towns and villages where there is no Tourism Information Centre showed the usefulness of such a scheme. But it was not until ERDF funding became available in 1995 that the project was able to go ahead.

Regarding tourism accommodation, participation in national classification schemes was made a compulsory requirement for all establishments in the North Pennines wishing to be featured in the *Where to Stay* guide. This was a measure to improve accommodation standards and increase confidence in the area as a quality destination. Serviced accommodation, self-catering holiday homes and caravan and holiday-home parks are affected.

Work has been undertaken to coordinate and promote public transport services, primarily through the leaflet *Across the Roof of England*. Roadsigns directing people to the North Pennines were also erected as part of the infrastructure strategy.

BUSINESS ADVICE AND TRAINING

A separate *North Pennines Business and Training Initiative* was established as a parallel project to the NPTP – working out of the same office and taking over the training and advisory work initiated by the NPTP. As a separate initiative, it was able to tap into different sources of funding, notably from training bodies. Take-up generally has been good, a key to success being the centrally-located office and the ability to deliver advice and training very locally, often on site. One third of the enquiries have come from would-be operators, the rest from existing enterprises. Most of the advice and training topics have related to marketing and general business advice, but environmental issues have also been covered.

ASSESSMENT

The CoCo report sums up the NPTP's achievements as follows: 'The NPTP has primarily performed a rural tourism marketing and training role in an area previously lacking in focus owing to isolation and its location on the fringes of a number of authorities' (CoCo, 1995).

The only reservation expressed in the report is that a greater involvement in development projects might have given the project a higher profile and left a more lasting benefit in the community.

The previous year, the Dronsfield report on the NPTP's performance as perceived by private-sector operators in the North Pennines had been extremely positive in its conclusions:

> 'All the objectives laid down by the Partnership are being met, the most obvious areas are: joint marketing initiatives, promotion of activities, promotion of rural arts and crafts, community representation and support and business support ... The NPTP has become an effective organisation; it is achieving the objectives which have been set for it. The ability to communicate and listen have proved to be a great strength. It is this great asset which has laid the foundation of a successful Partnership. Its profile has increased dramatically over the last three years; it is well positioned to continue helping maintain the community of the North Pennines through the controlled development of tourism.'
>
> *(Dronsfield, 1994)*

The NPTP's ability to communicate well with local businesses is demonstrated by the fact that 60% of the local operators interviewed in the Dronsfield survey had already made contact with the NPTP.

The theme of communication is also underlined in the CoCo list of the NPTP's particular achievements. These are as follows.

- There is excellent communication with small local businesses and communities. There appears to be a positive atmosphere in the area towards tourism and strong support for the project, which has been achieved by taking time to listen. Working in parallel with a focused training and advisory initiative has been valuable.
- There is a sense of genuine partnership. Use of the word 'partnership' has proved appropriate. A good balance has been achieved and the structure has meant that many organisations and individuals have become involved.
- There is a greater acceptance of the relationship between tourism and the environment. The embracing of conservation principles by the private sector has flowed from the NPTP's work. In 1994, a North Pennines Tourism Association was formed with 42 private sector members – it works closely with the NPTP and was nurtured by it: the North Pennines Tourist Association espouses conservation principles and will provide a useful vehicle for taking forward some projects in the future.
- They have succeeded in generating an 'awareness' of tourism. The logo and slogan have been effectively taken up – with limited resources, good promotion has been achieved on the back of others (CoCo, 1995).

POLICIES AND PLANS

The work of the NPTP has taken place within the context of a number of policies and plans relevant to the marketing and development of tourism in the North Pennines. At the same time, the NPTP has had an input into those plans and policies affecting the tourism aspect of the area.

NORTH PENNINES AONB MANAGEMENT PLAN

The **North Pennines AONB Management Plan** is a non-statutory plan produced by the North Pennines AONB Steering Group, which is composed of nine local authorities, the Countryside Commission and the Rural Development Commission. It identifies a range of issues which are of concern in ensuring that the character and quality of the AONB landscape may be conserved, enhanced and enjoyed, and develops an action programme with proposals for implementation by the principal partners in the management of the North Pennines area.

The objectives which AONB designation seeks to achieve in general were described on page 153 of this book. The AONB Management Plan notes that in the North Pennines area, these objectives are achieved:

- by practical conservation management
- by raising awareness of the value of the North Pennines as an AONB, thus generating local partnership and informed visitor support
- by guiding development to that which is sympathetic to the purposes of designation, through the planning system (NP AONB, 1995).

The AONB Management Plan addresses the first two of these methods, while the planning issues are addressed in the Structure and Local Plans of the County and District Planning authorities (see below).

The AONB Management Plan has the following guiding objectives:

- identify initiatives to secure the conservation and enhancement of the North Pennines Landscape
- ensure management initiatives and associated expenditure are to the benefit of the local community and economy
- ensure effective coordination between authorities, agencies, organisations and groups with responsibility for landscape management
- provide a mechanism to attract additional resources to the North Pennines from existing management partners and from central government and the European Union.

The AONB Management Plan maintains that the North Pennines of the future should be based on:

- a reshaped but viable hill farming regime
- a more diverse local economy
- an important tourism industry which is low-key in character.

The central tenet is to conserve the North Pennines landscape in a manner which does not break the bond between local people and the land – conserving the landscape through the activities of the local community, *not* through the imposition of a restrictive conservation regime.

Accordingly, the AONB Management Plan sets out three programmes for action:

1 Management of land (including promoting awareness of the economic problems of hill farming, encouraging farm diversification).
2 Management of historic buildings and features (including encouraging good design).
3 Promotion of enjoyment and understanding.

Under the third of these, the AONB Management Plan proposes the following objectives: 'Enhance visitor enjoyment and understanding of the North Pennines landscape and heritage; encourage recreation and access provision which is compatible with conservation and community aims; develop a sustainable tourism industry which benefits from the character of the North Pennines' (*ibid*).

It is therefore the aim of the AONB Management Plan to seek a balance between enjoying the countryside and conserving the special qualities and character of the North Pennines landscape. In this respect, it draws its inspiration from the guidelines, drawn up by the ETB, RDC and CoCo in 1989 (*Principles for Tourism in the Countryside*).

The AONB Management Plan proposes an Action Programme, setting out how the Management Plan's objectives can be implemented. Out of a total of 89 separate measures proposed in the Action Programme, 27 are related to the management of the land, 16 to the management of historic buildings and features, and 46 are directly related to tourism. For the implementation of most of the tourism-related measures, the NPTP is cited either as the lead body or as a partner organisation.

A major objective of the AONB Management Plan is related to the funding methods applied in the North Pennines. Its aims are to:

- encourage existing funding bodies to accord a higher priority to spending within the AONB
- stimulate expenditure across all action programmes to achieve a balanced programme of work
- adjust existing spending patterns to ensure that expenditure in the AONB is directed towards achieving priority action.

In addition, the AONB Management Plan is used to support bids for national and European funding from relevant programmes. As well as supporting applications for direct grants from government agencies (e.g. the RDC), the Plan is also an important element in bidding for funds from EU programmes of particular relevance to the North Pennines, notably European Regional Funding (Objective 2 and 5b), the LIFE programme (which has environmental objectives), and the LEADER programme.

In its assessment of the NPTP's work, the 1995 CoCo report commended the NPTP on influencing the AONB Management Plan 'which properly reflects the role of tourism'.

NORTH PENNINES INTERPRETATION STRATEGY

Interpretation is of considerable importance in the North Pennines, particularly as the art of conveying a sense of place – involving questions concerning which aspects of the North Pennines should be interpreted, how these should be interpreted and for what audience. Issues of physical appearance and design (e.g. of visitor centres, interpretive panels, publications) are also relevant.

The North Pennines Interpretation Strategy, prepared by the NPTP with the involvement of local people, outlines the principles and objectives for interpretation in the North Pennines. The AONB Management Plan has as one of its action points the implementation of this strategy.

OTHER PLANS

LAND USE AND ECONOMIC DEVELOPMENT

Being located on the fringes of a number of different local authorities, the North Pennines are affected by each local authority's measures, including the preparation and implementation of local economic development strategies and statutory development plans. Some of these include tourism development. For example, Eden District Council has sought to include the facilitation of tourism development as a form of economic diversification within its land-use planning objectives, with the emphasis on the need for environmentally-sensitive tourism development in its area. The 1991 Local Plan contains the following statement:

> 'Proposals for the development of recreation and tourism facilities need to be assessed in the light of their ability not only to contribute to the economy of the area but also to maintain the essential quality and character of the landscape ... With the confirmation of the designation of the North Pennines AONB, it is necessary to consider the AONB in a positive light, not only to evaluate measures for its protection but also to assess the economic and recreational opportunities created ... How can the designation of the North Pennines AONB be used to the social and economic benefit of the area's residents and of the district as a whole?'
>
> *(Eden District Council Local Plan, 1991)*

In this case, the local authority's approach to tourism in the North Pennines is compatible with that of the NPTP, but many local authorities' ambiguous attitude to AONB designation (on the grounds that it could stifle economic development) is recalled by Prentice (1993), who concludes: 'In both the general case, and that of the AONB, it is fair to conclude that in the 1990s, environment is seen by public authorities as an opportunity to aid tourism development in the North Pennines, as well as a constraint on such development.'

TOURISM

The NPTP is of course not the only local organisation involved in the tourism marketing of the area. The North Pennines are also affected by the tourism policies of two regional tourist boards (Northumbria and Cumbria) as well as several local authority tourism departments – many of whom are increasingly promoting the North Pennines as a means of stemming out-migration and assisting the regeneration of the local economy.

However, the marketing perspective of these

organisations does not always concur with that of the NPTP. In particular, the Cumbria Tourist Board has promoted tourism development in the west of the North Pennines as a means of seeking to divert tourism demand away from the Lake District, its traditional tourism area (Prentice, 1993, cites Cumbria Tourist Board); and Durham County Council promotes the North Pennines as the 'Durham Dales', with the emphasis on the area's lead mining past.

A PROFILE OF TOURISM IN THE NORTH PENNINES

Since 1990, a number of studies have traced the development of tourism in the North Pennines and offer some insight into the relative and growing importance of this sector for the local economy.

Tourism's impact on the local job market was highlighted by Heap and Wylie's (1992) study of the effect of tourism upon employment in the North Pennines. This estimated that over one third (35.5%) of all permanent jobs in the AONB area were directly attributable to, or induced by, tourism, while over 80% of all seasonal employment in the area was attributable to tourism (see Figure E.3).

The part-time and seasonal opportunities created by tourism fit into a general pattern of this type of work which, in the North Pennines, is (for all sectors) the rule rather than the exception. For example, the Heap and Wylie study shows that over a quarter of all permanent employees in the area's farming and manufacturing sectors work part-time, and almost half of all permanent employees in tourism and retail also work part-time. Over all sectors, the figures for part-time seasonal employees are much higher still.

Another relevant observation arising from the study concerns the age of local businesses:

'Tourism businesses are younger than farming, manufacturing and services in the [North Pennines]. A majority of tourism businesses are under five years old. This can be contrasted with farming and manufacturing in which businesses are generally over ten years old. The growth of tourism in the recent past and its forecast future expansion can be contrasted with a predicted decline in employment in the manufacturing and the service sectors.'

(Heap and Wylie, 1992)

The optimism surrounding the expectations for tourism in the early 1990s is also demonstrated in employers' recruitment intentions at the time, as shown in Figure E.4.

The key contrast emerging from Figure E.4 is that between the predictions of employers in the manufacturing sector (who expected to see their numbers of employees decline) and those of operators in the retailing and tourism sectors (who generally expected to increase their workforces).

However, as Heap and Wylie state in their conclusion to the study, *seasonality* is a major factor in limiting the contribution which tourism can make to the North Pennines economy:

'Though tourism is of great importance to the communities in the (North Pennines), its full employment potential would appear constrained by its seasonality. In the context of forecast declines in non-tourism service and manufacturing employment, the extension of the season for day and holiday tourism must be a priority for the . . . near future.'

(Heap and Wylie, 1992)

TOURISM IN THE NORTH PENNINES AREA (BETWEEN 1990 AND 1994)

Further insights into the development of tourism in the North Pennines are given in the Dronsfield survey of 150 local tourism businesses, which was undertaken to evaluate the

Employment	(A) Total employment	(B) Directly in tourism	(C) Induced by tourism	(D) Total (B + C)	(E) Tourism as % of all employment
Permanent employees					
Professional/managerial	831	210	84	294	35.3
Scientific/technical	59	4	15	19	32.2
Buying/marketing/selling	52	8	15	23	44.2
Clerical/secretary	84	3	20	23	27.3
Manual supervisory	46	5	12	17	37.0
Semi/unskilled manual	793	157	130	387	36.1
Total permanent employment	**1 865**	**387**	**276**	**663**	**35.5**
Seasonal employees					
Professional/managerial	53	33	2	35	66.0
Scientific/technical	0	–	–	–	–
Buying/marketing/selling	0	–	–	–	–
Clerical/secretary	0	–	–	–	–
Manual supervisory	0	–	–	–	–
Semi/unskilled manual	477	377	29	406	85.1
Total seasonal employment	**530**	**410**	**31**	**441**	**83.2**

Source: Heap and Wylie, 1992

FIGURE E.3 *Employment in the North Pennines AONB*

	Tourism	Manufacturing	Retail	Service	Farming
Increase	8.9	25.0*	10.7	0.0	0.0
Decrease	0.0	37.5	7.2	7.5	0.0
Remain the same	90.0	37.5	82.1	92.5	100.0
Don't know	1.1	0.0	0.0	0.0	0.0
Total %	**100**	**100**	**100**	**100**	**100**

* The most significant of the two employers in the manufacturing category who expected to increase their workforce in the following 12 months was in reality a hybrid business deriving at least 50% of his turnover from tourism-related activity. Therefore an expected increase in tourism and leisure day-trip activity is responsible for at least half of the 'increase in expected manufacturing employment' stated.

Source: Heap and Wylie, 1992

FIGURE E.4 *Expected change in employees in the next 12 months*

effectiveness of the NPTP from the point of view of the private sector.

In response to the question, 'What has happened to tourism business turnover within the last four years?' the answers were as follows:

- increased: 45.1%
- remained unchanged: 23.9%
- decreased: 21.8%
- not answered: 9.2%.

As well as an increase in visitor numbers, the report (through operators' responses) also identified apparent increases in the length of the visitor season, number of couples, retired visitors, repeat bookings and second holidays. The operators' answers also suggested a noticeable decrease in the number of families visiting the area and the average length of visitor stay.

However, in addition to this quantitative data, an interesting point emerged when operators were asked about their own priorities for the future. Increasing the number of tourists and conservation of the environment came only second equal in the list of priorities. What clearly emerged was that the top priority was by far the creation of *jobs* for local people. This echoed the results of a study undertaken the year before, when a survey of North Pennines residents' views (not only those directly involved in tourism) on local tourism development had also shown that:

> 'An unambiguous preference placing job creation before environment concerns would seem to exist within the North Pennines communities. This preference would concur with the stance of several of the local authorities in the 1980s to oppose the designation of these uplands for landscape conservation through the AONB ...'
>
> *(Prentice, 1993)*

This prioritising of jobs over the conservation of the environment raises an important point, to which we shall return in the conclusion to this case study.

Several tourist surveys undertaken in the North Pennines during the 1990s offer snapshot profiles of visitors to the area. The key findings of the 1995 Visitor Questionnaire were analysed by Tim Heap of the Tourism Research Centre at the University of Derby as follows.

- There has been an increase from 6% to 16.6% of overseas visitors since 1990. One reason may have been the weakness of the pound against other European currencies that year. But it was noted by 22% of the overseas market that the reason for them coming to the North Pennines was BTA publicity.
- The Midlands and London areas are dominant in the domestic market.
- A large number of people were visiting the area for the first time as a result of better signposting, publicity and brochures. None were disappointed or had dislikes, boding well for repeat visits.
- 84.4% visited the area as a holiday destination, similar to figures produced by earlier surveys. However, there was a 10% increase in business visitors – indicating an improved industrial performance in the area?
- As in earlier surveys, the most commonly-given responses to the question, 'What did you like most about the North Pennines' were: 'beautiful countryside', 'peace and quiet', 'uncrowded roads' and 'visiting historical and other sites'.

The majority of visitors were aged between 45 to 65 years, suggesting a group with a combination of high disposable incomes and increasing amounts of leisure time. This segment of the market usually takes more than one holiday a year and is seeking new and unusual destinations.

Finally, visitor spending patterns are shown by the following 1994 estimates of tourist spending in the North Pennines area, based on a combination of regionally- and locally-collected data:

Serviced accommodation: £10,485,900	30.9%
Self-catering: £1,964,000	5.8%
Caravan/camping: £3,465,500	10.2%
Group accommodation: £357,700	1.1%
VFR: £1,610,000	4.8%
Day visitors: £5,648,500	16.7%
Additional indirect spend: £10,355,600	30.5%

Source: NPTP (1994b)

FIGURE E.5 *Visitor spending in the North Pennines*

Taking all of this data into account, the NPTP was able to state in its 1994 review of its own activities that: tourism is worth over £33 million per annum to the North Pennines, in direct and indirect spending; it sustains approximately 1,250 jobs; and approximately 800,000 visitor nights are spent in the area each year (NPTP, 1994b).

All of the preceding information on the profile of tourism in the North Pennines may be represented on our 'tourism product portfolio' and 'tourism dominance' grids (see Figures E.6 and E.7).

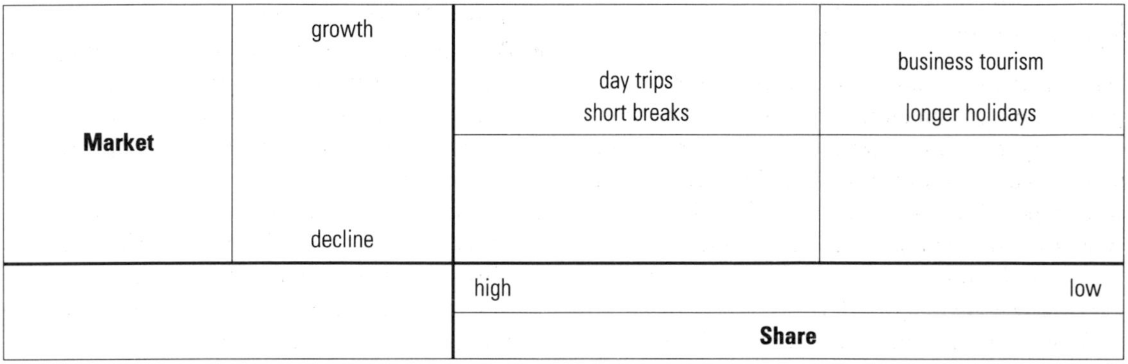

Market	growth	day trips short breaks	business tourism longer holidays
	decline		
		high	low
		Share	

FIGURE E.6 *Tourism product portfolio: North Pennines*

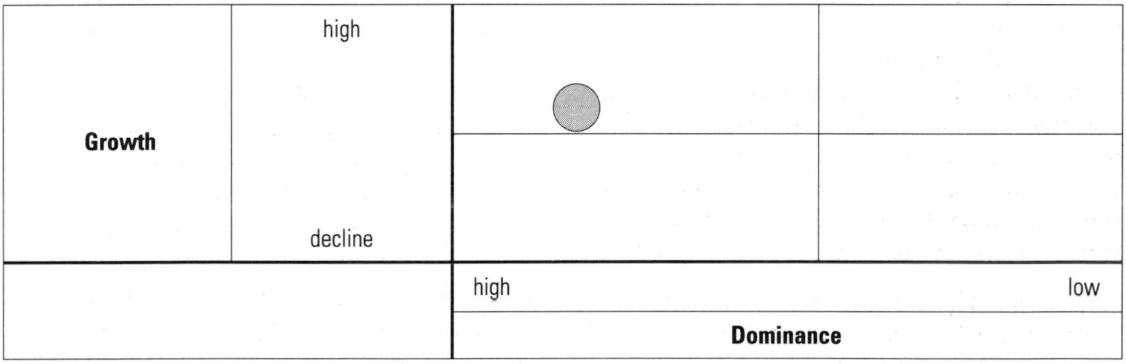

Growth	high		
	decline		
		high	low
		Dominance	

FIGURE E.7 *Tourism dominance and growth: North Pennines*

CONCLUSION

1 THE PARTNERSHIP APPROACH TO TOURISM PLANNING WAS EFFECTIVE IN AVOIDING CONFLICT

The data in Figures E.5, E.6 and E.7 suggest that tourism in the North Pennines is growing gradually and assuming greater importance in the local economy, in particular regarding employment. How much of this growth is due to the efforts of the NPTP is difficult to estimate. More monitoring by the NPTP itself might have made it easier to identify the amount of new tourism generated by it, as well as the economic benefits obtained.

The main effectiveness of the NPTP lies in its uniting the two sides of the conservation versus development issue in the North Pennines, using environmentally-sensitive tourism as a form of acceptable economic development in the area.

This approach helped make the AONB designation acceptable to the inhabitants of the area and the local authorities who represent them.

Nevertheless, the potential for conflict runs deep, with the North Pennines communities' 'unambiguous preference placing job creation before environment concerns' clearly expressed in questionnaire surveys, and most recently, in Prentice's investigation into the community dimension of support for local tourism development (Prentice, 1993). Even the title 'England's Last Wilderness' has been criticised by some as conveying a desolate image of the North Pennines, making the area 'that much less attractive to the real industry that it needs' (Phillips, 1991).

As Prentice concludes,

'The preference for jobs sets a challenge for tourism planning: the need to avoid employment–environmental conflicts. If such conflicts arise, the local preference may be to resolve them contrary to more widely felt priorities.'

(Prentice, 1993)

In other words, although a national priority may be to set aside certain areas of high landscape quality for conservation, the residents of those areas may not necessarily concur with those priorities, preferring economic development, as in the case of the North Pennines.

The challenge for the different agencies represented through the NPTP has been to demonstrate that there is a type of tourism development which goes hand-in-hand with protecting the landscape upon which it depends. The NPTP has consistently promoted tourism development based on principles of sustainability, and embracing landscape conservation through its origins linked to AONB designation.

2 THE COMMUNITY-BASED APPROACH WAS USED – BUT WHICH COMMUNITY?

Much of the NPTP's success has been attributed to the excellent communication it has achieved with the local business community. Almost every assessment of the NPTP's work commends it for the extensive contacts it has constructed with local tourism operators.

Elsewhere, the NPTP's claim to 'work through local people' has been called into question e.g. Phillips (1991) and Prentice (1993) caution generally against equating community preferences solely with the preferences of entrepreneurs.

The degree of public support for 'community-driven' tourism development, such as that in the North Pennines, is notoriously difficult to measure. Prentice's attempt to do so predictably detected a distinction in views between beneficiaries and non-beneficiaries of tourism in the area (with more support for tourism development coming from the former group). To qualify as truly community-based, the support of those who perceive themselves as non-beneficiaries needs to be enlisted. To be effective, this raises the general question of PR and education of the local population, which in turn depends on the reliable monitoring of economic and social benefits.

3 TOURISM INITIATIVES WERE FOSTERED BY PUBLIC FUNDS

Few of the NPTP's achievements would have been possible without the injections of public funds from the various European, national and local sources. But while national and EU funds may be welcomed by the public as money coming into the region, doubts have been raised over the willingness of local people to see the rates that *they* pay being used for this purpose.

The Prentice survey showed that although most residents would in general support economic development through tourism, there was far less support for locally-funded public investment in tourism, particularly among those not directly benefiting from tourism in the area: '. . . support does not generally extend into the conspicuous expenditure of locally-generated public resources on tourism development.'

An implication for tourism development may be that private-sector initiatives are generally acceptable as a form of economic development through tourism, but that the enabling role of public agencies as facilitators of this may be constrained if overtly reliant on the expenditure of substantially locally-derived public resources (Prentice, 1993).

REFERENCES

CoCo (1995) *Sustainable Rural Tourism: Opportunities for Local Action*, Countryside Commission, Department of National Heritage, English Tourist Board and Rural Development Commission, Cheltenham.

Dronsfield, J (1994) *A study of the effectiveness of the North Pennines Tourism Partnership as perceived by the private sector tourism operators located within the partnership area*, RDC/NPTP.

Heap, T. and Wylie, R. (1992) 'The volume of employment attributable to tourism and leisure day-trip activity' in *North Pennines AONB*, North Pennines Tourism Partnership, Alston.

NP AONB (1995) *The North Pennines AONB Management Plan*, The North Pennines AONB Steering Group, Countryside Commission, Newcastle upon Tyne.

NPTP (1994a) *1990–1993 Review*, North Pennines Tourism Partnership, Alston.

NPTP (1994b) *Tourism Partnership News*, Autumn 1994, North Pennines Tourism Partnership, Alston.

Phillips, D. (1991) 'UK issues in England's Last Wilderness' in *In Focus*, Autumn 1991, Tourism Concern, London.

Prentice, R. (1993) 'Community-driven tourism planning and residents' preferences' in *Tourism Management*, 14(3).

Tym, R. (1988) *Tourism in the North Pennines – Action Programme*, Cumbria Tourist Board (*et al.*), Windermere.

Index